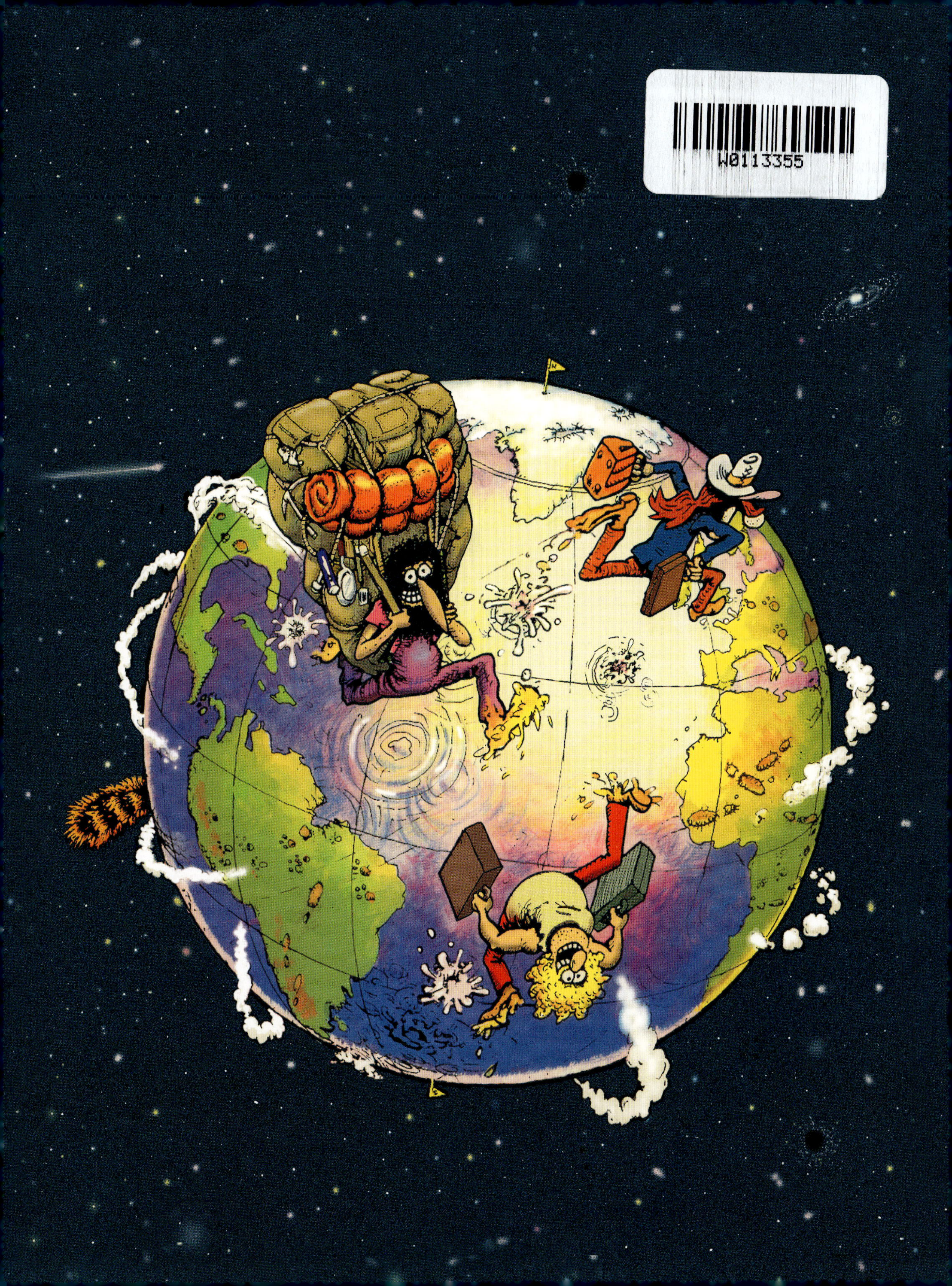

FREEWHEELIN'
FRANKLIN
FAT
FREDDY
PHINEAS
& FAT FREDDY'S CAT

THE FABULOUS FURRY FREAK BROTHERS

The Idiots Abroad and Other Follies

by Gilbert Shelton and Paul Mavrides

Publisher: GARY GROTH
Senior Editor: J. MICHAEL CATRON
Designer: JUSTIN ALLAN-SPENCER
Production: PAUL BARESH
VP / Associate Publisher: ERIC REYNOLDS

 The Fabulous Furry Freak Brothers Follies is a chronological collection of the adventures of The Fabulous Furry Freak Brothers, but the volumes are being released in a different order. This is Volume 6.

Fantagraphics Books, Inc.
7563 Lake City Way NE
Seattle, WA 98115
(800) 657-1100
Fantagraphics.com · Twitter: @fantagraphics · facebook.com/fantagraphics

Special thanks to Fred Todd, Glenn Bray, and Gary Panter.

First Fantagraphics Books edition: April 2022
ISBN 978 1 68396 510 7
Library of Congress Control Number: 2021944325
Printed in China

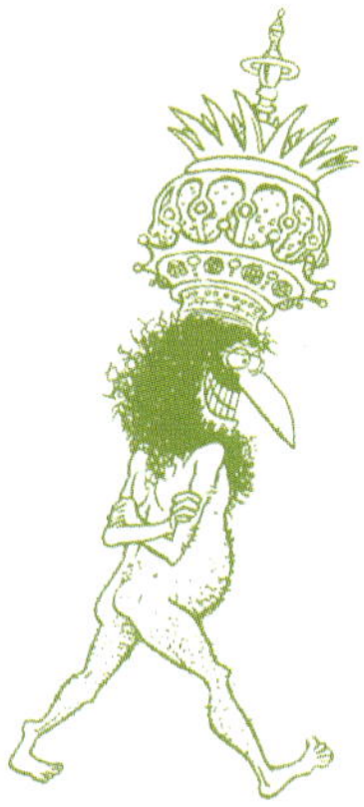

FIRST APPEARANCES

The comics stories and illustrations in this book were originally published in:

Rip Off #11, 1982
Rip Off #12, 1983
The Fabulous Furry Freak Brothers in "The Idiots Abroad" (*Part One*) (*Freak Brothers* #8), 1984
The Fabulous Furry Freak Brothers in "The Idiots Abroad" (*Part Two*) (*Freak Brothers* #9), 1985
The Fabulous Furry Freak Brothers in "The Idiots Abroad" (*Part Three*) (*Freak Brothers* #10), 1987
The Adventures of Fat Freddy's Cat Book 6 (*Fat Freddy's Cat* #6), 1986

COMING SOON:

The Freak Brothers in the 21st Century and Other Follies (Volume 5)

THE FABULOUS FURRY FREAK BROTHERS

The Idiots Abroad and Other Follies

by Gilbert Shelton and Paul Mavrides

Fantagraphics Books
Seattle

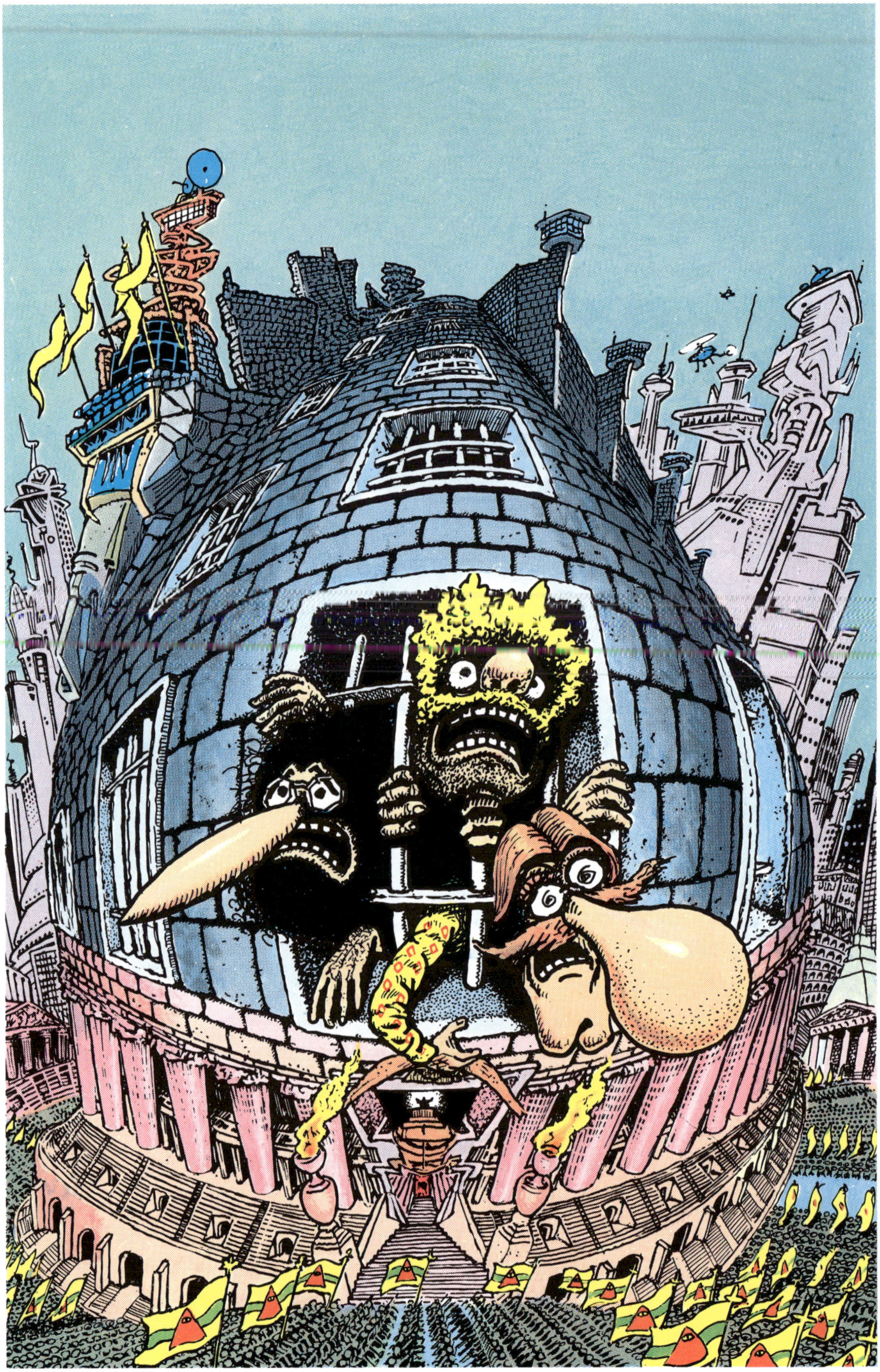

CONTENTS

THE FABULOUS FURRY FREAK BROTHERS
in
THE IDIOTS ABROAD

by Gilbert Shelton and Paul Mavrides
Color by Paul Mavrides and Guy Colwell

✸ ✸ ✸

FAT FREDDY'S CAT

by Gilbert Shelton

✸ ✸ ✸

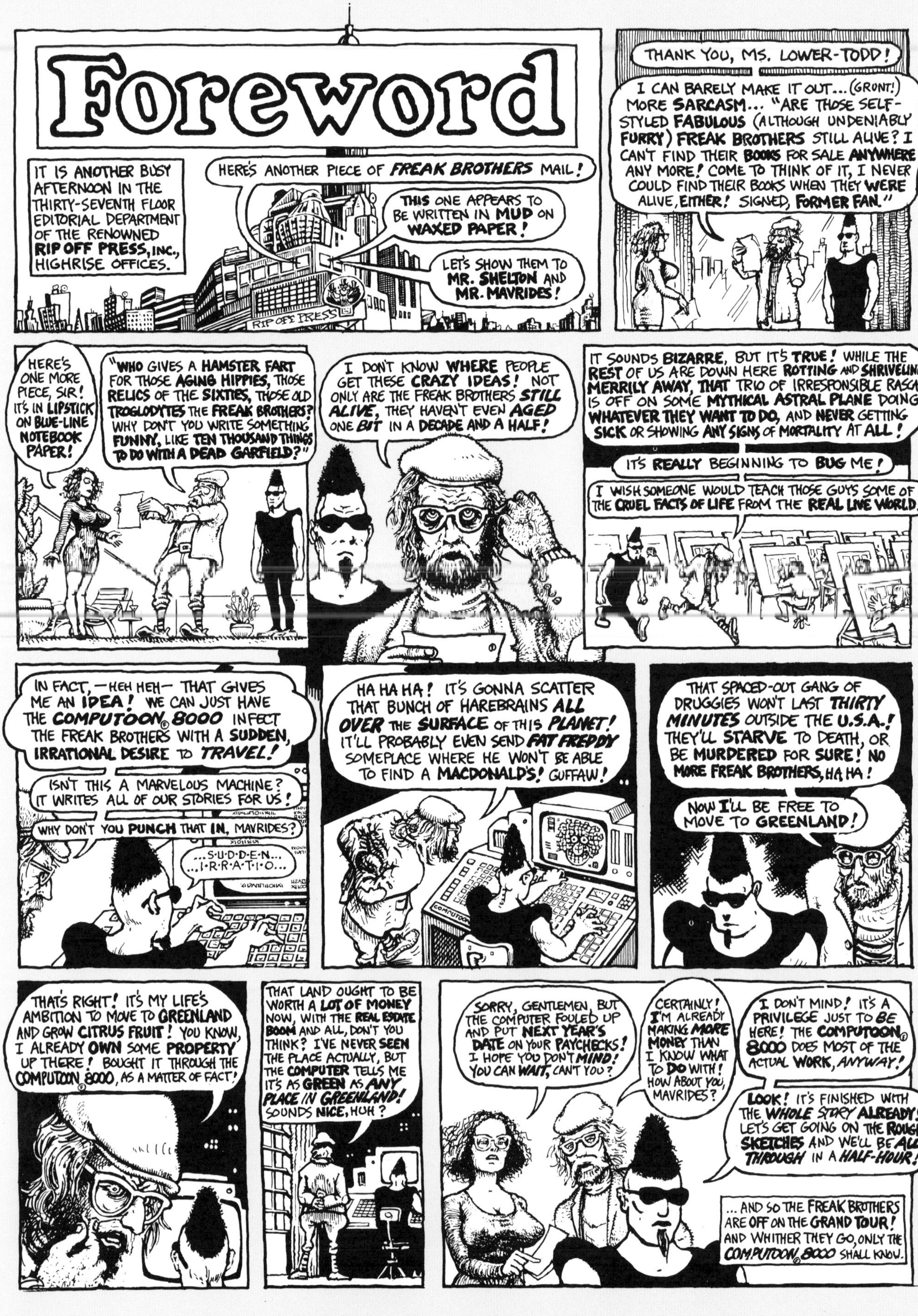

Foreword
IT IS ANOTHER BUSY AFTERNOON IN THE THIRTY-SEVENTH FLOOR EDITORIAL DEPARTMENT OF THE RENOWNED RIP OFF PRESS, INC., HIGHRISE OFFICES.
HERE'S ANOTHER PIECE OF FREAK BROTHERS MAIL!
THIS ONE APPEARS TO BE WRITTEN IN MUD ON WAXED PAPER!
LET'S SHOW THEM TO MR. SHELTON AND MR. MAVRIDES!
RIP OFF PRESS
THANK YOU, MS. LOWER-TODD!
I CAN BARELY MAKE IT OUT... (GRUNT!) MORE SARCASM... "ARE THOSE SELF-STYLED FABULOUS (ALTHOUGH UNDENIABLY FURRY) FREAK BROTHERS STILL ALIVE? I CAN'T FIND THEIR BOOKS FOR SALE ANYWHERE ANY MORE! COME TO THINK OF IT, I NEVER COULD FIND THEIR BOOKS WHEN THEY WERE ALIVE, EITHER! SIGNED, FORMER FAN."
HERE'S ONE MORE PIECE, SIR! IT'S IN LIPSTICK ON BLUE-LINE NOTEBOOK PAPER!
"WHO GIVES A HAMSTER FART FOR THOSE AGING HIPPIES, THOSE RELICS OF THE SIXTIES, THOSE OLD TROGLODYTES THE FREAK BROTHERS? WHY DON'T YOU WRITE SOMETHING FUNNY, LIKE TEN THOUSAND THINGS TO DO WITH A DEAD GARFIELD?"
I DON'T KNOW WHERE PEOPLE GET THESE CRAZY IDEAS! NOT ONLY ARE THE FREAK BROTHERS STILL ALIVE, THEY HAVEN'T EVEN AGED ONE BIT IN A DECADE AND A HALF!
IT SOUNDS BIZARRE, BUT IT'S TRUE! WHILE THE REST OF US ARE DOWN HERE ROTTING AND SHRIVELING MERRILY AWAY, THAT TRIO OF IRRESPONSIBLE RASCALS IS OFF ON SOME MYTHICAL ASTRAL PLANE DOING WHATEVER THEY WANT TO DO, AND NEVER GETTING SICK OR SHOWING ANY SIGNS OF MORTALITY AT ALL!
IT'S REALLY BEGINNING TO BUG ME!
I WISH SOMEONE WOULD TEACH THOSE GUYS SOME OF THE CRUEL FACTS OF LIFE FROM THE REAL LIVE WORLD!
IN FACT, —HEH HEH— THAT GIVES ME AN IDEA! WE CAN JUST HAVE THE COMPUTOON© 8000 INFECT THE FREAK BROTHERS WITH A SUDDEN, IRRATIONAL DESIRE TO TRAVEL!
ISN'T THIS A MARVELOUS MACHINE? IT WRITES ALL OF OUR STORIES FOR US!
WHY DON'T YOU PUNCH THAT IN, MAVRIDES?
...S·U·D·D·E·N... ...I·R·R·A·T·I·O...
HA HA HA! IT'S GONNA SCATTER THAT BUNCH OF HAREBRAINS ALL OVER THE SURFACE OF THIS PLANET! IT'LL PROBABLY EVEN SEND FAT FREDDY SOMEPLACE WHERE HE WON'T BE ABLE TO FIND A MACDONALD'S! GUFFAW!
THAT SPACED-OUT GANG OF DRUGGIES WON'T LAST THIRTY MINUTES OUTSIDE THE U.S.A.! THEY'LL STARVE TO DEATH, OR BE MURDERED FOR SURE! NO MORE FREAK BROTHERS, HA HA!
NOW I'LL BE FREE TO MOVE TO GREENLAND!
THAT'S RIGHT! IT'S MY LIFE'S AMBITION TO MOVE TO GREENLAND AND GROW CITRUS FRUIT! YOU KNOW, I ALREADY OWN SOME PROPERTY UP THERE! BOUGHT IT THROUGH THE COMPUTOON© 8000, AS A MATTER OF FACT!
THAT LAND OUGHT TO BE WORTH A LOT OF MONEY NOW, WITH THE REAL ESTATE BOOM AND ALL, DON'T YOU THINK? I'VE NEVER SEEN THE PLACE ACTUALLY, BUT THE COMPUTER TELLS ME IT'S AS GREEN AS ANY PLACE IN GREENLAND! SOUNDS NICE, HUH?
SORRY, GENTLEMEN, BUT THE COMPUTER FOULED UP AND PUT NEXT YEAR'S DATE ON YOUR PAYCHECKS! I HOPE YOU DON'T MIND! YOU CAN WAIT, CAN'T YOU?
CERTAINLY! I'M ALREADY MAKING MORE MONEY THAN I KNOW WHAT TO DO WITH! HOW ABOUT YOU, MAVRIDES?
I DON'T MIND! IT'S A PRIVILEGE JUST TO BE HERE! THE COMPUTOON© 8000 DOES MOST OF THE ACTUAL WORK, ANYWAY!
LOOK! IT'S FINISHED WITH THE WHOLE STORY ALREADY! LET'S GET GOING ON THE ROUGH SKETCHES AND WE'LL BE ALL THROUGH IN A HALF-HOUR!
...AND SO THE FREAK BROTHERS ARE OFF ON THE GRAND TOUR! AND WHITHER THEY GO, ONLY THE COMPUTOON© 8000 SHALL KNOW.

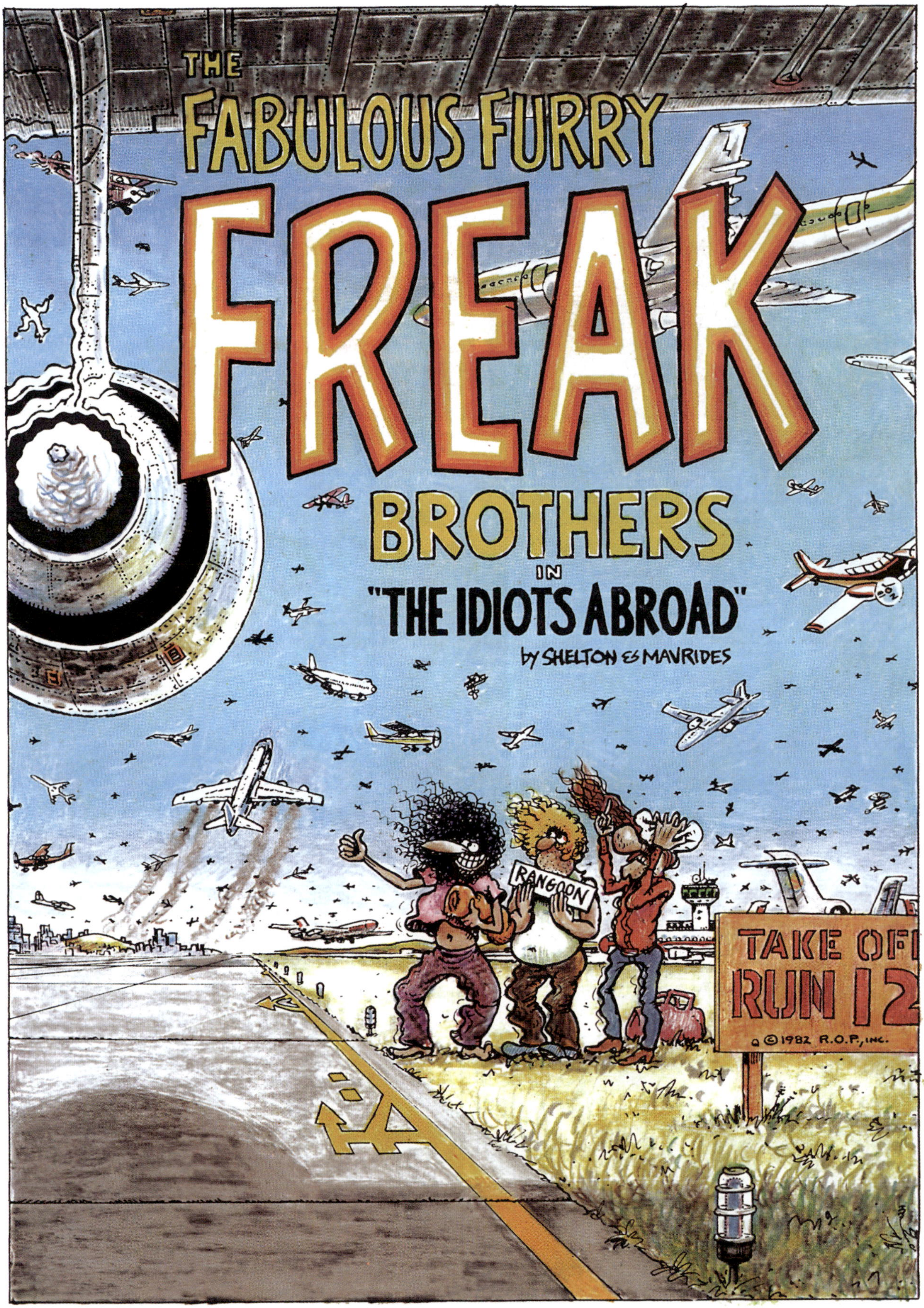
THE
FABULOUS FURRY
FREAK
BROTHERS
IN
"THE IDIOTS ABROAD"
by SHELTON & MAVRIDES
RANGOON
TAKE OF
RUN 12
© 1982 R.O.P., INC.

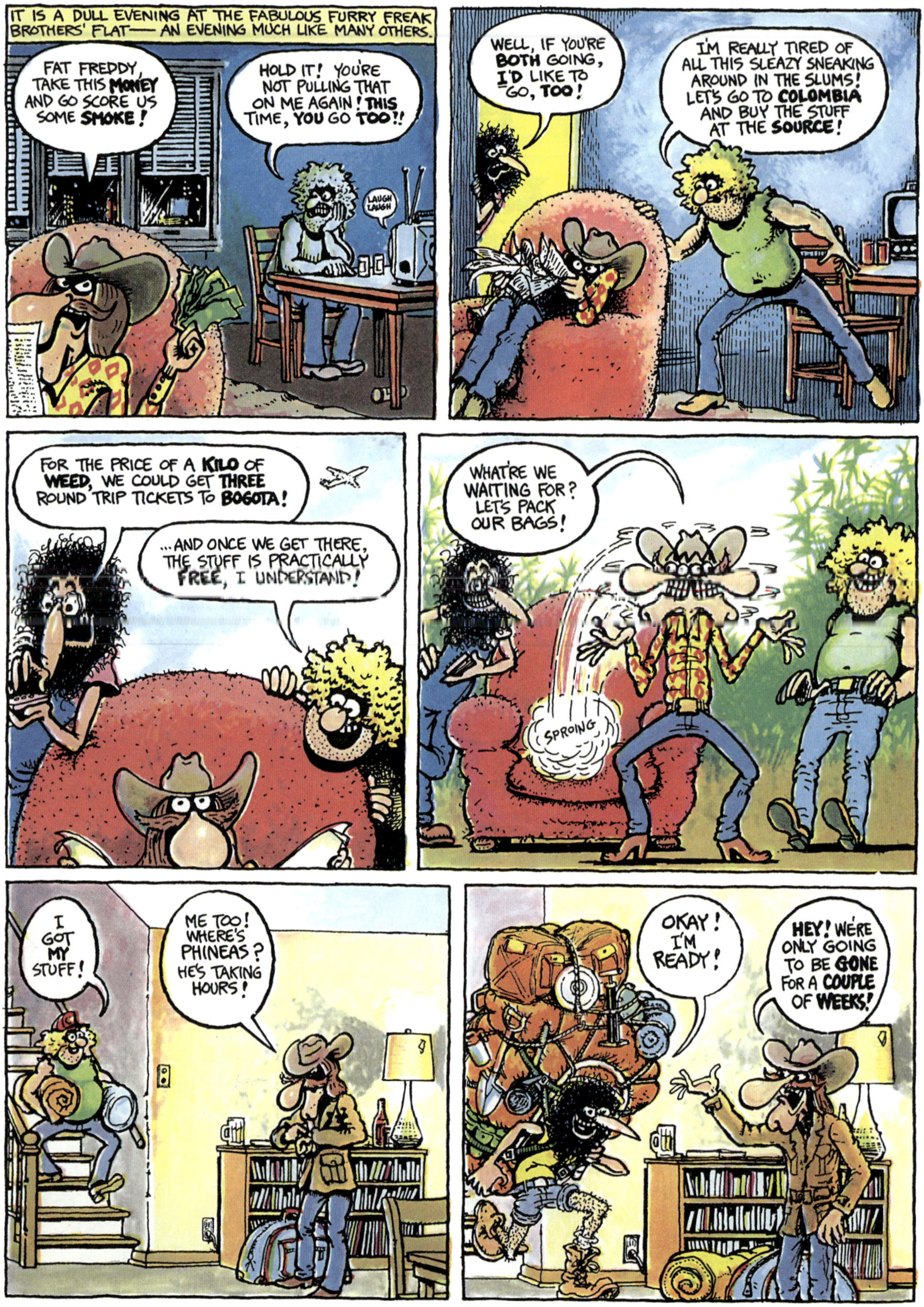
IT IS A DULL EVENING AT THE FABULOUS FURRY FREAK BROTHERS' FLAT— AN EVENING MUCH LIKE MANY OTHERS.
FAT FREDDY, TAKE THIS MONEY AND GO SCORE US SOME SMOKE!
HOLD IT! YOU'RE NOT PULLING THAT ON ME AGAIN! THIS TIME, YOU GO TOO!!
LAUGH LAUGH
WELL, IF YOU'RE BOTH GOING, I'D LIKE TO GO, TOO!
I'M REALLY TIRED OF ALL THIS SLEAZY SNEAKING AROUND IN THE SLUMS! LET'S GO TO COLOMBIA AND BUY THE STUFF AT THE SOURCE!
FOR THE PRICE OF A KILO OF WEED, WE COULD GET THREE ROUND TRIP TICKETS TO BOGOTA!
...AND ONCE WE GET THERE, THE STUFF IS PRACTICALLY FREE, I UNDERSTAND!
WHAT'RE WE WAITING FOR? LET'S PACK OUR BAGS!
SPROING
I GOT MY STUFF!
ME TOO! WHERE'S PHINEAS? HE'S TAKING HOURS!
OKAY! I'M READY!
HEY! WE'RE ONLY GOING TO BE GONE FOR A COUPLE OF WEEKS!

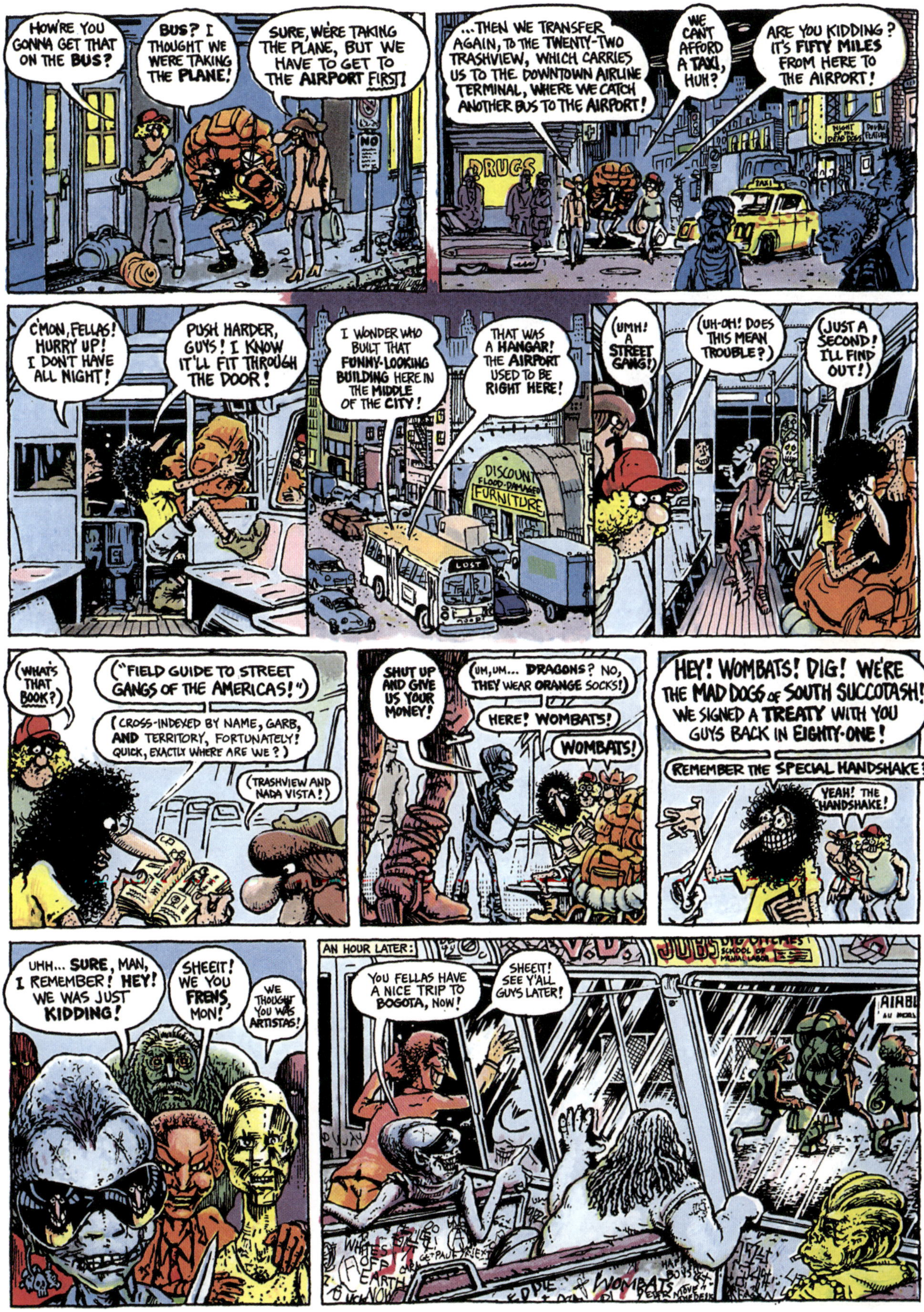
HOW'RE YOU GONNA GET THAT ON THE BUS?
BUS? I THOUGHT WE WERE TAKING THE PLANE!
SURE, WE'RE TAKING THE PLANE, BUT WE HAVE TO GET TO THE AIRPORT FIRST!
NO
...THEN WE TRANSFER AGAIN, TO THE TWENTY-TWO TRASHVIEW, WHICH CARRIES US TO THE DOWNTOWN AIRLINE TERMINAL, WHERE WE CATCH ANOTHER BUS TO THE AIRPORT!
WE CAN'T AFFORD A TAXI, HUH?
ARE YOU KIDDING? IT'S FIFTY MILES FROM HERE TO THE AIRPORT!
DRUGS
TAXI
C'MON, FELLAS! HURRY UP! I DON'T HAVE ALL NIGHT!
PUSH HARDER, GUYS! I KNOW IT'LL FIT THROUGH THE DOOR!
I WONDER WHO BUILT THAT FUNNY-LOOKING BUILDING HERE IN THE MIDDLE OF THE CITY!
THAT WAS A HANGAR! THE AIRPORT USED TO BE RIGHT HERE!
DISCOUNT FLOOD-DAMAGED FURNITURE
LOST
(UMH! A STREET GANG!)
(UH-OH! DOES THIS MEAN TROUBLE?)
(JUST A SECOND! I'LL FIND OUT!)
(WHAT'S THAT BOOK?)
("FIELD GUIDE TO STREET GANGS OF THE AMERICAS!")
(CROSS-INDEXED BY NAME, GARB, AND TERRITORY, FORTUNATELY! QUICK, EXACTLY WHERE ARE WE?)
(TRASHVIEW AND NADA VISTA!)
SHUT UP AND GIVE US YOUR MONEY!
(UM, UM... DRAGONS? NO, THEY WEAR ORANGE SOCKS!)
HERE! WOMBATS!
WOMBATS!
HEY! WOMBATS! DIG! WE'RE THE MAD DOGS OF SOUTH SUCCOTASH! WE SIGNED A TREATY WITH YOU GUYS BACK IN EIGHTY-ONE!
REMEMBER THE SPECIAL HANDSHAKE?
YEAH! THE HANDSHAKE!
UHH... SURE, MAN, I REMEMBER! HEY! WE WAS JUST KIDDING!
SHEEIT! WE YOU FRENS, MON!
WE THOUGHT YOU WAS ARTISTAS!
AN HOUR LATER:
YOU FELLAS HAVE A NICE TRIP TO BOGOTA, NOW!
SHEEIT! SEE Y'ALL GUYS LATER!
WOMBATS

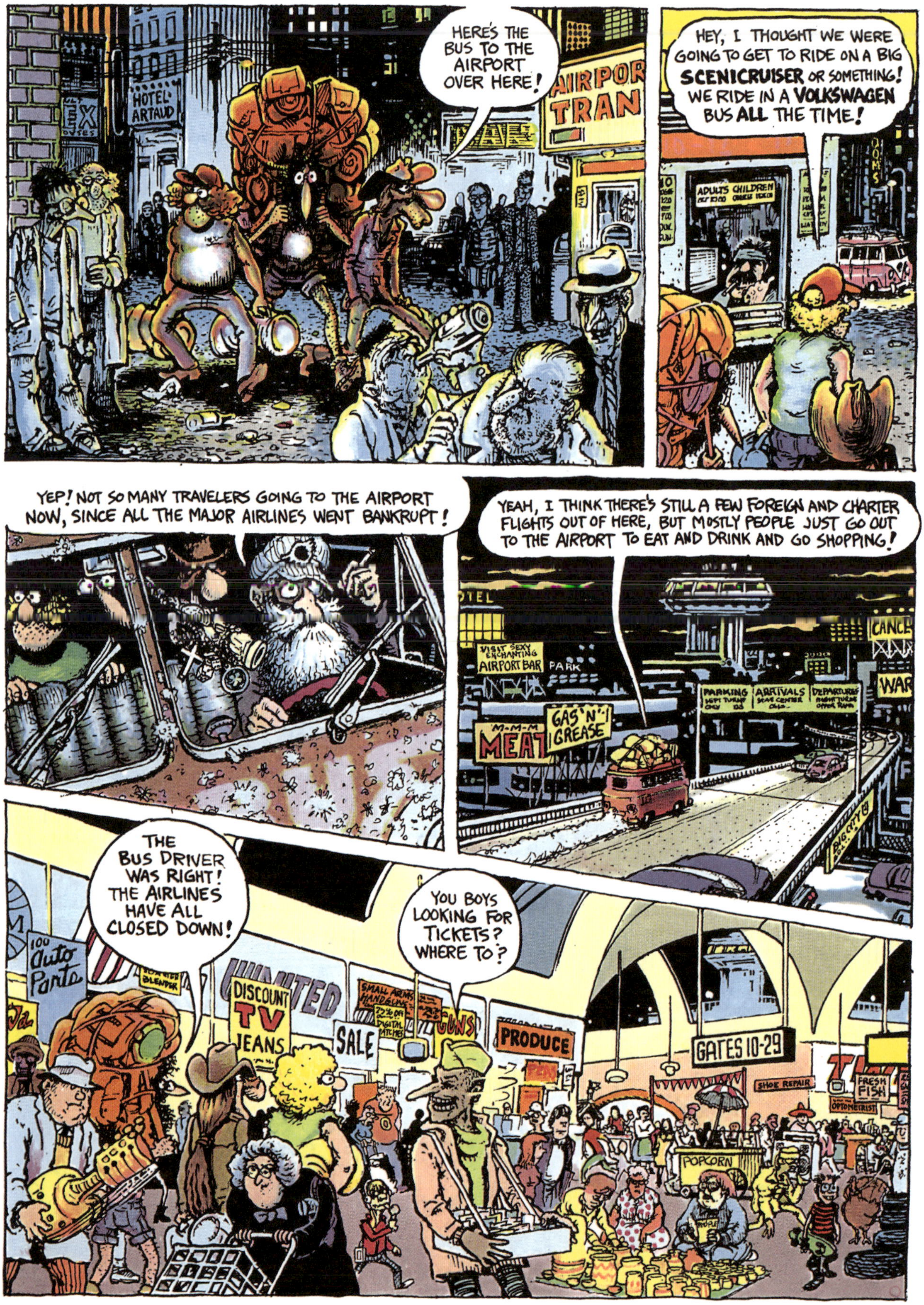

HERE'S THE BUS TO THE AIRPORT OVER HERE!
HOTEL ARTAUD
AIRPOR TRAN
HEY, I THOUGHT WE WERE GOING TO GET TO RIDE ON A BIG SCENICRUISER OR SOMETHING! WE RIDE IN A VOLKSWAGEN BUS ALL THE TIME!
ADULTS CHILDREN
YEP! NOT SO MANY TRAVELERS GOING TO THE AIRPORT NOW, SINCE ALL THE MAJOR AIRLINES WENT BANKRUPT!
YEAH, I THINK THERE'S STILL A FEW FOREIGN AND CHARTER FLIGHTS OUT OF HERE, BUT MOSTLY PEOPLE JUST GO OUT TO THE AIRPORT TO EAT AND DRINK AND GO SHOPPING!
VISIT SEXY ENCHANTING AIRPORT BAR
PARK
PARKING
ARRIVALS
DEPARTURES
GAS 'N' GREASE
M-M-M MEAT
THE BUS DRIVER WAS RIGHT! THE AIRLINES HAVE ALL CLOSED DOWN!
YOU BOYS LOOKING FOR TICKETS? WHERE TO?
100 auto Parts
DISCOUNT TV JEANS
SALE
GUNS
PRODUCE
GATES 10-29
SHOE REPAIR
FRESH FISH
OPTOMETRIST
POPCORN

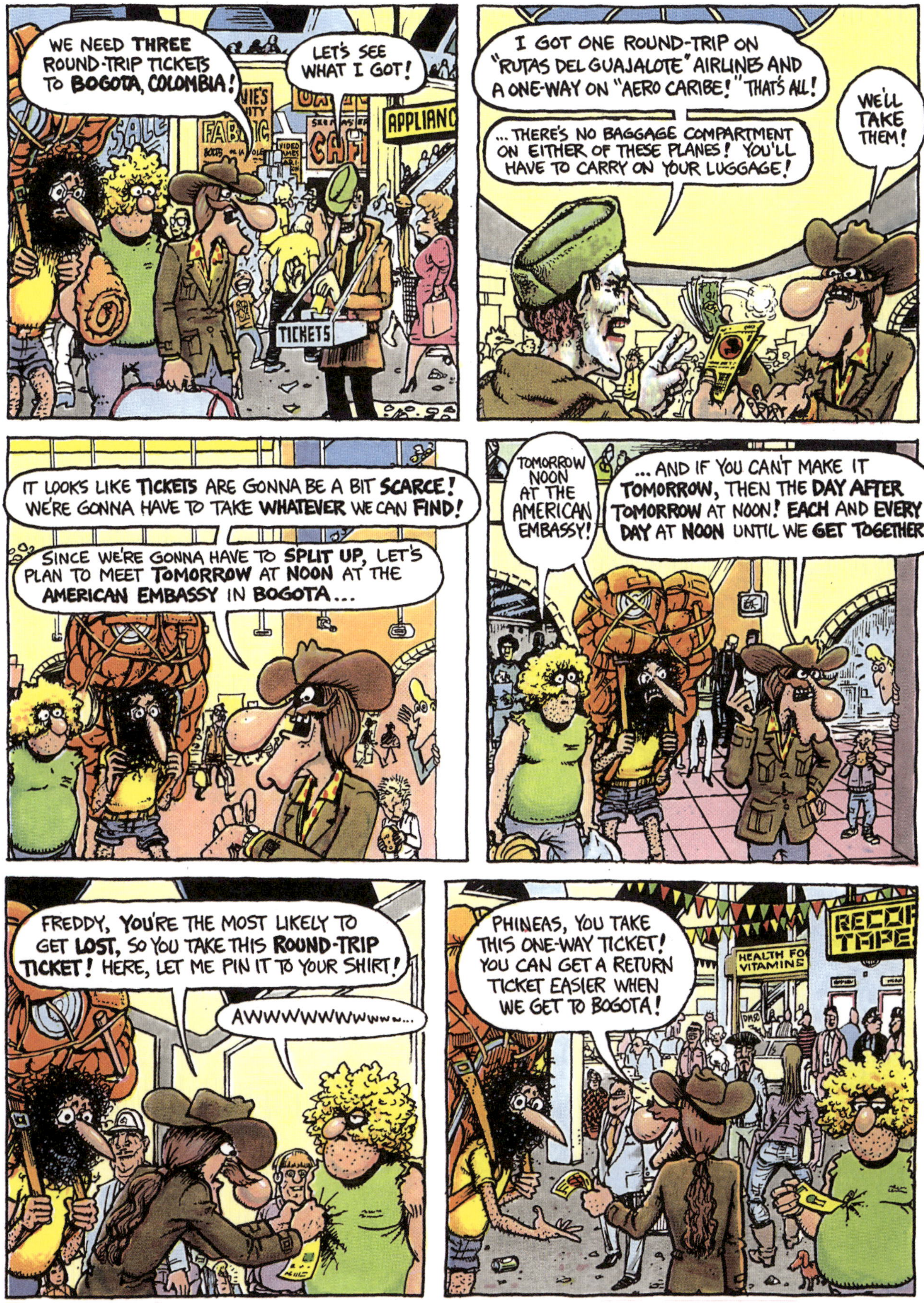
WE NEED THREE ROUND-TRIP TICKETS TO BOGOTA, COLOMBIA!
LET'S SEE WHAT I GOT!
TICKETS
I GOT ONE ROUND-TRIP ON "RUTAS DEL GUAJALOTE" AIRLINES AND A ONE-WAY ON "AERO CARIBE!" THAT'S ALL!
...THERE'S NO BAGGAGE COMPARTMENT ON EITHER OF THESE PLANES! YOU'LL HAVE TO CARRY ON YOUR LUGGAGE!
WE'LL TAKE THEM!
IT LOOKS LIKE TICKETS ARE GONNA BE A BIT SCARCE! WE'RE GONNA HAVE TO TAKE WHATEVER WE CAN FIND!
SINCE WE'RE GONNA HAVE TO SPLIT UP, LET'S PLAN TO MEET TOMORROW AT NOON AT THE AMERICAN EMBASSY IN BOGOTA...
TOMORROW NOON AT THE AMERICAN EMBASSY!
...AND IF YOU CAN'T MAKE IT TOMORROW, THEN THE DAY AFTER TOMORROW AT NOON! EACH AND EVERY DAY AT NOON UNTIL WE GET TOGETHER!
FREDDY, YOU'RE THE MOST LIKELY TO GET LOST, SO YOU TAKE THIS ROUND-TRIP TICKET! HERE, LET ME PIN IT TO YOUR SHIRT!
AWWWWWWWwww...
PHINEAS, YOU TAKE THIS ONE-WAY TICKET! YOU CAN GET A RETURN TICKET EASIER WHEN WE GET TO BOGOTA!

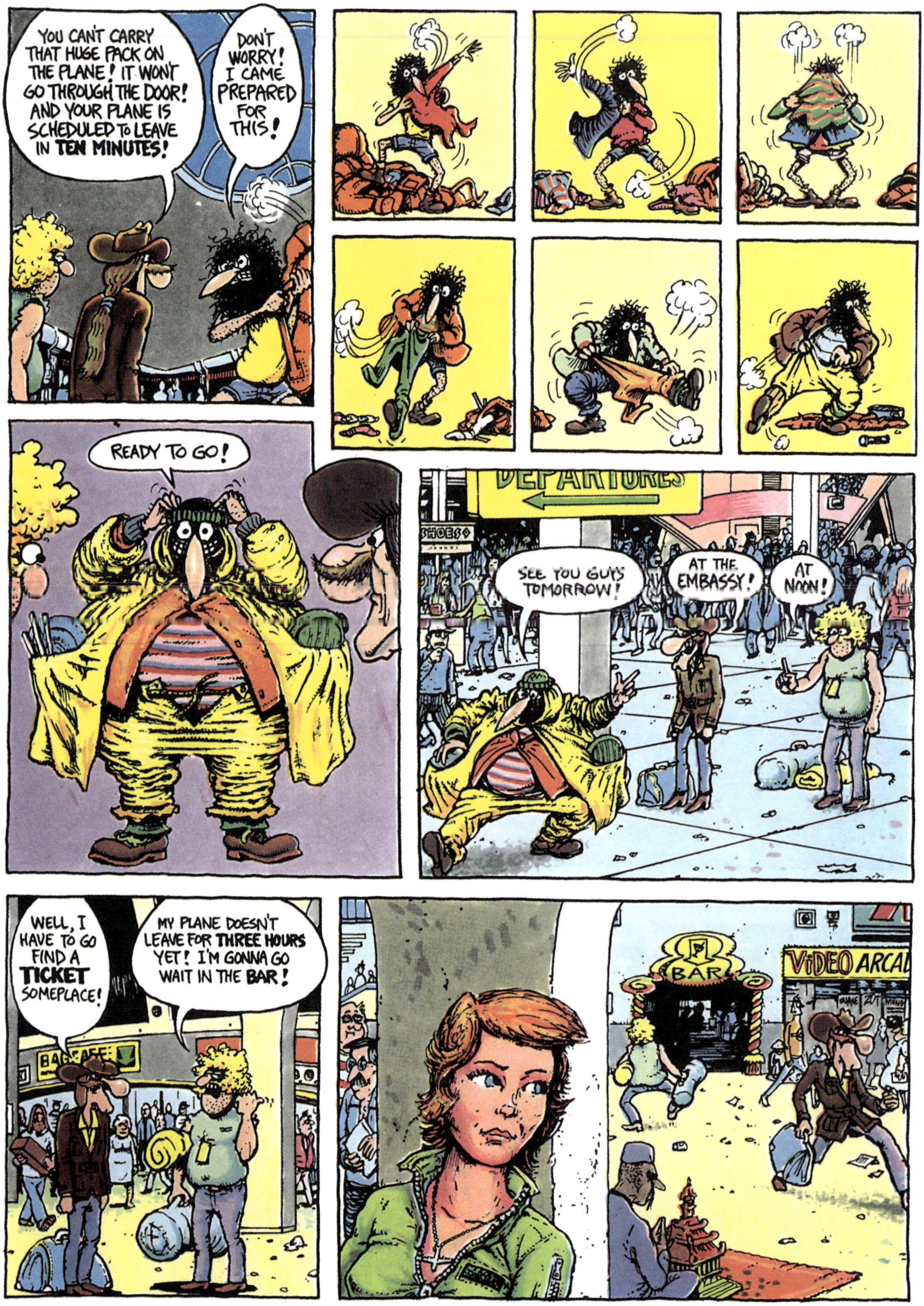
YOU CAN'T CARRY THAT HUGE PACK ON THE PLANE! IT WON'T GO THROUGH THE DOOR! AND YOUR PLANE IS SCHEDULED TO LEAVE IN TEN MINUTES!
DON'T WORRY! I CAME PREPARED FOR THIS!
READY TO GO!
DEPARTURES
SHOES
SEE YOU GUYS TOMORROW!
AT THE EMBASSY!
AT NOON!
WELL, I HAVE TO GO FIND A TICKET SOMEPLACE!
MY PLANE DOESN'T LEAVE FOR THREE HOURS YET! I'M GONNA GO WAIT IN THE BAR!
BAR
VIDEO ARCAD

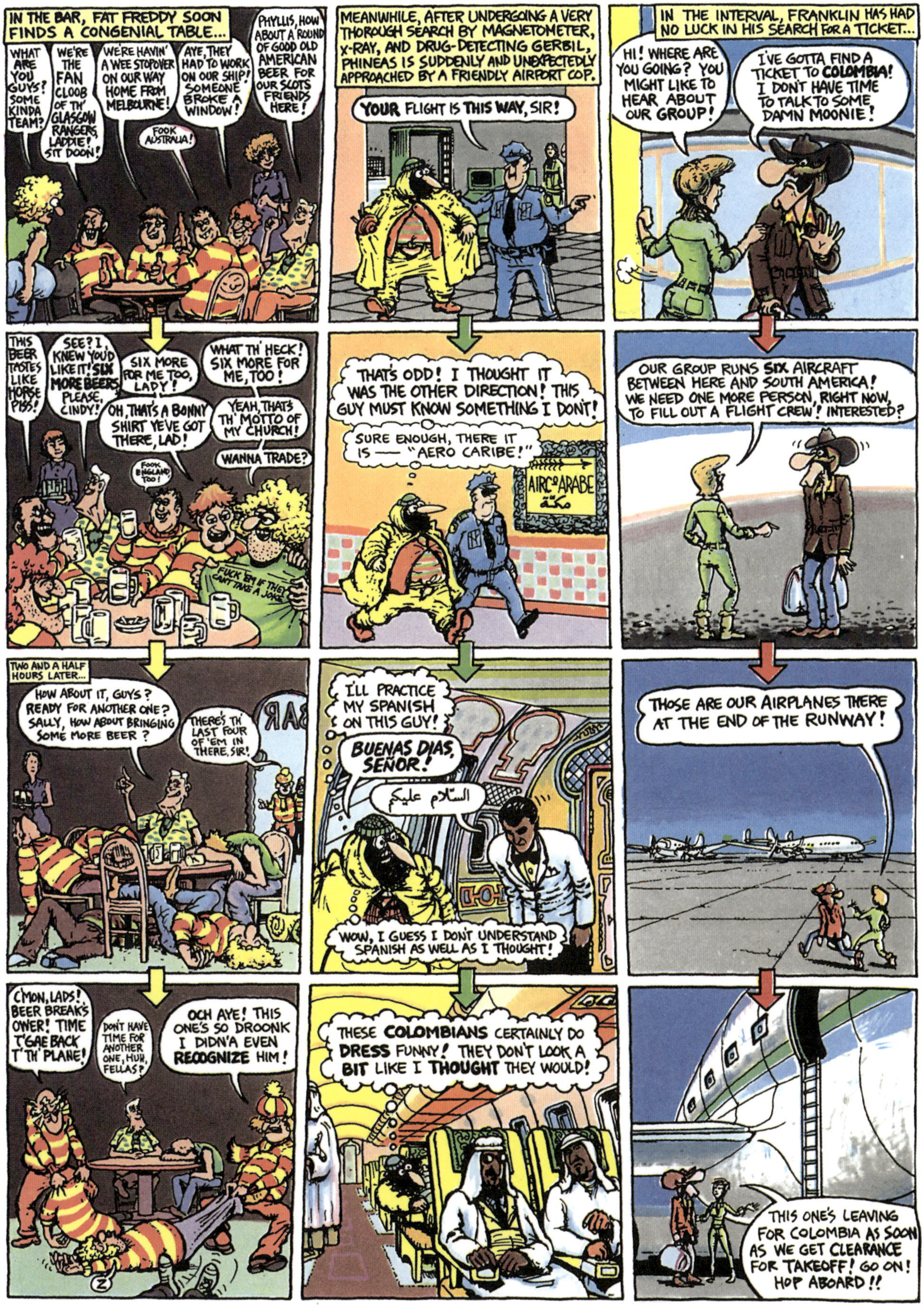
IN THE BAR, FAT FREDDY SOON FINDS A CONGENIAL TABLE...
WHAT ARE YOU GUYS? SOME KINDA TEAM?
WE'RE THE FAN CLOOB OF TH' GLASGOW RANGERS, LADDIE! SIT DOON!
WE'RE HAVIN' A WEE STOPOVER ON OUR WAY HOME FROM MELBOURNE!
AYE, THEY HAD TO WORK ON OUR SHIP! SOMEONE BROKE A WINDOW!
PHYLLIS, HOW ABOUT A ROUND OF GOOD OLD AMERICAN BEER FOR OUR SCOTS FRIENDS HERE!
FOOK AUSTRALIA!
THIS BEER TASTES LIKE HORSE PISS!
SEE? I KNEW YOU'D LIKE IT! SIX MORE BEERS, PLEASE, CINDY!
SIX MORE FOR ME TOO, LADY!
WHAT TH' HECK! SIX MORE FOR ME, TOO!
OH, THAT'S A BONNY SHIRT YE'VE GOT THERE, LAD!
YEAH, THAT'S TH' MOTTO OF MY CHURCH!
WANNA TRADE?
FOOK ENGLAND TOO!
FUCK 'EM IF THEY CAN'T TAKE A JOKE
TWO AND A HALF HOURS LATER...
HOW ABOUT IT, GUYS? READY FOR ANOTHER ONE? SALLY, HOW ABOUT BRINGING SOME MORE BEER?
THERE'S TH' LAST FOUR OF 'EM IN THERE, SIR!
BAR
C'MON, LADS! BEER BREAK'S OWER! TIME T'GAE BACK T' TH' PLANE!
DON'T HAVE TIME FOR ANOTHER ONE, HUH, FELLAS?
OCH AYE! THIS ONE'S SO DROONK I DIDN'A EVEN RECOGNIZE HIM!
Z
MEANWHILE, AFTER UNDERGOING A VERY THOROUGH SEARCH BY MAGNETOMETER, X-RAY, AND DRUG-DETECTING GERBIL, PHINEAS IS SUDDENLY AND UNEXPECTEDLY APPROACHED BY A FRIENDLY AIRPORT COP.
YOUR FLIGHT IS THIS WAY, SIR!
THAT'S ODD! I THOUGHT IT WAS THE OTHER DIRECTION! THIS GUY MUST KNOW SOMETHING I DON'T!
SURE ENOUGH, THERE IT IS — "AERO CARIBE!"
AIRCo ARABE
I'LL PRACTICE MY SPANISH ON THIS GUY!
BUENAS DIAS, SEÑOR!
السلام عليكم
WOW, I GUESS I DON'T UNDERSTAND SPANISH AS WELL AS I THOUGHT!
THESE COLOMBIANS CERTAINLY DO DRESS FUNNY! THEY DON'T LOOK A BIT LIKE I THOUGHT THEY WOULD!
IN THE INTERVAL, FRANKLIN HAS HAD NO LUCK IN HIS SEARCH FOR A TICKET...
HI! WHERE ARE YOU GOING? YOU MIGHT LIKE TO HEAR ABOUT OUR GROUP!
I'VE GOTTA FIND A TICKET TO COLOMBIA! I DON'T HAVE TIME TO TALK TO SOME DAMN MOONIE!
OUR GROUP RUNS SIX AIRCRAFT BETWEEN HERE AND SOUTH AMERICA! WE NEED ONE MORE PERSON, RIGHT NOW, TO FILL OUT A FLIGHT CREW! INTERESTED?
THOSE ARE OUR AIRPLANES THERE AT THE END OF THE RUNWAY!
THIS ONE'S LEAVING FOR COLOMBIA AS SOON AS WE GET CLEARANCE FOR TAKEOFF! GO ON! HOP ABOARD!!

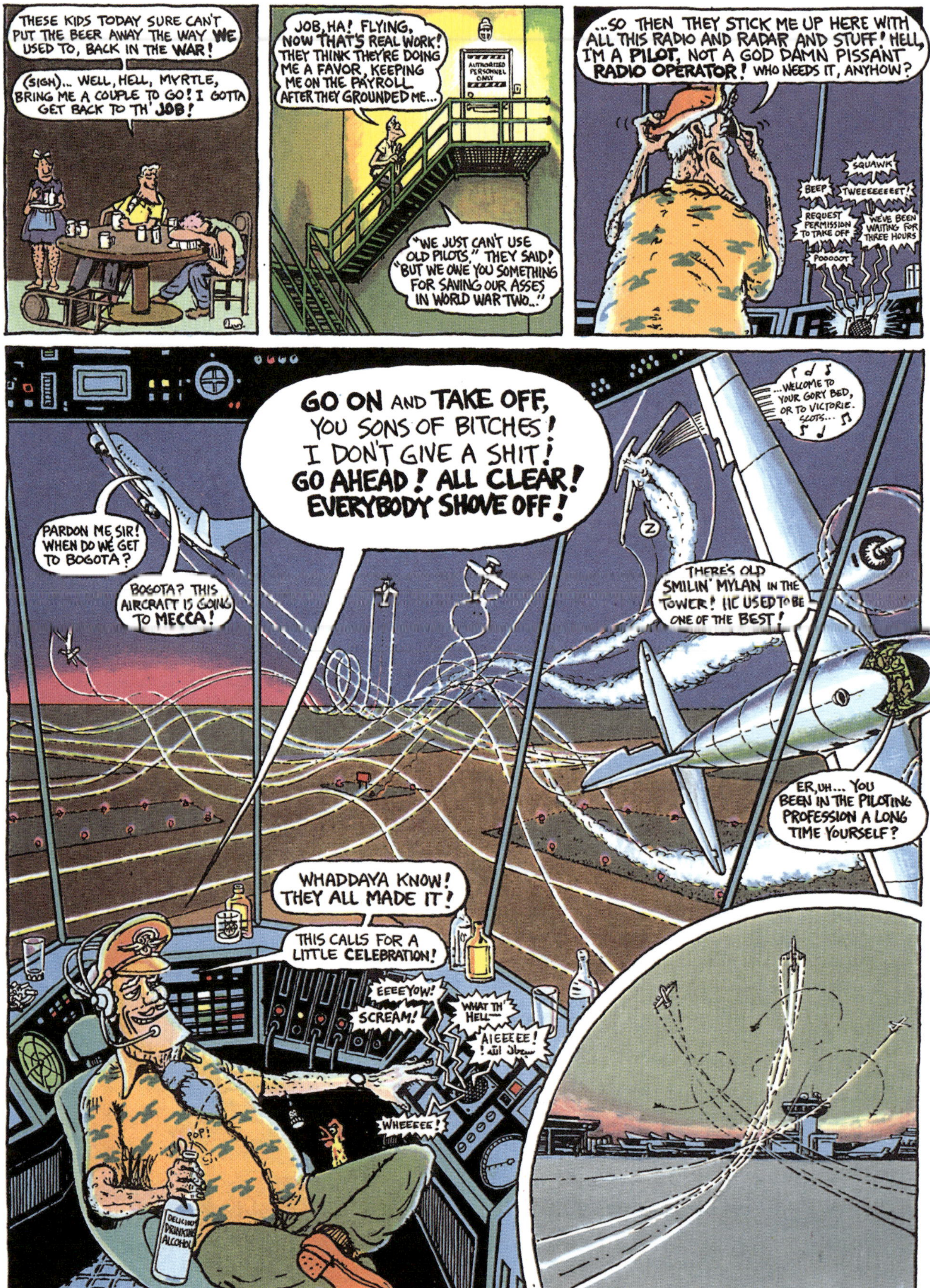
THESE KIDS TODAY SURE CAN'T PUT THE BEER AWAY THE WAY WE USED TO, BACK IN THE WAR!
(SIGH)... WELL, HELL, MYRTLE, BRING ME A COUPLE TO GO! I GOTTA GET BACK TO TH' JOB!
JOB, HA! FLYING, NOW THAT'S REAL WORK! THEY THINK THEY'RE DOING ME A FAVOR, KEEPING ME ON THE PAYROLL AFTER THEY GROUNDED ME...
AUTHORIZED PERSONNEL ONLY
"WE JUST CAN'T USE OLD PILOTS," THEY SAID! "BUT WE OWE YOU SOMETHING FOR SAVING OUR ASSES IN WORLD WAR TWO..."
...SO THEN THEY STICK ME UP HERE WITH ALL THIS RADIO AND RADAR AND STUFF! HELL, I'M A PILOT, NOT A GOD DAMN PISSANT RADIO OPERATOR! WHO NEEDS IT, ANYHOW?
SQUAWK
BEEP
TWEEEEEEEET!
REQUEST PERMISSION TO TAKE OFF
WE'VE BEEN WAITING FOR THREE HOURS
POOOOOT
GO ON AND TAKE OFF, YOU SONS OF BITCHES! I DON'T GIVE A SHIT! GO AHEAD! ALL CLEAR! EVERYBODY SHOVE OFF!
...WELCOME TO YOUR GORY BED, OR TO VICTORIE. SCOTS...
PARDON ME SIR! WHEN DO WE GET TO BOGOTA?
BOGOTA? THIS AIRCRAFT IS GOING TO MECCA!
Z
THERE'S OLD SMILIN' MYLAN IN THE TOWER! HE USED TO BE ONE OF THE BEST!
ER, UH... YOU BEEN IN THE PILOTING PROFESSION A LONG TIME YOURSELF?
WHADDAYA KNOW! THEY ALL MADE IT!
THIS CALLS FOR A LITTLE CELEBRATION!
EEEEYOW!
SCREAM!
WHAT TH' HELL—
AIEEEEE!
WHEEEEE!
POP!
DELICIOUS DRINKING ALCOHOL

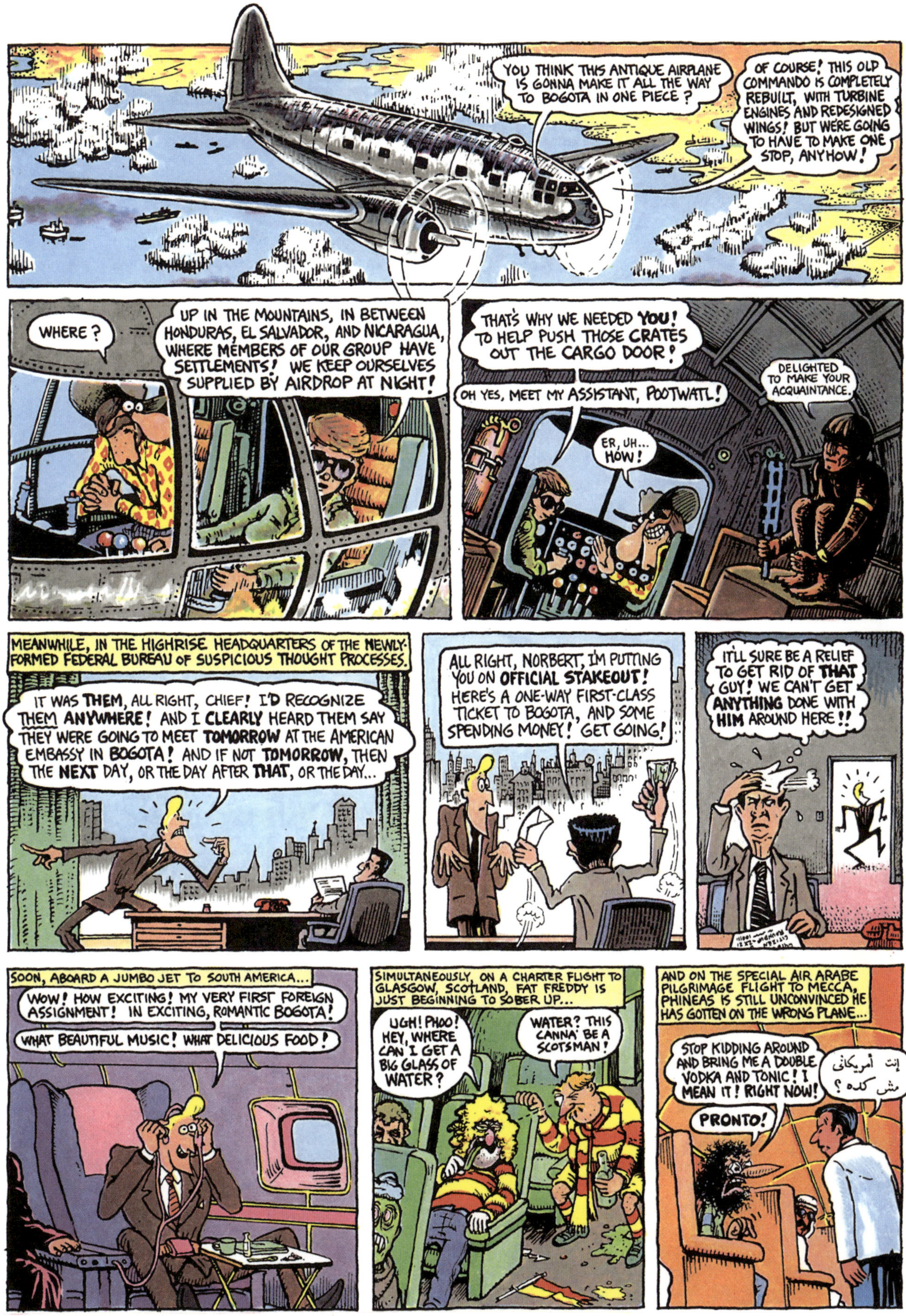

YOU THINK THIS ANTIQUE AIRPLANE IS GONNA MAKE IT ALL THE WAY TO BOGOTA IN ONE PIECE?
OF COURSE! THIS OLD COMMANDO IS COMPLETELY REBUILT, WITH TURBINE ENGINES AND REDESIGNED WINGS! BUT WE'RE GOING TO HAVE TO MAKE ONE STOP, ANYHOW!
WHERE?
UP IN THE MOUNTAINS, IN BETWEEN HONDURAS, EL SALVADOR, AND NICARAGUA, WHERE MEMBERS OF OUR GROUP HAVE SETTLEMENTS! WE KEEP OURSELVES SUPPLIED BY AIRDROP AT NIGHT!
THAT'S WHY WE NEEDED YOU! TO HELP PUSH THOSE CRATES OUT THE CARGO DOOR!
OH YES, MEET MY ASSISTANT, POOTWATL!
DELIGHTED TO MAKE YOUR ACQUAINTANCE.
ER, UH... HOW!
MEANWHILE, IN THE HIGHRISE HEADQUARTERS OF THE NEWLY-FORMED FEDERAL BUREAU OF SUSPICIOUS THOUGHT PROCESSES.
IT WAS THEM, ALL RIGHT, CHIEF! I'D RECOGNIZE THEM ANYWHERE! AND I CLEARLY HEARD THEM SAY THEY WERE GOING TO MEET TOMORROW AT THE AMERICAN EMBASSY IN BOGOTA! AND IF NOT TOMORROW, THEN THE NEXT DAY, OR THE DAY AFTER THAT, OR THE DAY...
ALL RIGHT, NORBERT, I'M PUTTING YOU ON OFFICIAL STAKEOUT! HERE'S A ONE-WAY FIRST-CLASS TICKET TO BOGOTA, AND SOME SPENDING MONEY! GET GOING!
IT'LL SURE BE A RELIEF TO GET RID OF THAT GUY! WE CAN'T GET ANYTHING DONE WITH HIM AROUND HERE!!
SOON, ABOARD A JUMBO JET TO SOUTH AMERICA...
WOW! HOW EXCITING! MY VERY FIRST FOREIGN ASSIGNMENT! IN EXCITING, ROMANTIC BOGOTA!
WHAT BEAUTIFUL MUSIC! WHAT DELICIOUS FOOD!
SIMULTANEOUSLY, ON A CHARTER FLIGHT TO GLASGOW, SCOTLAND, FAT FREDDY IS JUST BEGINNING TO SOBER UP...
UGH! PHOO! HEY, WHERE CAN I GET A BIG GLASS OF WATER?
WATER? THIS CANNA' BE A SCOTSMAN!
AND ON THE SPECIAL AIR ARABE PILGRIMAGE FLIGHT TO MECCA, PHINEAS IS STILL UNCONVINCED HE HAS GOTTEN ON THE WRONG PLANE...
STOP KIDDING AROUND AND BRING ME A DOUBLE VODKA AND TONIC! I MEAN IT! RIGHT NOW!
إنت أمريكاني مش كده ؟
PRONTO!

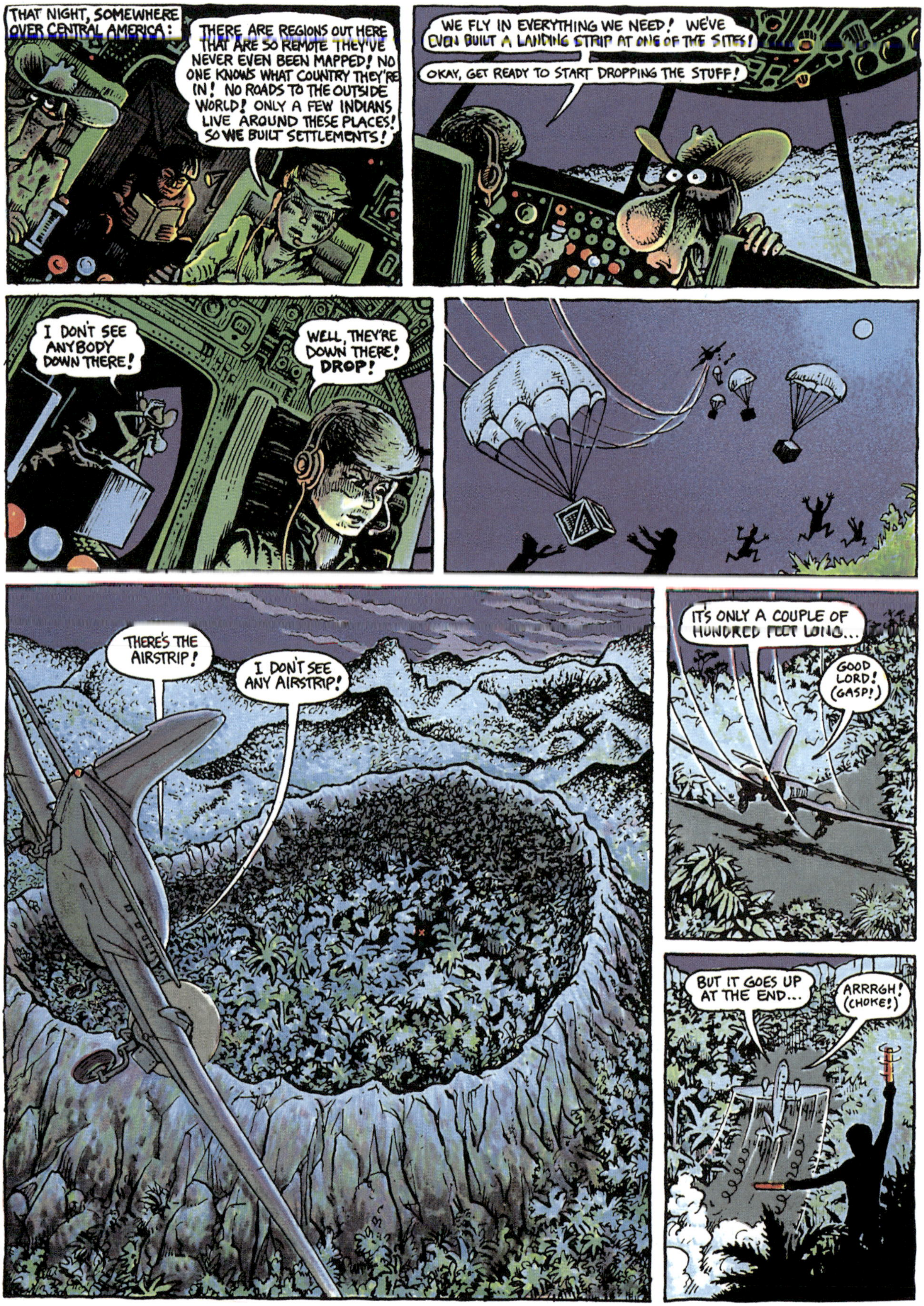

THAT NIGHT, SOMEWHERE OVER CENTRAL AMERICA:
THERE ARE REGIONS OUT HERE THAT ARE SO REMOTE THEY'VE NEVER EVEN BEEN MAPPED! NO ONE KNOWS WHAT COUNTRY THEY'RE IN! NO ROADS TO THE OUTSIDE WORLD! ONLY A FEW INDIANS LIVE AROUND THESE PLACES! SO WE BUILT SETTLEMENTS!
WE FLY IN EVERYTHING WE NEED! WE'VE EVEN BUILT A LANDING STRIP AT ONE OF THE SITES!
OKAY, GET READY TO START DROPPING THE STUFF!
I DON'T SEE ANYBODY DOWN THERE!
WELL, THEY'RE DOWN THERE! DROP!
THERE'S THE AIRSTRIP!
I DON'T SEE ANY AIRSTRIP!
IT'S ONLY A COUPLE OF HUNDRED FEET LONG...
GOOD LORD! (GASP!)
BUT IT GOES UP AT THE END...
ARRRGH! (CHOKE!)

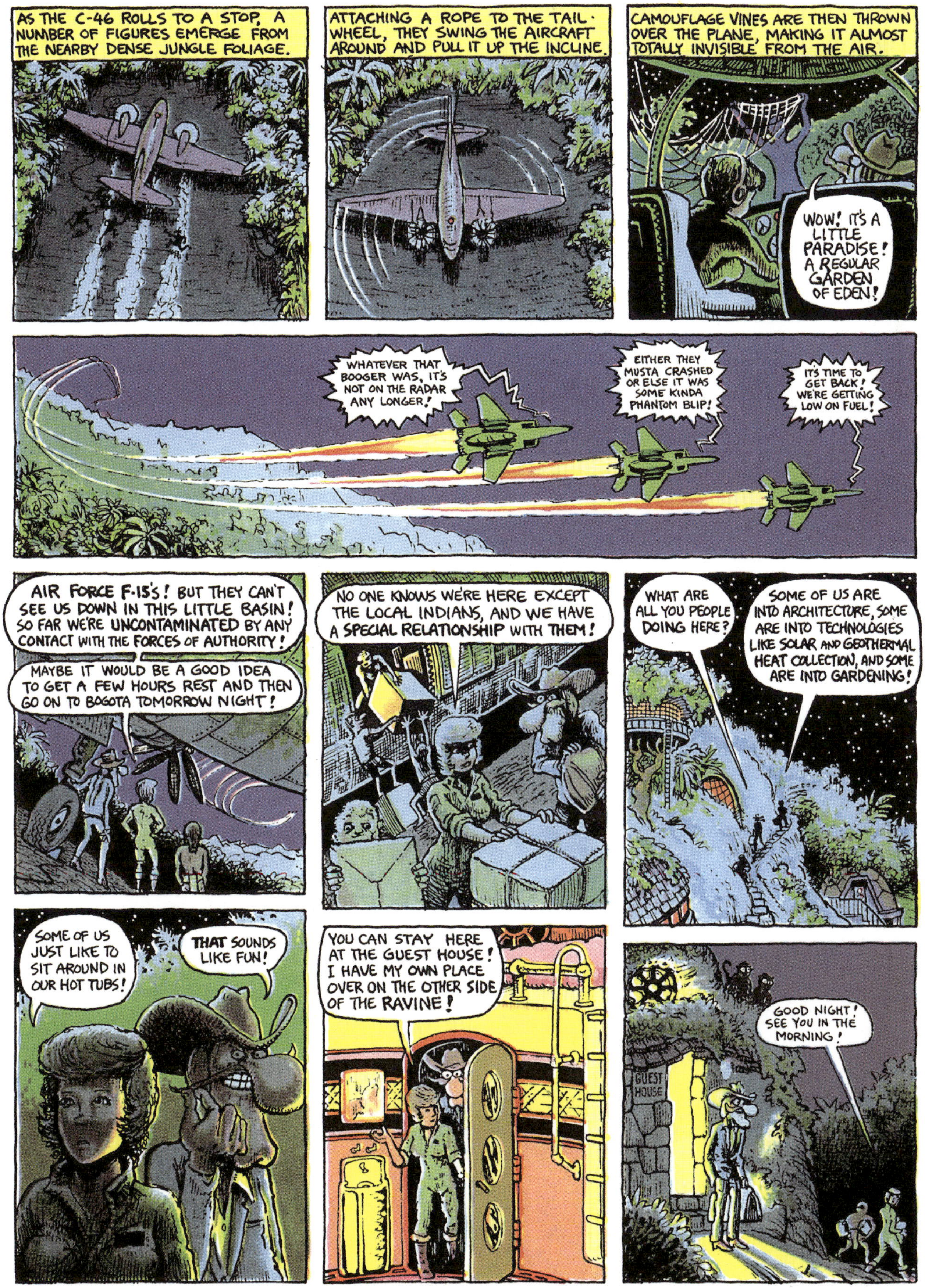
AS THE C-46 ROLLS TO A STOP, A NUMBER OF FIGURES EMERGE FROM THE NEARBY DENSE JUNGLE FOLIAGE.
ATTACHING A ROPE TO THE TAIL-WHEEL, THEY SWING THE AIRCRAFT AROUND AND PULL IT UP THE INCLINE.
CAMOUFLAGE VINES ARE THEN THROWN OVER THE PLANE, MAKING IT ALMOST TOTALLY INVISIBLE FROM THE AIR.
WOW! IT'S A LITTLE PARADISE! A REGULAR GARDEN OF EDEN!
WHATEVER THAT BOOGER WAS, IT'S NOT ON THE RADAR ANY LONGER!
EITHER THEY MUSTA CRASHED OR ELSE IT WAS SOME KINDA PHANTOM BLIP!
IT'S TIME TO GET BACK! WE'RE GETTING LOW ON FUEL!
AIR FORCE F-15'S! BUT THEY CAN'T SEE US DOWN IN THIS LITTLE BASIN! SO FAR WE'RE UNCONTAMINATED BY ANY CONTACT WITH THE FORCES OF AUTHORITY!
MAYBE IT WOULD BE A GOOD IDEA TO GET A FEW HOURS REST AND THEN GO ON TO BOGOTA TOMORROW NIGHT!
NO ONE KNOWS WE'RE HERE EXCEPT THE LOCAL INDIANS, AND WE HAVE A SPECIAL RELATIONSHIP WITH THEM!
WHAT ARE ALL YOU PEOPLE DOING HERE?
SOME OF US ARE INTO ARCHITECTURE, SOME ARE INTO TECHNOLOGIES LIKE SOLAR AND GEOTHERMAL HEAT COLLECTION, AND SOME ARE INTO GARDENING!
SOME OF US JUST LIKE TO SIT AROUND IN OUR HOT TUBS!
THAT SOUNDS LIKE FUN!
YOU CAN STAY HERE AT THE GUEST HOUSE! I HAVE MY OWN PLACE OVER ON THE OTHER SIDE OF THE RAVINE!
GUEST HOUSE
GOOD NIGHT! SEE YOU IN THE MORNING!

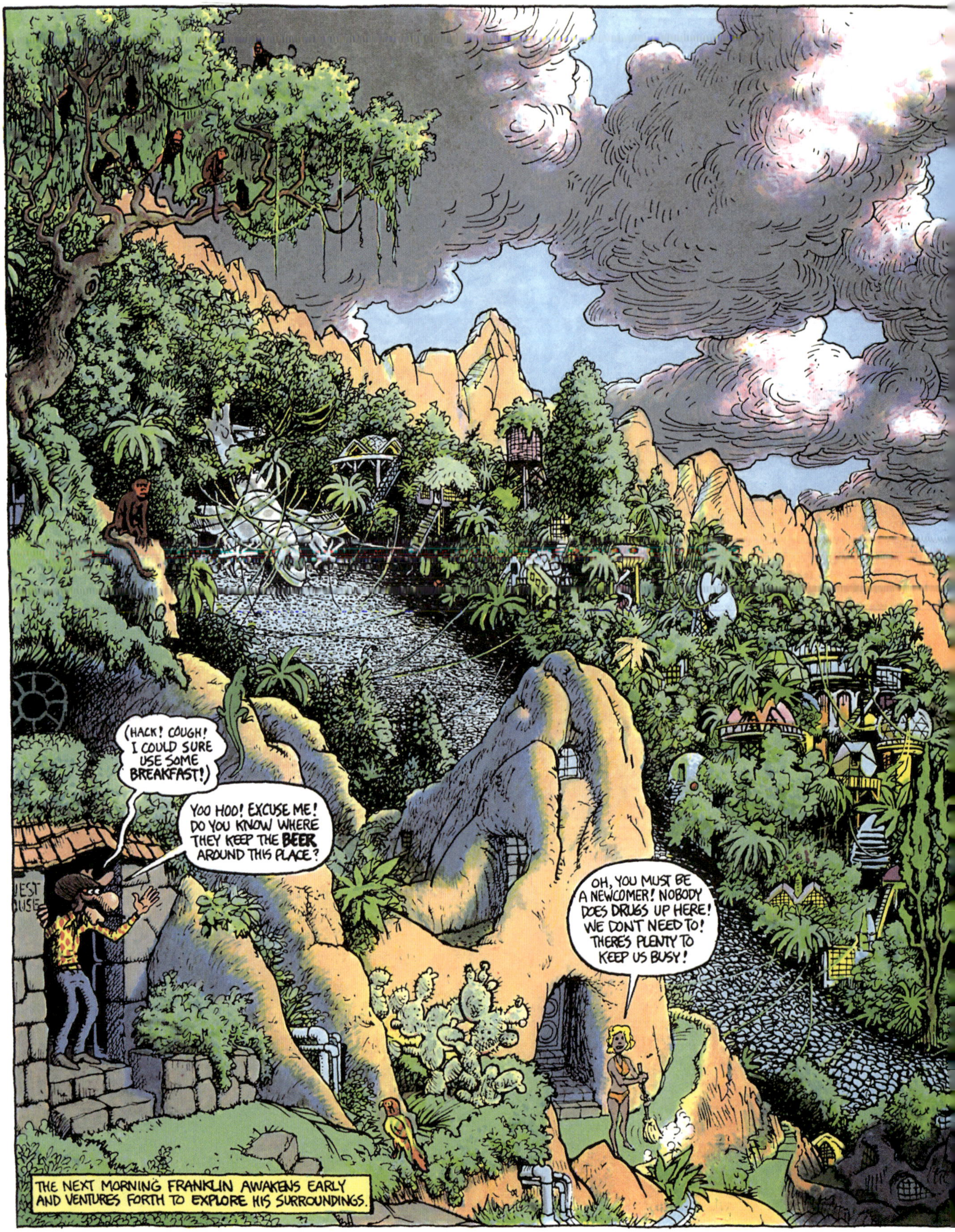
(HACK! COUGH! I COULD SURE USE SOME BREAKFAST!)
YOO HOO! EXCUSE ME! DO YOU KNOW WHERE THEY KEEP THE BEER AROUND THIS PLACE?
GUEST HOUSE
OH, YOU MUST BE A NEWCOMER! NOBODY DOES DRUGS UP HERE! WE DON'T NEED TO! THERE'S PLENTY TO KEEP US BUSY!
THE NEXT MORNING FRANKLIN AWAKENS EARLY AND VENTURES FORTH TO EXPLORE HIS SURROUNDINGS.

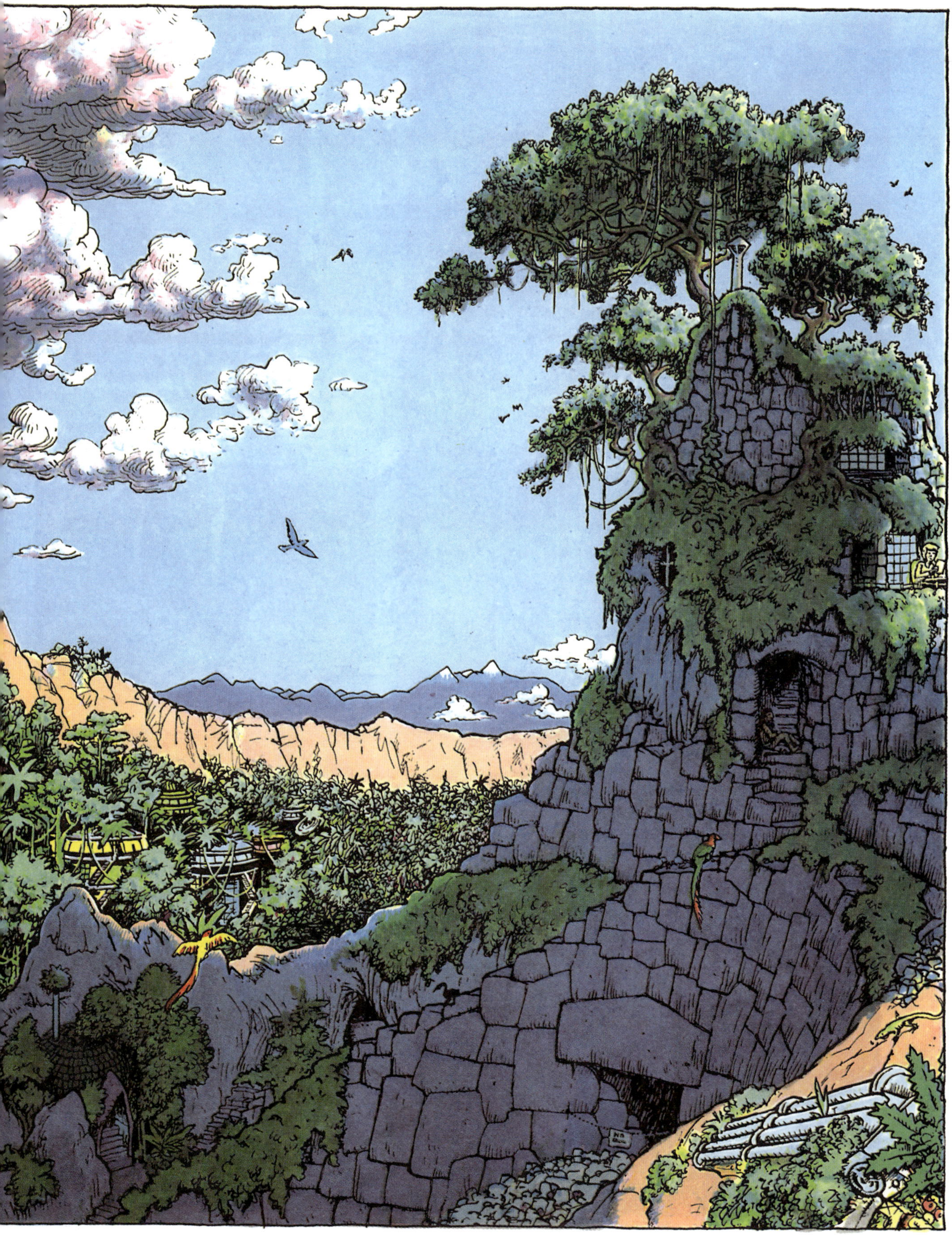

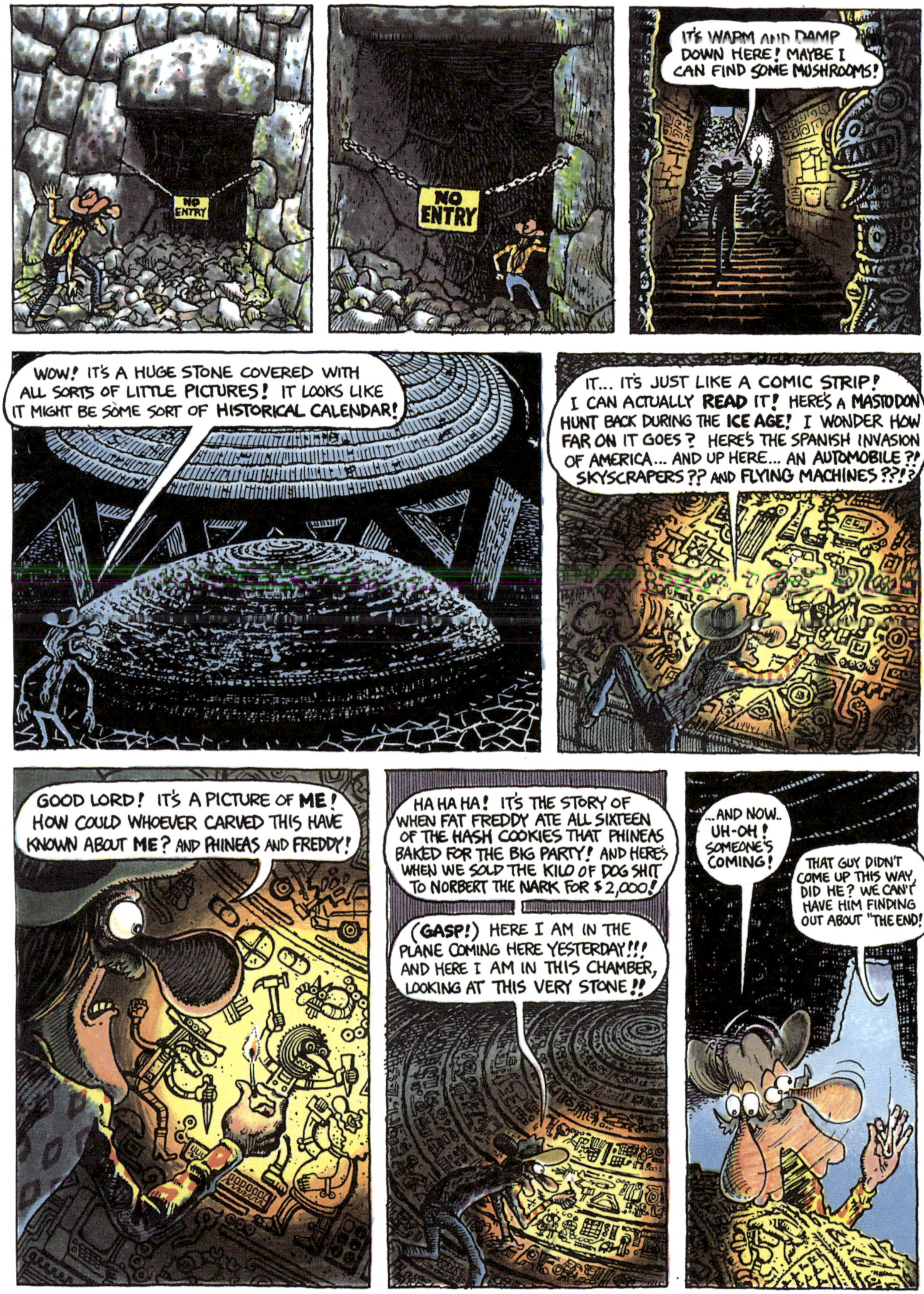
NO ENTRY
NO ENTRY
IT'S WARM AND DAMP DOWN HERE! MAYBE I CAN FIND SOME MUSHROOMS!
WOW! IT'S A HUGE STONE COVERED WITH ALL SORTS OF LITTLE PICTURES! IT LOOKS LIKE IT MIGHT BE SOME SORT OF HISTORICAL CALENDAR!
IT... IT'S JUST LIKE A COMIC STRIP! I CAN ACTUALLY READ IT! HERE'S A MASTODON HUNT BACK DURING THE ICE AGE! I WONDER HOW FAR ON IT GOES? HERE'S THE SPANISH INVASION OF AMERICA... AND UP HERE... AN AUTOMOBILE?! SKYSCRAPERS?? AND FLYING MACHINES??!?
GOOD LORD! IT'S A PICTURE OF ME! HOW COULD WHOEVER CARVED THIS HAVE KNOWN ABOUT ME? AND PHINEAS AND FREDDY!
HA HA HA! IT'S THE STORY OF WHEN FAT FREDDY ATE ALL SIXTEEN OF THE HASH COOKIES THAT PHINEAS BAKED FOR THE BIG PARTY! AND HERE'S WHEN WE SOLD THE KILO OF DOG SHIT TO NORBERT THE NARK FOR $2,000!
(GASP!) HERE I AM IN THE PLANE COMING HERE YESTERDAY!!! AND HERE I AM IN THIS CHAMBER, LOOKING AT THIS VERY STONE!!
...AND NOW... UH-OH! SOMEONE'S COMING!
THAT GUY DIDN'T COME UP THIS WAY, DID HE? WE CAN'T HAVE HIM FINDING OUT ABOUT "THE END!"

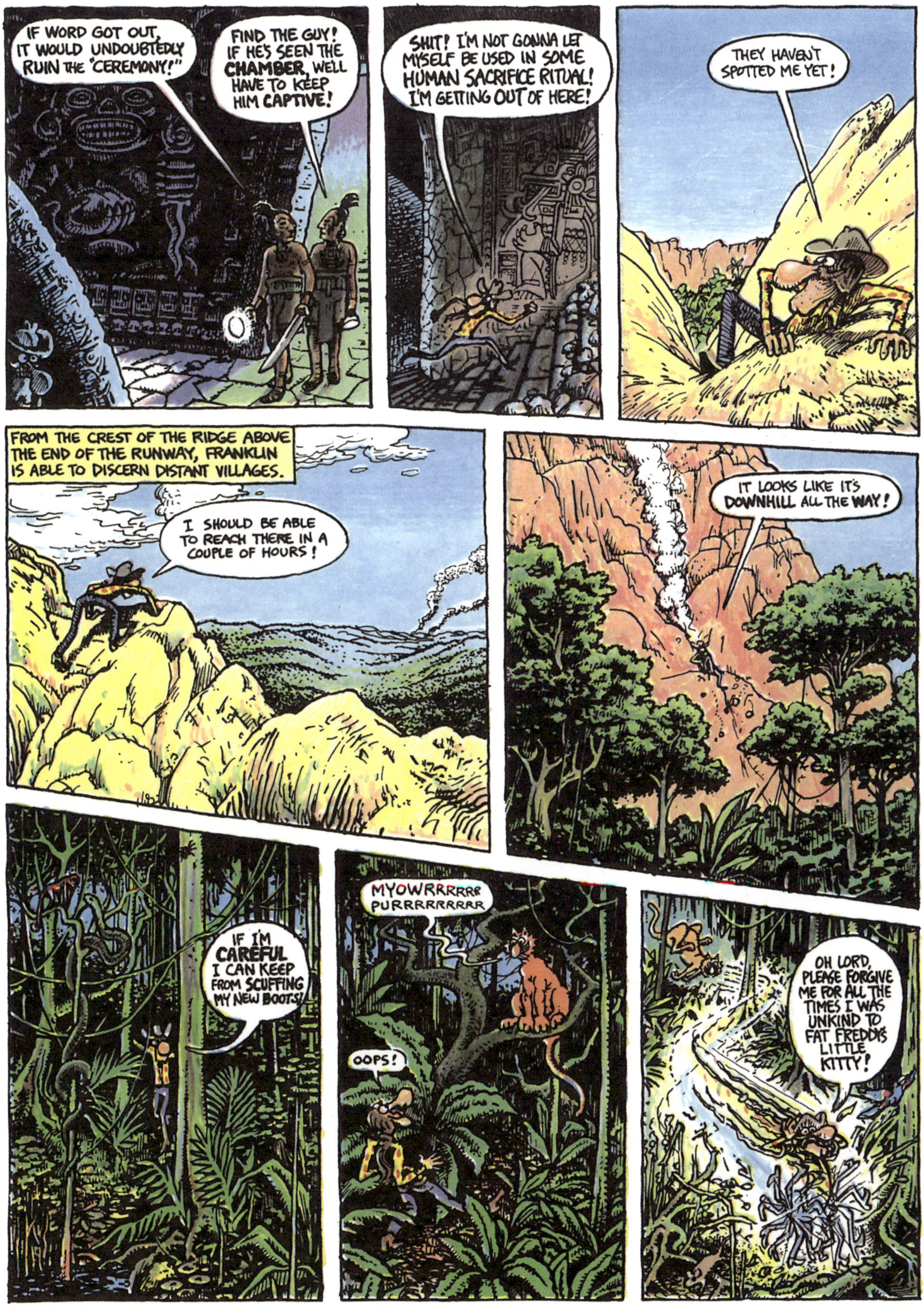
IF WORD GOT OUT, IT WOULD UNDOUBTEDLY RUIN THE "CEREMONY!"
FIND THE GUY! IF HE'S SEEN THE CHAMBER, WE'LL HAVE TO KEEP HIM CAPTIVE!
SHIT! I'M NOT GONNA LET MYSELF BE USED IN SOME HUMAN SACRIFICE RITUAL! I'M GETTING OUT OF HERE!
THEY HAVEN'T SPOTTED ME YET!
FROM THE CREST OF THE RIDGE ABOVE THE END OF THE RUNWAY, FRANKLIN IS ABLE TO DISCERN DISTANT VILLAGES.
I SHOULD BE ABLE TO REACH THERE IN A COUPLE OF HOURS!
IT LOOKS LIKE IT'S DOWNHILL ALL THE WAY!
IF I'M CAREFUL I CAN KEEP FROM SCUFFING MY NEW BOOTS!
MYOWRRRRRR PURRRRRRRRR
OOPS!
OH LORD, PLEASE FORGIVE ME FOR ALL THE TIMES I WAS UNKIND TO FAT FREDDY'S LITTLE KITTY!

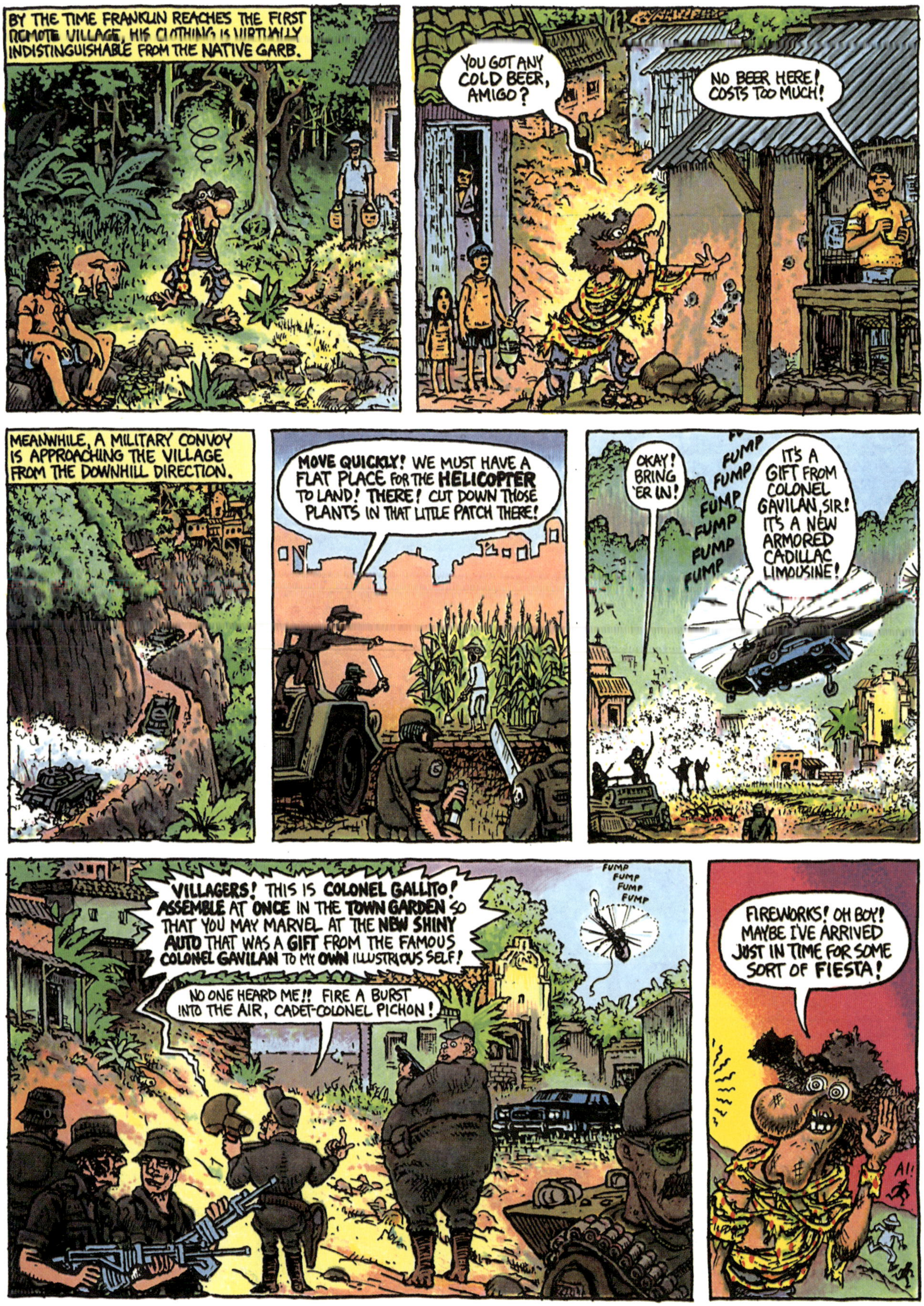

BY THE TIME FRANKLIN REACHES THE FIRST REMOTE VILLAGE, HIS CLOTHING IS VIRTUALLY INDISTINGUISHABLE FROM THE NATIVE GARB.
YOU GOT ANY COLD BEER, AMIGO?
NO BEER HERE! COSTS TOO MUCH!
MEANWHILE, A MILITARY CONVOY IS APPROACHING THE VILLAGE FROM THE DOWNHILL DIRECTION.
MOVE QUICKLY! WE MUST HAVE A FLAT PLACE FOR THE HELICOPTER TO LAND! THERE! CUT DOWN THOSE PLANTS IN THAT LITTLE PATCH THERE!
OKAY! BRING 'ER IN!
FUMP FUMP FUMP FUMP FUMP FUMP
IT'S A GIFT FROM COLONEL GAVILAN, SIR! IT'S A NEW ARMORED CADILLAC LIMOUSINE!
VILLAGERS! THIS IS COLONEL GALLITO! ASSEMBLE AT ONCE IN THE TOWN GARDEN SO THAT YOU MAY MARVEL AT THE NEW SHINY AUTO THAT WAS A GIFT FROM THE FAMOUS COLONEL GAVILAN TO MY OWN ILLUSTRIOUS SELF!
NO ONE HEARD ME!! FIRE A BURST INTO THE AIR, CADET-COLONEL PICHON!
FUMP FUMP FUMP FUMP
FIREWORKS! OH BOY! MAYBE I'VE ARRIVED JUST IN TIME FOR SOME SORT OF FIESTA!
AI!

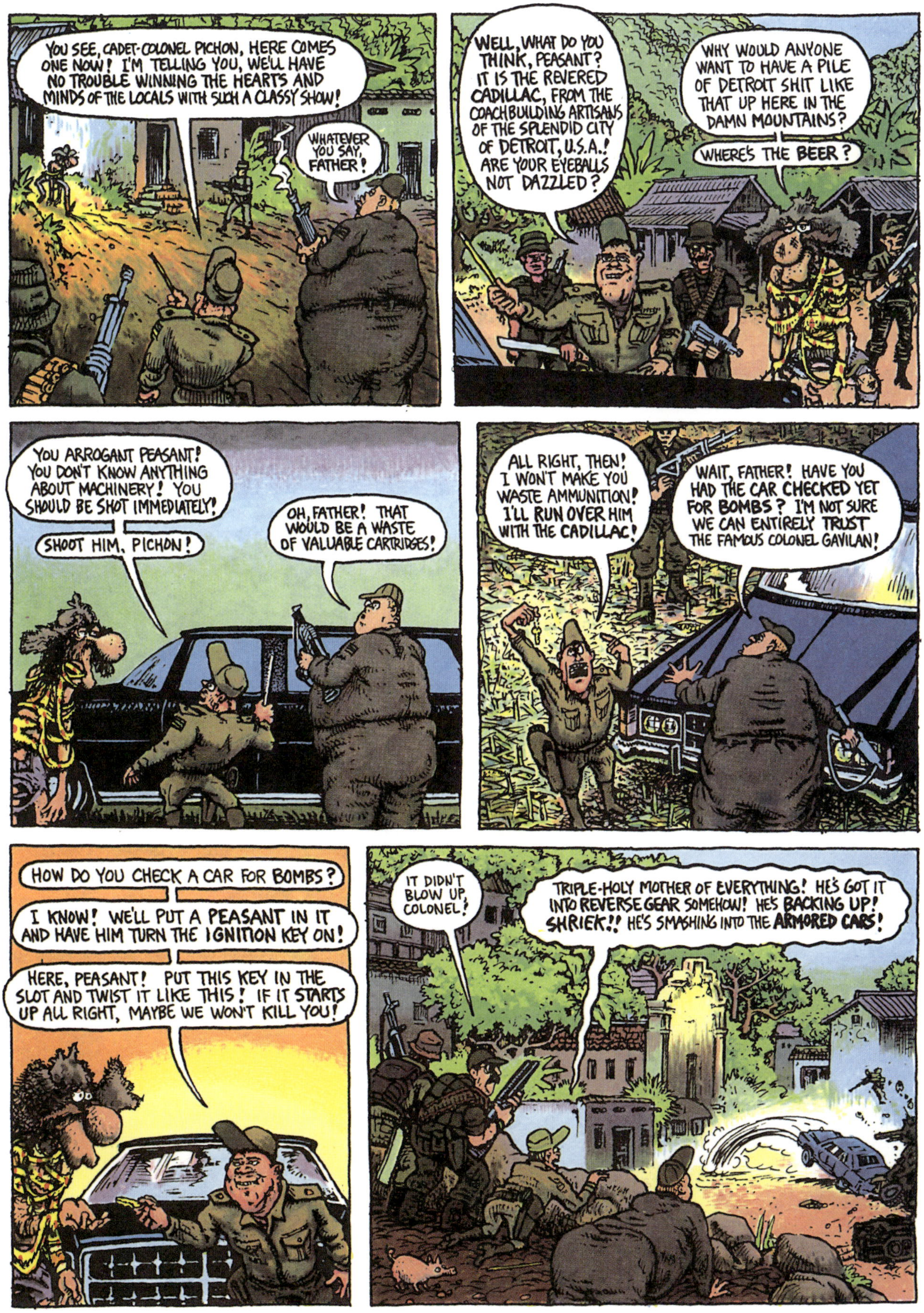

YOU SEE, CADET-COLONEL PICHON, HERE COMES ONE NOW! I'M TELLING YOU, WE'LL HAVE NO TROUBLE WINNING THE HEARTS AND MINDS OF THE LOCALS WITH SUCH A CLASSY SHOW!
WHATEVER YOU SAY, FATHER!
WELL, WHAT DO YOU THINK, PEASANT? IT IS THE REVERED CADILLAC, FROM THE COACHBUILDING ARTISANS OF THE SPLENDID CITY OF DETROIT, U.S.A.! ARE YOUR EYEBALLS NOT DAZZLED?
WHY WOULD ANYONE WANT TO HAVE A PILE OF DETROIT SHIT LIKE THAT UP HERE IN THE DAMN MOUNTAINS?
WHERE'S THE BEER?
YOU ARROGANT PEASANT! YOU DON'T KNOW ANYTHING ABOUT MACHINERY! YOU SHOULD BE SHOT IMMEDIATELY!
SHOOT HIM, PICHON!
OH, FATHER! THAT WOULD BE A WASTE OF VALUABLE CARTRIDGES!
ALL RIGHT, THEN! I WON'T MAKE YOU WASTE AMMUNITION! I'LL RUN OVER HIM WITH THE CADILLAC!
WAIT, FATHER! HAVE YOU HAD THE CAR CHECKED YET FOR BOMBS? I'M NOT SURE WE CAN ENTIRELY TRUST THE FAMOUS COLONEL GAVILAN!
HOW DO YOU CHECK A CAR FOR BOMBS?
I KNOW! WE'LL PUT A PEASANT IN IT AND HAVE HIM TURN THE IGNITION KEY ON!
HERE, PEASANT! PUT THIS KEY IN THE SLOT AND TWIST IT LIKE THIS! IF IT STARTS UP ALL RIGHT, MAYBE WE WON'T KILL YOU!
IT DIDN'T BLOW UP, COLONEL!
TRIPLE-HOLY MOTHER OF EVERYTHING! HE'S GOT IT INTO REVERSE GEAR SOMEHOW! HE'S BACKING UP! SHRIEK!! HE'S SMASHING INTO THE ARMORED CARS!

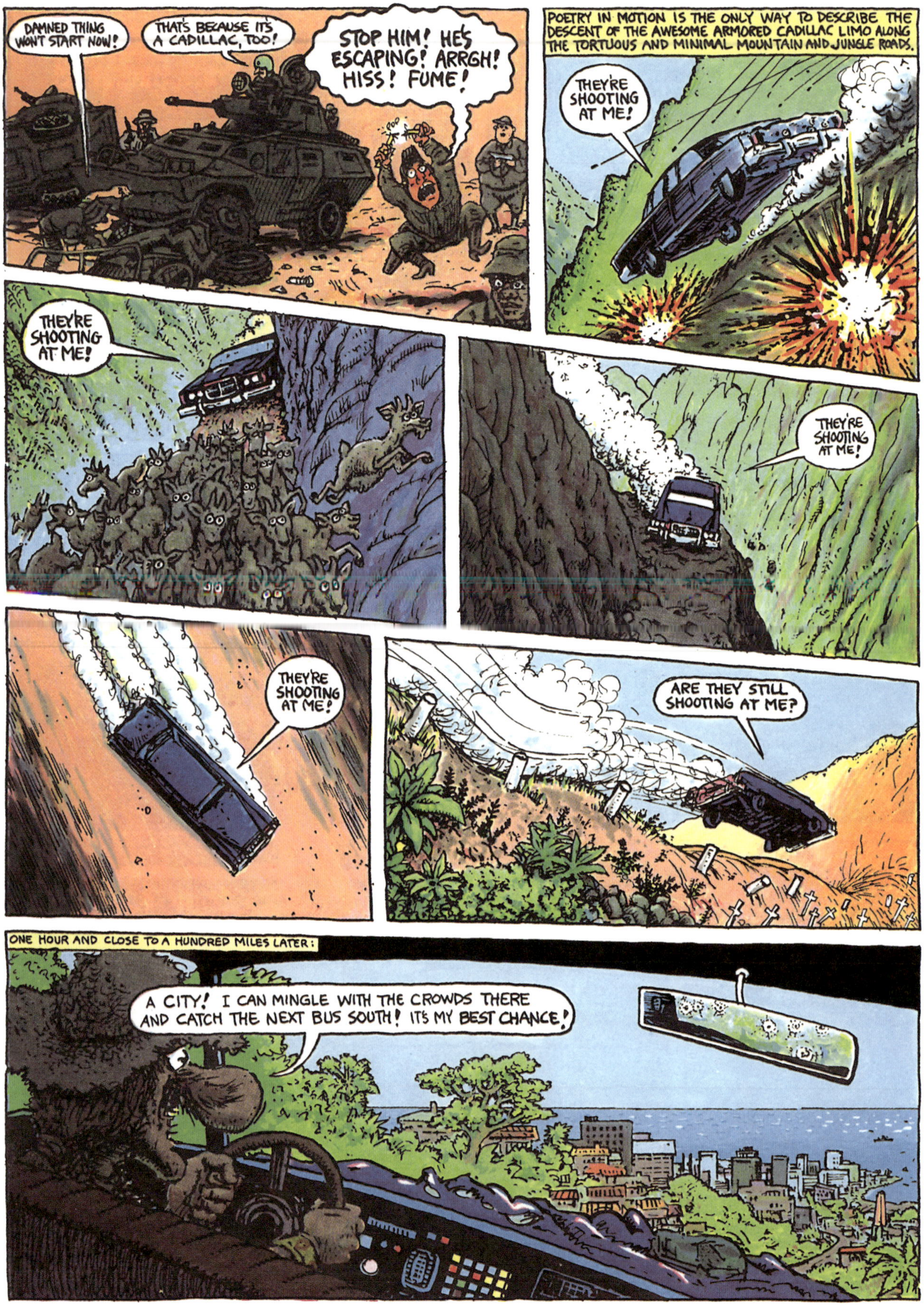
DAMNED THING WON'T START NOW!
THAT'S BECAUSE IT'S A CADILLAC, TOO!
STOP HIM! HE'S ESCAPING! ARRGH! HISS! FUME!
POETRY IN MOTION IS THE ONLY WAY TO DESCRIBE THE DESCENT OF THE AWESOME ARMORED CADILLAC LIMO ALONG THE TORTUOUS AND MINIMAL MOUNTAIN AND JUNGLE ROADS.
THEY'RE SHOOTING AT ME!
THEY'RE SHOOTING AT ME!
THEY'RE SHOOTING AT ME!
THEY'RE SHOOTING AT ME!
ARE THEY STILL SHOOTING AT ME?
ONE HOUR AND CLOSE TO A HUNDRED MILES LATER:
A CITY! I CAN MINGLE WITH THE CROWDS THERE AND CATCH THE NEXT BUS SOUTH! IT'S MY BEST CHANCE!

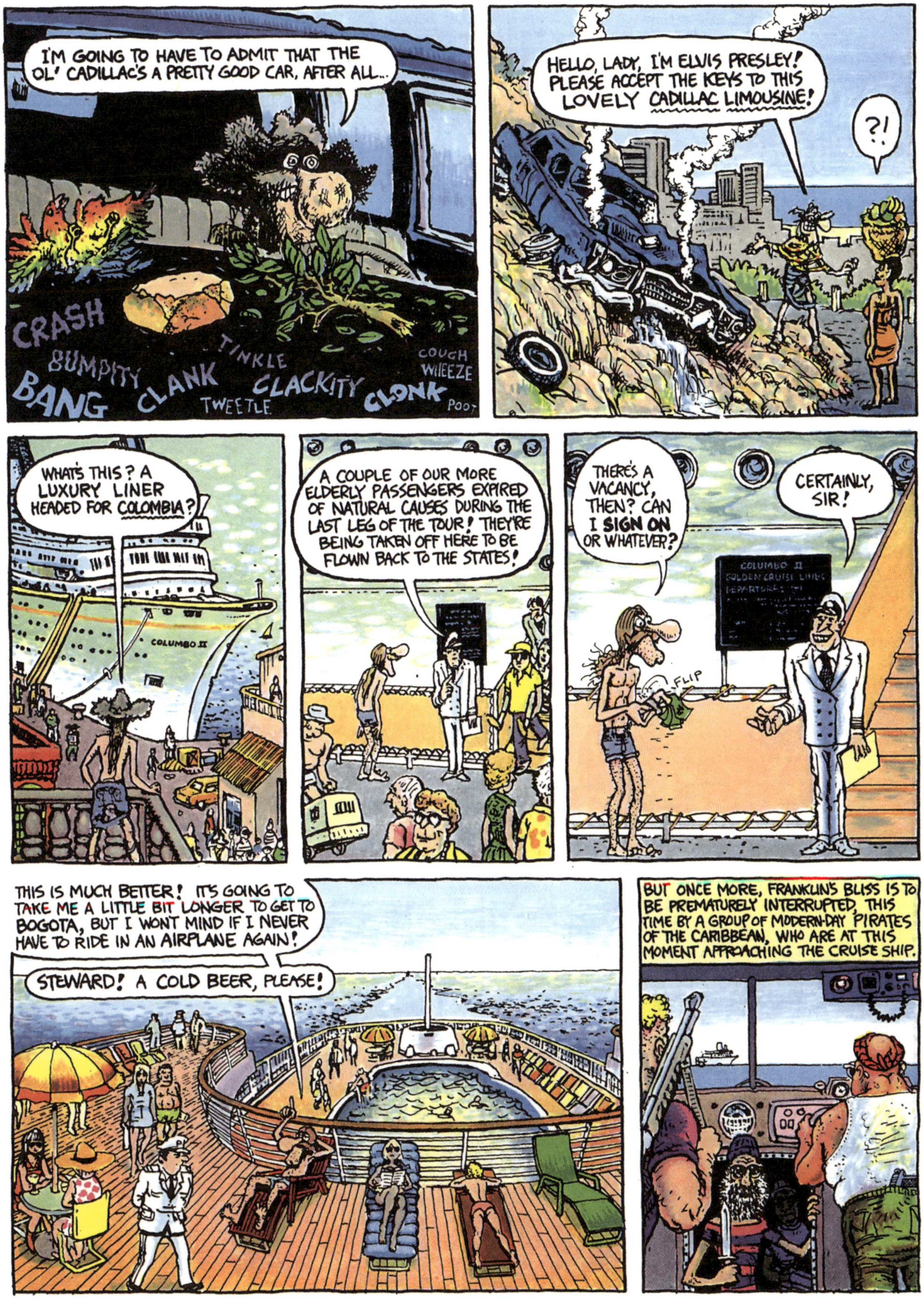

I'M GOING TO HAVE TO ADMIT THAT THE OL' CADILLAC'S A PRETTY GOOD CAR, AFTER ALL...
CRASH
BUMPITY
BANG
CLANK
TINKLE
TWEETLE
CLACKITY
COUGH
WHEEZE
CLONK
POOT
HELLO, LADY, I'M ELVIS PRESLEY! PLEASE ACCEPT THE KEYS TO THIS LOVELY CADILLAC LIMOUSINE!
?!
WHAT'S THIS? A LUXURY LINER HEADED FOR COLOMBIA?
COLUMBO II
A COUPLE OF OUR MORE ELDERLY PASSENGERS EXPIRED OF NATURAL CAUSES DURING THE LAST LEG OF THE TOUR! THEY'RE BEING TAKEN OFF HERE TO BE FLOWN BACK TO THE STATES!
THERE'S A VACANCY, THEN? CAN I SIGN ON OR WHATEVER?
CERTAINLY, SIR!
FLIP
THIS IS MUCH BETTER! IT'S GOING TO TAKE ME A LITTLE BIT LONGER TO GET TO BOGOTA, BUT I WON'T MIND IF I NEVER HAVE TO RIDE IN AN AIRPLANE AGAIN!
STEWARD! A COLD BEER, PLEASE!
BUT ONCE MORE, FRANKLIN'S BLISS IS TO BE PREMATURELY INTERRUPTED, THIS TIME BY A GROUP OF MODERN-DAY PIRATES OF THE CARIBBEAN, WHO ARE AT THIS MOMENT APPROACHING THE CRUISE SHIP.

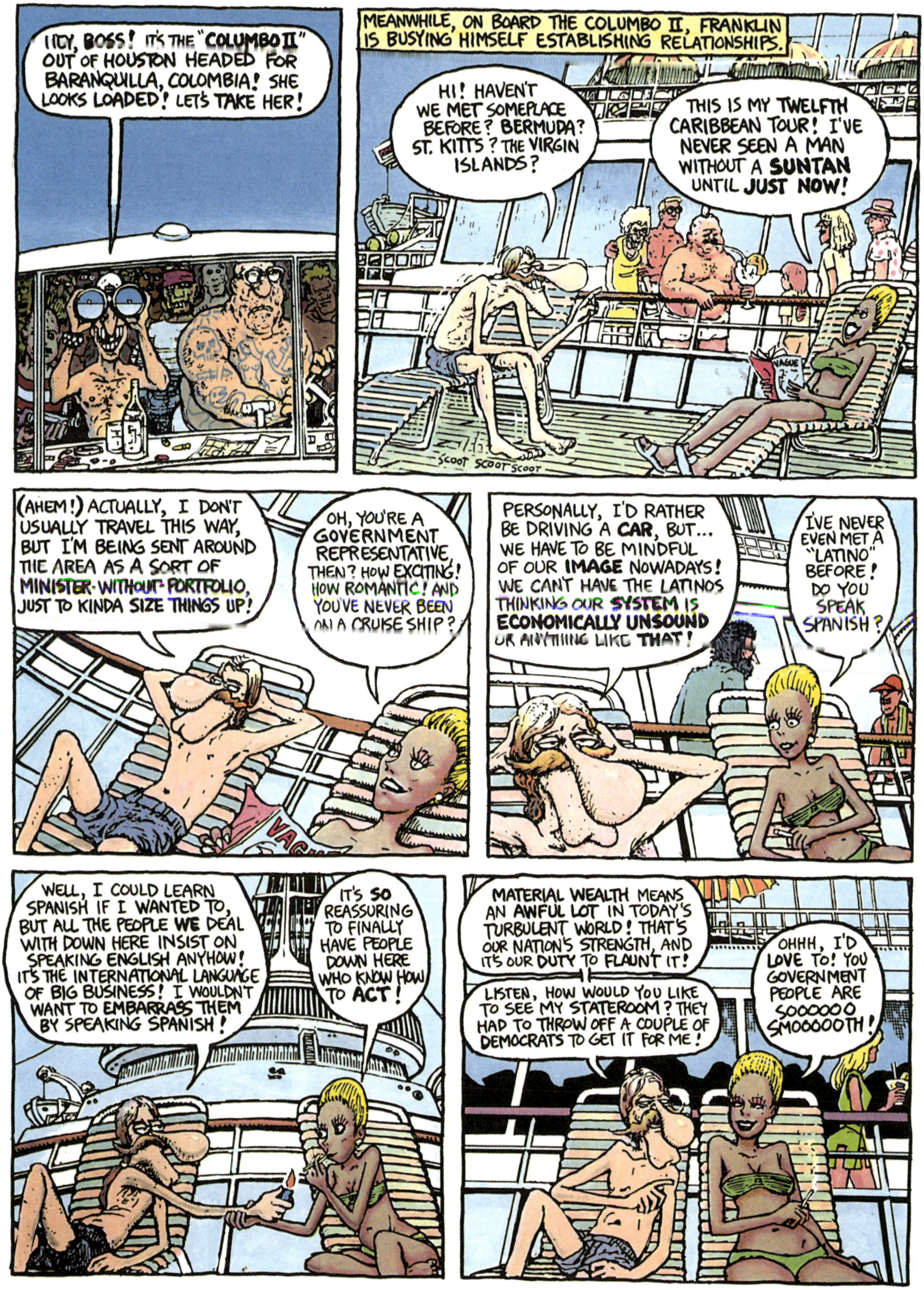
HEY, BOSS! IT'S THE "COLUMBO II" OUT OF HOUSTON HEADED FOR BARANQUILLA, COLOMBIA! SHE LOOKS LOADED! LET'S TAKE HER!
MEANWHILE, ON BOARD THE COLUMBO II, FRANKLIN IS BUSYING HIMSELF ESTABLISHING RELATIONSHIPS.
HI! HAVEN'T WE MET SOMEPLACE BEFORE? BERMUDA? ST. KITTS? THE VIRGIN ISLANDS?
THIS IS MY TWELFTH CARIBBEAN TOUR! I'VE NEVER SEEN A MAN WITHOUT A SUNTAN UNTIL JUST NOW!
SCOOT SCOOT SCOOT
(AHEM!) ACTUALLY, I DON'T USUALLY TRAVEL THIS WAY, BUT I'M BEING SENT AROUND THE AREA AS A SORT OF MINISTER-WITHOUT-PORTFOLIO, JUST TO KINDA SIZE THINGS UP!
OH, YOU'RE A GOVERNMENT REPRESENTATIVE, THEN? HOW EXCITING! HOW ROMANTIC! AND YOU'VE NEVER BEEN ON A CRUISE SHIP?
PERSONALLY, I'D RATHER BE DRIVING A CAR, BUT... WE HAVE TO BE MINDFUL OF OUR IMAGE NOWADAYS! WE CAN'T HAVE THE LATINOS THINKING OUR SYSTEM IS ECONOMICALLY UNSOUND OR ANYTHING LIKE THAT!
I'VE NEVER EVEN MET A "LATINO" BEFORE! DO YOU SPEAK SPANISH?
WELL, I COULD LEARN SPANISH IF I WANTED TO, BUT ALL THE PEOPLE WE DEAL WITH DOWN HERE INSIST ON SPEAKING ENGLISH ANYHOW! IT'S THE INTERNATIONAL LANGUAGE OF BIG BUSINESS! I WOULDN'T WANT TO EMBARRASS THEM BY SPEAKING SPANISH!
IT'S SO REASSURING TO FINALLY HAVE PEOPLE DOWN HERE WHO KNOW HOW TO ACT!
MATERIAL WEALTH MEANS AN AWFUL LOT IN TODAY'S TURBULENT WORLD! THAT'S OUR NATION'S STRENGTH, AND IT'S OUR DUTY TO FLAUNT IT!
LISTEN, HOW WOULD YOU LIKE TO SEE MY STATEROOM? THEY HAD TO THROW OFF A COUPLE OF DEMOCRATS TO GET IT FOR ME!
OHHH, I'D LOVE TO! YOU GOVERNMENT PEOPLE ARE SOOOOOO SMOOOOOTH!

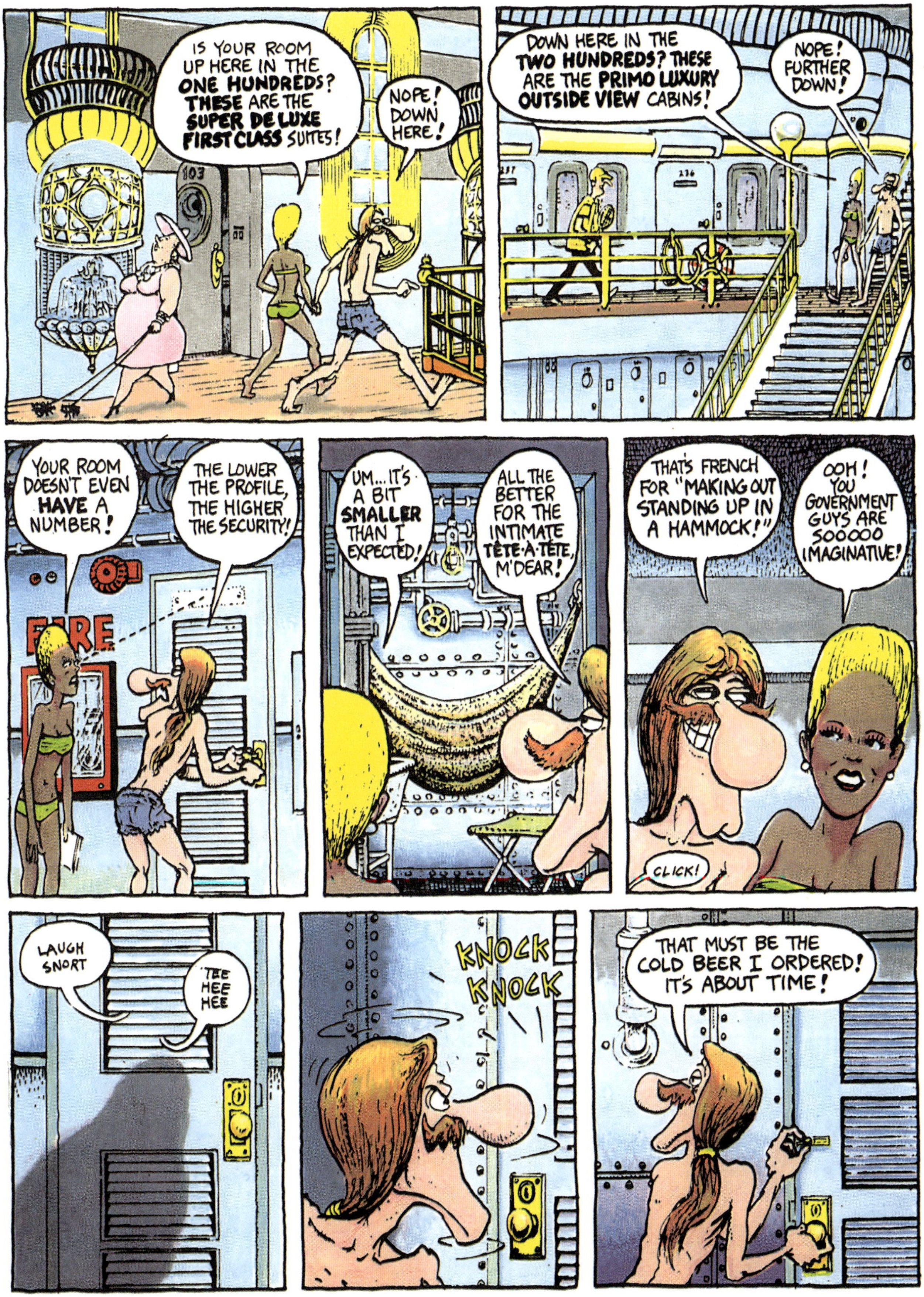
IS YOUR ROOM UP HERE IN THE ONE HUNDREDS? THESE ARE THE SUPER DE LUXE FIRST CLASS SUITES!
NOPE! DOWN HERE!
DOWN HERE IN THE TWO HUNDREDS? THESE ARE THE PRIMO LUXURY OUTSIDE VIEW CABINS!
NOPE! FURTHER DOWN!
YOUR ROOM DOESN'T EVEN HAVE A NUMBER!
THE LOWER THE PROFILE, THE HIGHER THE SECURITY!
FIRE
UM... IT'S A BIT SMALLER THAN I EXPECTED!
ALL THE BETTER FOR THE INTIMATE TÊTE-À-TÊTE, M'DEAR!
THAT'S FRENCH FOR "MAKING OUT STANDING UP IN A HAMMOCK!"
OOH! YOU GOVERNMENT GUYS ARE SOOOOO IMAGINATIVE!
CLICK!
LAUGH SNORT
TEE HEE HEE
KNOCK KNOCK
THAT MUST BE THE COLD BEER I ORDERED! IT'S ABOUT TIME!

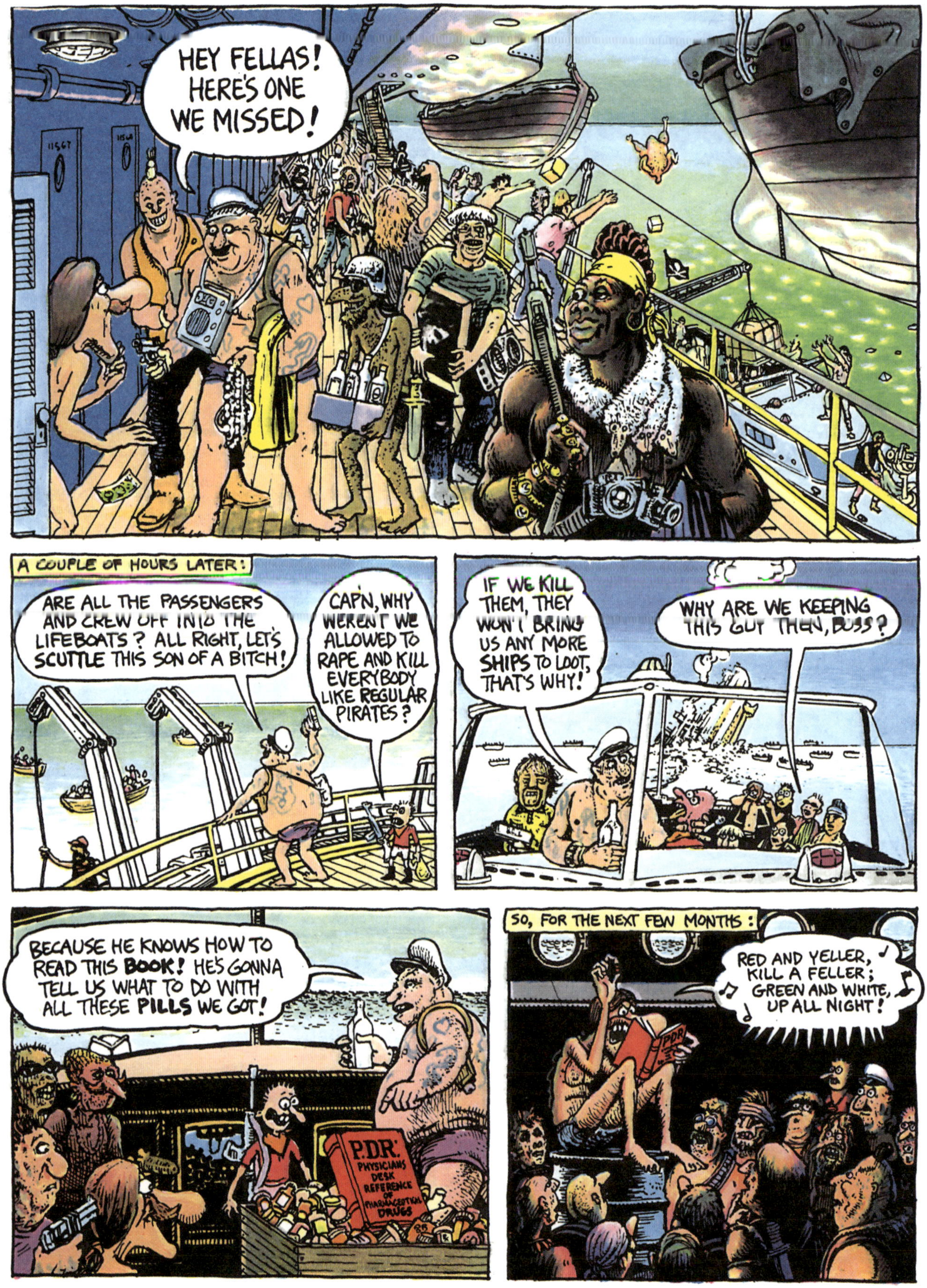
HEY FELLAS! HERE'S ONE WE MISSED!
A COUPLE OF HOURS LATER:
ARE ALL THE PASSENGERS AND CREW OFF INTO THE LIFEBOATS? ALL RIGHT, LET'S SCUTTLE THIS SON OF A BITCH!
CAP'N, WHY WEREN'T WE ALLOWED TO RAPE AND KILL EVERYBODY LIKE REGULAR PIRATES?
IF WE KILL THEM, THEY WON'T BRING US ANY MORE SHIPS TO LOOT, THAT'S WHY!
WHY ARE WE KEEPING THIS GUY THEN, BOSS?
BECAUSE HE KNOWS HOW TO READ THIS BOOK! HE'S GONNA TELL US WHAT TO DO WITH ALL THESE PILLS WE GOT!
P.D.R. PHYSICIANS DESK REFERENCE OF PHARMACEUTICAL DRUGS
SO, FOR THE NEXT FEW MONTHS:
RED AND YELLER, KILL A FELLER; GREEN AND WHITE, UP ALL NIGHT!
PDR

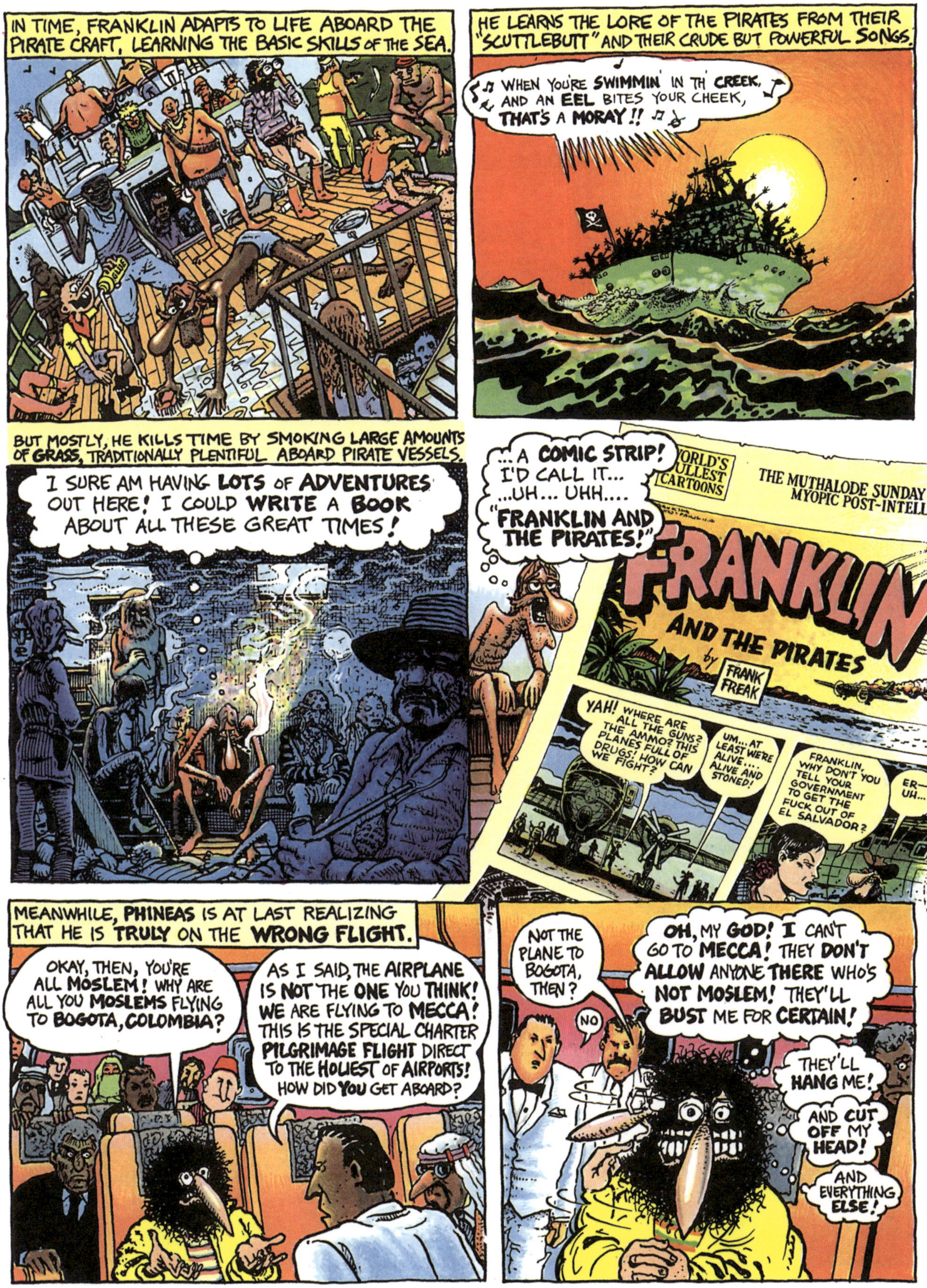
IN TIME, FRANKLIN ADAPTS TO LIFE ABOARD THE PIRATE CRAFT, LEARNING THE BASIC SKILLS OF THE SEA.
HE LEARNS THE LORE OF THE PIRATES FROM THEIR "SCUTTLEBUTT" AND THEIR CRUDE BUT POWERFUL SONGS.
WHEN YOU'RE SWIMMIN' IN TH' CREEK, AND AN EEL BITES YOUR CHEEK, THAT'S A MORAY!!
BUT MOSTLY, HE KILLS TIME BY SMOKING LARGE AMOUNTS OF GRASS, TRADITIONALLY PLENTIFUL ABOARD PIRATE VESSELS.
I SURE AM HAVING LOTS OF ADVENTURES OUT HERE! I COULD WRITE A BOOK ABOUT ALL THESE GREAT TIMES!
...A COMIC STRIP! I'D CALL IT... ...UH... UHH.... "FRANKLIN AND THE PIRATES!"
ORLD'S ULLEST CARTOONS
THE MUTHALODE SUNDAY MOR
MYOPIC POST-INTELLIGE
FRANKLIN AND THE PIRATES
by FRANK FREAK
YAH! WHERE ARE ALL THE GUNS? THE AMMO? THIS PLANES FULL OF DRUGS! HOW CAN WE FIGHT?
UM... AT LEAST WE'RE ALIVE... ALIVE AND STONED!
FRANKLIN, WHY DON'T YOU TELL YOUR GOVERNMENT TO GET THE FUCK OUT OF EL SALVADOR?
ER— UH...
MEANWHILE, PHINEAS IS AT LAST REALIZING THAT HE IS TRULY ON THE WRONG FLIGHT.
OKAY, THEN, YOU'RE ALL MOSLEM! WHY ARE ALL YOU MOSLEMS FLYING TO BOGOTA, COLOMBIA?
AS I SAID, THE AIRPLANE IS NOT THE ONE YOU THINK! WE ARE FLYING TO MECCA! THIS IS THE SPECIAL CHARTER PILGRIMAGE FLIGHT DIRECT TO THE HOLIEST OF AIRPORTS! HOW DID YOU GET ABOARD?
NOT THE PLANE TO BOGOTA, THEN?
NO
OH, MY GOD! I CAN'T GO TO MECCA! THEY DON'T ALLOW ANYONE THERE WHO'S NOT MOSLEM! THEY'LL BUST ME FOR CERTAIN!
THEY'LL HANG ME!
AND CUT OFF MY HEAD!
AND EVERYTHING ELSE!

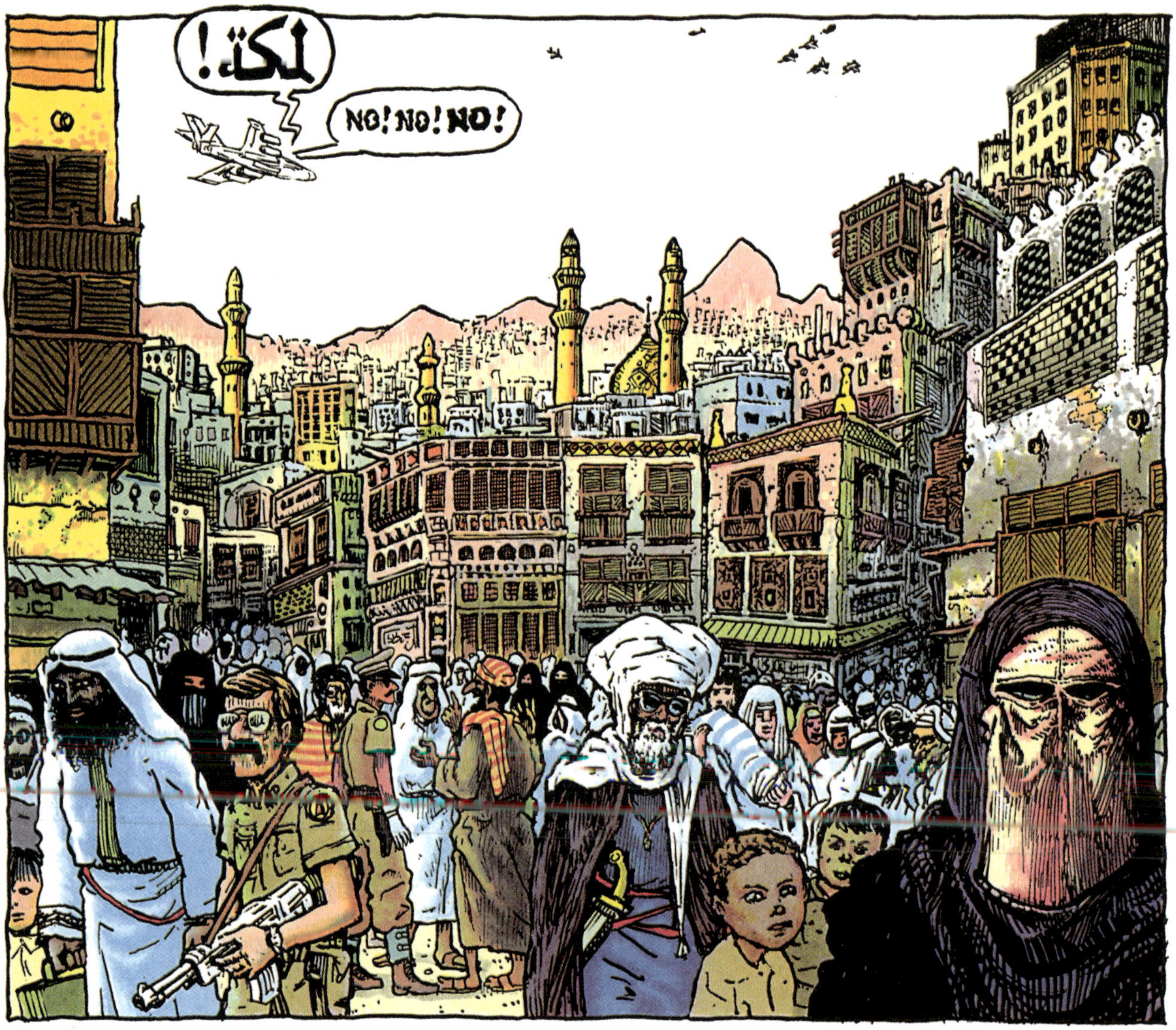
لكة!
NO! NO! NO!

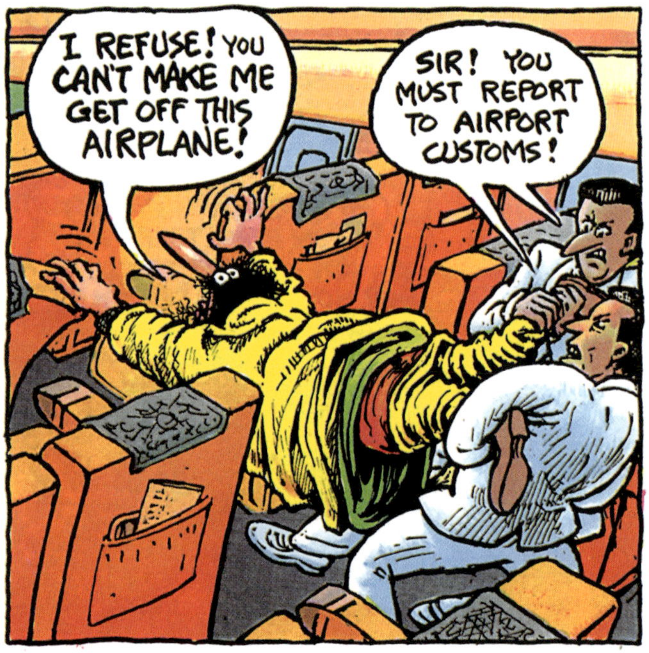
I REFUSE! YOU CAN'T MAKE ME GET OFF THIS AIRPLANE!
SIR! YOU MUST REPORT TO AIRPORT CUSTOMS!

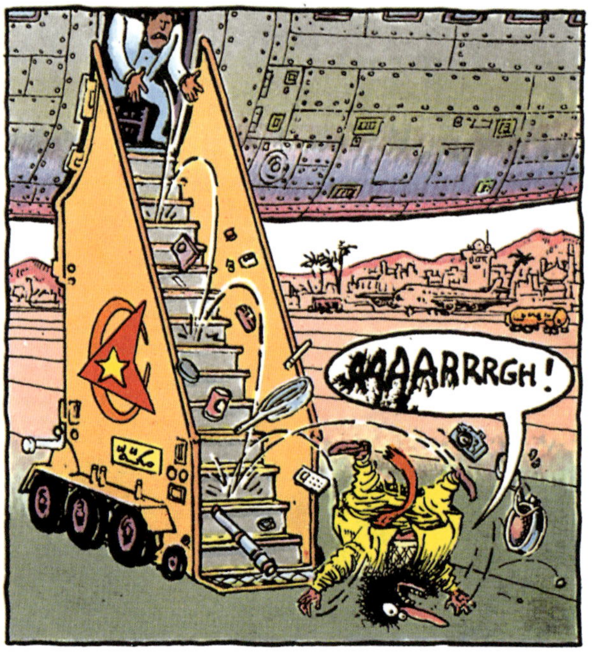
AAAARRRGH!

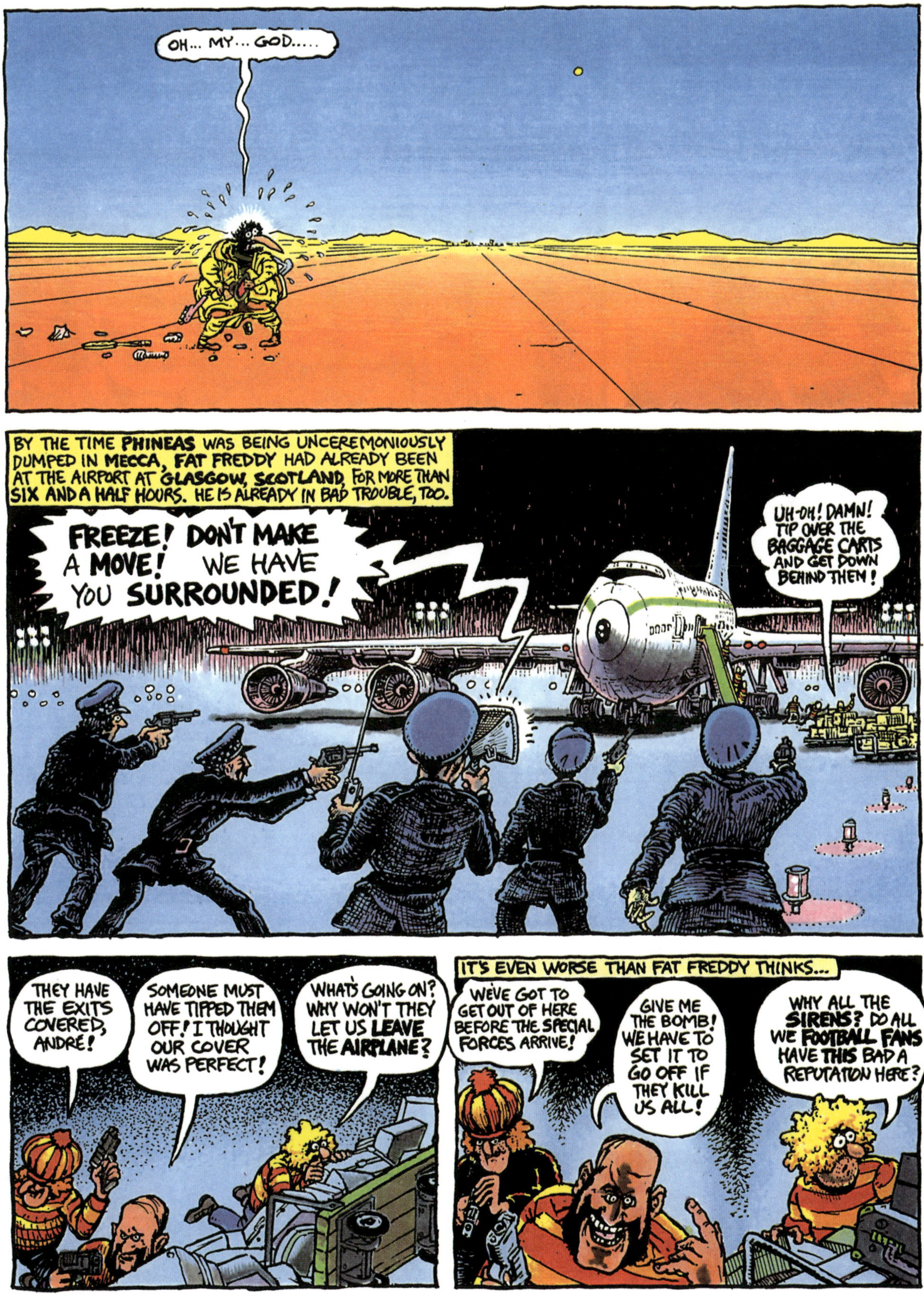

OH... MY... GOD.....
BY THE TIME PHINEAS WAS BEING UNCEREMONIOUSLY DUMPED IN MECCA, FAT FREDDY HAD ALREADY BEEN AT THE AIRPORT AT GLASGOW, SCOTLAND, FOR MORE THAN SIX AND A HALF HOURS. HE IS ALREADY IN BAD TROUBLE, TOO.
FREEZE! DON'T MAKE A MOVE! WE HAVE YOU SURROUNDED!
UH-OH! DAMN! TIP OVER THE BAGGAGE CARTS AND GET DOWN BEHIND THEM!
THEY HAVE THE EXITS COVERED, ANDRÉ!
SOMEONE MUST HAVE TIPPED THEM OFF! I THOUGHT OUR COVER WAS PERFECT!
WHAT'S GOING ON? WHY WON'T THEY LET US LEAVE THE AIRPLANE?
IT'S EVEN WORSE THAN FAT FREDDY THINKS...
WE'VE GOT TO GET OUT OF HERE BEFORE THE SPECIAL FORCES ARRIVE!
GIVE ME THE BOMB! WE HAVE TO SET IT TO GO OFF IF THEY KILL US ALL!
WHY ALL THE SIRENS? DO ALL WE FOOTBALL FANS HAVE THIS BAD A REPUTATION HERE?

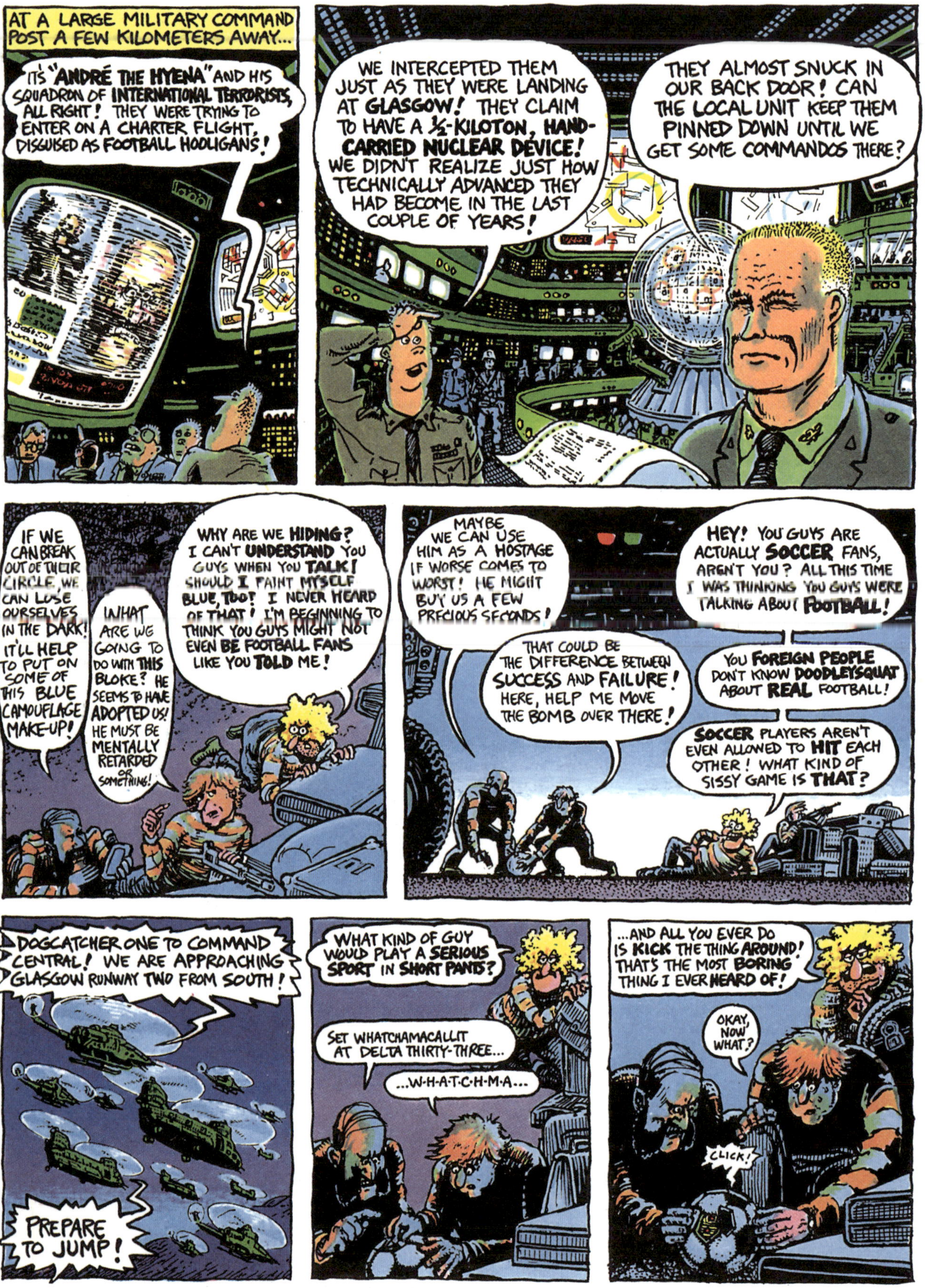
AT A LARGE MILITARY COMMAND POST A FEW KILOMETERS AWAY...
IT'S "ANDRÉ THE HYENA" AND HIS SQUADRON OF INTERNATIONAL TERRORISTS, ALL RIGHT! THEY WERE TRYING TO ENTER ON A CHARTER FLIGHT, DISGUISED AS FOOTBALL HOOLIGANS!
WE INTERCEPTED THEM JUST AS THEY WERE LANDING AT GLASGOW! THEY CLAIM TO HAVE A ½-KILOTON, HAND-CARRIED NUCLEAR DEVICE! WE DIDN'T REALIZE JUST HOW TECHNICALLY ADVANCED THEY HAD BECOME IN THE LAST COUPLE OF YEARS!
THEY ALMOST SNUCK IN OUR BACK DOOR! CAN THE LOCAL UNIT KEEP THEM PINNED DOWN UNTIL WE GET SOME COMMANDOS THERE?
IF WE CAN BREAK OUT OF THEIR CIRCLE, WE CAN LOSE OURSELVES IN THE DARK! IT'LL HELP TO PUT ON SOME OF THIS BLUE CAMOUFLAGE MAKE-UP!
WHAT ARE WE GOING TO DO WITH THIS BLOKE? HE SEEMS TO HAVE ADOPTED US! HE MUST BE MENTALLY RETARDED OR SOMETHING!
WHY ARE WE HIDING? I CAN'T UNDERSTAND YOU GUYS WHEN YOU TALK! SHOULD I PAINT MYSELF BLUE, TOO? I NEVER HEARD OF THAT! I'M BEGINNING TO THINK YOU GUYS MIGHT NOT EVEN BE FOOTBALL FANS LIKE YOU TOLD ME!
MAYBE WE CAN USE HIM AS A HOSTAGE IF WORSE COMES TO WORST! HE MIGHT BUY US A FEW PRECIOUS SECONDS!
THAT COULD BE THE DIFFERENCE BETWEEN SUCCESS AND FAILURE! HERE, HELP ME MOVE THE BOMB OVER THERE!
HEY! YOU GUYS ARE ACTUALLY SOCCER FANS, AREN'T YOU? ALL THIS TIME I WAS THINKING YOU GUYS WERE TALKING ABOUT FOOTBALL!
YOU FOREIGN PEOPLE DON'T KNOW DOODLEYSQUAT ABOUT REAL FOOTBALL!
SOCCER PLAYERS AREN'T EVEN ALLOWED TO HIT EACH OTHER! WHAT KIND OF SISSY GAME IS THAT?
DOGCATCHER ONE TO COMMAND CENTRAL! WE ARE APPROACHING GLASGOW RUNWAY TWO FROM SOUTH!
PREPARE TO JUMP!
WHAT KIND OF GUY WOULD PLAY A SERIOUS SPORT IN SHORT PANTS?
SET WHATCHAMACALLIT AT DELTA THIRTY-THREE...
...W-H-A-T-C-H-M-A...
...AND ALL YOU EVER DO IS KICK THE THING AROUND! THAT'S THE MOST BORING THING I EVER HEARD OF!
OKAY, NOW WHAT?
CLICK!

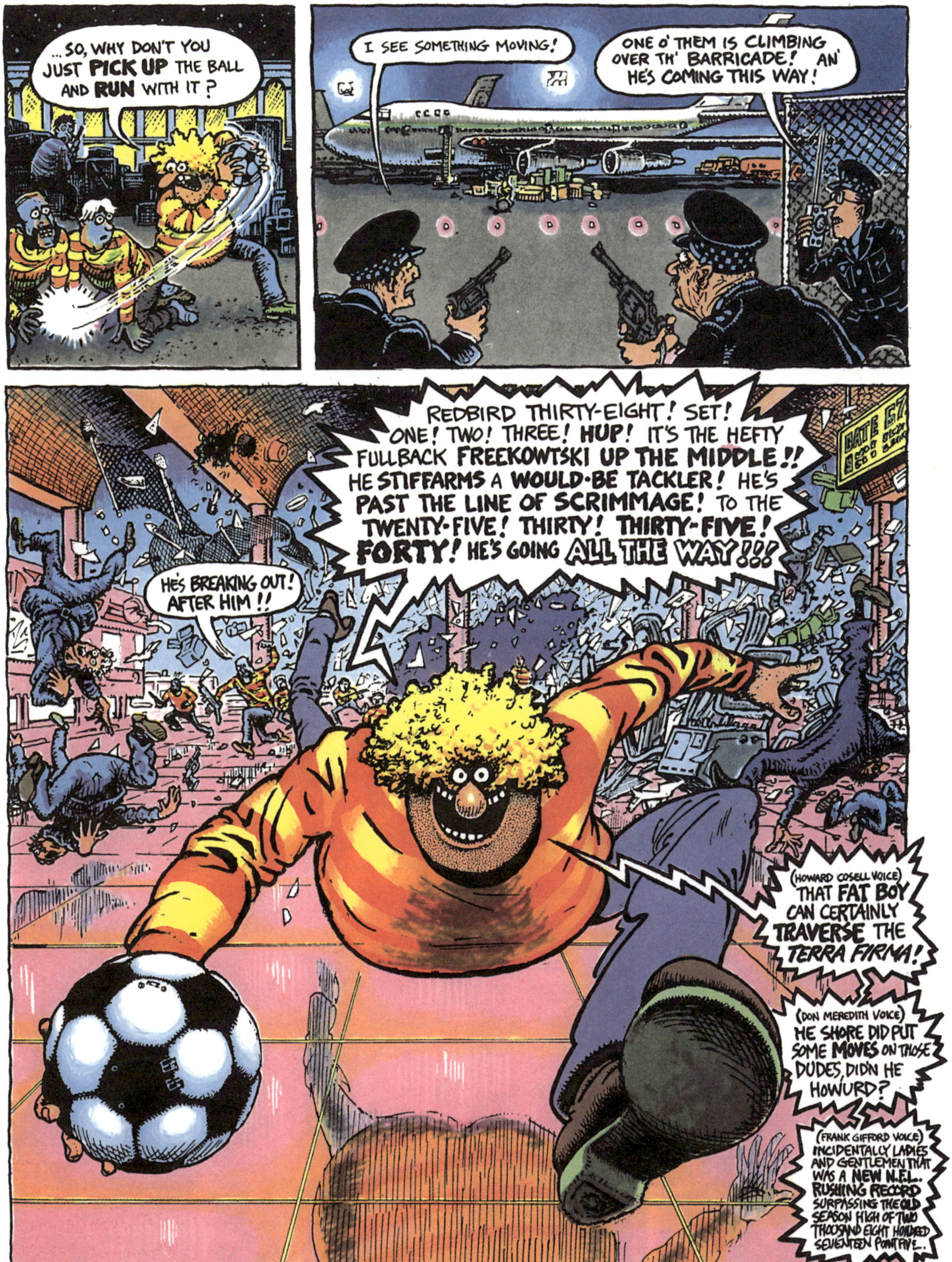
...SO, WHY DON'T YOU JUST PICK UP THE BALL AND RUN WITH IT?
I SEE SOMETHING MOVING!
ONE O' THEM IS CLIMBING OVER TH' BARRICADE! AN' HE'S COMING THIS WAY!
REDBIRD THIRTY-EIGHT! SET! ONE! TWO! THREE! HUP! IT'S THE HEFTY FULLBACK FREEKOWTSKI UP THE MIDDLE!! HE STIFFARMS A WOULD-BE TACKLER! HE'S PAST THE LINE OF SCRIMMAGE! TO THE TWENTY-FIVE! THIRTY! THIRTY-FIVE! FORTY! HE'S GOING ALL THE WAY!!!
HE'S BREAKING OUT! AFTER HIM!!
(HOWARD COSELL VOICE) THAT FAT BOY CAN CERTAINLY TRAVERSE THE TERRA FIRMA!
(DON MEREDITH VOICE) HE SHORE DID PUT SOME MOVES ON THOSE DUDES, DID'N HE HOWURD?
(FRANK GIFFORD VOICE) INCIDENTALLY LADIES AND GENTLEMEN THAT WAS A NEW N.F.L. RUSHING RECORD SURPASSING THE OLD SEASON HIGH OF TWO THOUSAND EIGHT HUNDRED SEVENTEEN POINT FIVE..

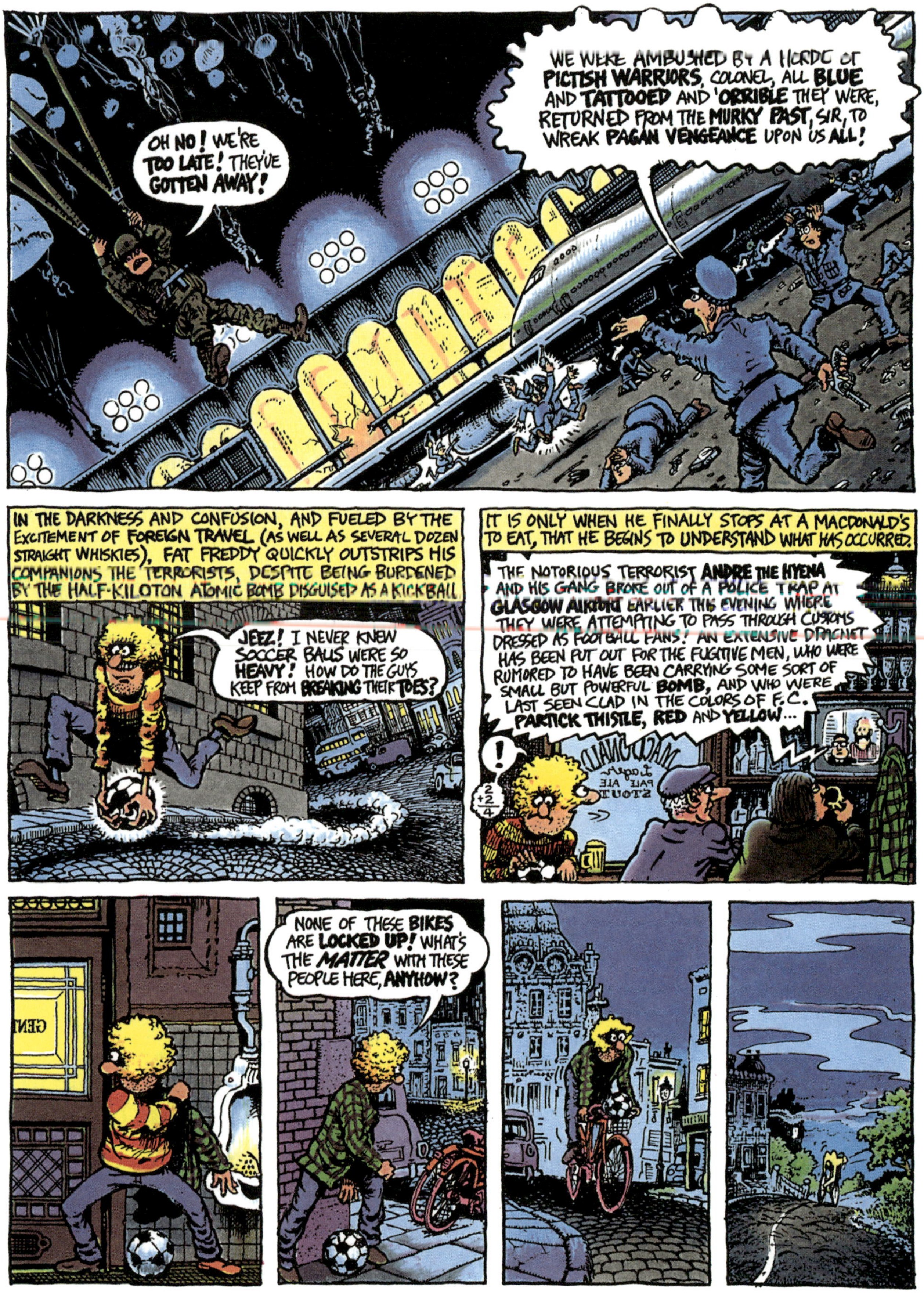
WE WERE AMBUSHED BY A HORDE OF PICTISH WARRIORS, COLONEL, ALL BLUE AND TATTOOED AND 'ORRIBLE THEY WERE, RETURNED FROM THE MURKY PAST, SIR, TO WREAK PAGAN VENGEANCE UPON US ALL!
OH NO! WE'RE TOO LATE! THEY'VE GOTTEN AWAY!
IN THE DARKNESS AND CONFUSION, AND FUELED BY THE EXCITEMENT OF FOREIGN TRAVEL (AS WELL AS SEVERAL DOZEN STRAIGHT WHISKIES), FAT FREDDY QUICKLY OUTSTRIPS HIS COMPANIONS THE TERRORISTS, DESPITE BEING BURDENED BY THE HALF-KILOTON ATOMIC BOMB DISGUISED AS A KICKBALL
JEEZ! I NEVER KNEW SOCCER BALLS WERE SO HEAVY! HOW DO THE GUYS KEEP FROM BREAKING THEIR TOES?
IT IS ONLY WHEN HE FINALLY STOPS AT A MACDONALD'S TO EAT, THAT HE BEGINS TO UNDERSTAND WHAT HAS OCCURRED.
THE NOTORIOUS TERRORIST ANDRE THE HYENA AND HIS GANG BROKE OUT OF A POLICE TRAP AT GLASGOW AIRPORT EARLIER THIS EVENING WHERE THEY WERE ATTEMPTING TO PASS THROUGH CUSTOMS DRESSED AS FOOTBALL FANS! AN EXTENSIVE DRAGNET HAS BEEN PUT OUT FOR THE FUGITIVE MEN, WHO WERE RUMORED TO HAVE BEEN CARRYING SOME SORT OF SMALL BUT POWERFUL BOMB, AND WHO WERE LAST SEEN CLAD IN THE COLORS OF F.C. PARTICK THISTLE, RED AND YELLOW...
!
NONE OF THESE BIKES ARE LOCKED UP! WHAT'S THE MATTER WITH THESE PEOPLE HERE, ANYHOW?

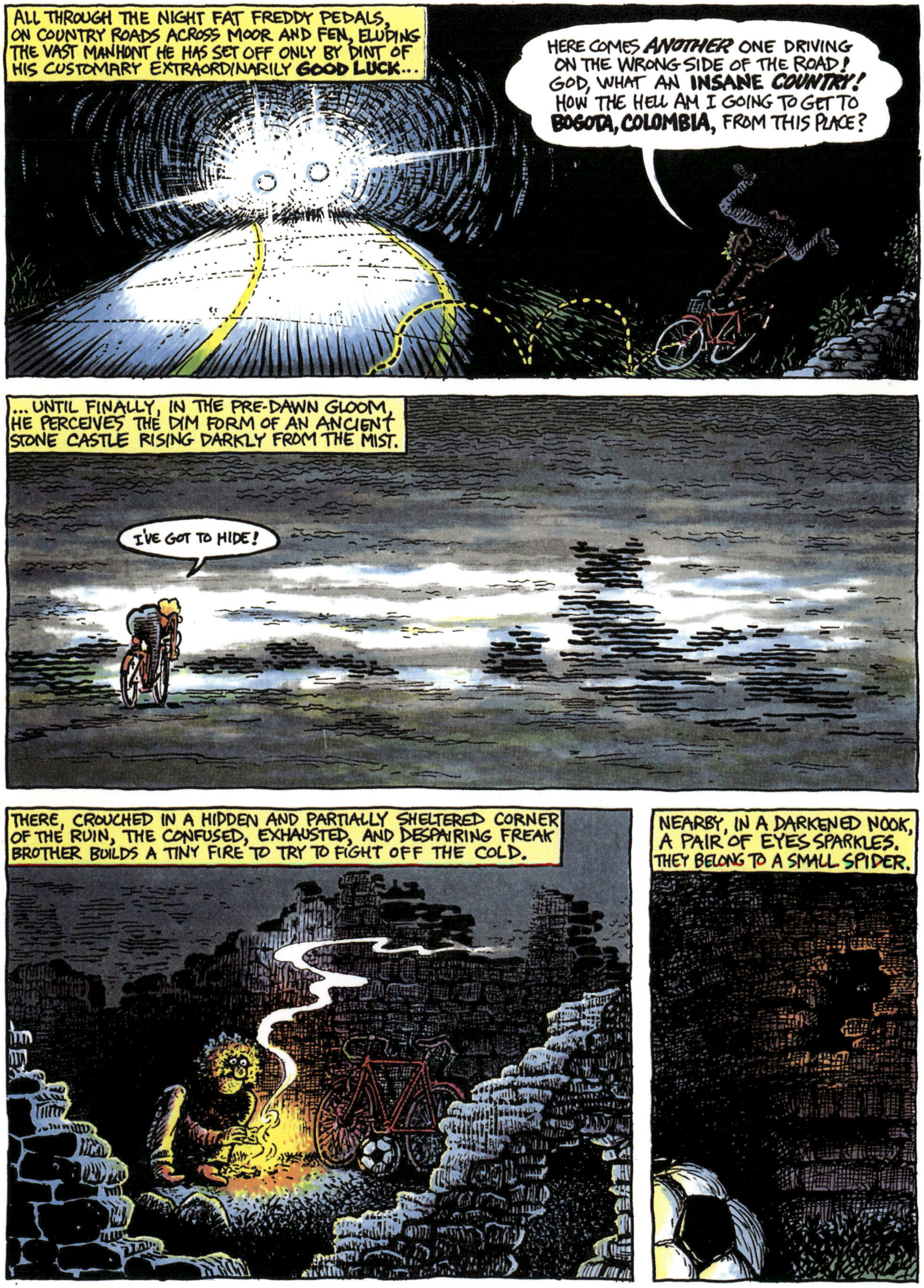
ALL THROUGH THE NIGHT FAT FREDDY PEDALS, ON COUNTRY ROADS ACROSS MOOR AND FEN, ELUDING THE VAST MANHUNT HE HAS SET OFF ONLY BY DINT OF HIS CUSTOMARY EXTRAORDINARILY GOOD LUCK...
HERE COMES ANOTHER ONE DRIVING ON THE WRONG SIDE OF THE ROAD! GOD, WHAT AN INSANE COUNTRY! HOW THE HELL AM I GOING TO GET TO BOGOTA, COLOMBIA, FROM THIS PLACE?
... UNTIL FINALLY, IN THE PRE-DAWN GLOOM, HE PERCEIVES THE DIM FORM OF AN ANCIENT STONE CASTLE RISING DARKLY FROM THE MIST.
I'VE GOT TO HIDE!
THERE, CROUCHED IN A HIDDEN AND PARTIALLY SHELTERED CORNER OF THE RUIN, THE CONFUSED, EXHAUSTED, AND DESPAIRING FREAK BROTHER BUILDS A TINY FIRE TO TRY TO FIGHT OFF THE COLD.
NEARBY, IN A DARKENED NOOK, A PAIR OF EYES SPARKLES. THEY BELONG TO A SMALL SPIDER.

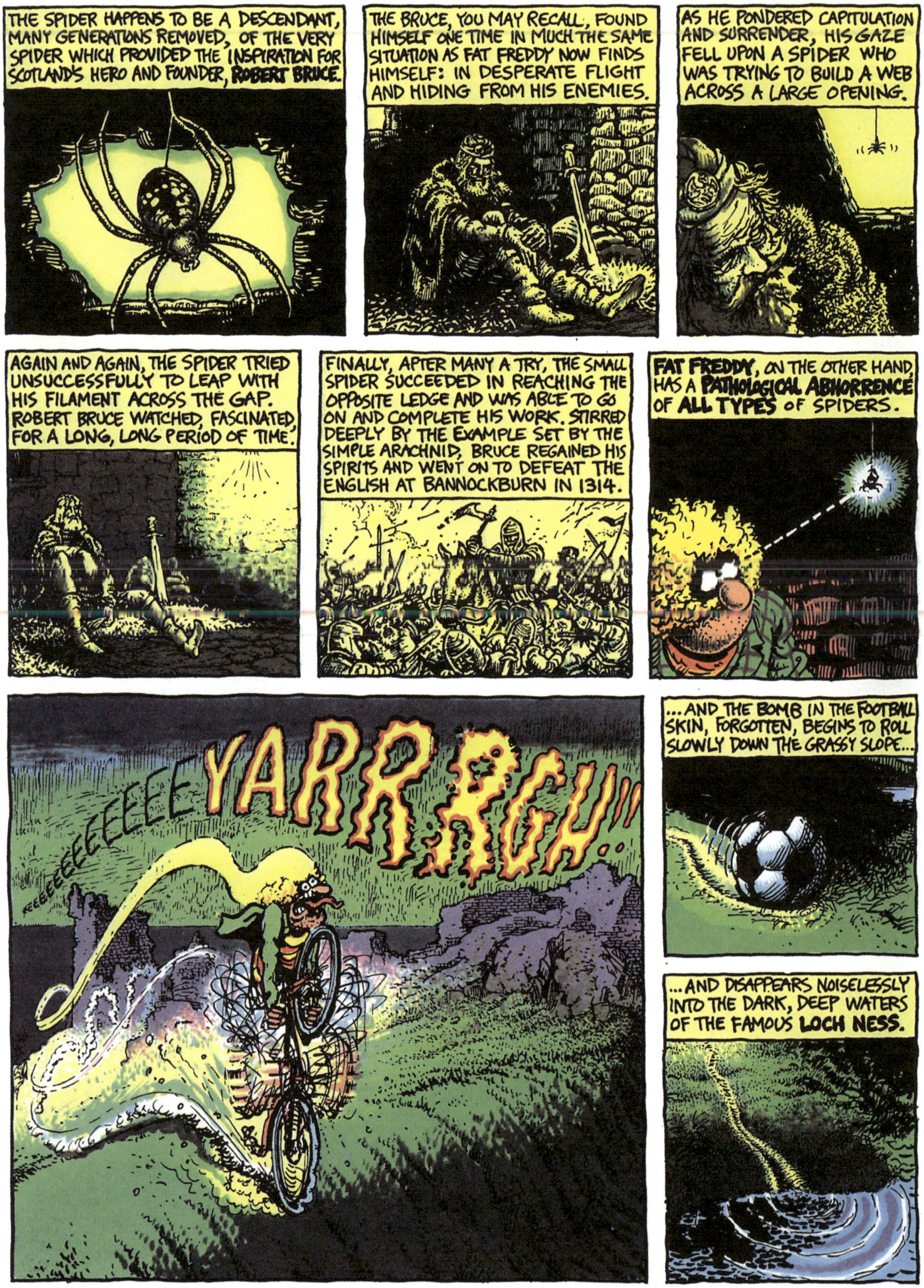
THE SPIDER HAPPENS TO BE A DESCENDANT, MANY GENERATIONS REMOVED, OF THE VERY SPIDER WHICH PROVIDED THE INSPIRATION FOR SCOTLAND'S HERO AND FOUNDER, ROBERT BRUCE.
THE BRUCE, YOU MAY RECALL, FOUND HIMSELF ONE TIME IN MUCH THE SAME SITUATION AS FAT FREDDY NOW FINDS HIMSELF: IN DESPERATE FLIGHT AND HIDING FROM HIS ENEMIES.
AS HE PONDERED CAPITULATION AND SURRENDER, HIS GAZE FELL UPON A SPIDER WHO WAS TRYING TO BUILD A WEB ACROSS A LARGE OPENING.
AGAIN AND AGAIN, THE SPIDER TRIED UNSUCCESSFULLY TO LEAP WITH HIS FILAMENT ACROSS THE GAP. ROBERT BRUCE WATCHED, FASCINATED, FOR A LONG, LONG PERIOD OF TIME.
FINALLY, AFTER MANY A TRY, THE SMALL SPIDER SUCCEEDED IN REACHING THE OPPOSITE LEDGE AND WAS ABLE TO GO ON AND COMPLETE HIS WORK. STIRRED DEEPLY BY THE EXAMPLE SET BY THE SIMPLE ARACHNID, BRUCE REGAINED HIS SPIRITS AND WENT ON TO DEFEAT THE ENGLISH AT BANNOCKBURN IN 1314.
FAT FREDDY, ON THE OTHER HAND, HAS A PATHOLOGICAL ABHORRENCE OF ALL TYPES OF SPIDERS.
EEEEEEEEEEEEEEEYARRRGH!!
...AND THE BOMB IN THE FOOTBALL SKIN, FORGOTTEN, BEGINS TO ROLL SLOWLY DOWN THE GRASSY SLOPE...
...AND DISAPPEARS NOISELESSLY INTO THE DARK, DEEP WATERS OF THE FAMOUS LOCH NESS.

Editorial Comment

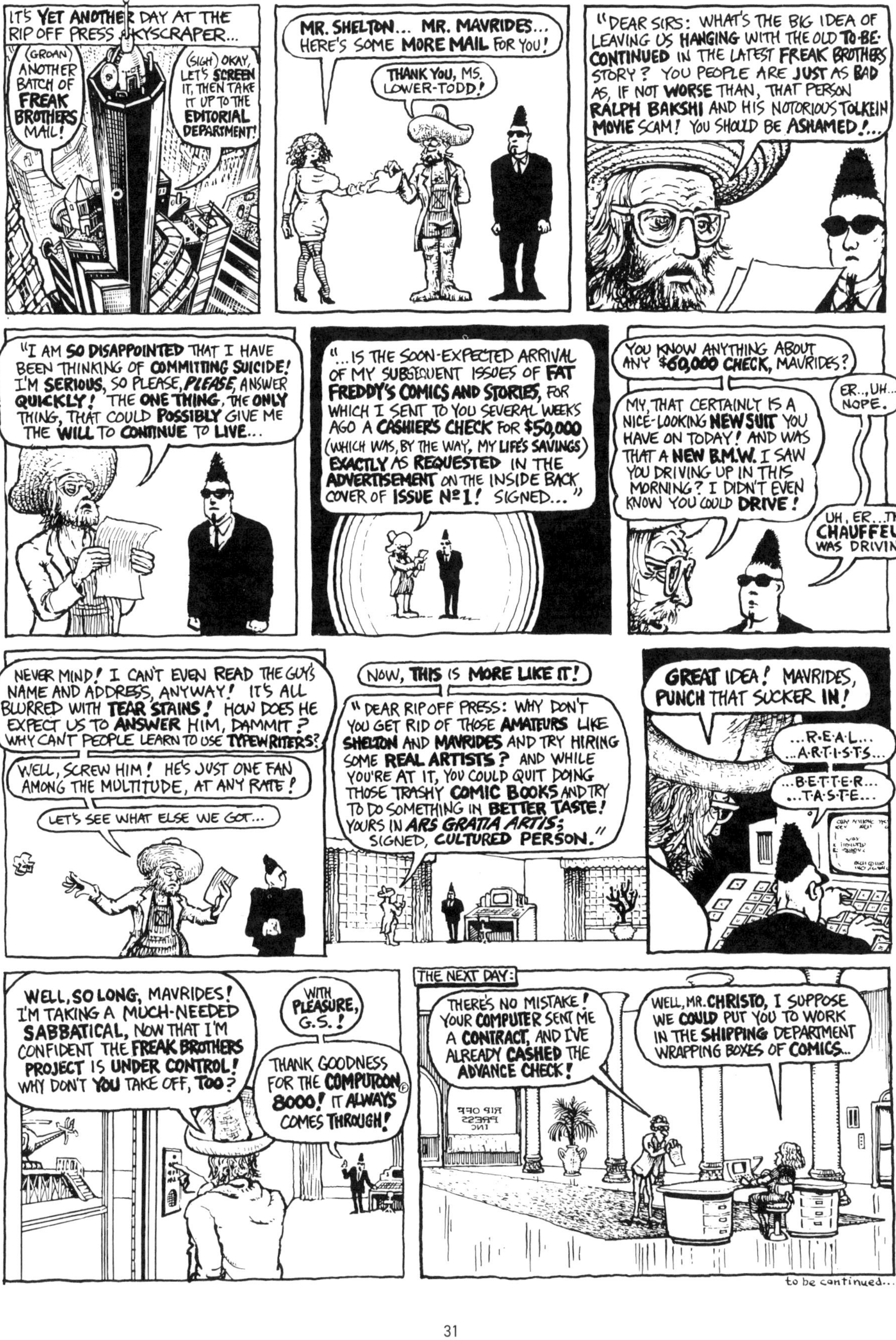

IT'S YET ANOTHER DAY AT THE RIP OFF PRESS SKYSCRAPER...
(GROAN) ANOTHER BATCH OF FREAK BROTHERS MAIL!
(SIGH) OKAY, LET'S SCREEN IT, THEN TAKE IT UP TO THE EDITORIAL DEPARTMENT!
MR. SHELTON... MR. MAVRIDES... HERE'S SOME MORE MAIL FOR YOU!
THANK YOU, MS. LOWER-TODD!
"DEAR SIRS: WHAT'S THE BIG IDEA OF LEAVING US HANGING WITH THE OLD TO-BE-CONTINUED IN THE LATEST FREAK BROTHERS STORY? YOU PEOPLE ARE JUST AS BAD AS, IF NOT WORSE THAN, THAT PERSON RALPH BAKSHI AND HIS NOTORIOUS TOLKEIN MOVIE SCAM! YOU SHOULD BE ASHAMED!...
"I AM SO DISAPPOINTED THAT I HAVE BEEN THINKING OF COMMITTING SUICIDE! I'M SERIOUS, SO PLEASE, PLEASE, ANSWER QUICKLY! THE ONE THING, THE ONLY THING, THAT COULD POSSIBLY GIVE ME THE WILL TO CONTINUE TO LIVE...
"...IS THE SOON-EXPECTED ARRIVAL OF MY SUBSEQUENT ISSUES OF FAT FREDDY'S COMICS AND STORIES, FOR WHICH I SENT TO YOU SEVERAL WEEKS AGO A CASHIER'S CHECK FOR $50,000 (WHICH WAS, BY THE WAY, MY LIFE'S SAVINGS) EXACTLY AS REQUESTED IN THE ADVERTISEMENT ON THE INSIDE BACK COVER OF ISSUE No 1! SIGNED..."
YOU KNOW ANYTHING ABOUT ANY $60,000 CHECK, MAVRIDES?
ER.., UH... NOPE.
MY, THAT CERTAINLY IS A NICE-LOOKING NEW SUIT YOU HAVE ON TODAY! AND WAS THAT A NEW B.M.W. I SAW YOU DRIVING UP IN THIS MORNING? I DIDN'T EVEN KNOW YOU COULD DRIVE!
UH, ER...THE CHAUFFEUR WAS DRIVING!
NEVER MIND! I CAN'T EVEN READ THE GUY'S NAME AND ADDRESS, ANYWAY! IT'S ALL BLURRED WITH TEAR STAINS! HOW DOES HE EXPECT US TO ANSWER HIM, DAMMIT? WHY CAN'T PEOPLE LEARN TO USE TYPEWRITERS?
WELL, SCREW HIM! HE'S JUST ONE FAN AMONG THE MULTITUDE, AT ANY RATE!
LET'S SEE WHAT ELSE WE GOT...
NOW, THIS IS MORE LIKE IT!
"DEAR RIP OFF PRESS: WHY DON'T YOU GET RID OF THOSE AMATEURS LIKE SHELTON AND MAVRIDES AND TRY HIRING SOME REAL ARTISTS? AND WHILE YOU'RE AT IT, YOU COULD QUIT DOING THOSE TRASHY COMIC BOOKS AND TRY TO DO SOMETHING IN BETTER TASTE! YOURS IN ARS GRATIA ARTIS; SIGNED, CULTURED PERSON."
GREAT IDEA! MAVRIDES, PUNCH THAT SUCKER IN!
...R.E.A.L... ..A.R.T.I.S.T.S...
...B.E.T.T.E.R... ...T.A.S.T.E...
WELL, SO LONG, MAVRIDES! I'M TAKING A MUCH-NEEDED SABBATICAL, NOW THAT I'M CONFIDENT THE FREAK BROTHERS PROJECT IS UNDER CONTROL! WHY DON'T YOU TAKE OFF, TOO?
WITH PLEASURE, G.S.!
THANK GOODNESS FOR THE COMPUTOON 8000! IT ALWAYS COMES THROUGH!
THE NEXT DAY:
THERE'S NO MISTAKE! YOUR COMPUTER SENT ME A CONTRACT, AND I'VE ALREADY CASHED THE ADVANCE CHECK!
WELL, MR. CHRISTO, I SUPPOSE WE COULD PUT YOU TO WORK IN THE SHIPPING DEPARTMENT WRAPPING BOXES OF COMICS...
to be continued...

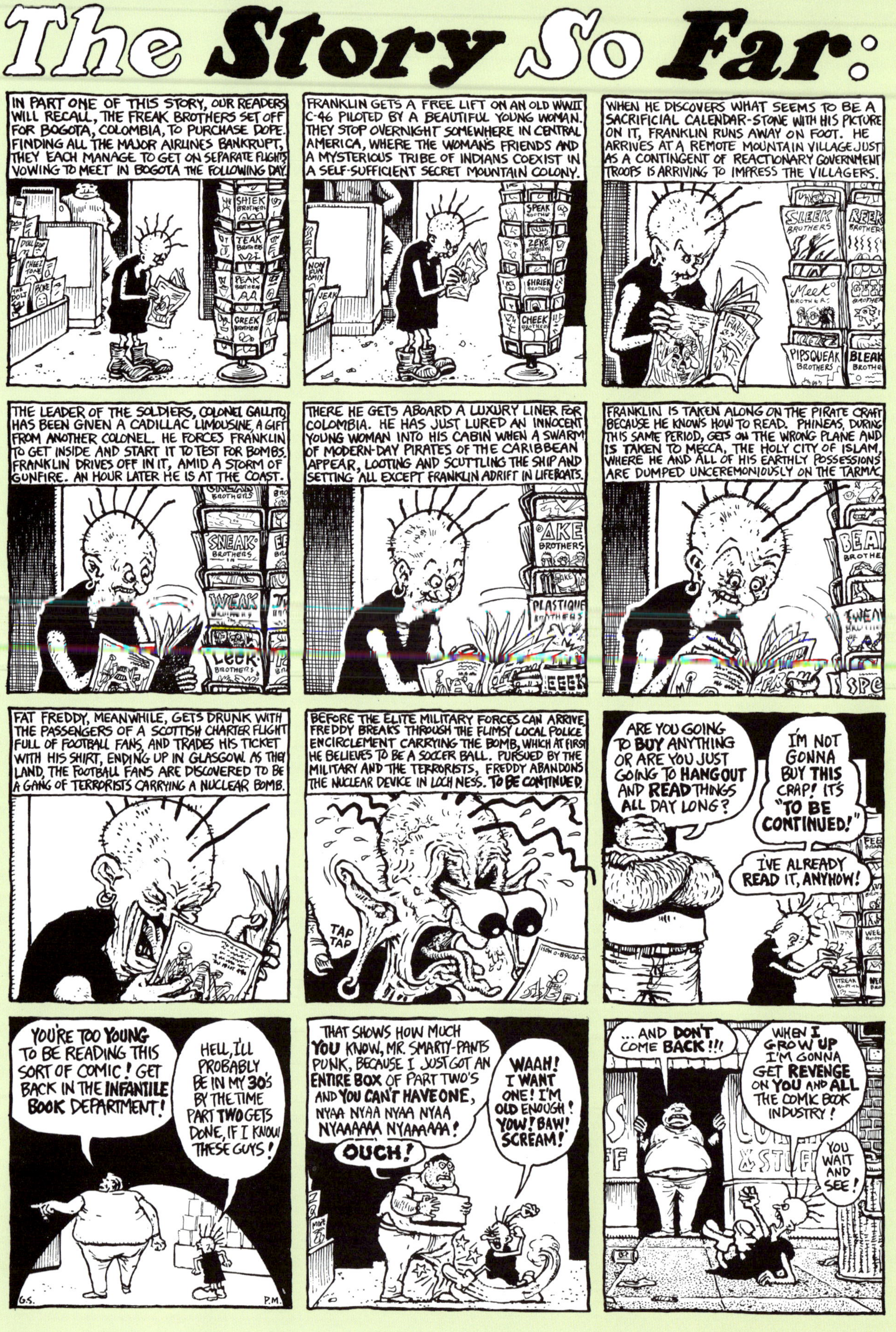
The Story So Far:
IN PART ONE OF THIS STORY, OUR READERS WILL RECALL, THE FREAK BROTHERS SET OFF FOR BOGOTA, COLOMBIA, TO PURCHASE DOPE. FINDING ALL THE MAJOR AIRLINES BANKRUPT, THEY EACH MANAGE TO GET ON SEPARATE FLIGHTS VOWING TO MEET IN BOGOTA THE FOLLOWING DAY.
FRANKLIN GETS A FREE LIFT ON AN OLD WWII C-46 PILOTED BY A BEAUTIFUL YOUNG WOMAN. THEY STOP OVERNIGHT SOMEWHERE IN CENTRAL AMERICA, WHERE THE WOMAN'S FRIENDS AND A MYSTERIOUS TRIBE OF INDIANS COEXIST IN A SELF-SUFFICIENT SECRET MOUNTAIN COLONY.
WHEN HE DISCOVERS WHAT SEEMS TO BE A SACRIFICIAL CALENDAR-STONE WITH HIS PICTURE ON IT, FRANKLIN RUNS AWAY ON FOOT. HE ARRIVES AT A REMOTE MOUNTAIN VILLAGE JUST AS A CONTINGENT OF REACTIONARY GOVERNMENT TROOPS IS ARRIVING TO IMPRESS THE VILLAGERS.
THE LEADER OF THE SOLDIERS, COLONEL GALLITO, HAS BEEN GIVEN A CADILLAC LIMOUSINE, A GIFT FROM ANOTHER COLONEL. HE FORCES FRANKLIN TO GET INSIDE AND START IT TO TEST FOR BOMBS. FRANKLIN DRIVES OFF IN IT, AMID A STORM OF GUNFIRE. AN HOUR LATER HE IS AT THE COAST.
THERE HE GETS ABOARD A LUXURY LINER FOR COLOMBIA. HE HAS JUST LURED AN INNOCENT YOUNG WOMAN INTO HIS CABIN WHEN A SWARM OF MODERN-DAY PIRATES OF THE CARIBBEAN APPEAR, LOOTING AND SCUTTLING THE SHIP AND SETTING ALL EXCEPT FRANKLIN ADRIFT IN LIFEBOATS.
FRANKLIN IS TAKEN ALONG ON THE PIRATE CRAFT BECAUSE HE KNOWS HOW TO READ. PHINEAS, DURING THIS SAME PERIOD, GETS ON THE WRONG PLANE AND IS TAKEN TO MECCA, THE HOLY CITY OF ISLAM, WHERE HE AND ALL OF HIS EARTHLY POSSESSIONS ARE DUMPED UNCEREMONIOUSLY ON THE TARMAC.
FAT FREDDY, MEANWHILE, GETS DRUNK WITH THE PASSENGERS OF A SCOTTISH CHARTER FLIGHT FULL OF FOOTBALL FANS, AND TRADES HIS TICKET WITH HIS SHIRT, ENDING UP IN GLASGOW. AS THEY LAND, THE FOOTBALL FANS ARE DISCOVERED TO BE A GANG OF TERRORISTS CARRYING A NUCLEAR BOMB.
BEFORE THE ELITE MILITARY FORCES CAN ARRIVE, FREDDY BREAKS THROUGH THE FLIMSY LOCAL POLICE ENCIRCLEMENT CARRYING THE BOMB, WHICH AT FIRST HE BELIEVES TO BE A SOCCER BALL. PURSUED BY THE MILITARY AND THE TERRORISTS, FREDDY ABANDONS THE NUCLEAR DEVICE IN LOCH NESS. TO BE CONTINUED.
TAP TAP
ARE YOU GOING TO BUY ANYTHING OR ARE YOU JUST GOING TO HANG OUT AND READ THINGS ALL DAY LONG?
I'M NOT GONNA BUY THIS CRAP! IT'S "TO BE CONTINUED!"
I'VE ALREADY READ IT, ANYHOW!
YOU'RE TOO YOUNG TO BE READING THIS SORT OF COMIC! GET BACK IN THE INFANTILE BOOK DEPARTMENT!
HELL, I'LL PROBABLY BE IN MY 30'S BY THE TIME PART TWO GETS DONE, IF I KNOW THESE GUYS!
G.S.
P.M.
THAT SHOWS HOW MUCH YOU KNOW, MR. SMARTY-PANTS PUNK, BECAUSE I JUST GOT AN ENTIRE BOX OF PART TWO'S AND YOU CAN'T HAVE ONE, NYAA NYAA NYAA NYAA NYAAAAAA NYAAAAAA!
WAAH! I WANT ONE! I'M OLD ENOUGH! YOW! BAW! SCREAM!
OUCH!
...AND DON'T COME BACK!!!
WHEN I GROW UP I'M GONNA GET REVENGE ON YOU AND ALL THE COMIC BOOK INDUSTRY!
YOU WAIT AND SEE!

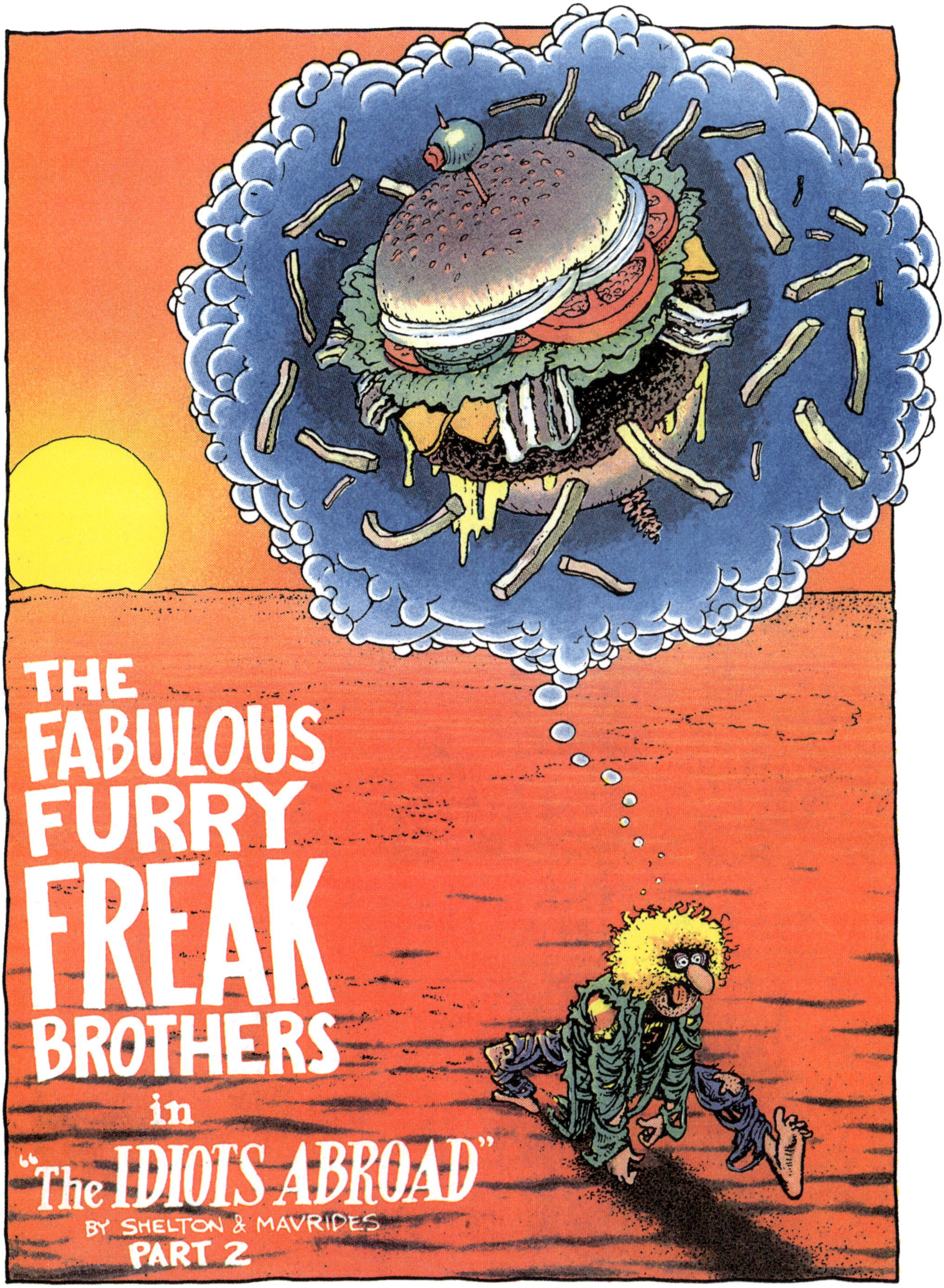
THE
FABULOUS
FURRY
FREAK
BROTHERS
in
"The IDIOTS ABROAD"
BY SHELTON & MAVRIDES
PART 2

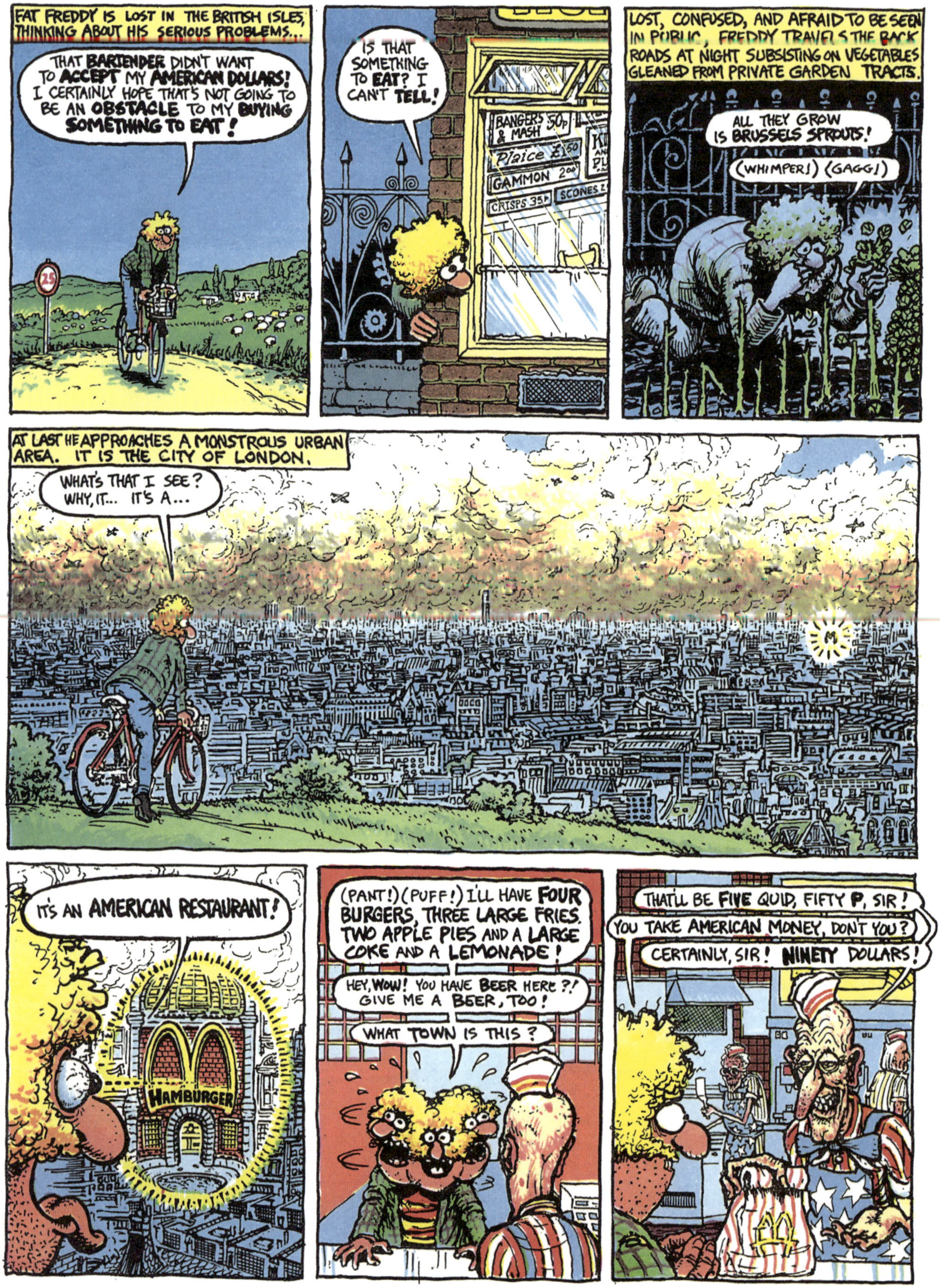

FAT FREDDY IS LOST IN THE BRITISH ISLES, THINKING ABOUT HIS SERIOUS PROBLEMS...
THAT BARTENDER DIDN'T WANT TO ACCEPT MY AMERICAN DOLLARS! I CERTAINLY HOPE THAT'S NOT GOING TO BE AN OBSTACLE TO MY BUYING SOMETHING TO EAT!
25
IS THAT SOMETHING TO EAT? I CAN'T TELL!
BANGERS & MASH 50p
Plaice £1.50
GAMMON 200
CRISPS 35p
LOST, CONFUSED, AND AFRAID TO BE SEEN IN PUBLIC, FREDDY TRAVELS THE BACK ROADS AT NIGHT SUBSISTING ON VEGETABLES GLEANED FROM PRIVATE GARDEN TRACTS.
ALL THEY GROW IS BRUSSELS SPROUTS!
(WHIMPER!) (GAGG!)
AT LAST HE APPROACHES A MONSTROUS URBAN AREA. IT IS THE CITY OF LONDON.
WHAT'S THAT I SEE? WHY, IT... IT'S A...
IT'S AN AMERICAN RESTAURANT!
HAMBURGER
(PANT!) (PUFF!) I'LL HAVE FOUR BURGERS, THREE LARGE FRIES, TWO APPLE PIES AND A LARGE COKE AND A LEMONADE!
HEY, WOW! YOU HAVE BEER HERE?! GIVE ME A BEER, TOO!
WHAT TOWN IS THIS?
THAT'LL BE FIVE QUID, FIFTY P, SIR!
YOU TAKE AMERICAN MONEY, DON'T YOU?
CERTAINLY, SIR! NINETY DOLLARS!

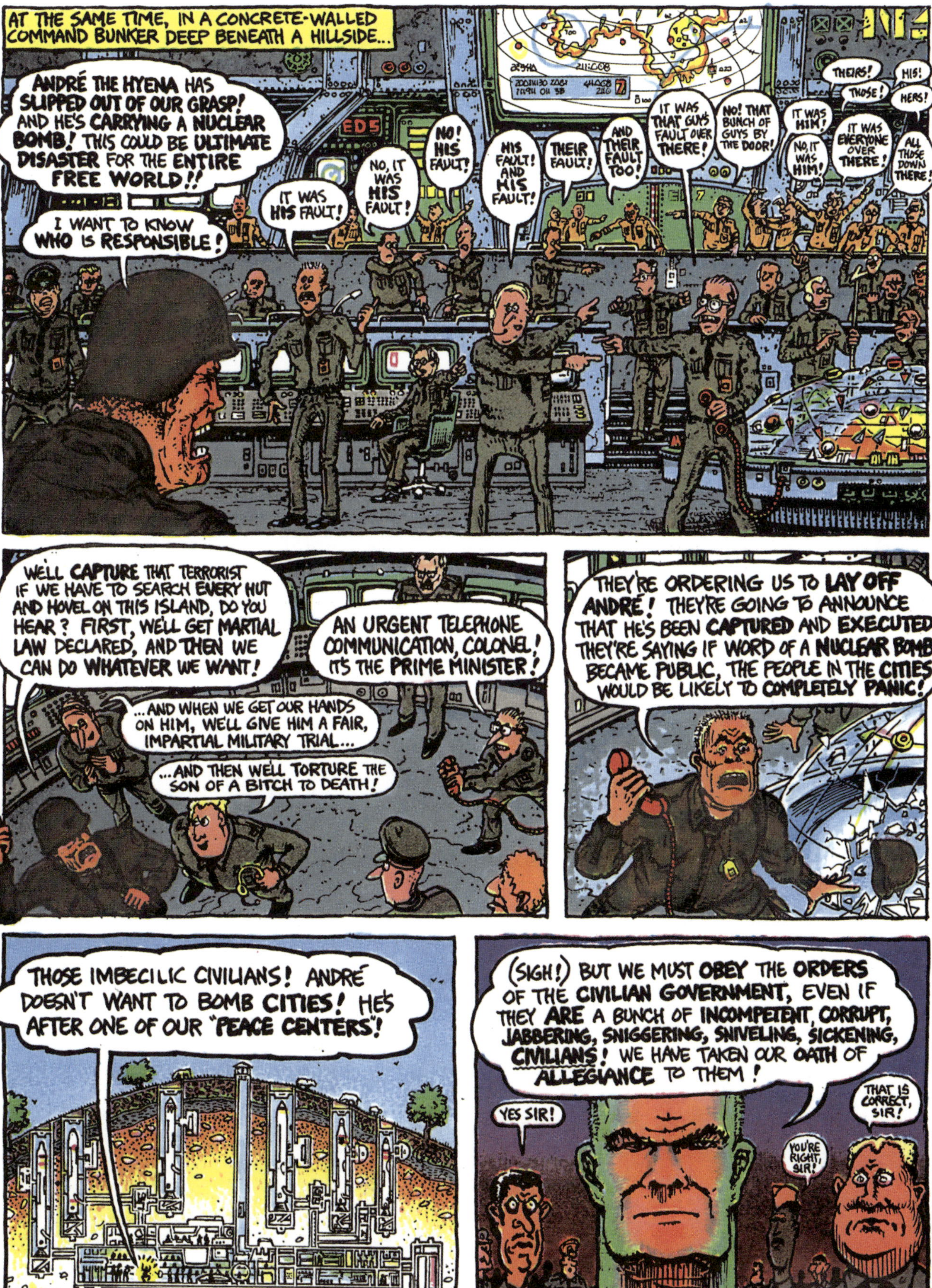
AT THE SAME TIME, IN A CONCRETE-WALLED COMMAND BUNKER DEEP BENEATH A HILLSIDE...
ANDRÉ THE HYENA HAS SLIPPED OUT OF OUR GRASP! AND HE'S CARRYING A NUCLEAR BOMB! THIS COULD BE ULTIMATE DISASTER FOR THE ENTIRE FREE WORLD!!
I WANT TO KNOW WHO IS RESPONSIBLE!
IT WAS HIS FAULT!
NO, IT WAS HIS FAULT!
NO! HIS FAULT!
HIS FAULT! AND HIS FAULT!
THEIR FAULT!
AND THEIR FAULT TOO!
IT WAS THAT GUY'S FAULT OVER THERE!
NO! THAT BUNCH OF GUYS BY THE DOOR!
IT WAS HIM!
NO, IT WAS HIM!
THEIRS!
HIS!
THOSE!
HERS!
IT WAS EVERYONE OVER THERE!
ALL THOSE DOWN THERE!
WE'LL CAPTURE THAT TERRORIST IF WE HAVE TO SEARCH EVERY HUT AND HOVEL ON THIS ISLAND, DO YOU HEAR? FIRST, WE'LL GET MARTIAL LAW DECLARED, AND THEN WE CAN DO WHATEVER WE WANT!
AN URGENT TELEPHONE COMMUNICATION, COLONEL! IT'S THE PRIME MINISTER!
...AND WHEN WE GET OUR HANDS ON HIM, WE'LL GIVE HIM A FAIR, IMPARTIAL MILITARY TRIAL...
...AND THEN WE'LL TORTURE THE SON OF A BITCH TO DEATH!
THEY'RE ORDERING US TO LAY OFF ANDRÉ! THEY'RE GOING TO ANNOUNCE THAT HE'S BEEN CAPTURED AND EXECUTED! THEY'RE SAYING IF WORD OF A NUCLEAR BOMB BECAME PUBLIC, THE PEOPLE IN THE CITIES WOULD BE LIKELY TO COMPLETELY PANIC!
THOSE IMBECILIC CIVILIANS! ANDRÉ DOESN'T WANT TO BOMB CITIES! HE'S AFTER ONE OF OUR "PEACE CENTERS"!
(SIGH!) BUT WE MUST OBEY THE ORDERS OF THE CIVILIAN GOVERNMENT, EVEN IF THEY ARE A BUNCH OF INCOMPETENT, CORRUPT, JABBERING, SNIGGERING, SNIVELING, SICKENING, CIVILIANS! WE HAVE TAKEN OUR OATH OF ALLEGIANCE TO THEM!
YES SIR!
YOU'RE RIGHT, SIR!
THAT IS CORRECT, SIR!

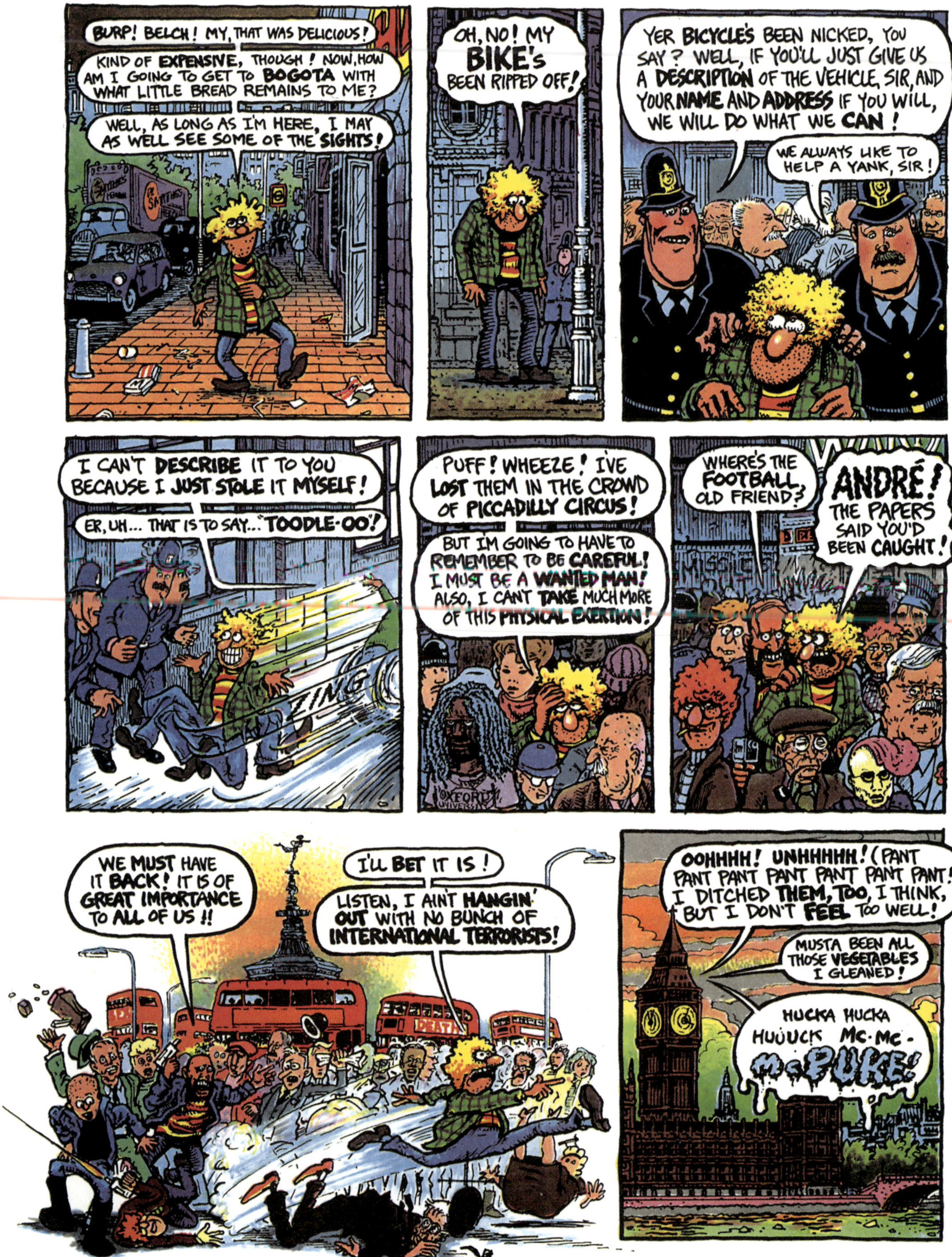

BURP! BELCH! MY, THAT WAS DELICIOUS!
KIND OF EXPENSIVE, THOUGH! NOW, HOW AM I GOING TO GET TO BOGOTA WITH WHAT LITTLE BREAD REMAINS TO ME?
WELL, AS LONG AS I'M HERE, I MAY AS WELL SEE SOME OF THE SIGHTS!
OH, NO! MY BIKE'S BEEN RIPPED OFF!
YER BICYCLE'S BEEN NICKED, YOU SAY? WELL, IF YOU'LL JUST GIVE US A DESCRIPTION OF THE VEHICLE, SIR, AND YOUR NAME AND ADDRESS IF YOU WILL, WE WILL DO WHAT WE CAN!
WE ALWAYS LIKE TO HELP A YANK, SIR!
I CAN'T DESCRIBE IT TO YOU BECAUSE I JUST STOLE IT MYSELF!
ER, UH... THAT IS TO SAY... TOODLE-OO!
ZING
PUFF! WHEEZE! I'VE LOST THEM IN THE CROWD OF PICCADILLY CIRCUS!
BUT I'M GOING TO HAVE TO REMEMBER TO BE CAREFUL! I MUST BE A WANTED MAN! ALSO, I CAN'T TAKE MUCH MORE OF THIS PHYSICAL EXERTION!
OXFORD
WHERE'S THE FOOTBALL, OLD FRIEND?
ANDRÉ! THE PAPERS SAID YOU'D BEEN CAUGHT!
WE MUST HAVE IT BACK! IT IS OF GREAT IMPORTANCE TO ALL OF US!!
I'LL BET IT IS!
LISTEN, I AIN'T HANGIN' OUT WITH NO BUNCH OF INTERNATIONAL TERRORISTS!
DEATH
OOHHHH! UNHHHHH! (PANT PANT PANT PANT PANT PANT PANT!) I DITCHED THEM, TOO, I THINK, BUT I DON'T FEEL TOO WELL!
MUSTA BEEN ALL THOSE VEGETABLES I GLEANED!
HUCKA HUCKA HUUUCK Mc-Mc-Mc PUKE!

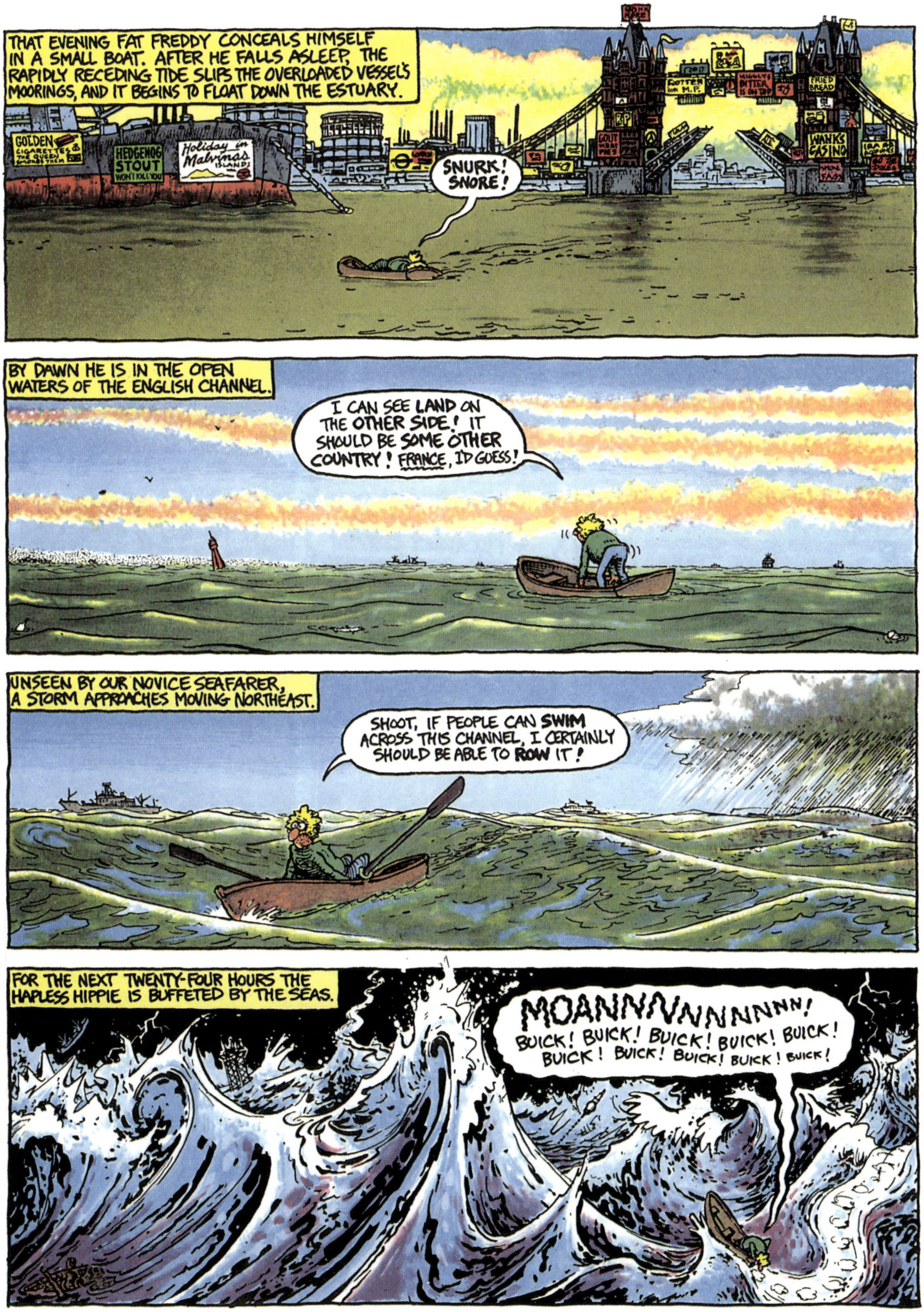
THAT EVENING FAT FREDDY CONCEALS HIMSELF IN A SMALL BOAT. AFTER HE FALLS ASLEEP, THE RAPIDLY RECEDING TIDE SLIPS THE OVERLOADED VESSEL'S MOORINGS, AND IT BEGINS TO FLOAT DOWN THE ESTUARY.
GOLDEN
HEDGEHOG STOUT WON'T KILL YOU
Holiday in Malvinas ISLAND!
ROTTER for M.P.
FRIED BREAD
WANKS CASINO
SNURK! SNORE!
BY DAWN HE IS IN THE OPEN WATERS OF THE ENGLISH CHANNEL.
I CAN SEE LAND ON THE OTHER SIDE! IT SHOULD BE SOME OTHER COUNTRY! FRANCE, I'D GUESS!
UNSEEN BY OUR NOVICE SEAFARER, A STORM APPROACHES MOVING NORTHEAST.
SHOOT, IF PEOPLE CAN SWIM ACROSS THIS CHANNEL, I CERTAINLY SHOULD BE ABLE TO ROW IT!
FOR THE NEXT TWENTY-FOUR HOURS THE HAPLESS HIPPIE IS BUFFETED BY THE SEAS.
MOANNNNNNNNN!
BUICK! BUICK! BUICK! BUICK! BUICK! BUICK! BUICK! BUICK! BUICK! BUICK!

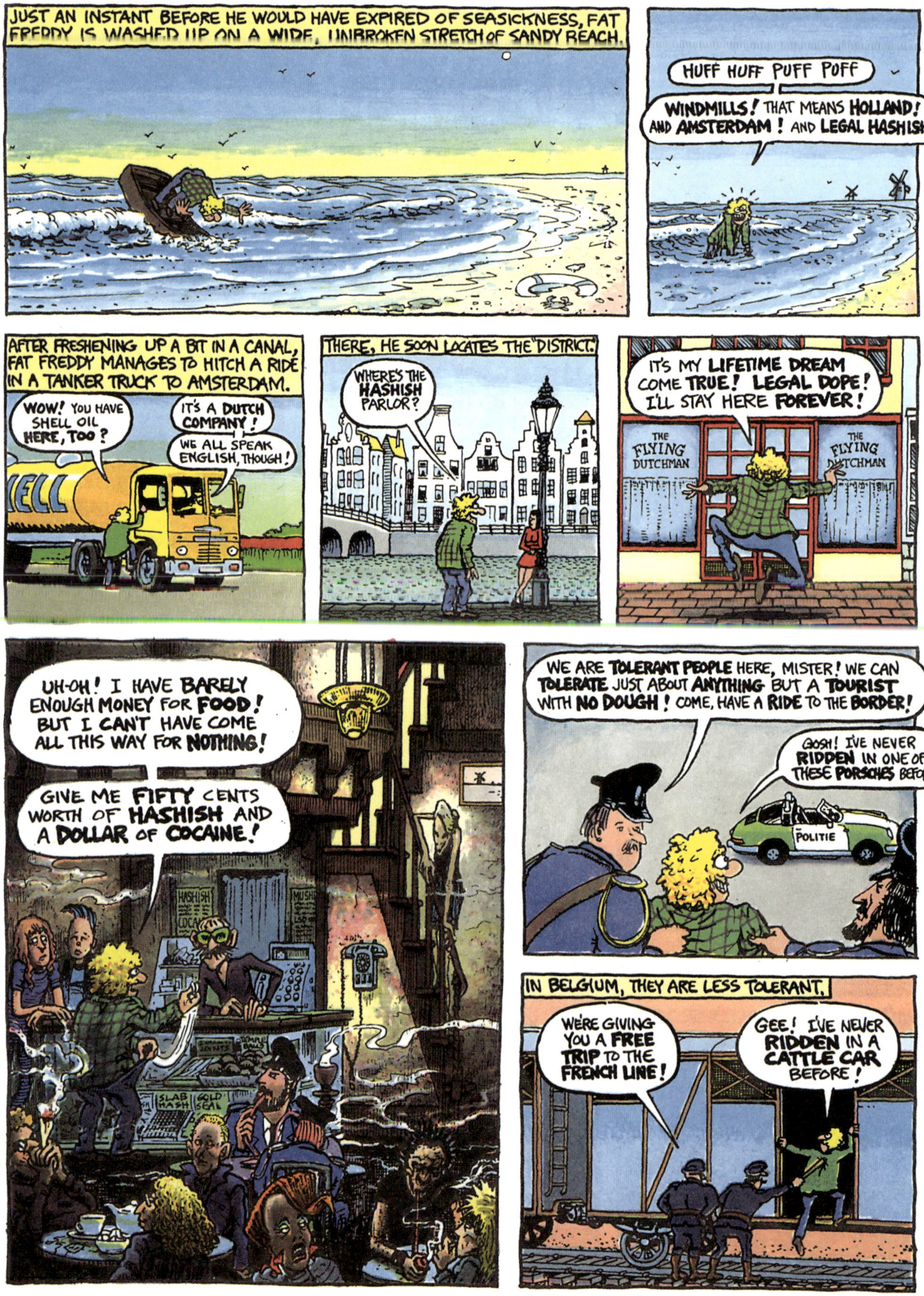
JUST AN INSTANT BEFORE HE WOULD HAVE EXPIRED OF SEASICKNESS, FAT FREDDY IS WASHED UP ON A WIDE, UNBROKEN STRETCH OF SANDY BEACH.
HUFF HUFF PUFF POFF
WINDMILLS! THAT MEANS HOLLAND! AND AMSTERDAM! AND LEGAL HASHISH!
AFTER FRESHENING UP A BIT IN A CANAL, FAT FREDDY MANAGES TO HITCH A RIDE IN A TANKER TRUCK TO AMSTERDAM.
WOW! YOU HAVE SHELL OIL HERE, TOO?
IT'S A DUTCH COMPANY!
WE ALL SPEAK ENGLISH, THOUGH!
THERE, HE SOON LOCATES THE "DISTRICT."
WHERE'S THE HASHISH PARLOR?
IT'S MY LIFETIME DREAM COME TRUE! LEGAL DOPE! I'LL STAY HERE FOREVER!
THE FLYING DUTCHMAN
THE FLYING DUTCHMAN
UH-OH! I HAVE BARELY ENOUGH MONEY FOR FOOD! BUT I CAN'T HAVE COME ALL THIS WAY FOR NOTHING!
GIVE ME FIFTY CENTS WORTH OF HASHISH AND A DOLLAR OF COCAINE!
HASHISH
SLAB HASH
GOLD SEAL
WE ARE TOLERANT PEOPLE HERE, MISTER! WE CAN TOLERATE JUST ABOUT ANYTHING BUT A TOURIST WITH NO DOUGH! COME, HAVE A RIDE TO THE BORDER!
GOSH! I'VE NEVER RIDDEN IN ONE OF THESE PORSCHES BEFORE!
POLITIE
IN BELGIUM, THEY ARE LESS TOLERANT.
WE'RE GIVING YOU A FREE TRIP TO THE FRENCH LINE!
GEE! I'VE NEVER RIDDEN IN A CATTLE CAR BEFORE!

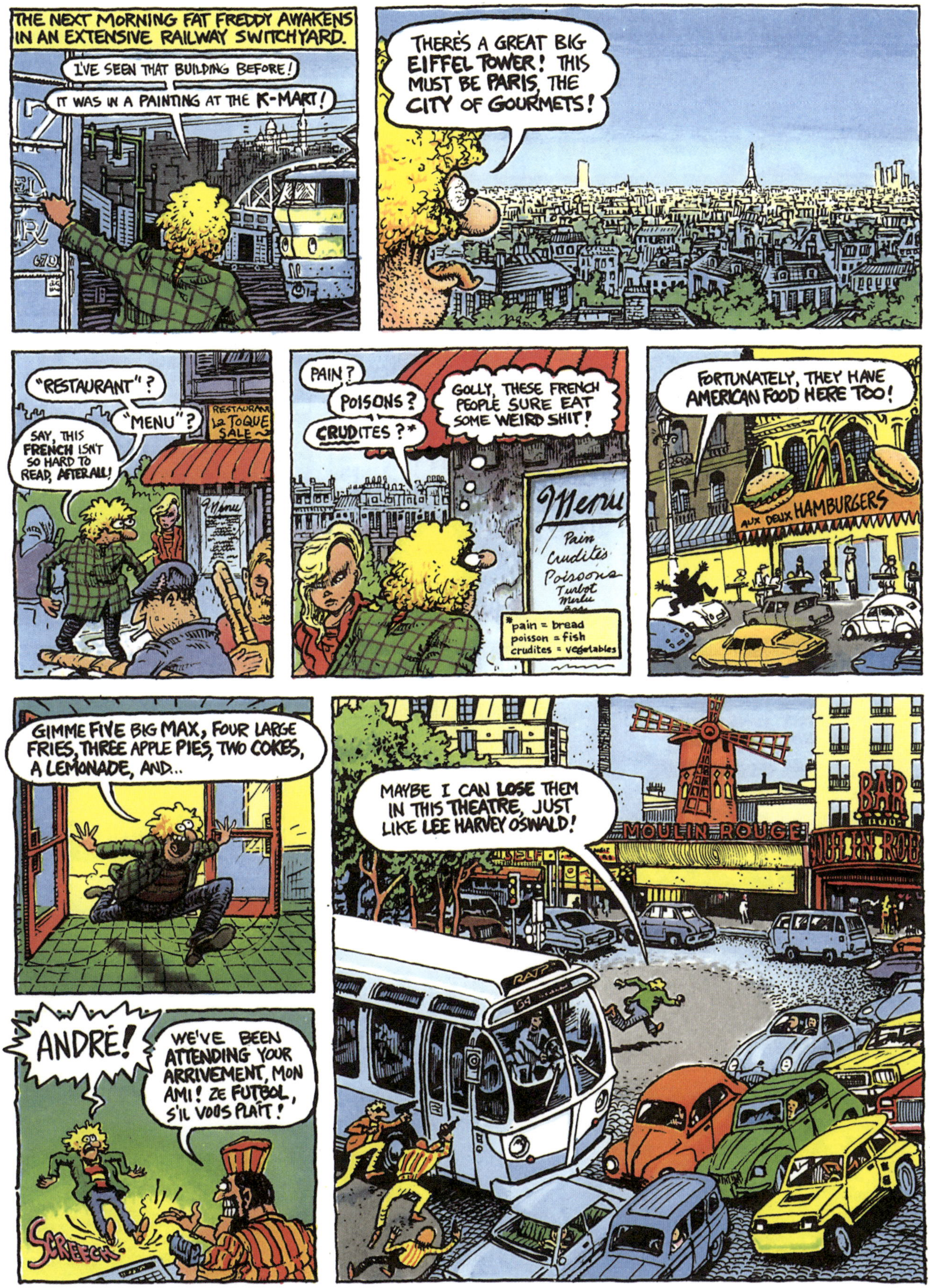
THE NEXT MORNING FAT FREDDY AWAKENS IN AN EXTENSIVE RAILWAY SWITCHYARD.
I'VE SEEN THAT BUILDING BEFORE!
IT WAS IN A PAINTING AT THE K-MART!
THERE'S A GREAT BIG EIFFEL TOWER! THIS MUST BE PARIS, THE CITY OF GOURMETS!
"RESTAURANT"?
"MENU"?
SAY, THIS FRENCH ISN'T SO HARD TO READ, AFTER ALL!
RESTAURANT La TOQUE SALE
PAIN?
POISONS?
CRUDITES?*
GOLLY, THESE FRENCH PEOPLE SURE EAT SOME WEIRD SHIT!
Menu
Pain
Crudités
Poissons
Turbot
*pain = bread
poisson = fish
crudites = vegetables
FORTUNATELY, THEY HAVE AMERICAN FOOD HERE TOO!
AUX DEUX HAMBURGERS
GIMME FIVE BIG MAX, FOUR LARGE FRIES, THREE APPLE PIES, TWO COKES, A LEMONADE, AND...
MAYBE I CAN LOSE THEM IN THIS THEATRE, JUST LIKE LEE HARVEY OSWALD!
MOULIN ROUGE
BAR
RATP
ANDRÉ!
WE'VE BEEN ATTENDING YOUR ARRIVEMENT, MON AMI! ZE FUTBOL, S'IL VOUS PLAÎT!
SCREECH

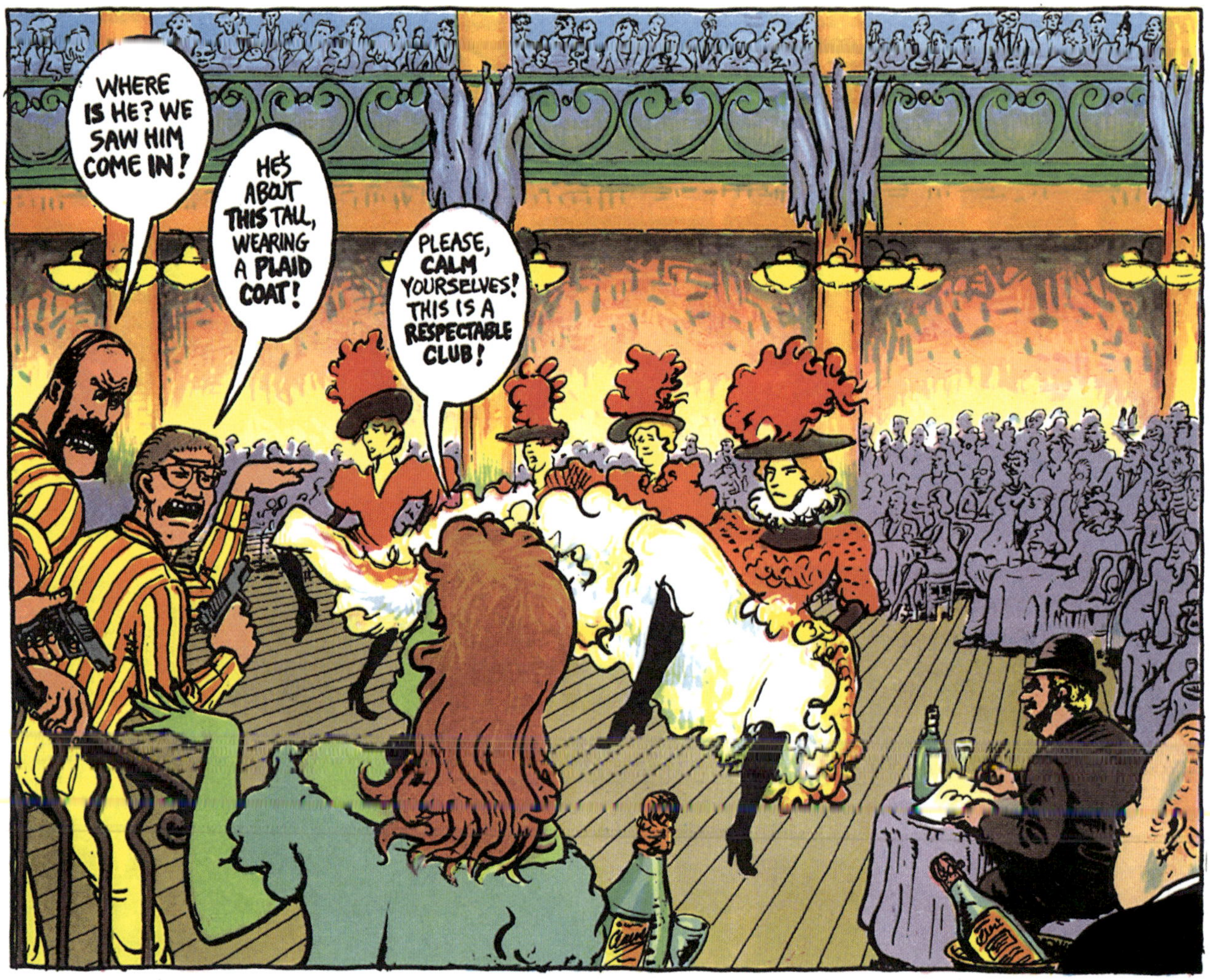
WHERE IS HE? WE SAW HIM COME IN!
HE'S ABOUT THIS TALL, WEARING A PLAID COAT!
PLEASE, CALM YOURSELVES! THIS IS A RESPECTABLE CLUB!

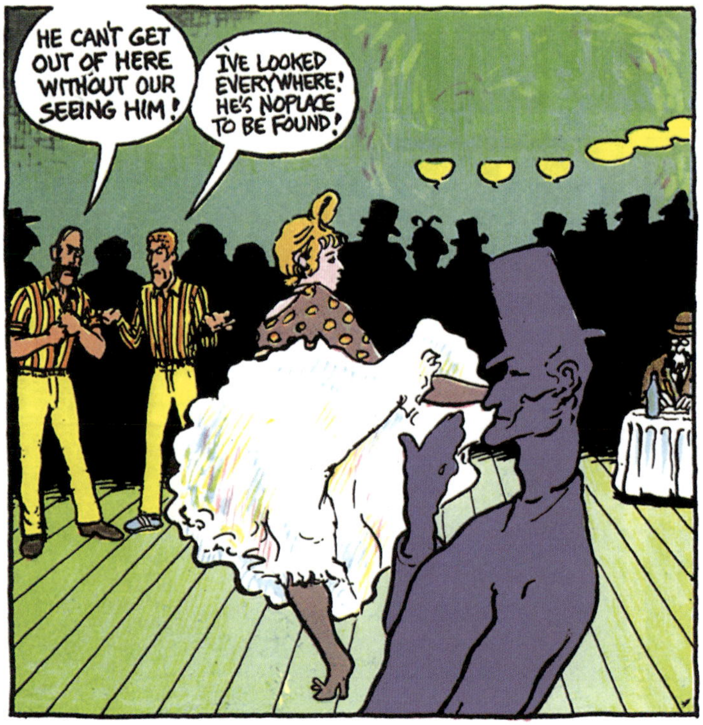
HE CAN'T GET OUT OF HERE WITHOUT OUR SEEING HIM!
I'VE LOOKED EVERYWHERE! HE'S NOPLACE TO BE FOUND!

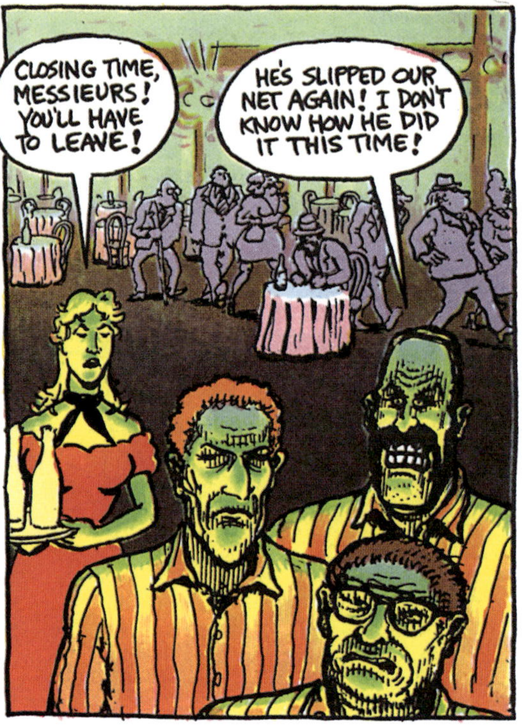
CLOSING TIME, MESSIEURS! YOU'LL HAVE TO LEAVE!
HE'S SLIPPED OUR NET AGAIN! I DON'T KNOW HOW HE DID IT THIS TIME!

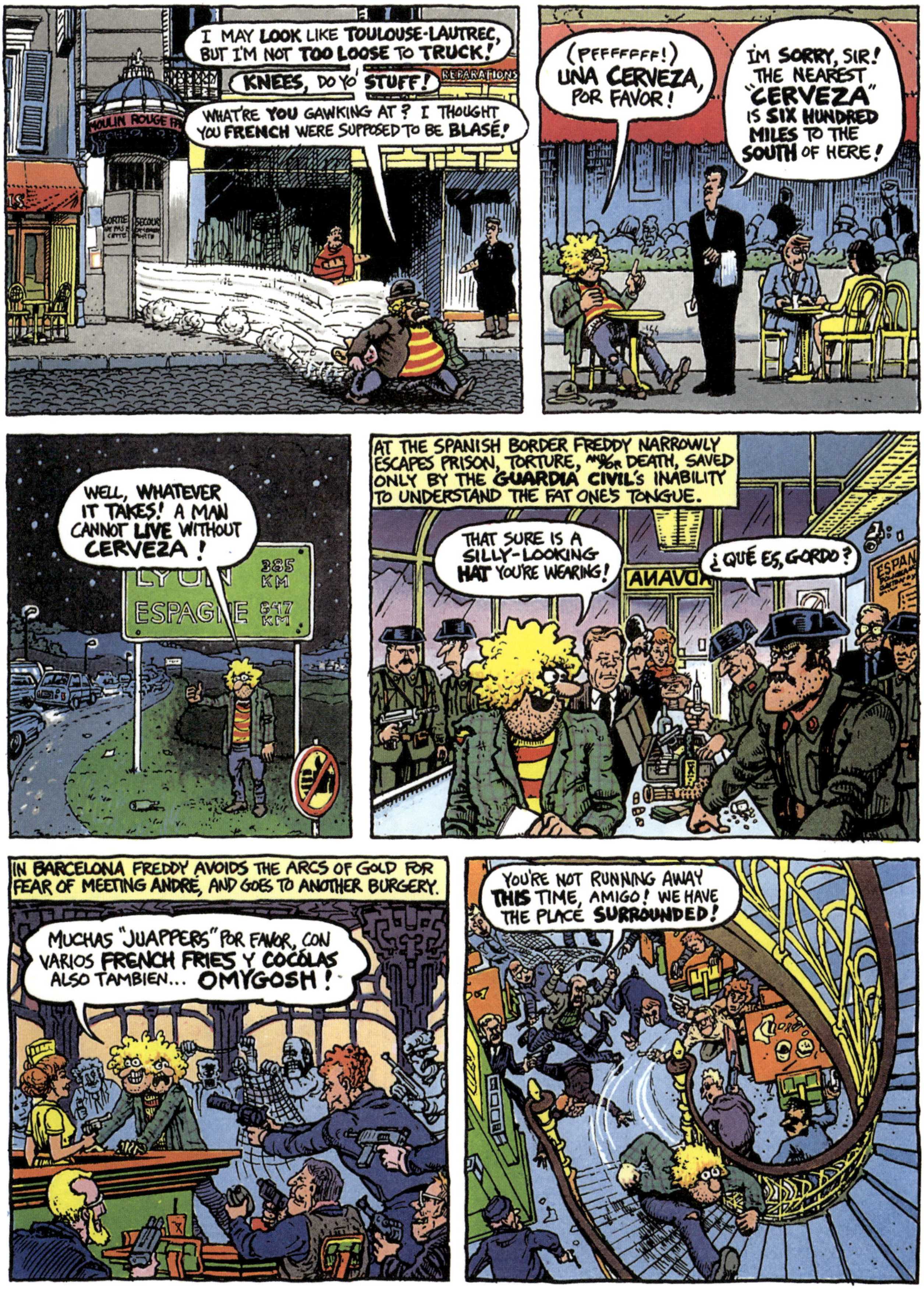
I MAY LOOK LIKE TOULOUSE-LAUTREC, BUT I'M NOT TOO LOOSE TO TRUCK!
KNEES, DO YO' STUFF!
WHAT'RE YOU GAWKING AT? I THOUGHT YOU FRENCH WERE SUPPOSED TO BE BLASÉ!
MOULIN ROUGE
REPARATIONS
(PFFFFFFF!) UNA CERVEZA, POR FAVOR!
I'M SORRY, SIR! THE NEAREST "CERVEZA" IS SIX HUNDRED MILES TO THE SOUTH OF HERE!
WELL, WHATEVER IT TAKES! A MAN CANNOT LIVE WITHOUT CERVEZA!
385 KM
847 KM
AT THE SPANISH BORDER FREDDY NARROWLY ESCAPES PRISON, TORTURE, AND/OR DEATH, SAVED ONLY BY THE GUARDIA CIVIL'S INABILITY TO UNDERSTAND THE FAT ONE'S TONGUE.
THAT SURE IS A SILLY-LOOKING HAT YOU'RE WEARING!
¿QUÉ ES, GORDO?
IN BARCELONA FREDDY AVOIDS THE ARCS OF GOLD FOR FEAR OF MEETING ANDRE, AND GOES TO ANOTHER BURGERY.
MUCHAS "JUAPPERS" POR FAVOR, CON VARIOS FRENCH FRIES Y COCÓLAS ALSO TAMBIEN... OMYGOSH!
YOU'RE NOT RUNNING AWAY THIS TIME, AMIGO! WE HAVE THE PLACE SURROUNDED!

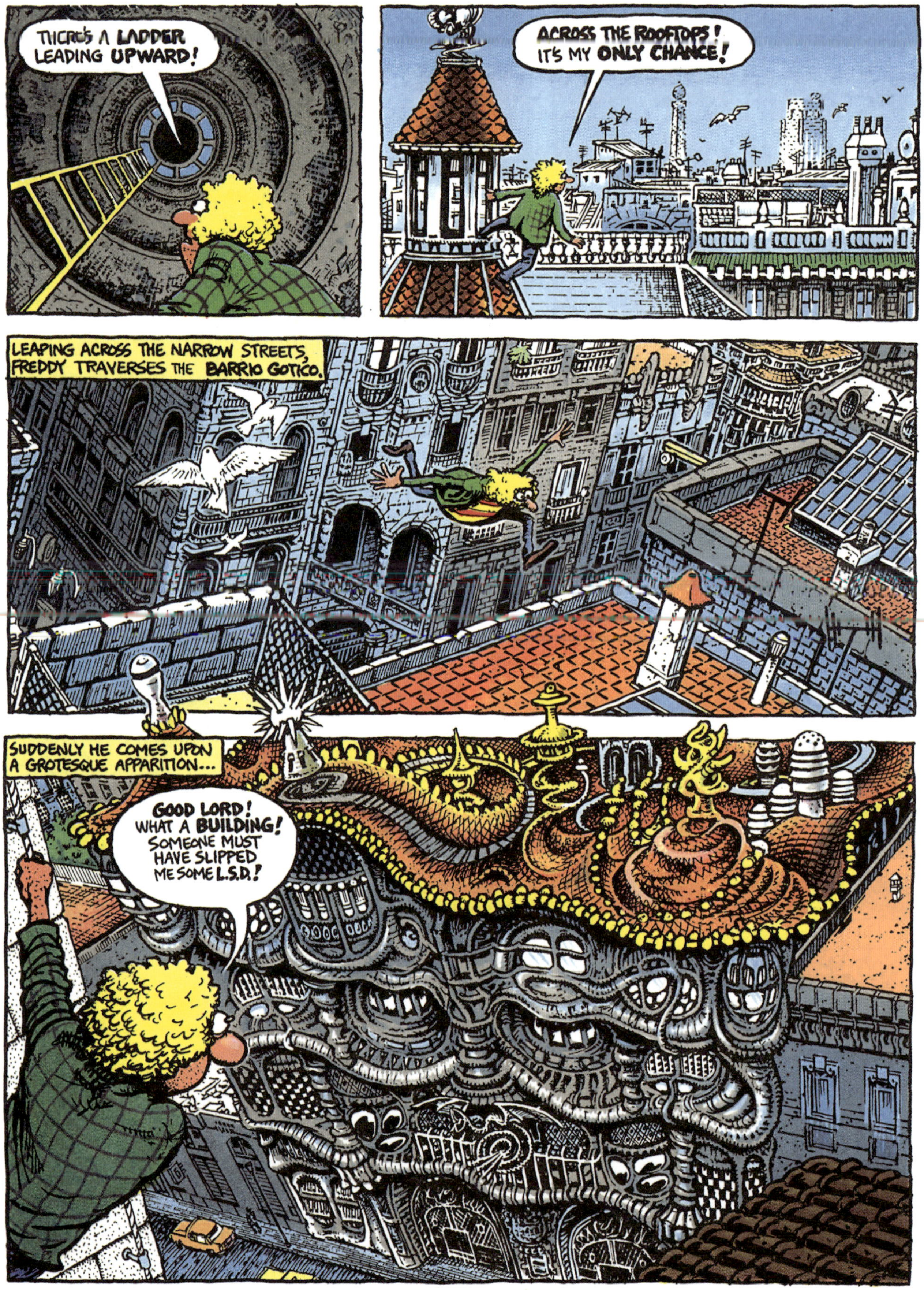

THERE'S A LADDER LEADING UPWARD!
ACROSS THE ROOFTOPS! IT'S MY ONLY CHANCE!
LEAPING ACROSS THE NARROW STREETS, FREDDY TRAVERSES THE BARRIO GOTICO.
SUDDENLY HE COMES UPON A GROTESQUE APPARITION...
GOOD LORD! WHAT A BUILDING! SOMEONE MUST HAVE SLIPPED ME SOME L.S.D.!

WHO DO YOU THINK YOU ARE? SUPERMAN?
WHY CAN'T YOU AMERICAN TOURISTS USE THE STREETS LIKE EVERYONE ELSE?
(GASP!) I... I DIDN'T SEE YOU!
DO YOU LIVE HERE? I'M BEING CHASED BY A BUNCH OF TERRORISTS!
HA HA HA! WHAT FERTILE IMAGINATIONS YOU YANKEES HAVE! OUR STREETS HERE ARE AS SAFE AS ANY PLACE IN THE WORLD, I ASSURE YOU!
PLEASE ALLOW ME TO INTRODUCE MYSELF! I AM PABLO PEGASO, ARTIST AND AUTOMOBILE AFICIONADO!
THIS IS MY STUDIO! WILL YOU COME IN?
HERE'S MY LATEST PIECE, "BERSERK ROAD-RUNNER"... WHAT DO YOU THINK?
VERY INTERESTING — BUT WHAT ABOUT...
GO ON! WIND IT UP!
POK POK POK POK POK POK!
NOW DO YOU BELIEVE ME?
QUICKLY! TO THE GARAGE!

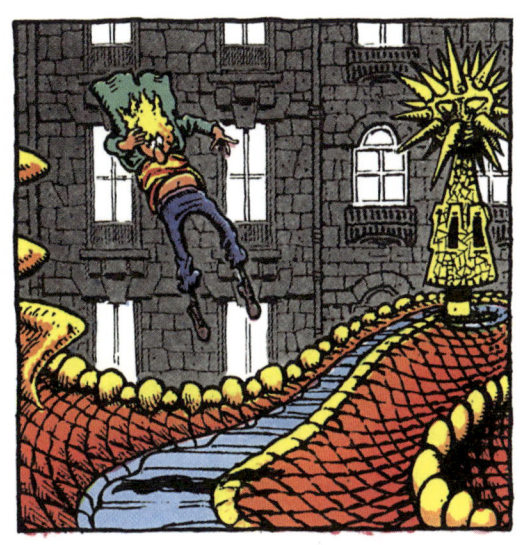

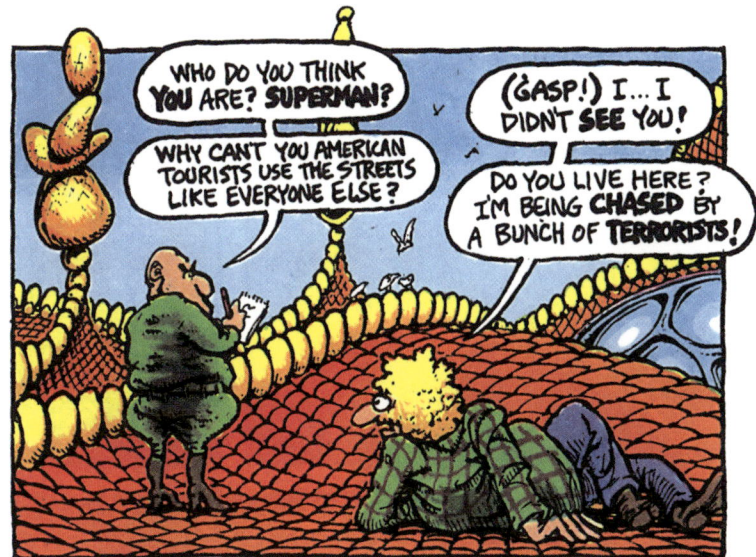

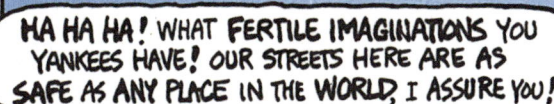

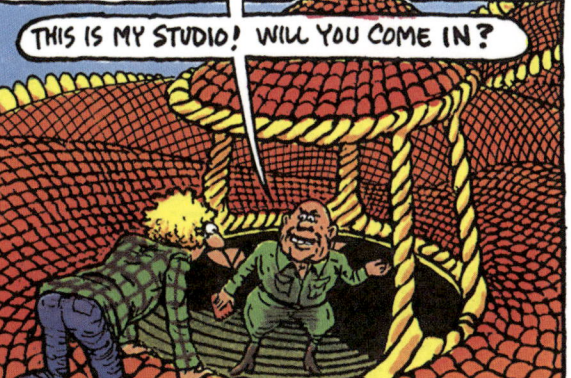

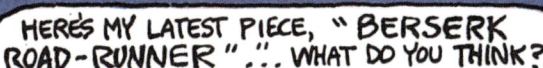

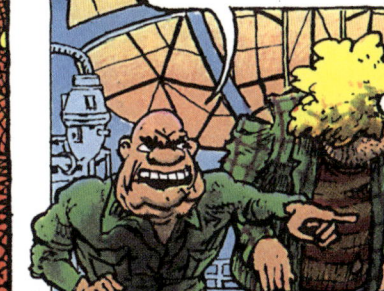

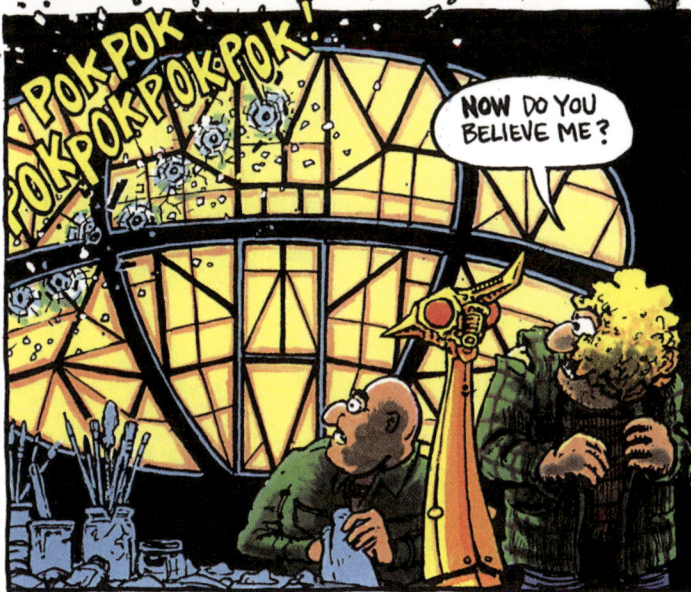

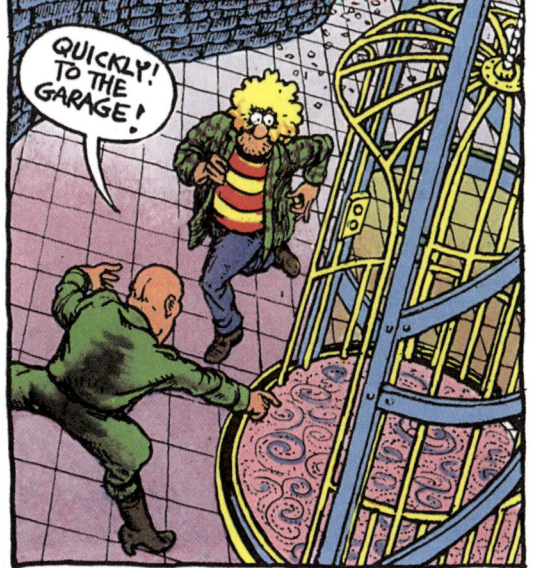

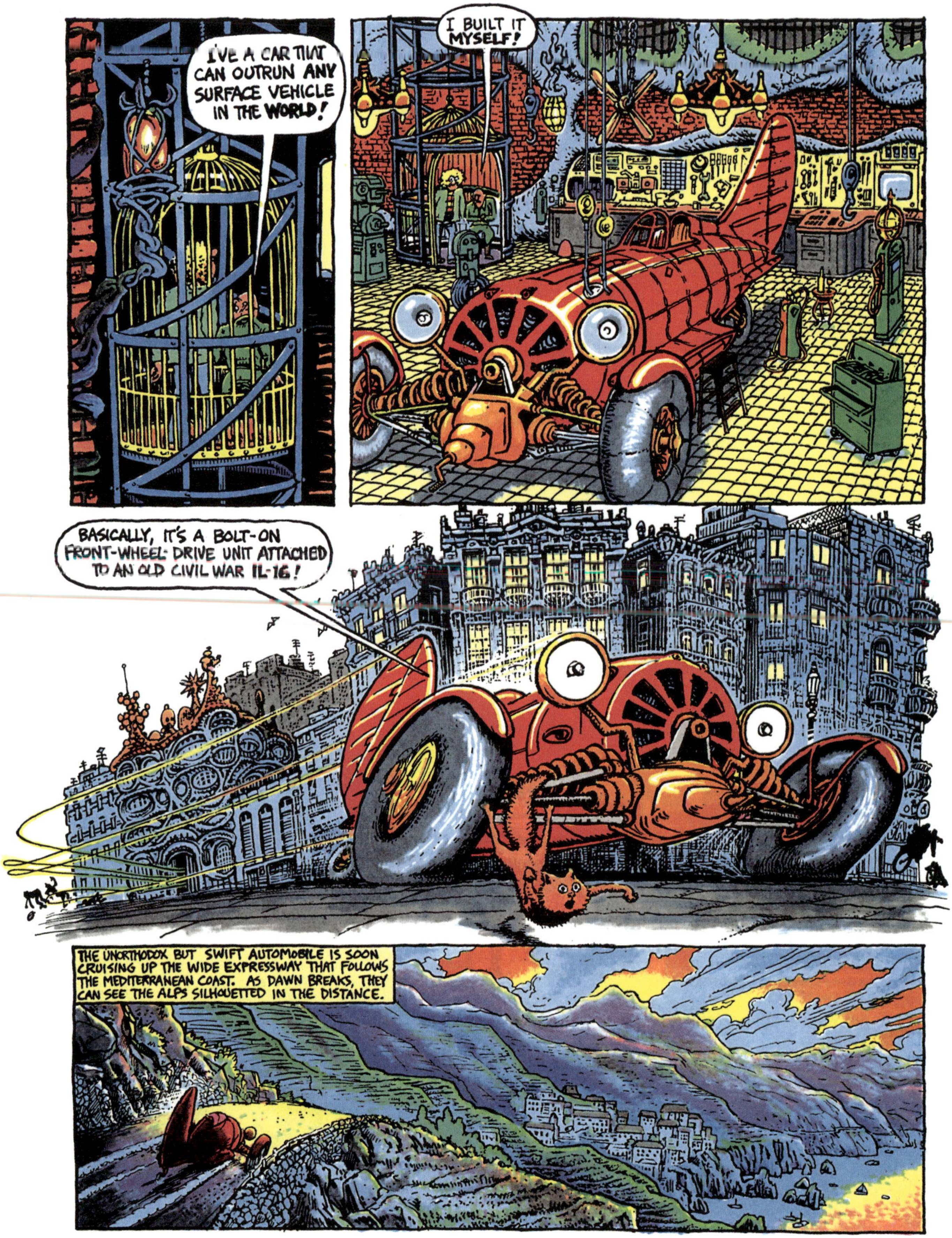
I'VE A CAR THAT CAN OUTRUN ANY SURFACE VEHICLE IN THE WORLD!
I BUILT IT MYSELF!
BASICALLY, IT'S A BOLT-ON FRONT-WHEEL-DRIVE UNIT ATTACHED TO AN OLD CIVIL WAR IL-16!
THE UNORTHODOX BUT SWIFT AUTOMOBILE IS SOON CRUISING UP THE WIDE EXPRESSWAY THAT FOLLOWS THE MEDITERRANEAN COAST. AS DAWN BREAKS, THEY CAN SEE THE ALPS SILHOUETTED IN THE DISTANCE.

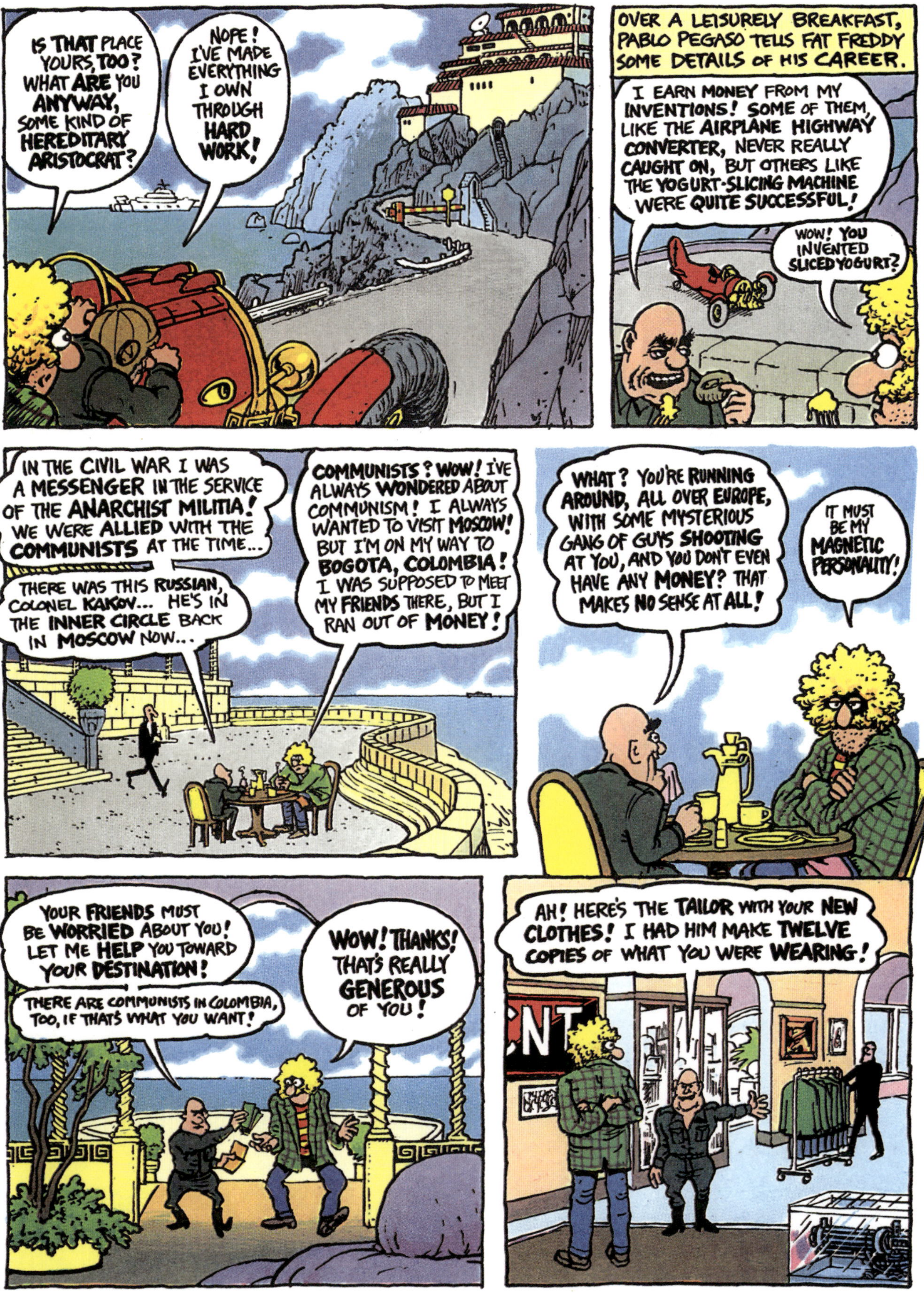

IS THAT PLACE YOURS, TOO? WHAT ARE YOU ANYWAY, SOME KIND OF HEREDITARY ARISTOCRAT?
NOPE! I'VE MADE EVERYTHING I OWN THROUGH HARD WORK!
OVER A LEISURELY BREAKFAST, PABLO PEGASO TELLS FAT FREDDY SOME DETAILS OF HIS CAREER.
I EARN MONEY FROM MY INVENTIONS! SOME OF THEM, LIKE THE AIRPLANE HIGHWAY CONVERTER, NEVER REALLY CAUGHT ON, BUT OTHERS LIKE THE YOGURT-SLICING MACHINE WERE QUITE SUCCESSFUL!
WOW! YOU INVENTED SLICED YOGURT?
IN THE CIVIL WAR I WAS A MESSENGER IN THE SERVICE OF THE ANARCHIST MILITIA! WE WERE ALLIED WITH THE COMMUNISTS AT THE TIME...
THERE WAS THIS RUSSIAN, COLONEL KAKOV... HE'S IN THE INNER CIRCLE BACK IN MOSCOW NOW...
COMMUNISTS? WOW! I'VE ALWAYS WONDERED ABOUT COMMUNISM! I ALWAYS WANTED TO VISIT MOSCOW! BUT I'M ON MY WAY TO BOGOTA, COLOMBIA! I WAS SUPPOSED TO MEET MY FRIENDS THERE, BUT I RAN OUT OF MONEY!
WHAT? YOU'RE RUNNING AROUND, ALL OVER EUROPE, WITH SOME MYSTERIOUS GANG OF GUYS SHOOTING AT YOU, AND YOU DON'T EVEN HAVE ANY MONEY? THAT MAKES NO SENSE AT ALL!
IT MUST BE MY MAGNETIC PERSONALITY!
YOUR FRIENDS MUST BE WORRIED ABOUT YOU! LET ME HELP YOU TOWARD YOUR DESTINATION!
THERE ARE COMMUNISTS IN COLOMBIA, TOO, IF THAT'S WHAT YOU WANT!
WOW! THANKS! THAT'S REALLY GENEROUS OF YOU!
AH! HERE'S THE TAILOR WITH YOUR NEW CLOTHES! I HAD HIM MAKE TWELVE COPIES OF WHAT YOU WERE WEARING!

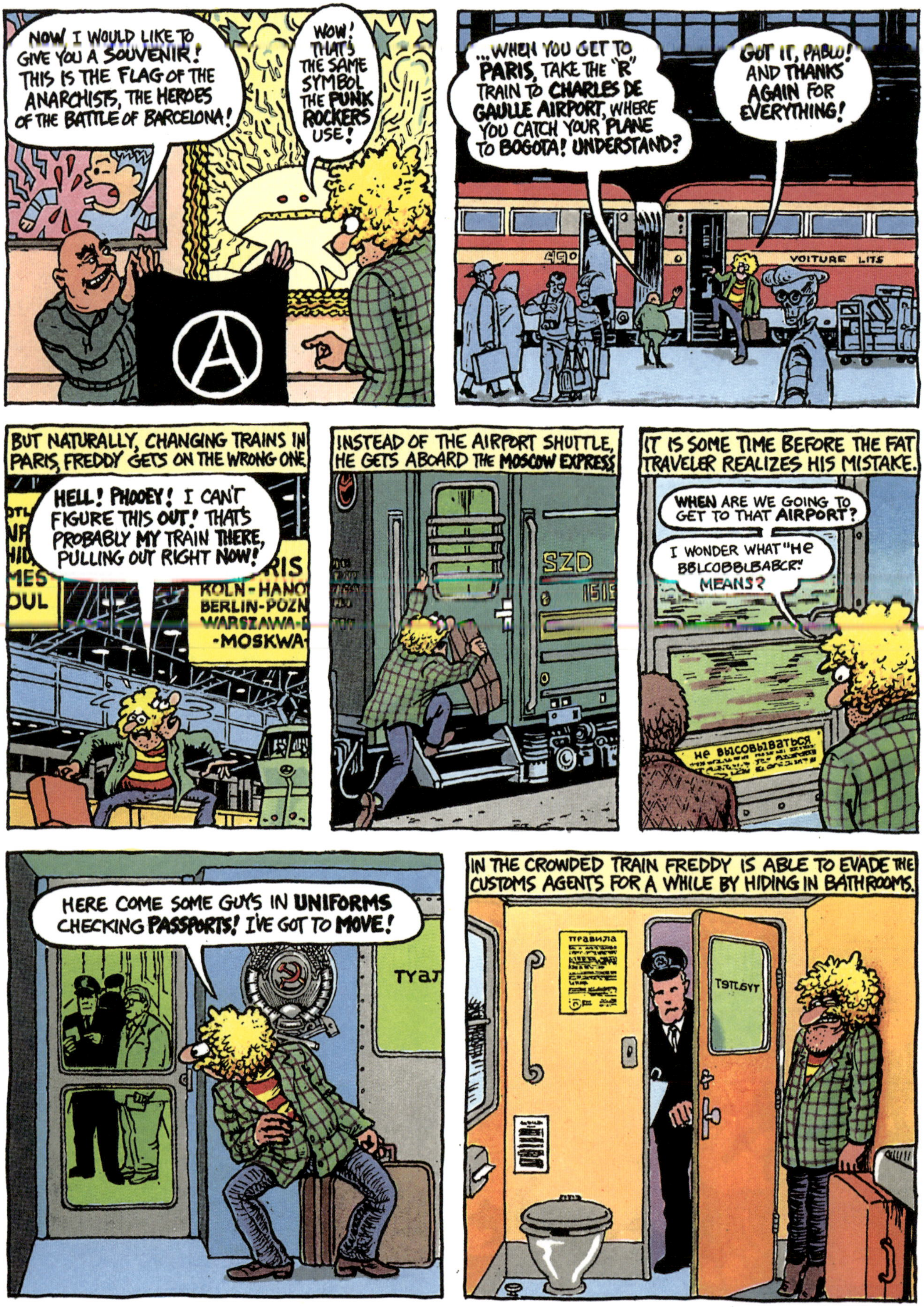
NOW I WOULD LIKE TO GIVE YOU A SOUVENIR! THIS IS THE FLAG OF THE ANARCHISTS, THE HEROES OF THE BATTLE OF BARCELONA!
WOW! THAT'S THE SAME SYMBOL THE PUNK ROCKERS USE!
...WHEN YOU GET TO PARIS, TAKE THE "R" TRAIN TO CHARLES DE GAULLE AIRPORT, WHERE YOU CATCH YOUR PLANE TO BOGOTA! UNDERSTAND?
GOT IT, PABLO! AND THANKS AGAIN FOR EVERYTHING!
490
VOITURE LITS
BUT NATURALLY, CHANGING TRAINS IN PARIS, FREDDY GETS ON THE WRONG ONE.
HELL! PHOOEY! I CAN'T FIGURE THIS OUT! THAT'S PROBABLY MY TRAIN THERE, PULLING OUT RIGHT NOW!
-MOSKWA-
INSTEAD OF THE AIRPORT SHUTTLE, HE GETS ABOARD THE MOSCOW EXPRESS.
SZD
IT IS SOME TIME BEFORE THE FAT TRAVELER REALIZES HIS MISTAKE.
WHEN ARE WE GOING TO GET TO THAT AIRPORT?
I WONDER WHAT "HE BBLCOBBLBABCR" MEANS?
НЕ ВЫСОВЫВАТЬСЯ
HERE COME SOME GUYS IN UNIFORMS CHECKING PASSPORTS! I'VE GOT TO MOVE!
IN THE CROWDED TRAIN FREDDY IS ABLE TO EVADE THE CUSTOMS AGENTS FOR A WHILE BY HIDING IN BATHROOMS.
Правила

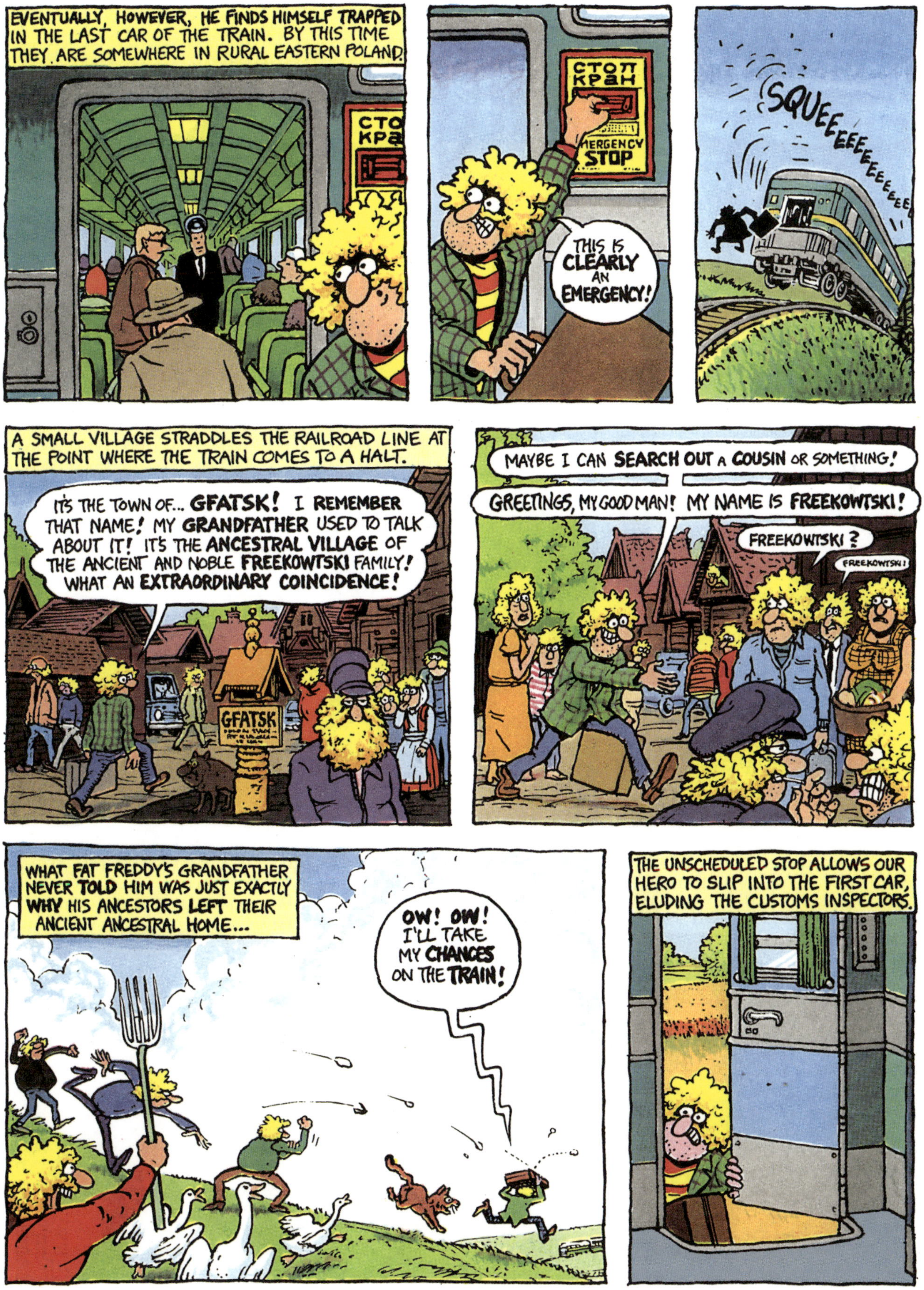

EVENTUALLY, HOWEVER, HE FINDS HIMSELF TRAPPED IN THE LAST CAR OF THE TRAIN. BY THIS TIME THEY ARE SOMEWHERE IN RURAL EASTERN POLAND.
СТОП КРАН
MERGENCY STOP
THIS IS CLEARLY AN EMERGENCY!
SQUEEEEEEEEEEEE
A SMALL VILLAGE STRADDLES THE RAILROAD LINE AT THE POINT WHERE THE TRAIN COMES TO A HALT.
IT'S THE TOWN OF... GFATSK! I REMEMBER THAT NAME! MY GRANDFATHER USED TO TALK ABOUT IT! IT'S THE ANCESTRAL VILLAGE OF THE ANCIENT AND NOBLE FREEKOWTSKI FAMILY! WHAT AN EXTRAORDINARY COINCIDENCE!
GFATSK
MAYBE I CAN SEARCH OUT A COUSIN OR SOMETHING!
GREETINGS, MY GOOD MAN! MY NAME IS FREEKOWTSKI!
FREEKOWTSKI?
FREEKOWTSKI!
WHAT FAT FREDDY'S GRANDFATHER NEVER TOLD HIM WAS JUST EXACTLY WHY HIS ANCESTORS LEFT THEIR ANCIENT ANCESTRAL HOME...
OW! OW! I'LL TAKE MY CHANCES ON THE TRAIN!
THE UNSCHEDULED STOP ALLOWS OUR HERO TO SLIP INTO THE FIRST CAR, ELUDING THE CUSTOMS INSPECTORS.

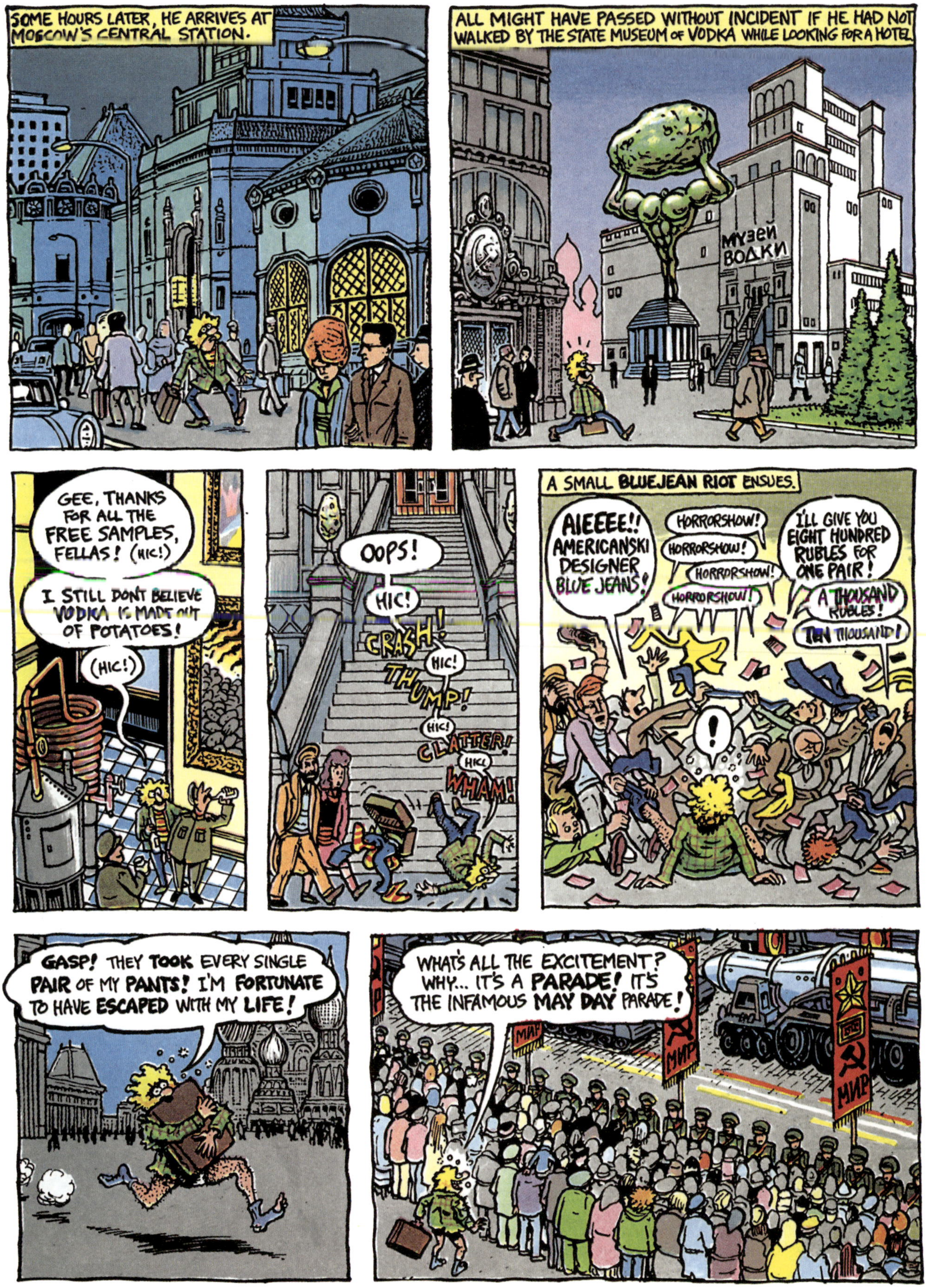

SOME HOURS LATER, HE ARRIVES AT MOSCOW'S CENTRAL STATION.
ALL MIGHT HAVE PASSED WITHOUT INCIDENT IF HE HAD NOT WALKED BY THE STATE MUSEUM OF VODKA WHILE LOOKING FOR A HOTEL.
МУЗЕЙ ВОДКИ
GEE, THANKS FOR ALL THE FREE SAMPLES, FELLAS! (HIC!)
I STILL DON'T BELIEVE VODKA IS MADE OUT OF POTATOES!
(HIC!)
OOPS!
HIC!
CRASH!
HIC!
THUMP!
HIC!
CLATTER!
HIC!
WHAM!
A SMALL BLUEJEAN RIOT ENSUES.
AIEEEE!! AMERICANSKI DESIGNER BLUE JEANS!
HORRORSHOW!
HORRORSHOW!
HORRORSHOW!
HORRORSHOW!
I'LL GIVE YOU EIGHT HUNDRED RUBLES FOR ONE PAIR!
A THOUSAND RUBLES!
TEN THOUSAND!
!
GASP! THEY TOOK EVERY SINGLE PAIR OF MY PANTS! I'M FORTUNATE TO HAVE ESCAPED WITH MY LIFE!
WHAT'S ALL THE EXCITEMENT? WHY... IT'S A PARADE! IT'S THE INFAMOUS MAY DAY PARADE!
МИР
МИР
МИР

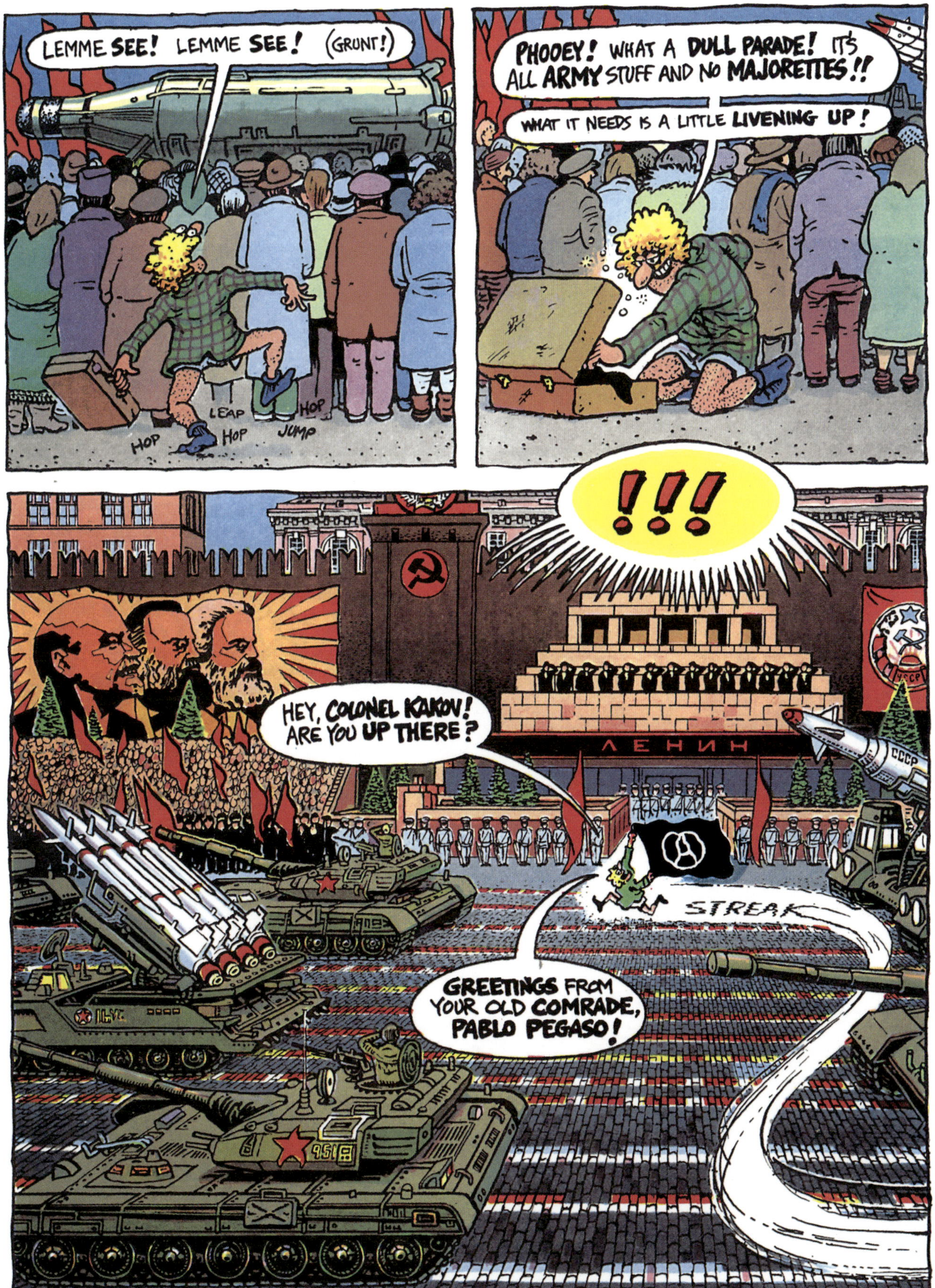
LEMME SEE! LEMME SEE! (GRUNT!)
HOP
LEAP
HOP
JUMP
HOP
PHOOEY! WHAT A DULL PARADE! IT'S ALL ARMY STUFF AND NO MAJORETTES!!
WHAT IT NEEDS IS A LITTLE LIVENING UP!
!!!
ЛЕНИН
CCCP
HEY, COLONEL KAKOV! ARE YOU UP THERE?
STREAK
GREETINGS FROM YOUR OLD COMRADE, PABLO PEGASO!

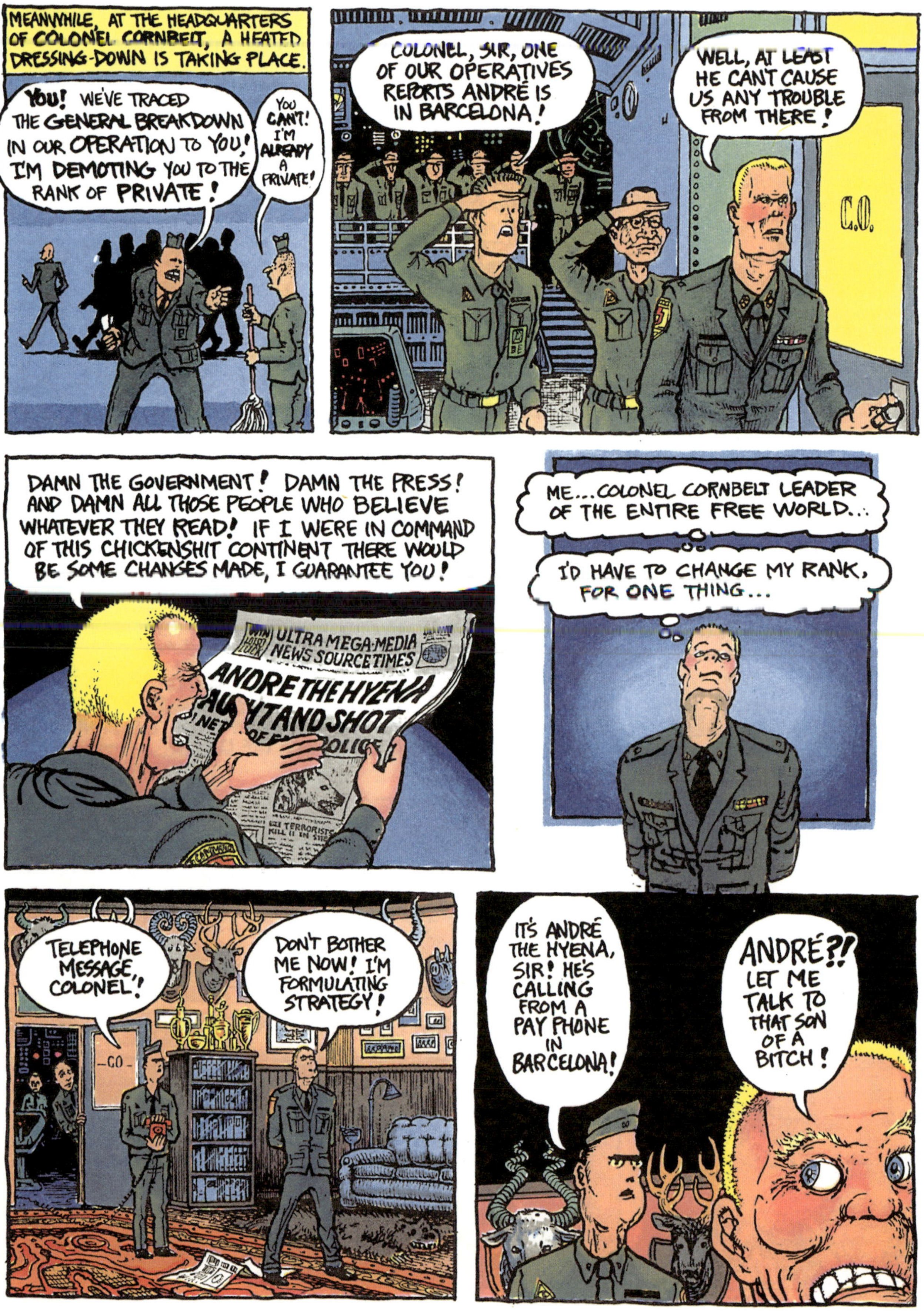
MEANWHILE, AT THE HEADQUARTERS OF COLONEL CORNBELT, A HEATED DRESSING-DOWN IS TAKING PLACE.
YOU! WE'VE TRACED THE GENERAL BREAKDOWN IN OUR OPERATION TO YOU! I'M DEMOTING YOU TO THE RANK OF PRIVATE!
YOU CAN'T! I'M ALREADY A PRIVATE!
COLONEL, SIR, ONE OF OUR OPERATIVES REPORTS ANDRÉ IS IN BARCELONA!
WELL, AT LEAST HE CAN'T CAUSE US ANY TROUBLE FROM THERE!
C.O.
DAMN THE GOVERNMENT! DAMN THE PRESS! AND DAMN ALL THOSE PEOPLE WHO BELIEVE WHATEVER THEY READ! IF I WERE IN COMMAND OF THIS CHICKENSHIT CONTINENT THERE WOULD BE SOME CHANGES MADE, I GUARANTEE YOU!
ULTRA MEGA-MEDIA NEWS SOURCE TIMES
ANDRE THE HYENA
ME... COLONEL CORNBELT LEADER OF THE ENTIRE FREE WORLD...
I'D HAVE TO CHANGE MY RANK, FOR ONE THING...
TELEPHONE MESSAGE, COLONEL!
DON'T BOTHER ME NOW! I'M FORMULATING STRATEGY!
-CO-
IT'S ANDRÉ THE HYENA, SIR! HE'S CALLING FROM A PAY PHONE IN BARCELONA!
ANDRÉ?! LET ME TALK TO THAT SON OF A BITCH!

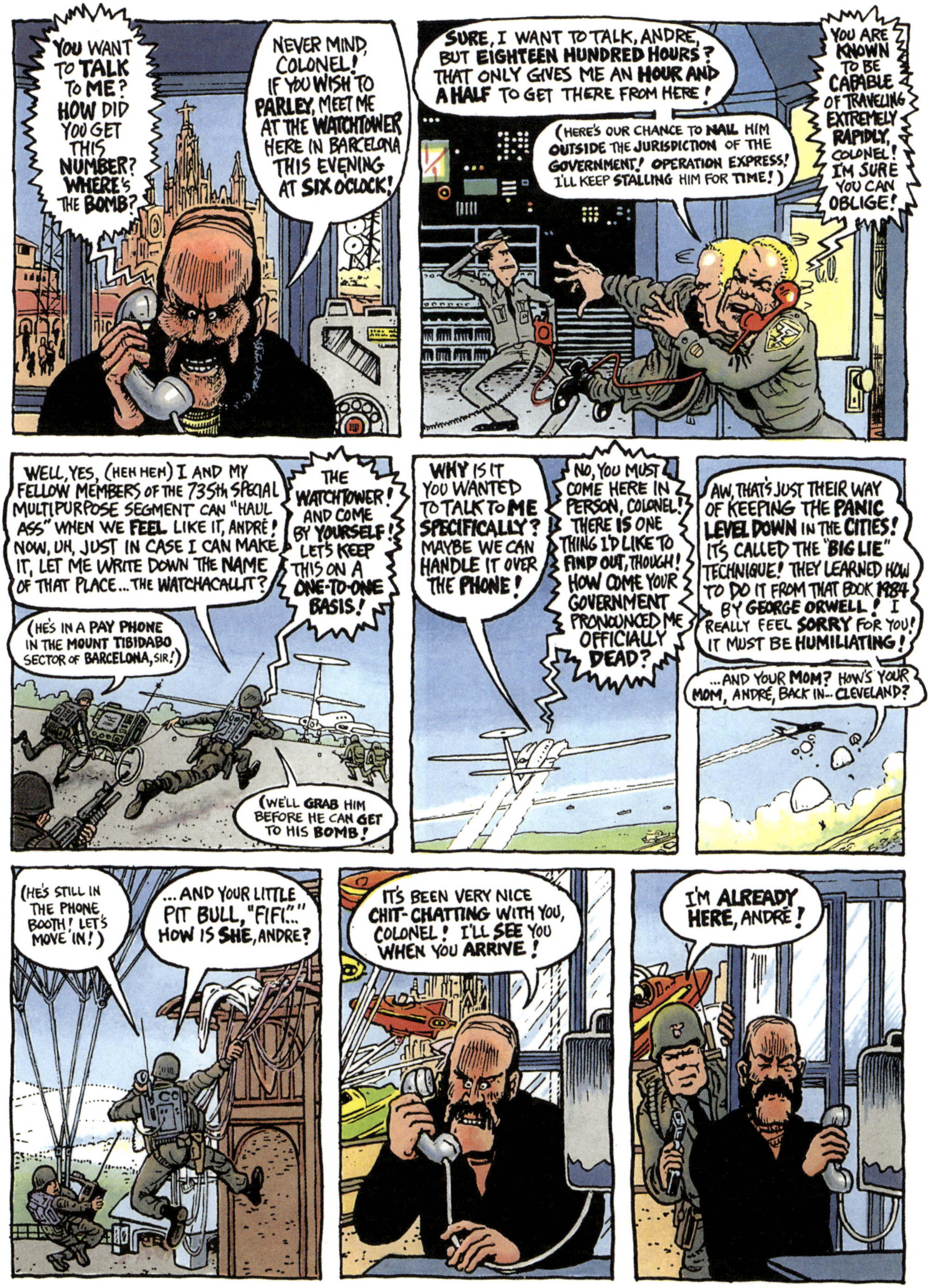
YOU WANT TO TALK TO ME? HOW DID YOU GET THIS NUMBER? WHERE'S THE BOMB?
NEVER MIND, COLONEL! IF YOU WISH TO PARLEY, MEET ME AT THE WATCHTOWER HERE IN BARCELONA THIS EVENING AT SIX O'CLOCK!
SURE, I WANT TO TALK, ANDRE, BUT EIGHTEEN HUNDRED HOURS? THAT ONLY GIVES ME AN HOUR AND A HALF TO GET THERE FROM HERE!
(HERE'S OUR CHANCE TO NAIL HIM OUTSIDE THE JURISDICTION OF THE GOVERNMENT! OPERATION EXPRESS! I'LL KEEP STALLING HIM FOR TIME!)
YOU ARE KNOWN TO BE CAPABLE OF TRAVELING EXTREMELY RAPIDLY, COLONEL! I'M SURE YOU CAN OBLIGE!
WELL, YES, (HEH HEH) I AND MY FELLOW MEMBERS OF THE 735th SPECIAL MULTIPURPOSE SEGMENT CAN "HAUL ASS" WHEN WE FEEL LIKE IT, ANDRÉ! NOW, UH, JUST IN CASE I CAN MAKE IT, LET ME WRITE DOWN THE NAME OF THAT PLACE... THE WATCHACALLIT?
THE WATCHTOWER! AND COME BY YOURSELF! LET'S KEEP THIS ON A ONE-TO-ONE BASIS!
(HE'S IN A PAY PHONE IN THE MOUNT TIBIDABO SECTOR OF BARCELONA, SIR!)
(WE'LL GRAB HIM BEFORE HE CAN GET TO HIS BOMB!
WHY IS IT YOU WANTED TO TALK TO ME SPECIFICALLY? MAYBE WE CAN HANDLE IT OVER THE PHONE!
NO, YOU MUST COME HERE IN PERSON, COLONEL! THERE IS ONE THING I'D LIKE TO FIND OUT, THOUGH! HOW COME YOUR GOVERNMENT PRONOUNCED ME OFFICIALLY DEAD?
AW, THAT'S JUST THEIR WAY OF KEEPING THE PANIC LEVEL DOWN IN THE CITIES! IT'S CALLED THE "BIG LIE" TECHNIQUE! THEY LEARNED HOW TO DO IT FROM THAT BOOK 1984 BY GEORGE ORWELL! I REALLY FEEL SORRY FOR YOU! IT MUST BE HUMILIATING!
...AND YOUR MOM? HOW'S YOUR MOM, ANDRÉ, BACK IN... CLEVELAND?
(HE'S STILL IN THE PHONE BOOTH! LET'S MOVE IN!)
...AND YOUR LITTLE PIT BULL, "FIFI"... HOW IS SHE, ANDRE?
IT'S BEEN VERY NICE CHIT-CHATTING WITH YOU, COLONEL! I'LL SEE YOU WHEN YOU ARRIVE!
I'M ALREADY HERE, ANDRÉ!

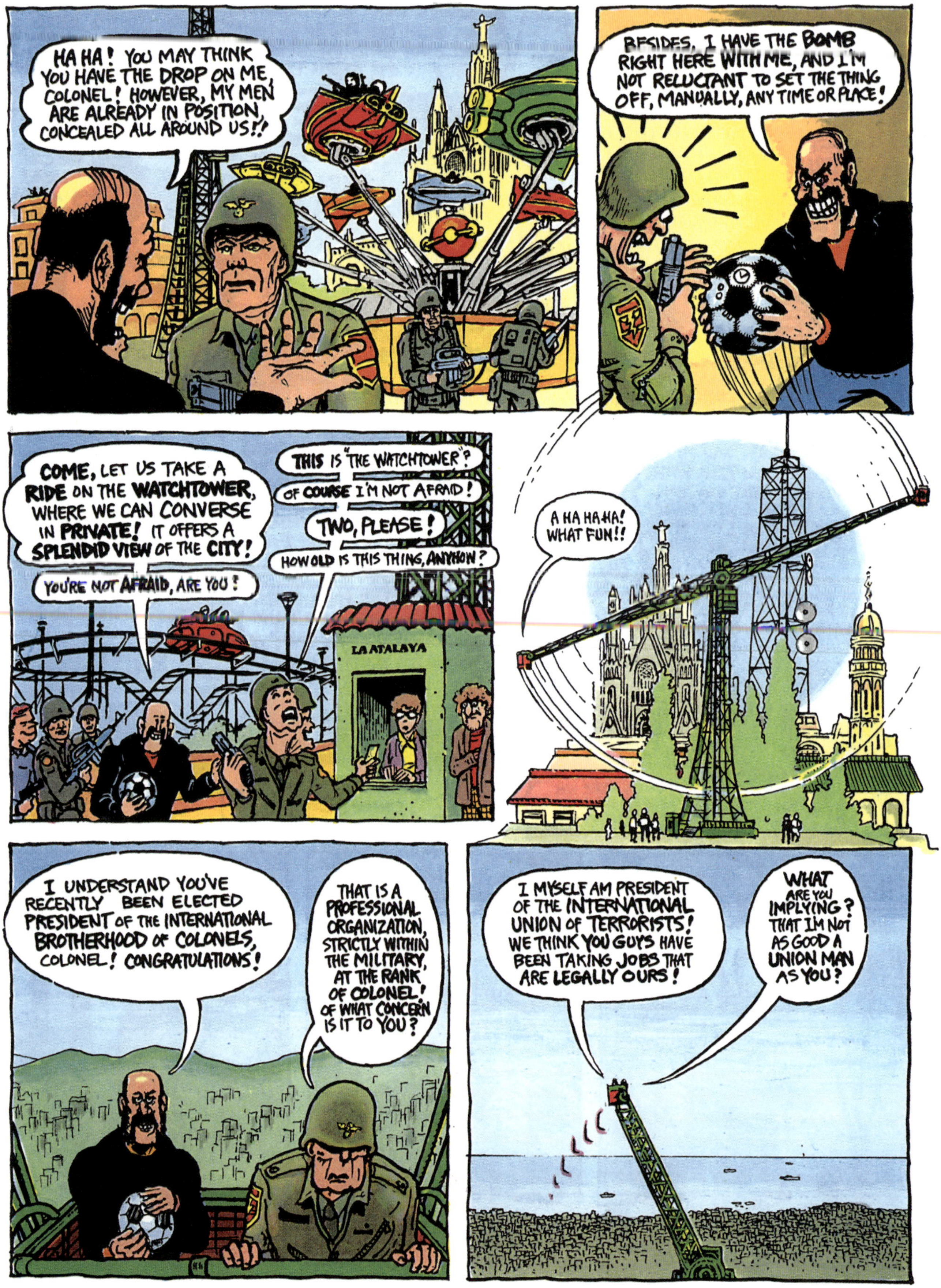
HA HA! YOU MAY THINK YOU HAVE THE DROP ON ME, COLONEL! HOWEVER, MY MEN ARE ALREADY IN POSITION, CONCEALED ALL AROUND US!?!
BESIDES, I HAVE THE BOMB RIGHT HERE WITH ME, AND I'M NOT RELUCTANT TO SET THE THING OFF, MANUALLY, ANY TIME OR PLACE!
COME, LET US TAKE A RIDE ON THE WATCHTOWER, WHERE WE CAN CONVERSE IN PRIVATE! IT OFFERS A SPLENDID VIEW OF THE CITY!
YOU'RE NOT AFRAID, ARE YOU?
THIS IS "THE WATCHTOWER"?
OF COURSE I'M NOT AFRAID!
TWO, PLEASE!
HOW OLD IS THIS THING, ANYHOW?
LA ATALAYA
A HA HA HA! WHAT FUN!!
I UNDERSTAND YOU'VE RECENTLY BEEN ELECTED PRESIDENT OF THE INTERNATIONAL BROTHERHOOD OF COLONELS, COLONEL! CONGRATULATIONS!
THAT IS A PROFESSIONAL ORGANIZATION, STRICTLY WITHIN THE MILITARY, AT THE RANK OF COLONEL! OF WHAT CONCERN IS IT TO YOU?
I MYSELF AM PRESIDENT OF THE INTERNATIONAL UNION OF TERRORISTS! WE THINK YOU GUYS HAVE BEEN TAKING JOBS THAT ARE LEGALLY OURS!
WHAT ARE YOU IMPLYING? THAT I'M NOT AS GOOD A UNION MAN AS YOU?

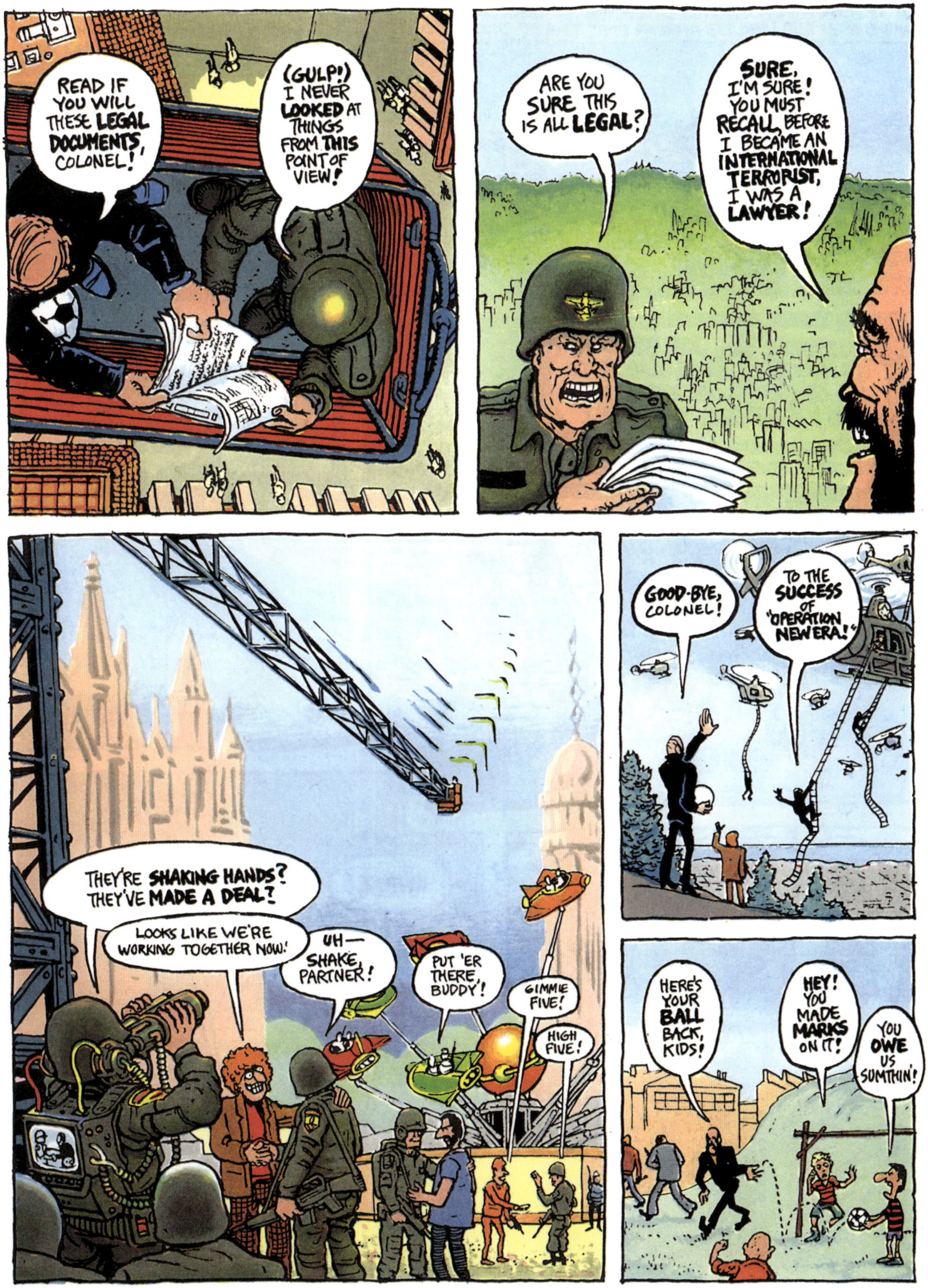
READ IF YOU WILL THESE LEGAL DOCUMENTS, COLONEL!
(GULP!) I NEVER LOOKED AT THINGS FROM THIS POINT OF VIEW!
ARE YOU SURE THIS IS ALL LEGAL?
SURE, I'M SURE! YOU MUST RECALL, BEFORE I BECAME AN INTERNATIONAL TERRORIST, I WAS A LAWYER!
THEY'RE SHAKING HANDS? THEY'VE MADE A DEAL?
LOOKS LIKE WE'RE WORKING TOGETHER NOW!
UH— SHAKE, PARTNER!
PUT 'ER THERE, BUDDY!
GIMMIE FIVE!
HIGH FIVE!
GOOD-BYE, COLONEL!
TO THE SUCCESS OF "OPERATION NEW ERA!"
HERE'S YOUR BALL BACK, KIDS!
HEY! YOU MADE MARKS ON IT!
YOU OWE US SUMTHIN'!

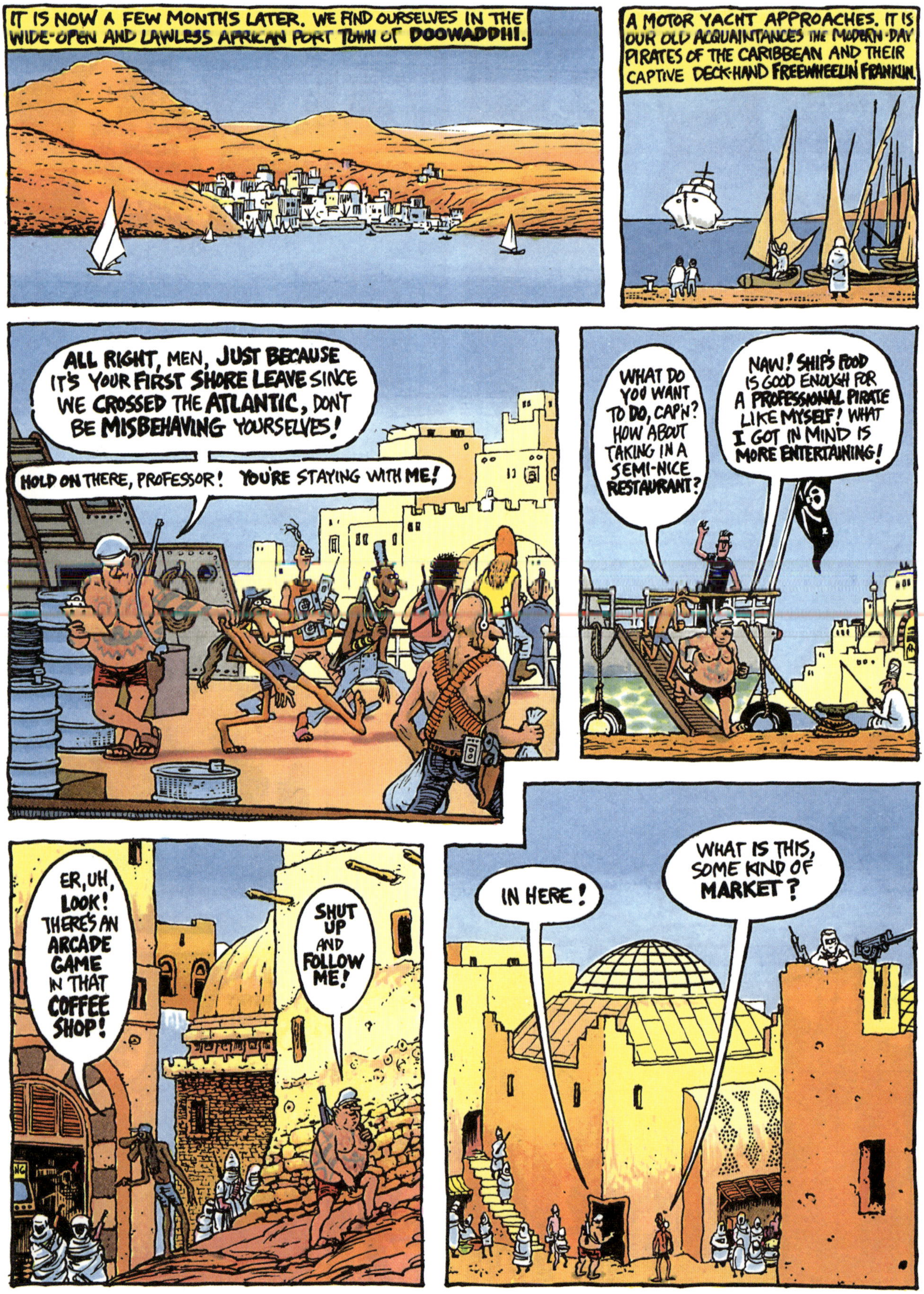

IT IS NOW A FEW MONTHS LATER. WE FIND OURSELVES IN THE WIDE-OPEN AND LAWLESS AFRICAN PORT TOWN OF DOOWADDHI.
A MOTOR YACHT APPROACHES. IT IS OUR OLD ACQUAINTANCES THE MODERN-DAY PIRATES OF THE CARIBBEAN AND THEIR CAPTIVE DECK-HAND FREEWHEELIN' FRANKLIN.
ALL RIGHT, MEN, JUST BECAUSE IT'S YOUR FIRST SHORE LEAVE SINCE WE CROSSED THE ATLANTIC, DON'T BE MISBEHAVING YOURSELVES!
HOLD ON THERE, PROFESSOR! YOU'RE STAYING WITH ME!
WHAT DO YOU WANT TO DO, CAP'N? HOW ABOUT TAKING IN A SEMI-NICE RESTAURANT?
NAW! SHIP'S FOOD IS GOOD ENOUGH FOR A PROFESSIONAL PIRATE LIKE MYSELF! WHAT I GOT IN MIND IS MORE ENTERTAINING!
ER, UH, LOOK! THERE'S AN ARCADE GAME IN THAT COFFEE SHOP!
SHUT UP AND FOLLOW ME!
IN HERE!
WHAT IS THIS, SOME KIND OF MARKET?

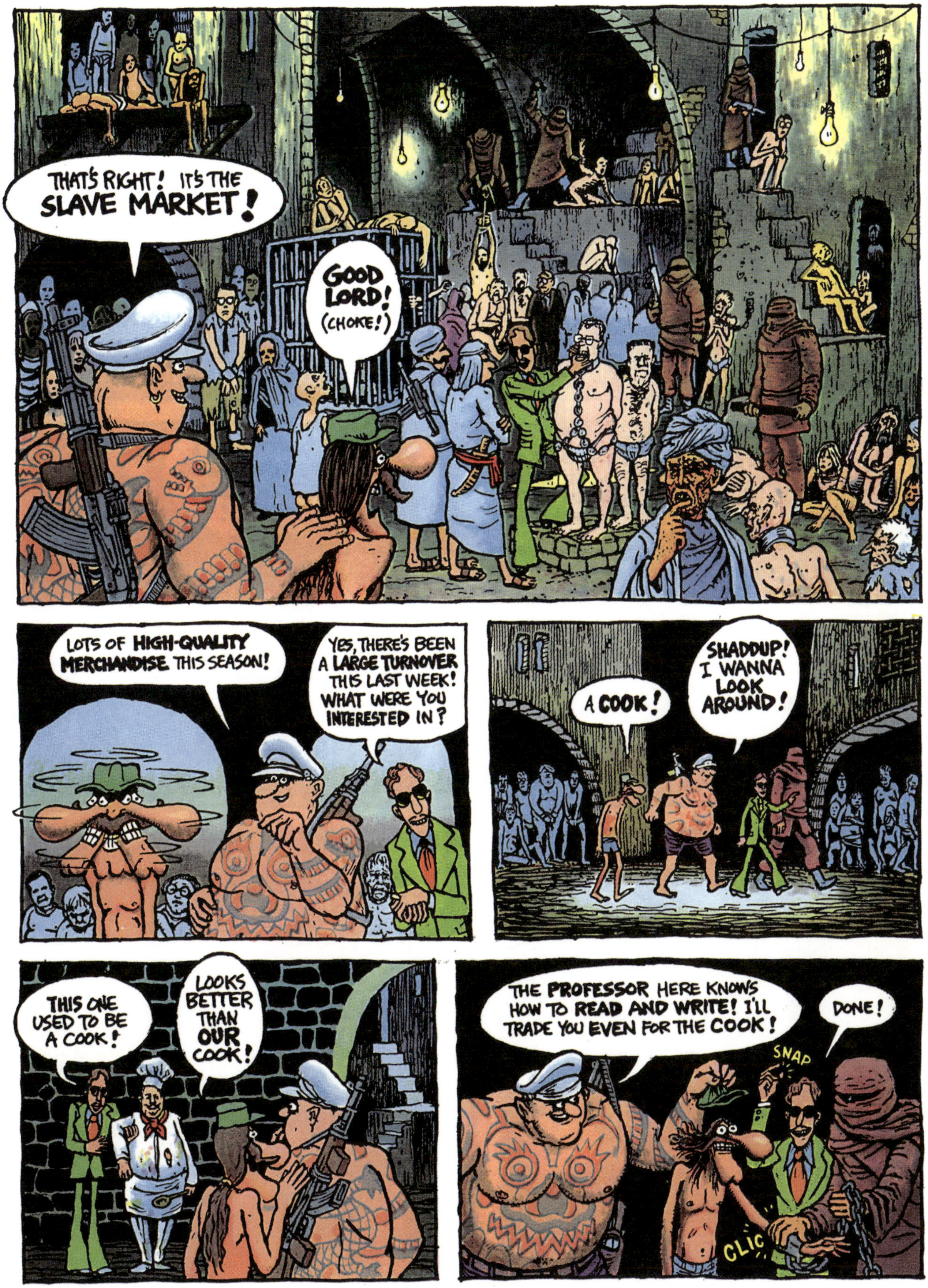
THAT'S RIGHT! IT'S THE SLAVE MARKET!
GOOD LORD! (CHOKE!)
LOTS OF HIGH-QUALITY MERCHANDISE THIS SEASON!
YES, THERE'S BEEN A LARGE TURNOVER THIS LAST WEEK! WHAT WERE YOU INTERESTED IN?
A COOK!
SHADDUP! I WANNA LOOK AROUND!
THIS ONE USED TO BE A COOK!
LOOKS BETTER THAN OUR COOK!
THE PROFESSOR HERE KNOWS HOW TO READ AND WRITE! I'LL TRADE YOU EVEN FOR THE COOK!
DONE!
SNAP
CLIC

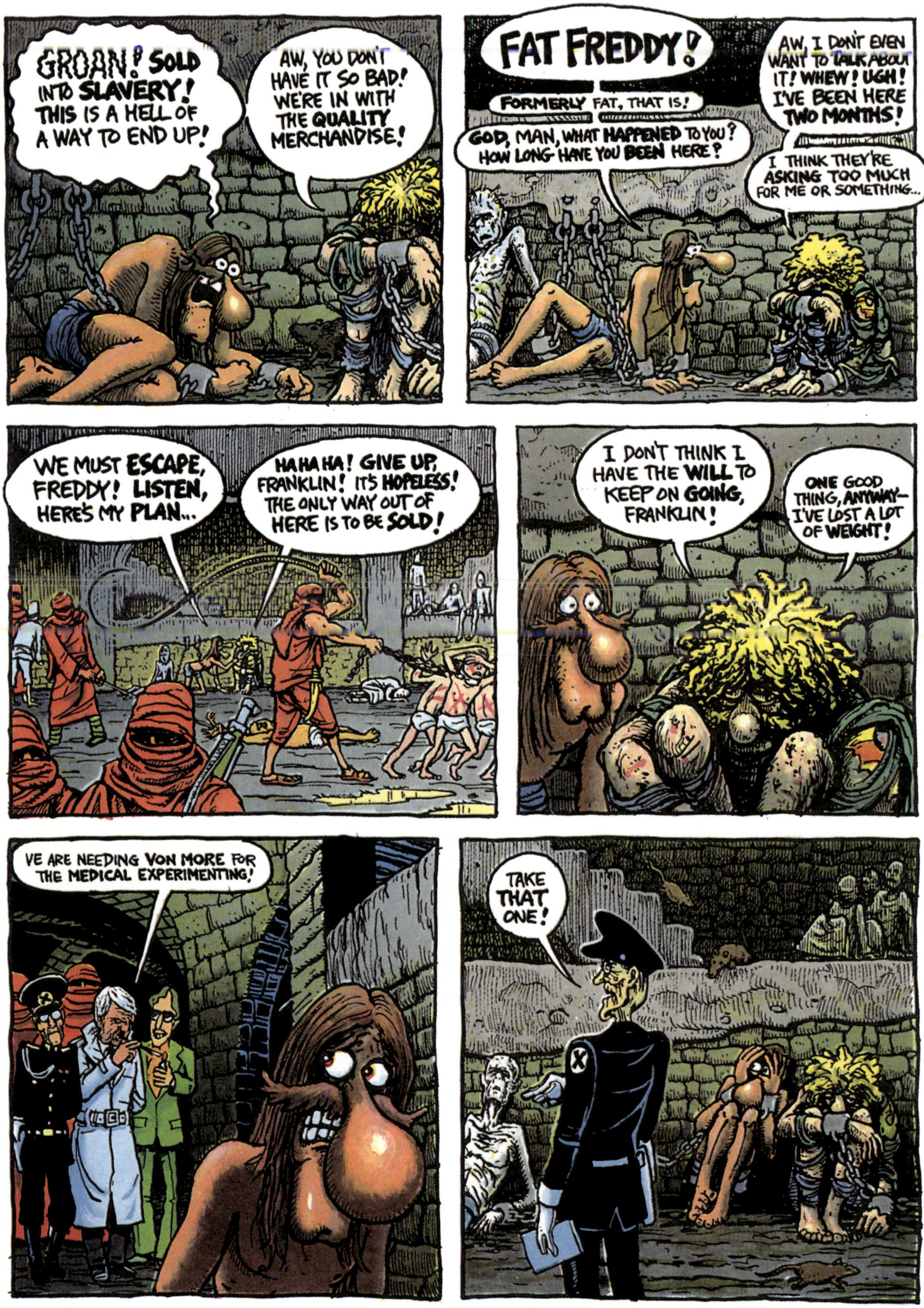
GROAN! SOLD INTO SLAVERY! THIS IS A HELL OF A WAY TO END UP!
AW, YOU DON'T HAVE IT SO BAD! WE'RE IN WITH THE QUALITY MERCHANDISE!
FAT FREDDY!
FORMERLY FAT, THAT IS!
GOD, MAN, WHAT HAPPENED TO YOU? HOW LONG HAVE YOU BEEN HERE?
AW, I DON'T EVEN WANT TO TALK ABOUT IT! WHEW! UGH! I'VE BEEN HERE TWO MONTHS!
I THINK THEY'RE ASKING TOO MUCH FOR ME OR SOMETHING...
WE MUST ESCAPE, FREDDY! LISTEN, HERE'S MY PLAN...
HA HA HA! GIVE UP, FRANKLIN! IT'S HOPELESS! THE ONLY WAY OUT OF HERE IS TO BE SOLD!
I DON'T THINK I HAVE THE WILL TO KEEP ON GOING, FRANKLIN!
ONE GOOD THING, ANYWAY— I'VE LOST A LOT OF WEIGHT!
VE ARE NEEDING VON MORE FOR THE MEDICAL EXPERIMENTING!
TAKE THAT ONE!

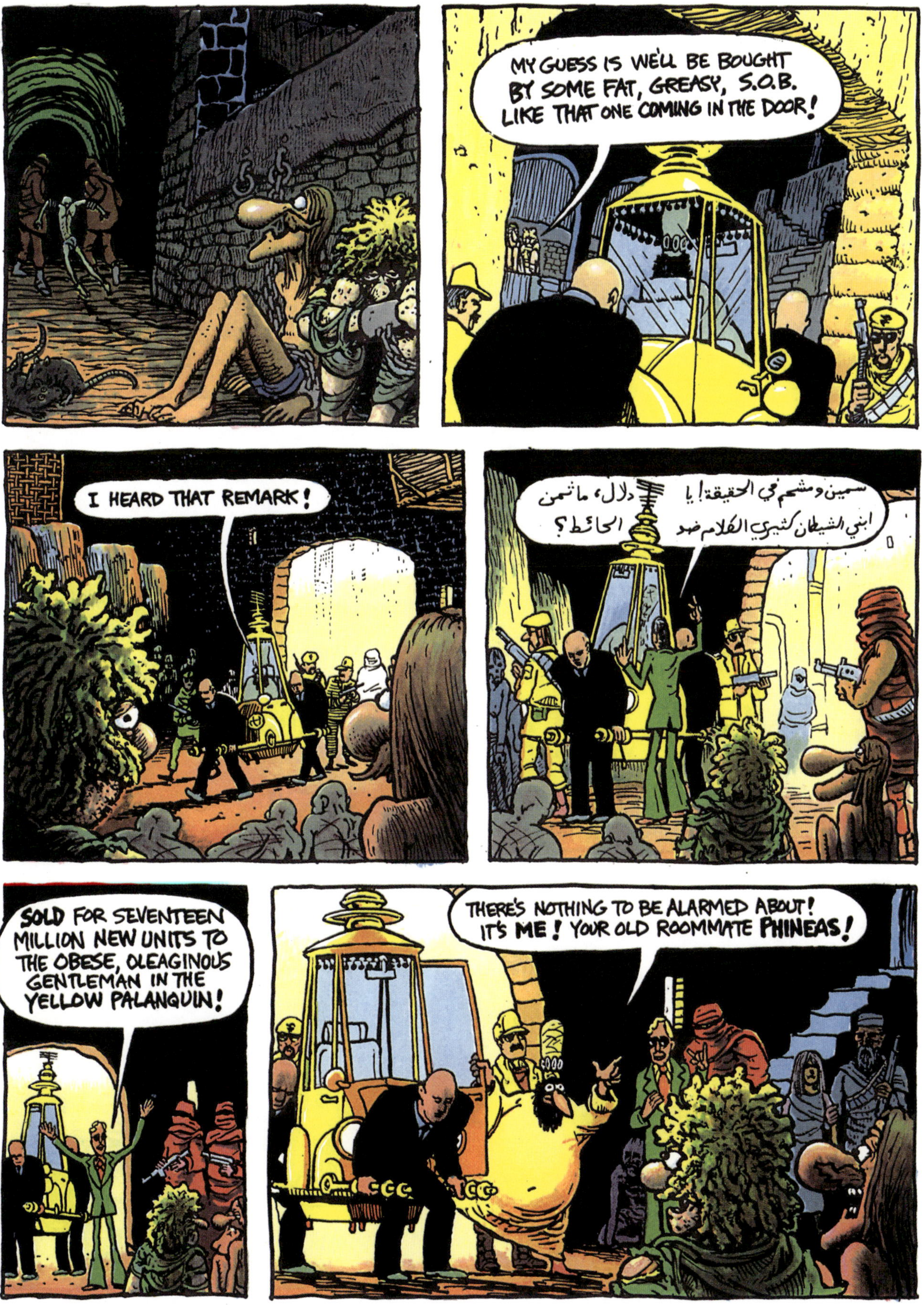
MY GUESS IS WE'LL BE BOUGHT BY SOME FAT, GREASY, S.O.B. LIKE THAT ONE COMING IN THE DOOR!
I HEARD THAT REMARK!
سمين ومشحم في الحقيقة! يا دلال، ما ثمن ابني الشيطان كثيري الكلام ضد الحائط؟
SOLD FOR SEVENTEEN MILLION NEW UNITS TO THE OBESE, OLEAGINOUS GENTLEMAN IN THE YELLOW PALANQUIN!
THERE'S NOTHING TO BE ALARMED ABOUT! IT'S ME! YOUR OLD ROOMMATE PHINEAS!

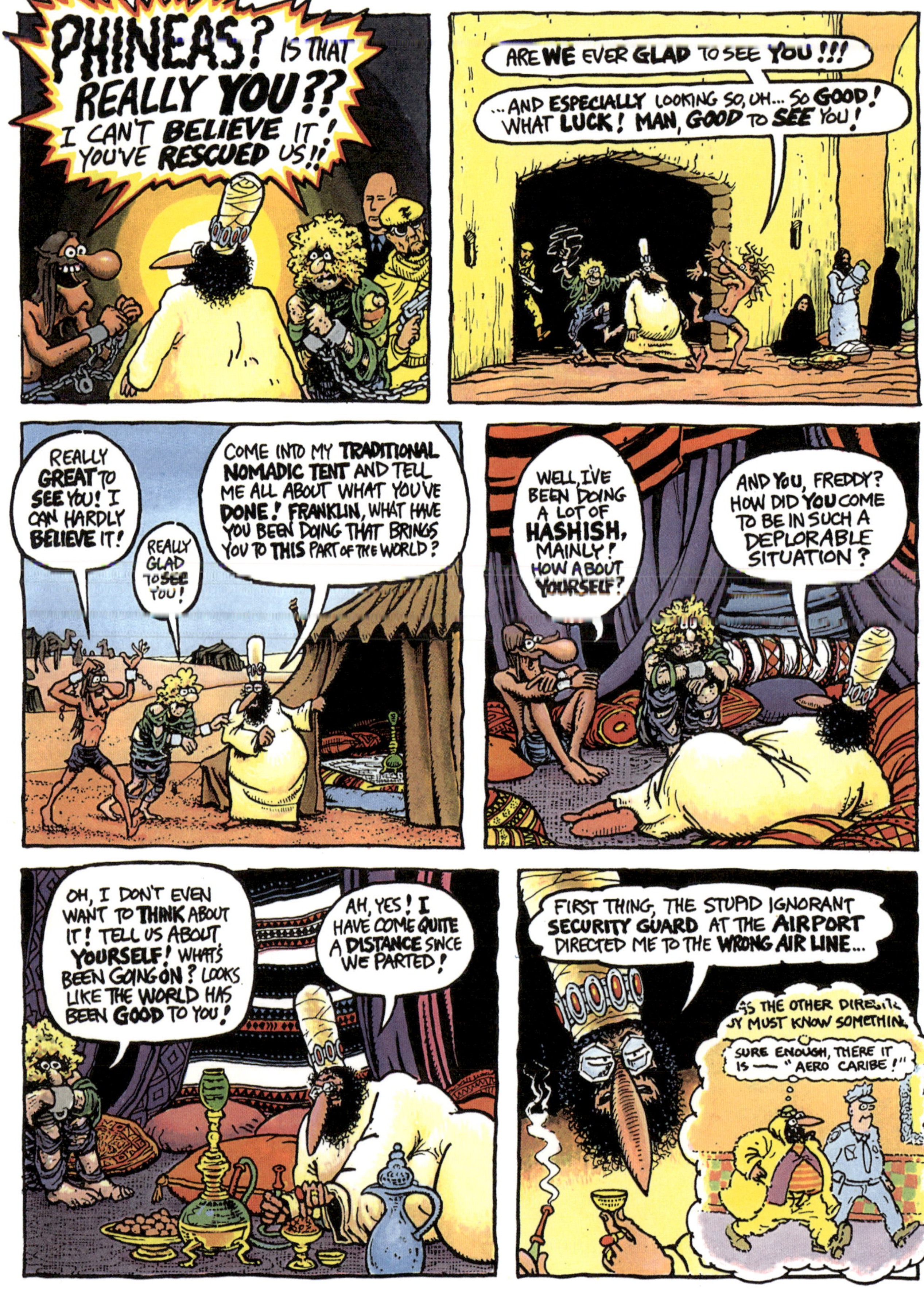

PHINEAS? IS THAT REALLY YOU?? I CAN'T BELIEVE IT! YOU'VE RESCUED US!!
ARE WE EVER GLAD TO SEE YOU!!!
...AND ESPECIALLY LOOKING SO, UH... SO GOOD! WHAT LUCK! MAN, GOOD TO SEE YOU!
REALLY GREAT TO SEE YOU! I CAN HARDLY BELIEVE IT!
REALLY GLAD TO SEE YOU!
COME INTO MY TRADITIONAL NOMADIC TENT AND TELL ME ALL ABOUT WHAT YOU'VE DONE! FRANKLIN, WHAT HAVE YOU BEEN DOING THAT BRINGS YOU TO THIS PART OF THE WORLD?
WELL, I'VE BEEN DOING A LOT OF HASHISH, MAINLY! HOW ABOUT YOURSELF?
AND YOU, FREDDY? HOW DID YOU COME TO BE IN SUCH A DEPLORABLE SITUATION?
OH, I DON'T EVEN WANT TO THINK ABOUT IT! TELL US ABOUT YOURSELF! WHAT'S BEEN GOING ON? LOOKS LIKE THE WORLD HAS BEEN GOOD TO YOU!
AH, YES! I HAVE COME QUITE A DISTANCE SINCE WE PARTED!
FIRST THING, THE STUPID IGNORANT SECURITY GUARD AT THE AIRPORT DIRECTED ME TO THE WRONG AIR LINE...
THE OTHER
MUST KNOW
SURE ENOUGH, THERE IT IS — "AERO CARIBE!"

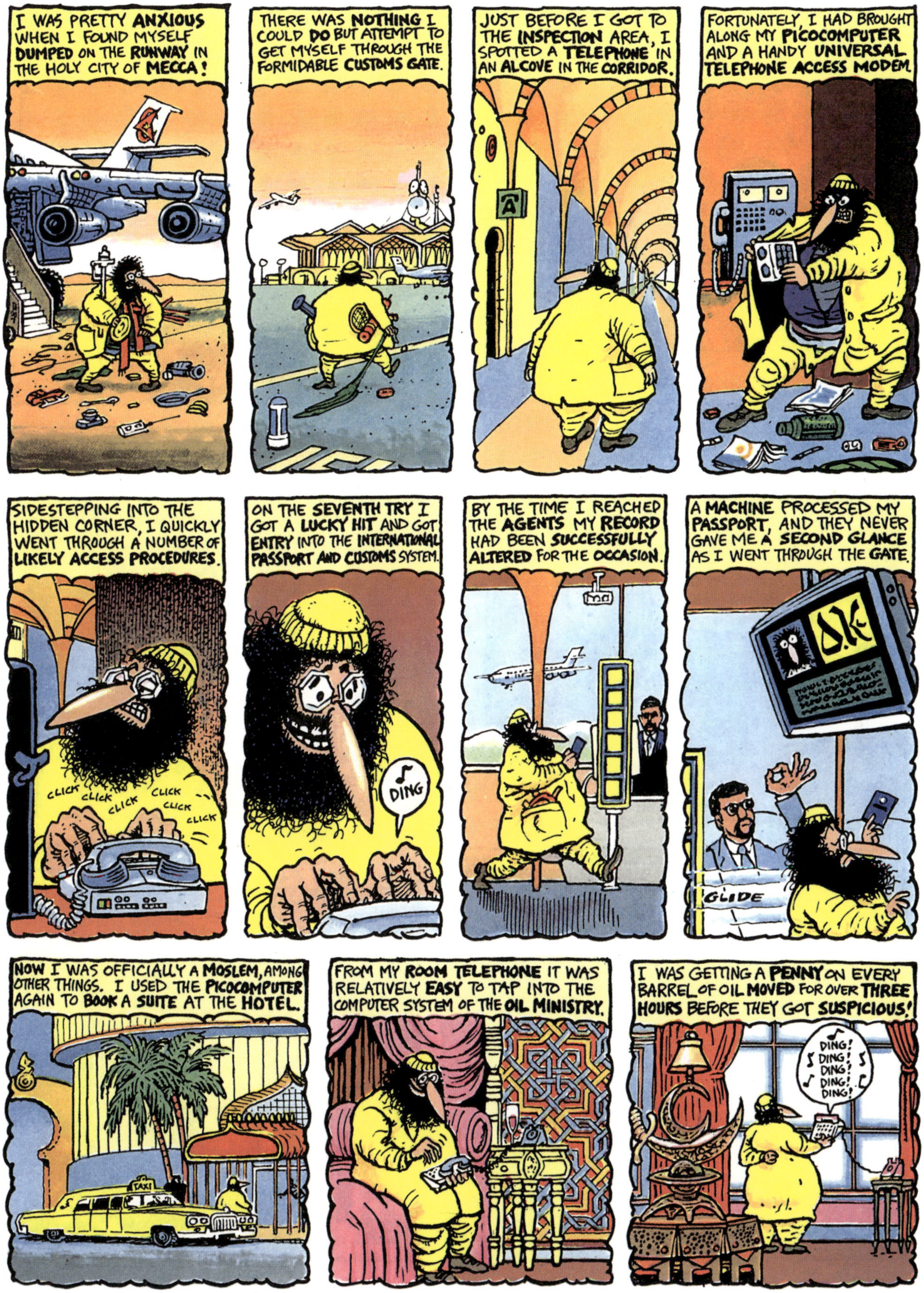
I WAS PRETTY ANXIOUS WHEN I FOUND MYSELF DUMPED ON THE RUNWAY IN THE HOLY CITY OF MECCA!
THERE WAS NOTHING I COULD DO BUT ATTEMPT TO GET MYSELF THROUGH THE FORMIDABLE CUSTOMS GATE.
JUST BEFORE I GOT TO THE INSPECTION AREA, I SPOTTED A TELEPHONE IN AN ALCOVE IN THE CORRIDOR.
FORTUNATELY, I HAD BROUGHT ALONG MY PICOCOMPUTER AND A HANDY UNIVERSAL TELEPHONE ACCESS MODEM.
SIDESTEPPING INTO THE HIDDEN CORNER, I QUICKLY WENT THROUGH A NUMBER OF LIKELY ACCESS PROCEDURES.
CLICK CLICK CLICK CLICK CLICK CLICK
ON THE SEVENTH TRY I GOT A LUCKY HIT AND GOT ENTRY INTO THE INTERNATIONAL PASSPORT AND CUSTOMS SYSTEM.
DING
BY THE TIME I REACHED THE AGENTS MY RECORD HAD BEEN SUCCESSFULLY ALTERED FOR THE OCCASION.
A MACHINE PROCESSED MY PASSPORT, AND THEY NEVER GAVE ME A SECOND GLANCE AS I WENT THROUGH THE GATE.
O.K.
GLIDE
NOW I WAS OFFICIALLY A MOSLEM, AMONG OTHER THINGS. I USED THE PICOCOMPUTER AGAIN TO BOOK A SUITE AT THE HOTEL.
TAXI
FROM MY ROOM TELEPHONE IT WAS RELATIVELY EASY TO TAP INTO THE COMPUTER SYSTEM OF THE OIL MINISTRY.
I WAS GETTING A PENNY ON EVERY BARREL OF OIL MOVED FOR OVER THREE HOURS BEFORE THEY GOT SUSPICIOUS!
DING! DING! DING! DING! DING!

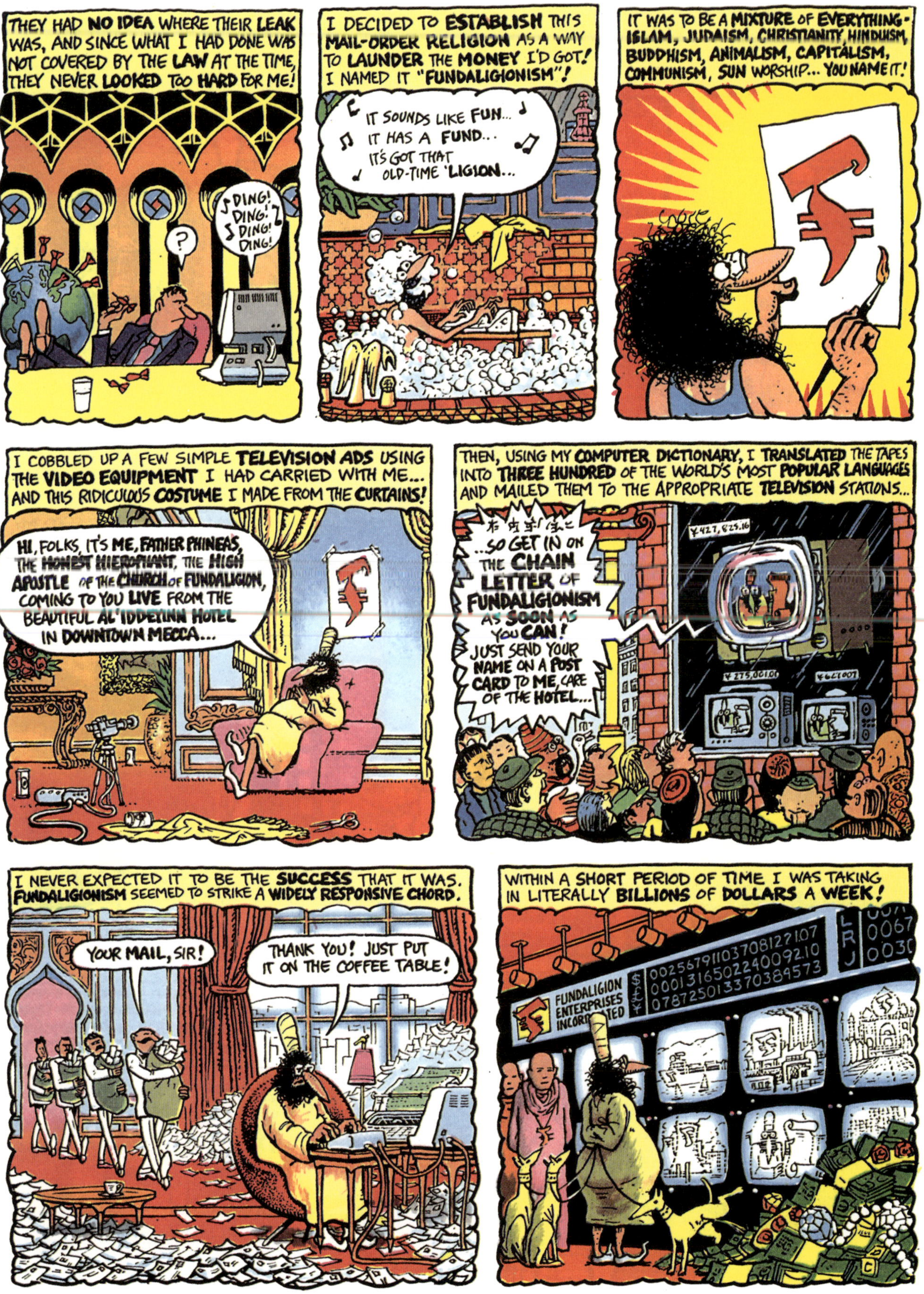
THEY HAD NO IDEA WHERE THEIR LEAK WAS, AND SINCE WHAT I HAD DONE WAS NOT COVERED BY THE LAW AT THE TIME, THEY NEVER LOOKED TOO HARD FOR ME!
?
DING! DING! DING! DING!
I DECIDED TO ESTABLISH THIS MAIL-ORDER RELIGION AS A WAY TO LAUNDER THE MONEY I'D GOT! I NAMED IT "FUNDALIGIONISM"!
IT SOUNDS LIKE FUN... IT HAS A FUND... IT'S GOT THAT OLD-TIME 'LIGION...
IT WAS TO BE A MIXTURE OF EVERYTHING- ISLAM, JUDAISM, CHRISTIANITY, HINDUISM, BUDDHISM, ANIMALISM, CAPITALISM, COMMUNISM, SUN WORSHIP... YOU NAME IT!
I COBBLED UP A FEW SIMPLE TELEVISION ADS USING THE VIDEO EQUIPMENT I HAD CARRIED WITH ME... AND THIS RIDICULOUS COSTUME I MADE FROM THE CURTAINS!
HI, FOLKS, IT'S ME, FATHER PHINEAS, THE HONEST HIEROPHANT, THE HIGH APOSTLE OF THE CHURCH OF FUNDALIGION, COMING TO YOU LIVE FROM THE BEAUTIFUL AL'IDDEYINN HOTEL IN DOWNTOWN MECCA...
THEN, USING MY COMPUTER DICTIONARY, I TRANSLATED THE TAPES INTO THREE HUNDRED OF THE WORLD'S MOST POPULAR LANGUAGES AND MAILED THEM TO THE APPROPRIATE TELEVISION STATIONS...
...SO GET IN ON THE CHAIN LETTER OF FUNDALIGIONISM AS SOON AS YOU CAN! JUST SEND YOUR NAME ON A POST CARD TO ME, CARE OF THE HOTEL...
¥427,825.16
¥275,001.00
I NEVER EXPECTED IT TO BE THE SUCCESS THAT IT WAS. FUNDALIGIONISM SEEMED TO STRIKE A WIDELY RESPONSIVE CHORD.
YOUR MAIL, SIR!
THANK YOU! JUST PUT IT ON THE COFFEE TABLE!
WITHIN A SHORT PERIOD OF TIME I WAS TAKING IN LITERALLY BILLIONS OF DOLLARS A WEEK!
FUNDALIGION ENTERPRISES INCORPORATED
002567911037081227107
000131650224009210
07872501337038457 3
0067
0030

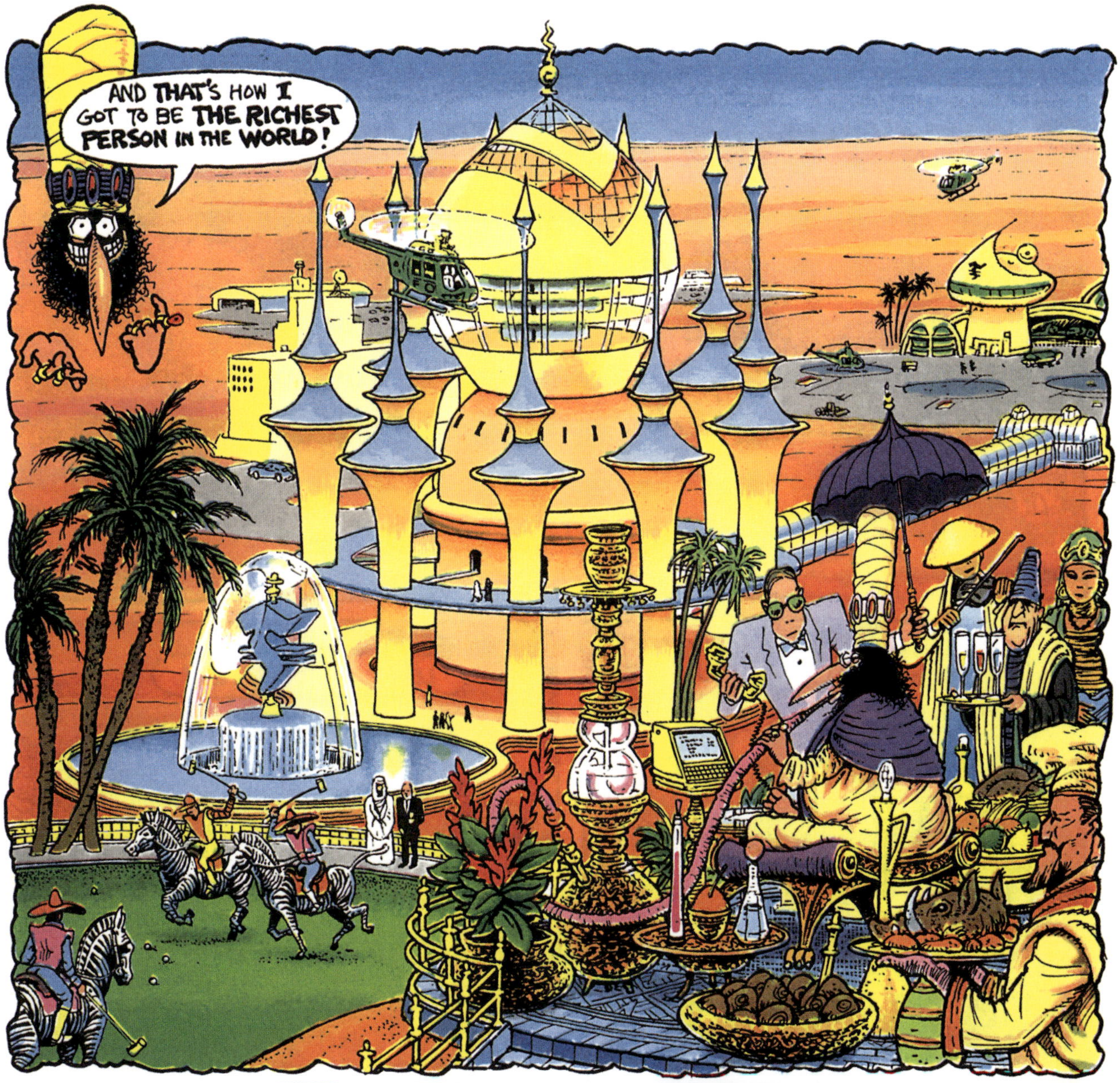
AND THAT'S HOW I GOT TO BE THE RICHEST PERSON IN THE WORLD!

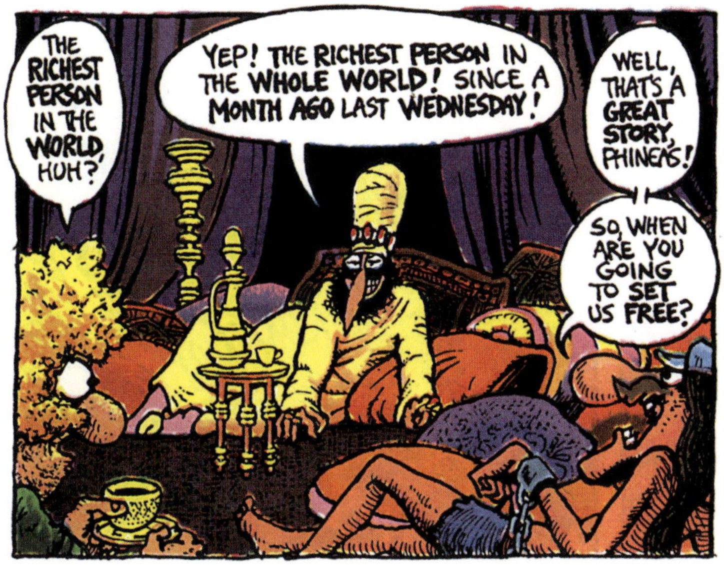
THE RICHEST PERSON IN THE WORLD, HUH?
YEP! THE RICHEST PERSON IN THE WHOLE WORLD! SINCE A MONTH AGO LAST WEDNESDAY!
WELL, THAT'S A GREAT STORY, PHINEAS!
SO, WHEN ARE YOU GOING TO SET US FREE?

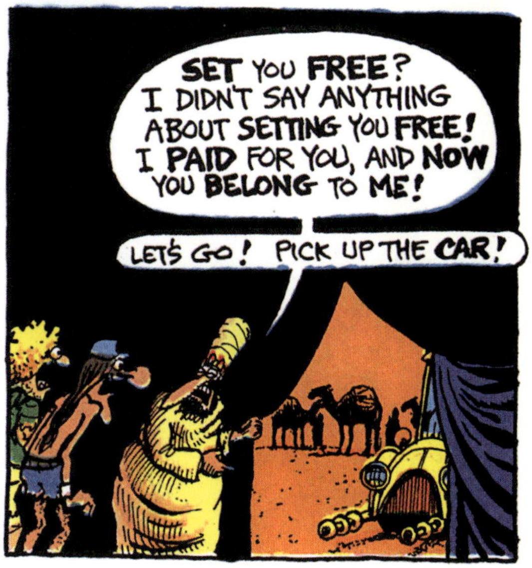
SET YOU FREE? I DIDN'T SAY ANYTHING ABOUT SETTING YOU FREE! I PAID FOR YOU, AND NOW YOU BELONG TO ME!
LET'S GO! PICK UP THE CAR!

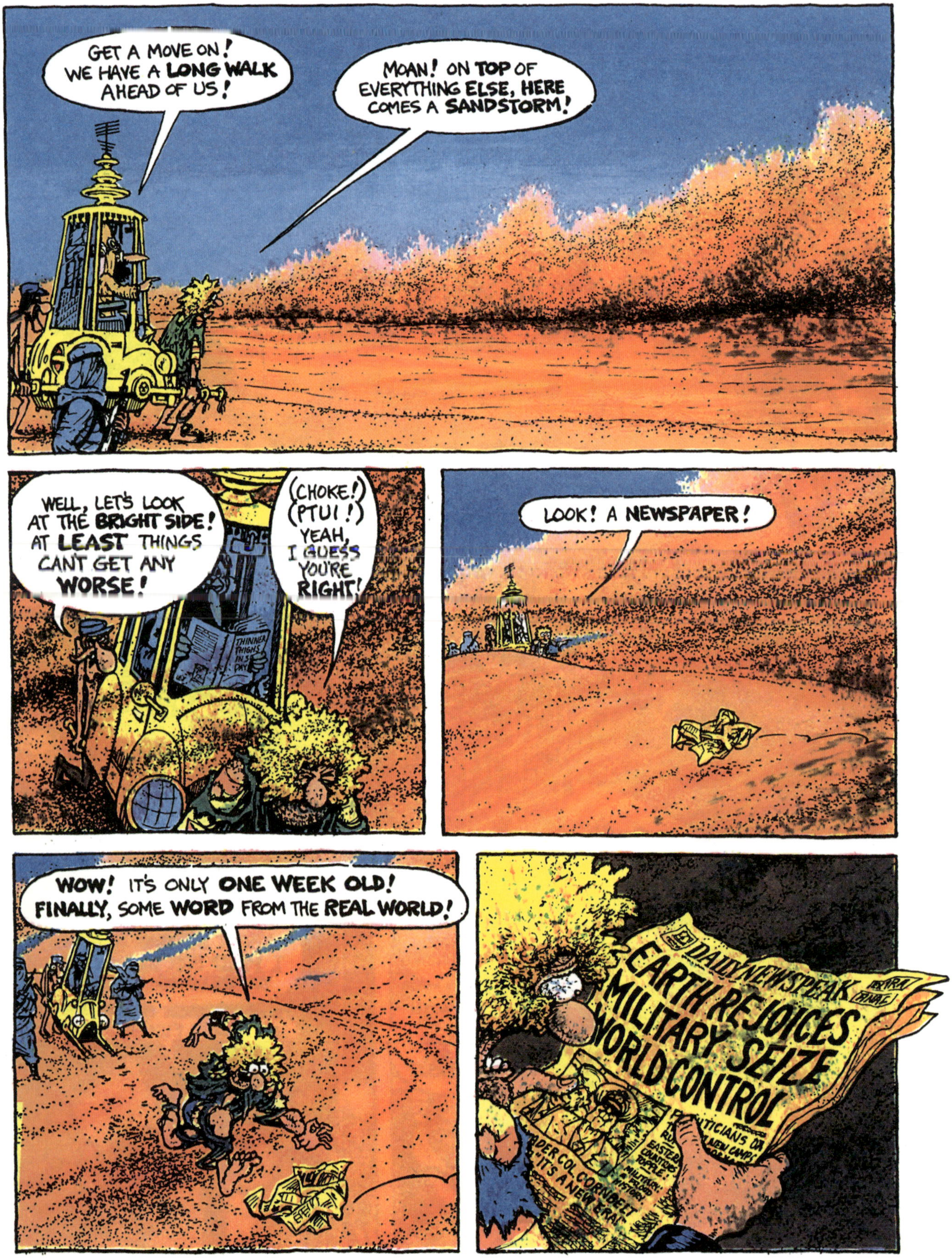
GET A MOVE ON! WE HAVE A LONG WALK AHEAD OF US!
MOAN! ON TOP OF EVERYTHING ELSE, HERE COMES A SANDSTORM!
WELL, LET'S LOOK AT THE BRIGHT SIDE! AT LEAST THINGS CAN'T GET ANY WORSE!
(CHOKE!) (PTUI!) YEAH, I GUESS YOU'RE RIGHT!
LOOK! A NEWSPAPER!
WOW! IT'S ONLY ONE WEEK OLD! FINALLY, SOME WORD FROM THE REAL WORLD!
DAILY NEWSPEAK
EARTH REJOICES
MILITARY SEIZE WORLD CONTROL

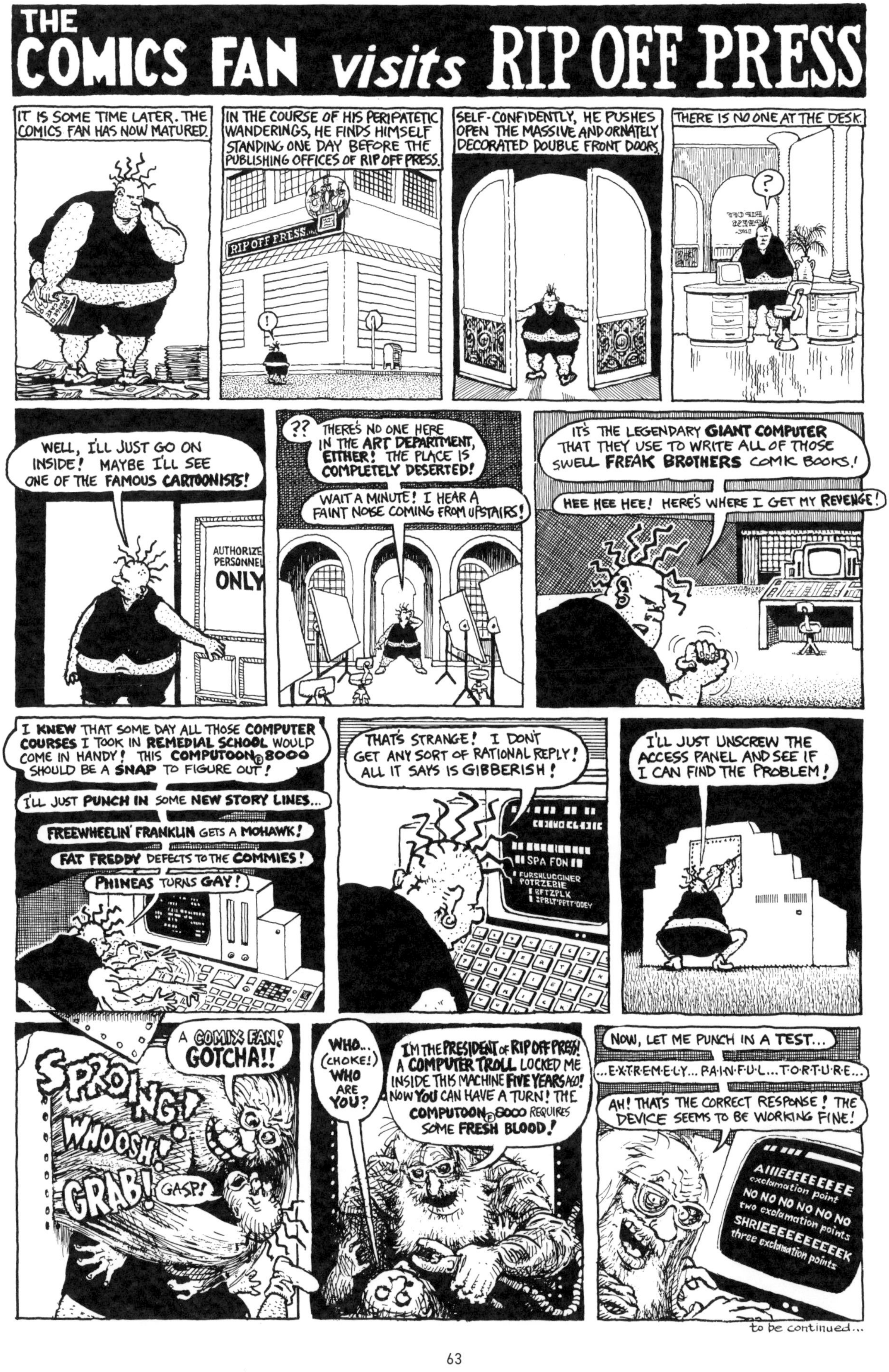
THE COMICS FAN visits RIP OFF PRESS
IT IS SOME TIME LATER. THE COMICS FAN HAS NOW MATURED.
IN THE COURSE OF HIS PERIPATETIC WANDERINGS, HE FINDS HIMSELF STANDING ONE DAY BEFORE THE PUBLISHING OFFICES OF RIP OFF PRESS.
RIP OFF PRESS...
!
SELF-CONFIDENTLY, HE PUSHES OPEN THE MASSIVE AND ORNATELY DECORATED DOUBLE FRONT DOORS.
THERE IS NO ONE AT THE DESK.
?
WELL, I'LL JUST GO ON INSIDE! MAYBE I'LL SEE ONE OF THE FAMOUS CARTOONISTS!
AUTHORIZE PERSONNEL ONLY
?? THERE'S NO ONE HERE IN THE ART DEPARTMENT, EITHER! THE PLACE IS COMPLETELY DESERTED!
WAIT A MINUTE! I HEAR A FAINT NOISE COMING FROM UPSTAIRS!
IT'S THE LEGENDARY GIANT COMPUTER THAT THEY USE TO WRITE ALL OF THOSE SWELL FREAK BROTHERS COMIK BOOKS!
HEE HEE HEE! HERE'S WHERE I GET MY REVENGE!
I KNEW THAT SOME DAY ALL THOSE COMPUTER COURSES I TOOK IN REMEDIAL SCHOOL WOULD COME IN HANDY! THIS COMPUTOON 8000 SHOULD BE A SNAP TO FIGURE OUT!
I'LL JUST PUNCH IN SOME NEW STORY LINES...
FREEWHEELIN' FRANKLIN GETS A MOHAWK!
FAT FREDDY DEFECTS TO THE COMMIES!
PHINEAS TURNS GAY!
THAT'S STRANGE! I DON'T GET ANY SORT OF RATIONAL REPLY! ALL IT SAYS IS GIBBERISH!
SPA FON
FURSHLUGGINER POTRZEBIE
BFTZPLK
SPBLT'PPTT'OOEY
I'LL JUST UNSCREW THE ACCESS PANEL AND SEE IF I CAN FIND THE PROBLEM!
A COMIX FAN! GOTCHA!!
SPROING!
WHOOSH!
GRAB!
GASP!
WHO... (CHOKE!) WHO ARE YOU?
I'M THE PRESIDENT OF RIP OFF PRESS! A COMPUTER TROLL LOCKED ME INSIDE THIS MACHINE FIVE YEARS AGO! NOW YOU CAN HAVE A TURN! THE COMPUTOON 8000 REQUIRES SOME FRESH BLOOD!
NOW, LET ME PUNCH IN A TEST...
...E·X·T·R·E·M·E·L·Y... P·A·I·N·F·U·L... T·O·R·T·U·R·E...
AH! THAT'S THE CORRECT RESPONSE! THE DEVICE SEEMS TO BE WORKING FINE!
AIIIEEEEEEEE exclamation point
NO NO NO NO NO NO two exclamation points
SHRIEEEEEEEEEEK three exclamation points
to be continued...

As You May Remember...

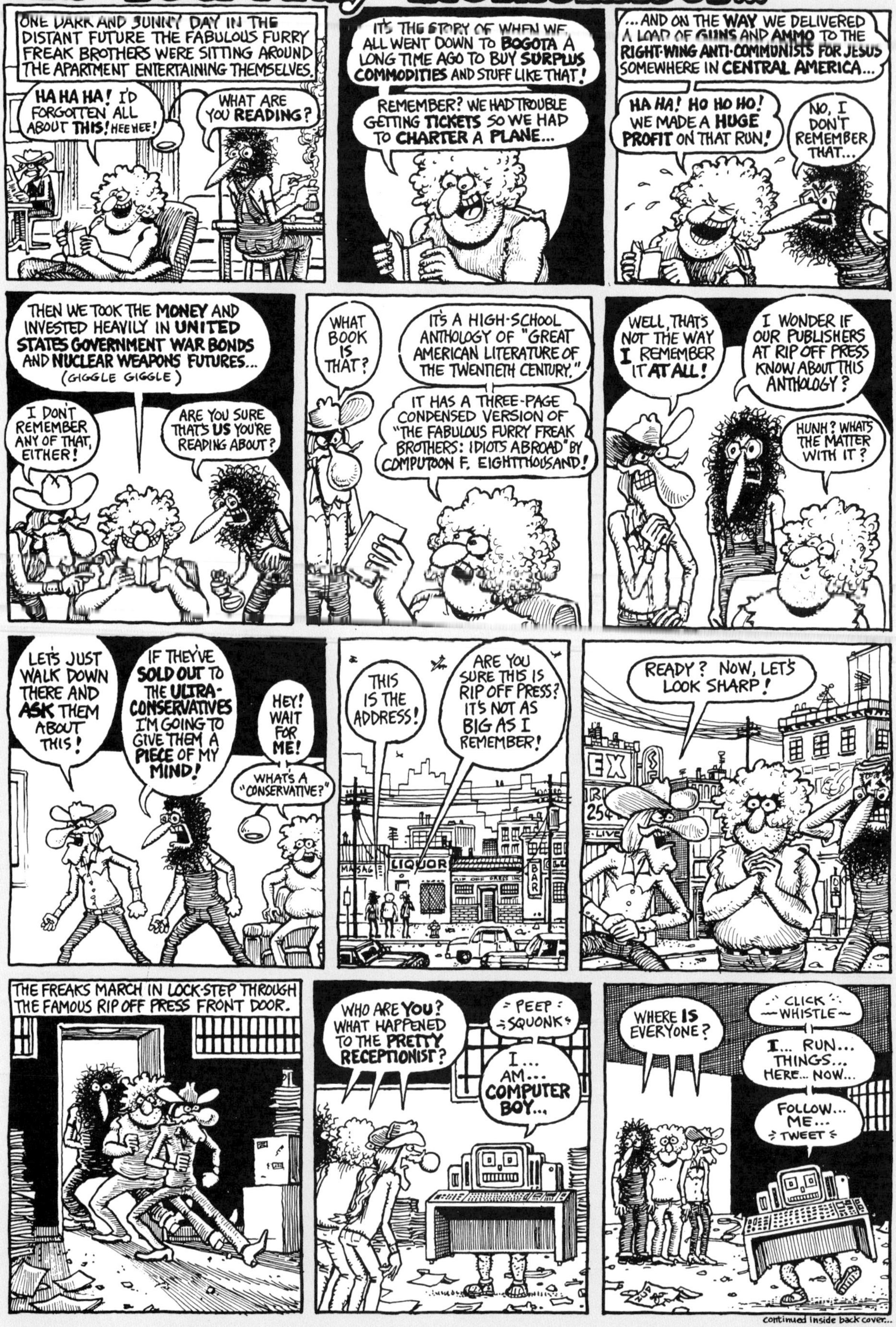

ONE DARK AND SUNNY DAY IN THE DISTANT FUTURE THE FABULOUS FURRY FREAK BROTHERS WERE SITTING AROUND THE APARTMENT ENTERTAINING THEMSELVES.
HA HA HA! I'D FORGOTTEN ALL ABOUT THIS! HEE HEE!
WHAT ARE YOU READING?
IT'S THE STORY OF WHEN WE ALL WENT DOWN TO BOGOTA A LONG TIME AGO TO BUY SURPLUS COMMODITIES AND STUFF LIKE THAT!
REMEMBER? WE HAD TROUBLE GETTING TICKETS SO WE HAD TO CHARTER A PLANE...
...AND ON THE WAY WE DELIVERED A LOAD OF GUNS AND AMMO TO THE RIGHT-WING ANTI-COMMUNISTS FOR JESUS SOMEWHERE IN CENTRAL AMERICA...
HA HA! HO HO HO! WE MADE A HUGE PROFIT ON THAT RUN!
NO, I DON'T REMEMBER THAT...
THEN WE TOOK THE MONEY AND INVESTED HEAVILY IN UNITED STATES GOVERNMENT WAR BONDS AND NUCLEAR WEAPONS FUTURES... (GIGGLE GIGGLE)
I DON'T REMEMBER ANY OF THAT, EITHER!
ARE YOU SURE THAT'S US YOU'RE READING ABOUT?
WHAT BOOK IS THAT?
IT'S A HIGH-SCHOOL ANTHOLOGY OF "GREAT AMERICAN LITERATURE OF THE TWENTIETH CENTURY."
IT HAS A THREE-PAGE CONDENSED VERSION OF "THE FABULOUS FURRY FREAK BROTHERS: IDIOTS ABROAD" BY COMPUTOON F. EIGHTTHOUSAND!
WELL, THAT'S NOT THE WAY I REMEMBER IT AT ALL!
I WONDER IF OUR PUBLISHERS AT RIP OFF PRESS KNOW ABOUT THIS ANTHOLOGY?
HUNH? WHAT'S THE MATTER WITH IT?
LET'S JUST WALK DOWN THERE AND ASK THEM ABOUT THIS!
IF THEY'VE SOLD OUT TO THE ULTRA-CONSERVATIVES I'M GOING TO GIVE THEM A PIECE OF MY MIND!
HEY! WAIT FOR ME!
WHAT'S A "CONSERVATIVE?"
THIS IS THE ADDRESS!
ARE YOU SURE THIS IS RIP OFF PRESS? IT'S NOT AS BIG AS I REMEMBER!
LIQUOR
RIP OFF PRESS INC
BAR
READY? NOW, LET'S LOOK SHARP!
THE FREAKS MARCH IN LOCK-STEP THROUGH THE FAMOUS RIP OFF PRESS FRONT DOOR.
WHO ARE YOU? WHAT HAPPENED TO THE PRETTY RECEPTIONIST?
PEEP SQUONK
I... AM... COMPUTER BOY...
WHERE IS EVERYONE?
CLICK WHISTLE
I... RUN... THINGS... HERE... NOW...
FOLLOW... ME... TWEET

continued inside back cover...

THE CAST OF CHARACTERS

AND A ONE-SENTENCE SYNOPSIS OF THE STORY SO FAR

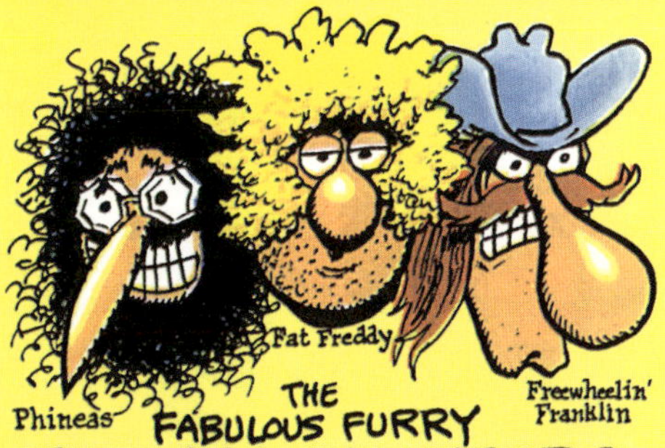
Phineas
Fat Freddy
Freewheelin' Franklin

THE FABULOUS FURRY FREAK BROTHERS

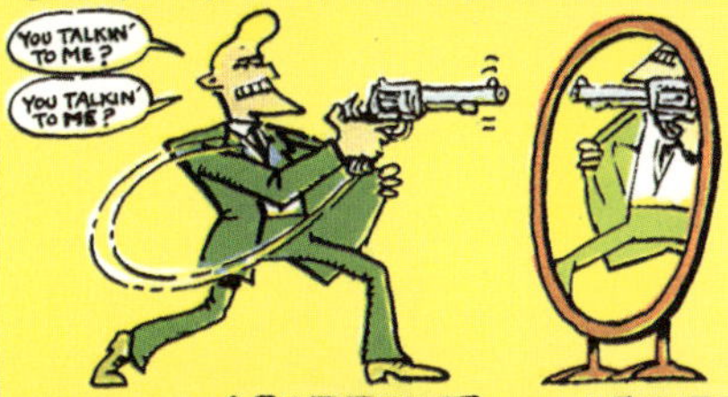
YOU TALKIN' TO ME?
YOU TALKIN' TO ME?

NOTORIOUS NORBERT THE NARK

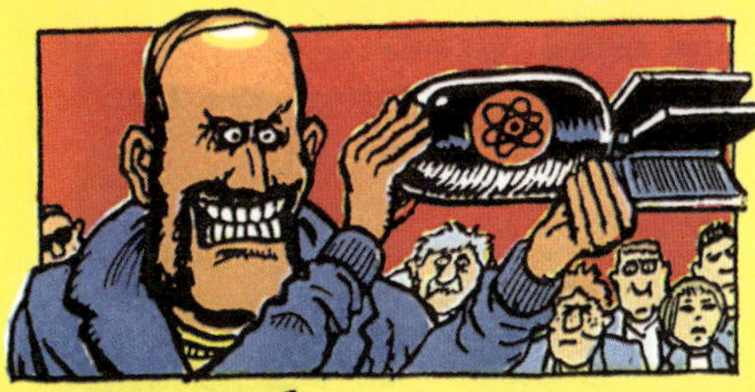

ANDRÉ THE HYENA
AND HIS GANG OF INTERNATIONAL TERRORISTS

THE **FABULOUS FURRY FREAK BROTHERS** HAD REALLY TRIED TO GO TO BOGOTA SOME TIME AGO AND HAD ACTUALLY GOTTEN AS FAR AS THE AIRPORT, TRAILED UNOBSERVED BY THE NOTORIOUS **NORBERT THE NARK**, WHEN THEY BECAME SEPARATED, **FREEWHEELIN' FRANKLIN** GOING FIRST TO CENTRAL AMERICA IN A RESTORED WWII C-46 PILOTED BY A MYSTERIOUS WOMAN WHO IS A MEMBER OF A **GROUP OF SURVIVALISTS**, THEN ALMOST BEING SHOT BY THE LEADER OF A RIGHT-WING DEATH SQUAD, **COLONEL GALLITO**, AND HIS SON **CADET-COLONEL PICHON**, THEN BEING CAPTURED BY A BOATFUL OF **MODERN-DAY PIRATES OF THE CARIBBEAN** AND FINALLY BEING SOLD AS A SLAVE IN AFRICA, WHILE **FAT FREDDY** WAS CONDUCTING A HIGH-SPEED CHASE SCENE THROUGHOUT EUROPE, PURSUED BY **ANDRÉ THE HYENA** AND HIS **GANG OF INTERNATIONAL TERRORISTS**, FREDDY HAVING UNWITTINGLY RUN OFF WITH ANDRÉ'S NUCLEAR BOMB AND LOST IT IN LOCH NESS, AND AFTER HAVING BEEN RESCUED BY THE ANARCHIST ARTIST-INVENTOR **PABLO PEGASO**, MAKING AN UNPLANNED SIDE TRIP TO MOSCOW, WHERE HE IS ARRESTED FOR SOME TRIVIAL OFFENSE, ONLY TO RESURFACE AT THE SAME AFRICAN SLAVE MARKET AS **FREEWHEELIN' FRANKLIN**, WHERE THEY ARE EVENTUALLY PURCHASED BY A FAT, OILY MAN OF INDETERMINABLE RACIAL ORIGIN WHO TURNS OUT TO BE THEIR OLD ROOMMATE **PHINEAS** AND WHO HAS NOW BEEN THE RICHEST MAN ON EARTH FOR OVER A MONTH THANKS TO HIS AMAZINGLY SUCCESSFUL TELEVISION MAIL-ORDER RELIGION "FUNDALIGIONISM" WHICH INCORPORATES THE SALIENT FEATURES OF ALL THE WORLDS' GREAT RELIGIONS OF ALL HISTORY, AMONG WHICH IS UNFORTUNATELY INCLUDED HUMAN SLAVERY, AND IT IS AS A SLAVE CARRYING PHINEAS IN A PALANQUIN THAT FAT FREDDY READS IN A DISCARDED NEWSPAPER HOW A MILITARY COUP LED BY THE AMERICAN MILITARY ADVISOR FOR EUROPE, **COLONEL CORNBELT**, HAS SEIZED (WITH THE AID OF **ANDRÉ**) CONTROL OF EVERY GOVERNMENT ON EARTH, INCLUDING CHINA AND THE U.S.S.R.

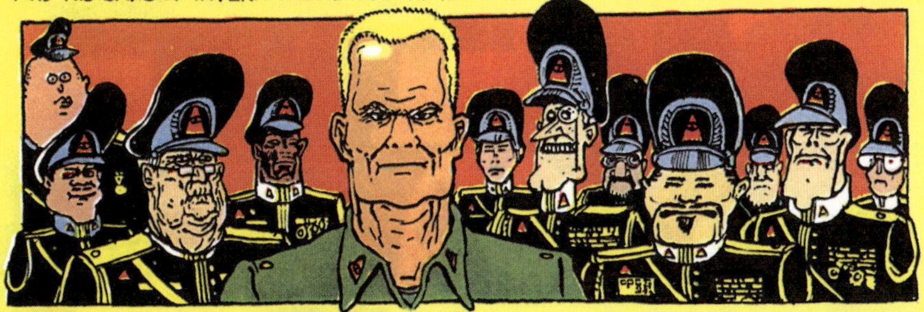

COLONEL CORNBELT AND THE AUTHORITY OF THE NEW ERA

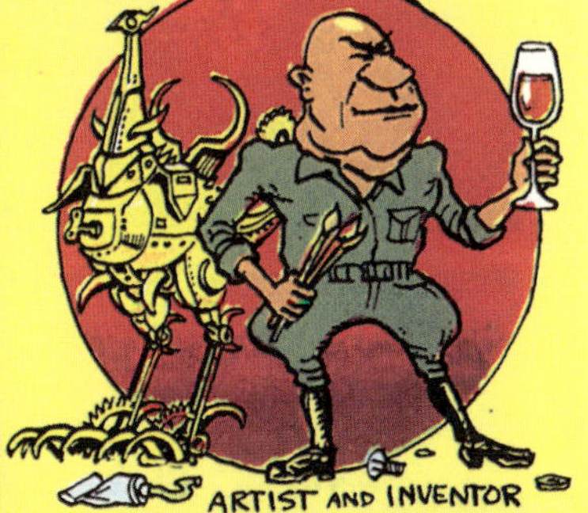

ARTIST AND INVENTOR
PABLO PEGASO
ANARCHIST AND GOURMET

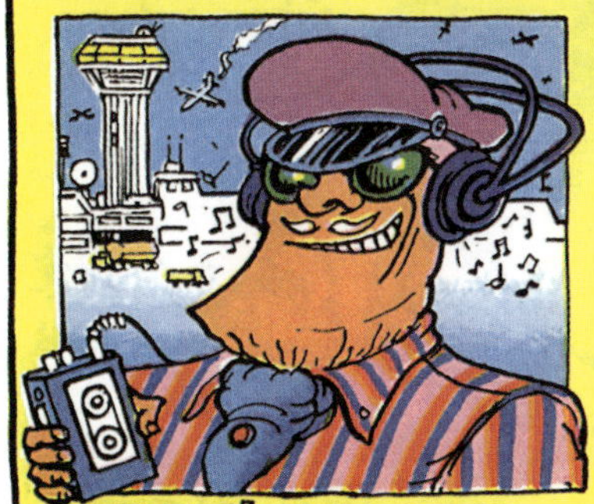

SMILIN' MYLAN
THE HAS-BEEN AIR ACE

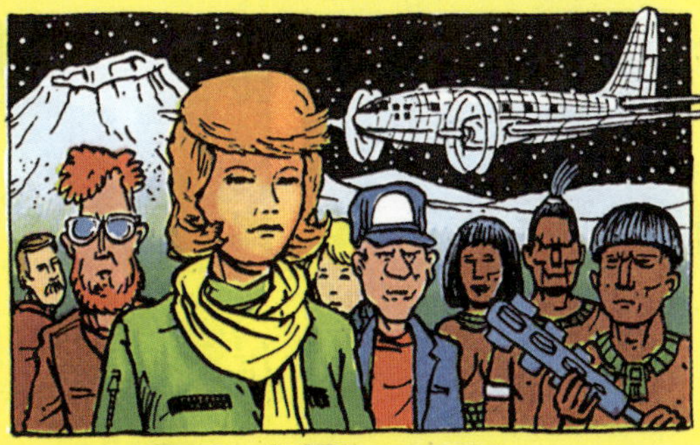

THE SURVIVALISTS OF THE CENTRAL AMERICAN MOUNTAINS & THEIR INDIAN FRIENDS

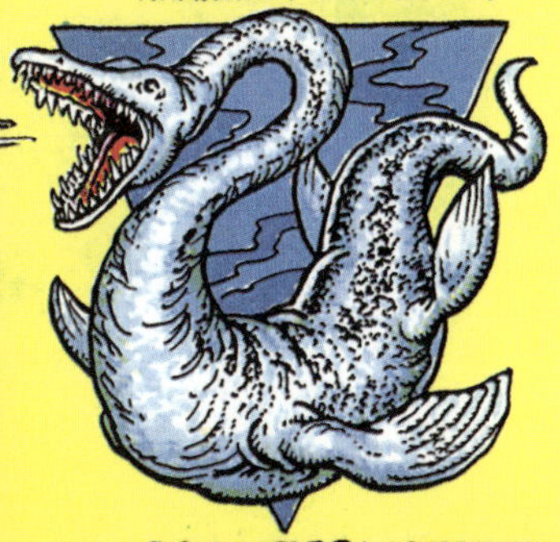

THE LOCH NESS MONSTER

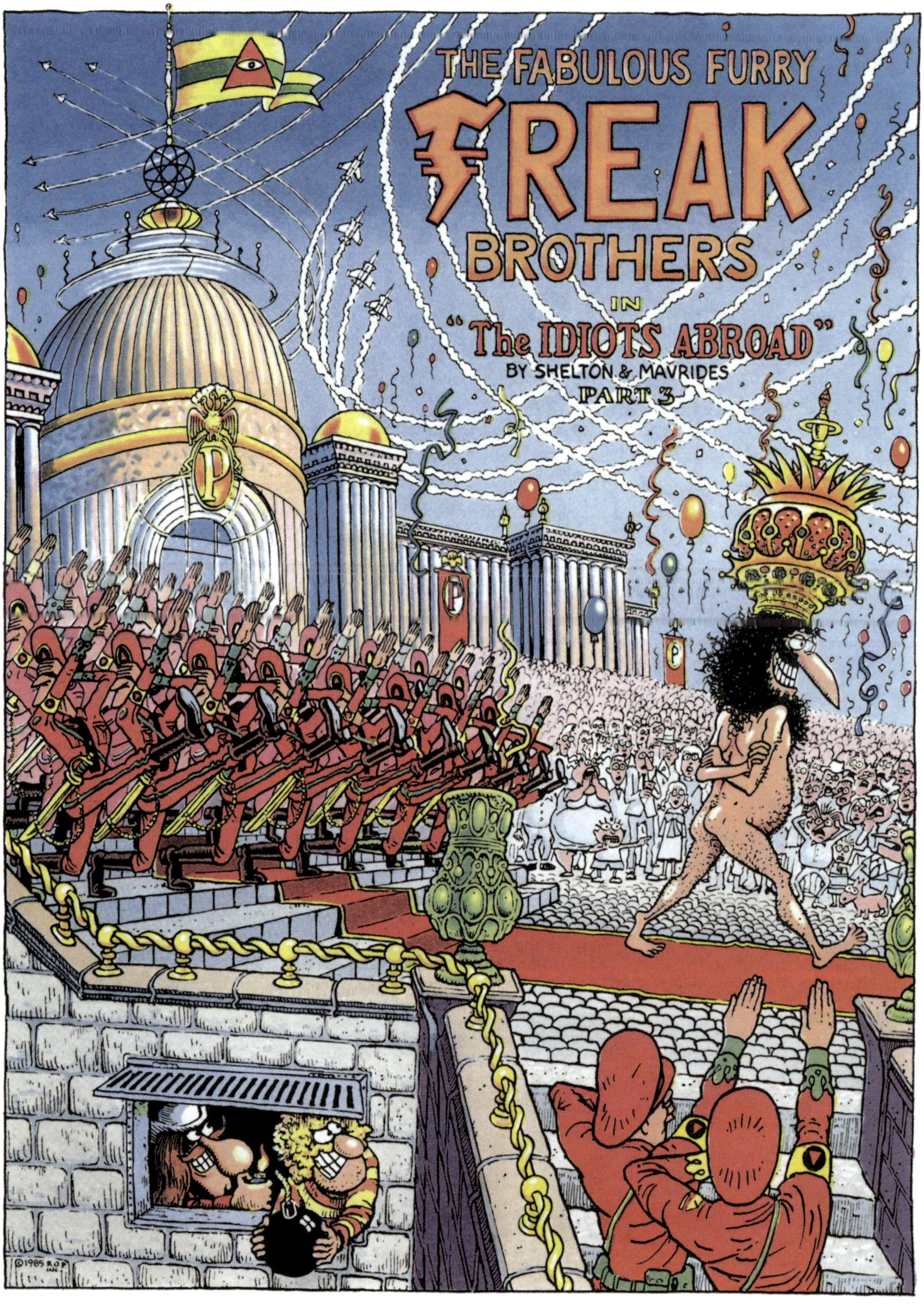
THE FABULOUS FURRY
FREAK
BROTHERS
IN
"The IDIOTS ABROAD"
BY SHELTON & MAVRIDES
PART 3
©1985 R.O.P.

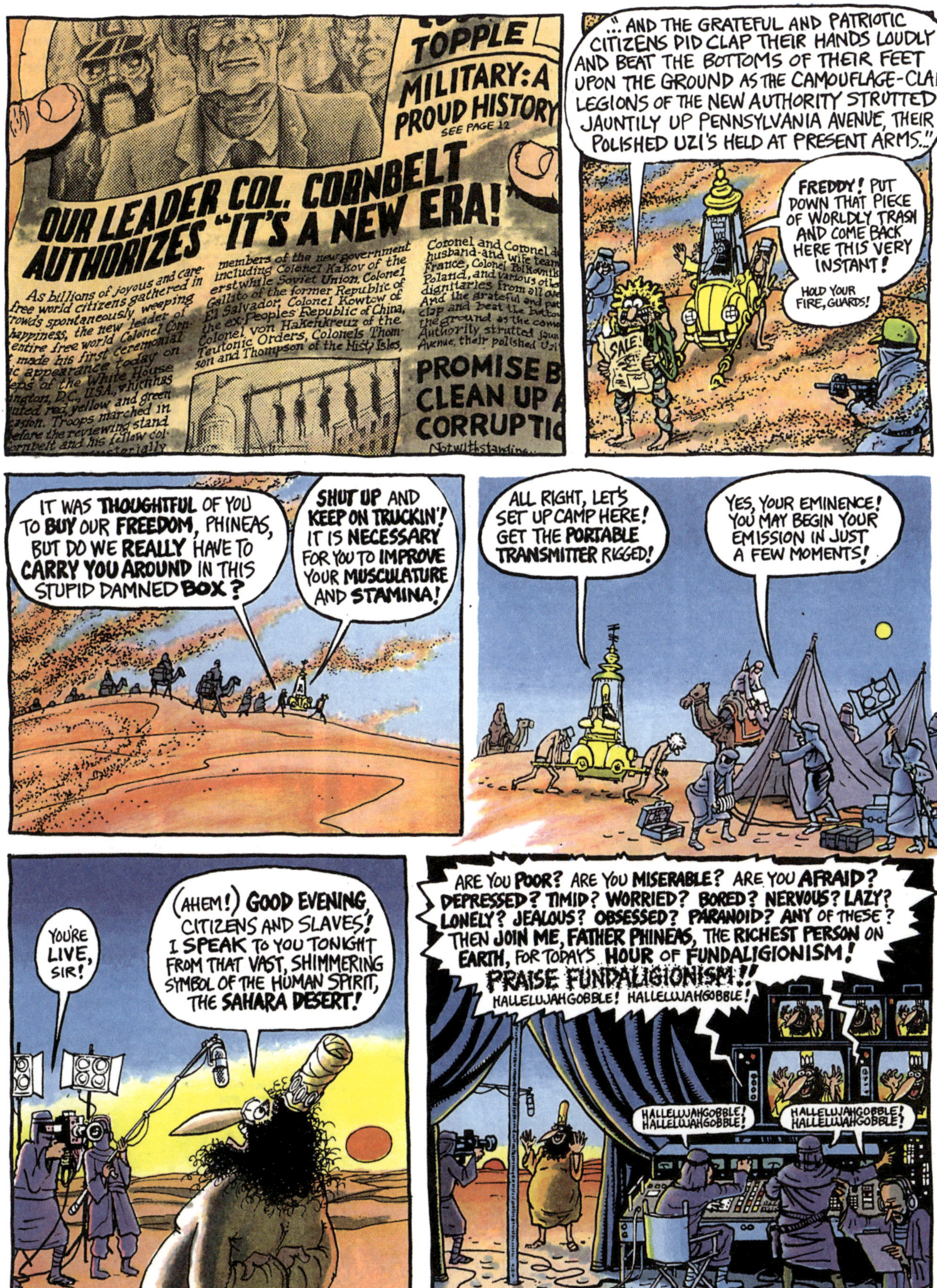
TOPPLE
MILITARY: A PROUD HISTORY
SEE PAGE 12
OUR LEADER COL. CORNBELT AUTHORIZES "IT'S A NEW ERA!"
members of the new government including Colonel Kakov of the erstwhile Soviet Union, Colonel Gallito of the former Republic of El Salvador, Colonel Kowtow of the ex-Peoples Republic of China, Colonel von Hakenkreuz of the Teutonic Orders, Colonels Thomson and Thompson of the Misty Isles,
"... AND THE GRATEFUL AND PATRIOTIC CITIZENS DID CLAP THEIR HANDS LOUDLY AND BEAT THE BOTTOMS OF THEIR FEET UPON THE GROUND AS THE CAMOUFLAGE-CLAD LEGIONS OF THE NEW AUTHORITY STRUTTED JAUNTILY UP PENNSYLVANIA AVENUE, THEIR POLISHED UZI'S HELD AT PRESENT ARMS..."
FREDDY! PUT DOWN THAT PIECE OF WORLDLY TRASH AND COME BACK HERE THIS VERY INSTANT!
HOLD YOUR FIRE, GUARDS!
SALE
IT WAS THOUGHTFUL OF YOU TO BUY OUR FREEDOM, PHINEAS, BUT DO WE REALLY HAVE TO CARRY YOU AROUND IN THIS STUPID DAMNED BOX?
SHUT UP AND KEEP ON TRUCKIN'! IT IS NECESSARY FOR YOU TO IMPROVE YOUR MUSCULATURE AND STAMINA!
ALL RIGHT, LET'S SET UP CAMP HERE! GET THE PORTABLE TRANSMITTER RIGGED!
YES, YOUR EMINENCE! YOU MAY BEGIN YOUR EMISSION IN JUST A FEW MOMENTS!
YOU'RE LIVE, SIR!
(AHEM!) GOOD EVENING, CITIZENS AND SLAVES! I SPEAK TO YOU TONIGHT FROM THAT VAST, SHIMMERING SYMBOL OF THE HUMAN SPIRIT, THE SAHARA DESERT!
ARE YOU POOR? ARE YOU MISERABLE? ARE YOU AFRAID? DEPRESSED? TIMID? WORRIED? BORED? NERVOUS? LAZY? LONELY? JEALOUS? OBSESSED? PARANOID? ANY OF THESE? THEN JOIN ME, FATHER PHINEAS, THE RICHEST PERSON ON EARTH, FOR TODAY'S HOUR OF FUNDALIGIONISM!
PRAISE FUNDALIGIONISM!!
HALLELUJAHGOBBLE! HALLELUJAHGOBBLE!
HALLELUJAHGOBBLE! HALLELUJAHGOBBLE!
HALLELUJAHGOBBLE! HALLELUJAHGOBBLE!

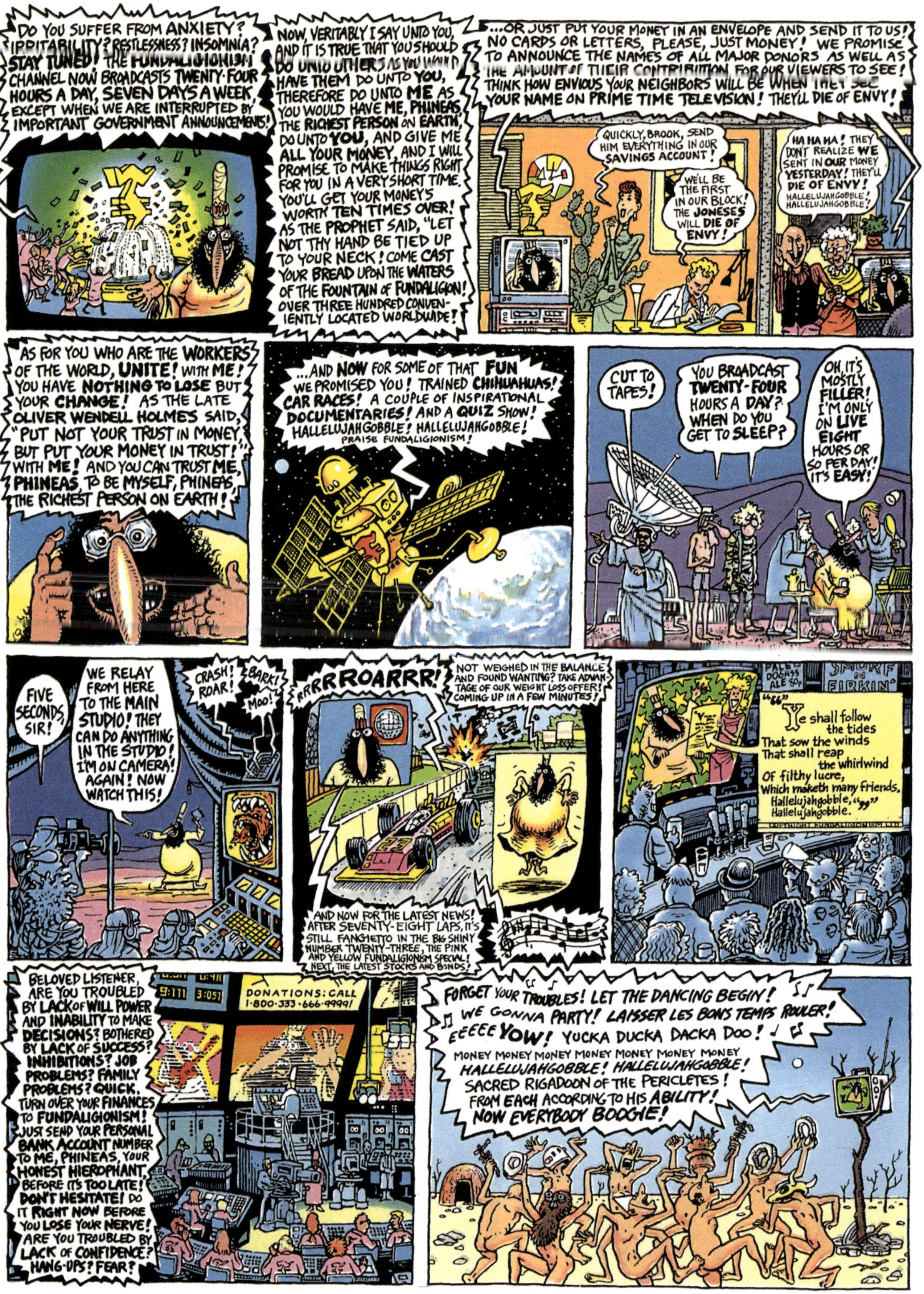
DO YOU SUFFER FROM ANXIETY? IRRITABILITY? RESTLESSNESS? INSOMNIA? STAY TUNED! THE FUNDALIGIONISM CHANNEL NOW BROADCASTS TWENTY-FOUR HOURS A DAY, SEVEN DAYS A WEEK, EXCEPT WHEN WE ARE INTERRUPTED BY IMPORTANT GOVERNMENT ANNOUNCEMENTS!
NOW, VERITABLY I SAY UNTO YOU, AND IT IS TRUE THAT YOU SHOULD DO UNTO OTHERS AS YOU WOULD HAVE THEM DO UNTO YOU, THEREFORE DO UNTO ME AS YOU WOULD HAVE ME, PHINEAS, THE RICHEST PERSON ON EARTH, DO UNTO YOU, AND GIVE ME ALL YOUR MONEY, AND I WILL PROMISE TO MAKE THINGS RIGHT FOR YOU IN A VERY SHORT TIME. YOU'LL GET YOUR MONEY'S WORTH TEN TIMES OVER! AS THE PROPHET SAID, "LET NOT THY HAND BE TIED UP TO YOUR NECK! COME CAST YOUR BREAD UPON THE WATERS OF THE FOUNTAIN OF FUNDALIGION! OVER THREE HUNDRED CONVENIENTLY LOCATED WORLDWIDE!
...OR JUST PUT YOUR MONEY IN AN ENVELOPE AND SEND IT TO US! NO CARDS OR LETTERS, PLEASE, JUST MONEY! WE PROMISE TO ANNOUNCE THE NAMES OF ALL MAJOR DONORS AS WELL AS THE AMOUNT OF THEIR CONTRIBUTION FOR OUR VIEWERS TO SEE! THINK HOW ENVIOUS YOUR NEIGHBORS WILL BE WHEN THEY SEE YOUR NAME ON PRIME TIME TELEVISION! THEY'LL DIE OF ENVY!
QUICKLY, BROOK, SEND HIM EVERYTHING IN OUR SAVINGS ACCOUNT!
WE'LL BE THE FIRST IN OUR BLOCK! THE JONESES WILL DIE OF ENVY!
HA HA HA! THEY DON'T REALIZE WE SENT IN OUR MONEY YESTERDAY! THEY'LL DIE OF ENVY! HALLELUJAHGOBBLE! HALLELUJAHGOBBLE!
AS FOR YOU WHO ARE THE WORKERS OF THE WORLD, UNITE! WITH ME! YOU HAVE NOTHING TO LOSE BUT YOUR CHANGE! AS THE LATE OLIVER WENDELL HOLMES SAID, "PUT NOT YOUR TRUST IN MONEY, BUT PUT YOUR MONEY IN TRUST!" WITH ME! AND YOU CAN TRUST ME, PHINEAS, TO BE MYSELF, PHINEAS, THE RICHEST PERSON ON EARTH!
...AND NOW FOR SOME OF THAT FUN WE PROMISED YOU! TRAINED CHIHUAHUAS! CAR RACES! A COUPLE OF INSPIRATIONAL DOCUMENTARIES! AND A QUIZ SHOW! HALLELUJAHGOBBLE! HALLELUJAHGOBBLE! PRAISE FUNDALIGIONISM!
CUT TO TAPES!
YOU BROADCAST TWENTY-FOUR HOURS A DAY? WHEN DO YOU GET TO SLEEP?
OH, IT'S MOSTLY FILLER! I'M ONLY ON LIVE EIGHT HOURS OR SO PER DAY! IT'S EASY!
FIVE SECONDS, SIR!
WE RELAY FROM HERE TO THE MAIN STUDIO! THEY CAN DO ANYTHING IN THE STUDIO! I'M ON CAMERA! AGAIN! NOW WATCH THIS!
CRASH! ROAR!
BARK!
MOO!
RRRRROARRR!
NOT WEIGHED IN THE BALANCE AND FOUND WANTING? TAKE ADVANTAGE OF OUR WEIGHT LOSS OFFER! COMING UP IN A FEW MINUTES!
AND NOW FOR THE LATEST NEWS! AFTER SEVENTY-EIGHT LAPS, IT'S STILL FANGHETTO IN THE BIG SHINY NUMBER TWENTY-THREE, THE PINK AND YELLOW FUNDALIGIONISM SPECIAL! NEXT, THE LATEST STOCKS AND BONDS!
SMURF & FIRKIN
"Ye shall follow the tides
That sow the winds
That shall reap the whirlwind
Of filthy lucre,
Which maketh many friends.
Hallelujahgobble,
Hallelujahgobble."
BELOVED LISTENER, ARE YOU TROUBLED BY LACK OF WILL POWER AND INABILITY TO MAKE DECISIONS? BOTHERED BY LACK OF SUCCESS? INHIBITIONS? JOB PROBLEMS? FAMILY PROBLEMS? QUICK, TURN OVER YOUR FINANCES TO FUNDALIGIONISM! JUST SEND YOUR PERSONAL BANK ACCOUNT NUMBER TO ME, PHINEAS, YOUR HONEST HIEROPHANT, BEFORE IT'S TOO LATE! DON'T HESITATE! DO IT RIGHT NOW BEFORE YOU LOSE YOUR NERVE! ARE YOU TROUBLED BY LACK OF CONFIDENCE? HANG-UPS? FEAR?
DONATIONS: CALL 1-800-333-666-9999!
FORGET YOUR TROUBLES! LET THE DANCING BEGIN! WE GONNA PARTY! LAISSER LES BONS TEMPS ROULER! EEEEE YOW! YUCKA DUCKA DACKA DOO! MONEY MONEY MONEY MONEY MONEY MONEY MONEY HALLELUJAHGOBBLE! HALLELUJAHGOBBLE! SACRED RIGADOON OF THE PERICLETES! FROM EACH ACCORDING TO HIS ABILITY! NOW EVERYBODY BOOGIE!

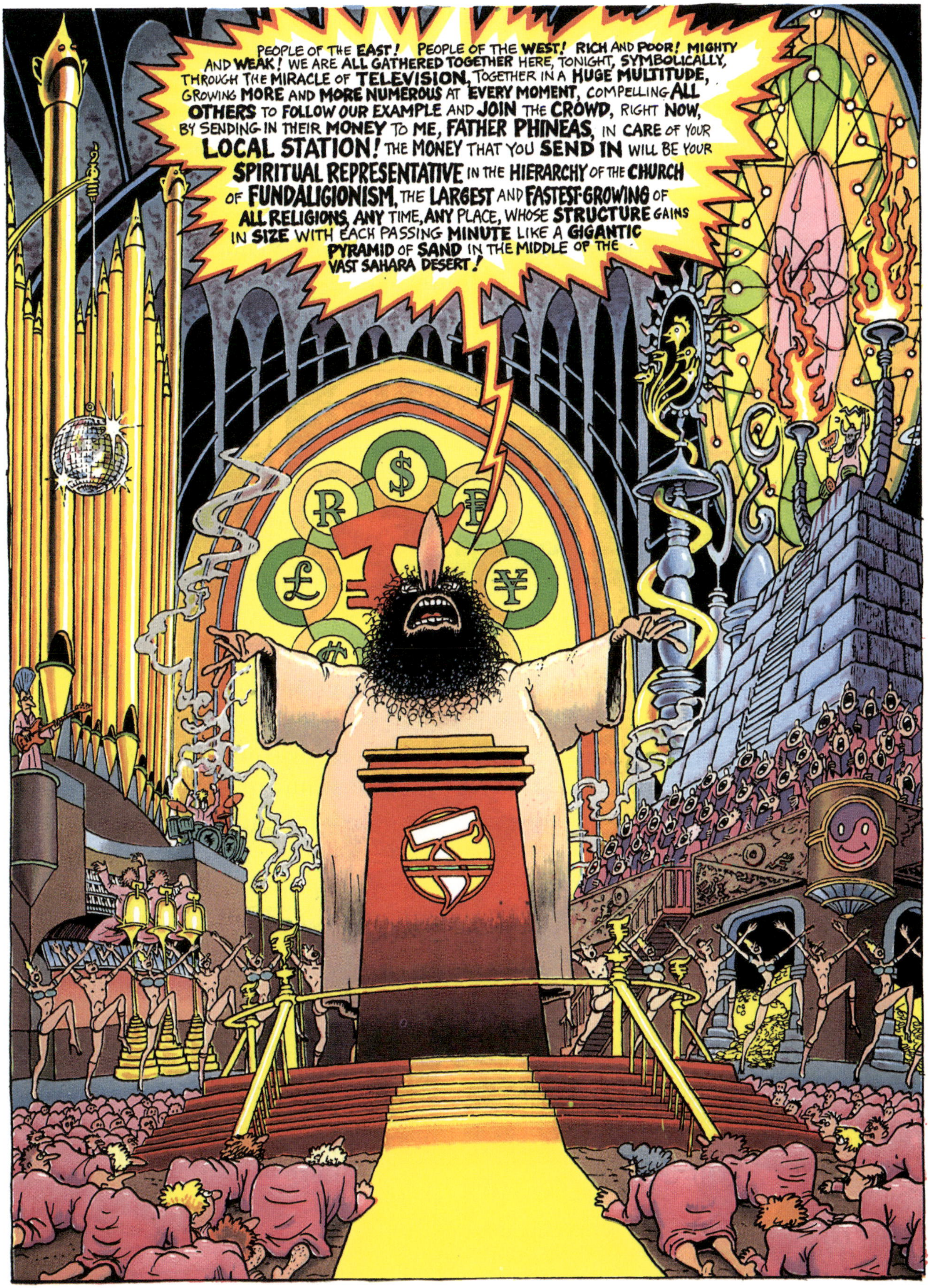
PEOPLE OF THE EAST! PEOPLE OF THE WEST! RICH AND POOR! MIGHTY AND WEAK! WE ARE ALL GATHERED TOGETHER HERE, TONIGHT, SYMBOLICALLY, THROUGH THE MIRACLE OF TELEVISION, TOGETHER IN A HUGE MULTITUDE, GROWING MORE AND MORE NUMEROUS AT EVERY MOMENT, COMPELLING ALL OTHERS TO FOLLOW OUR EXAMPLE AND JOIN THE CROWD, RIGHT NOW, BY SENDING IN THEIR MONEY TO ME, FATHER PHINEAS, IN CARE OF YOUR LOCAL STATION! THE MONEY THAT YOU SEND IN WILL BE YOUR SPIRITUAL REPRESENTATIVE IN THE HIERARCHY OF THE CHURCH OF FUNDALIGIONISM, THE LARGEST AND FASTEST-GROWING OF ALL RELIGIONS, ANY TIME, ANY PLACE, WHOSE STRUCTURE GAINS IN SIZE WITH EACH PASSING MINUTE LIKE A GIGANTIC PYRAMID OF SAND IN THE MIDDLE OF THE VAST SAHARA DESERT!

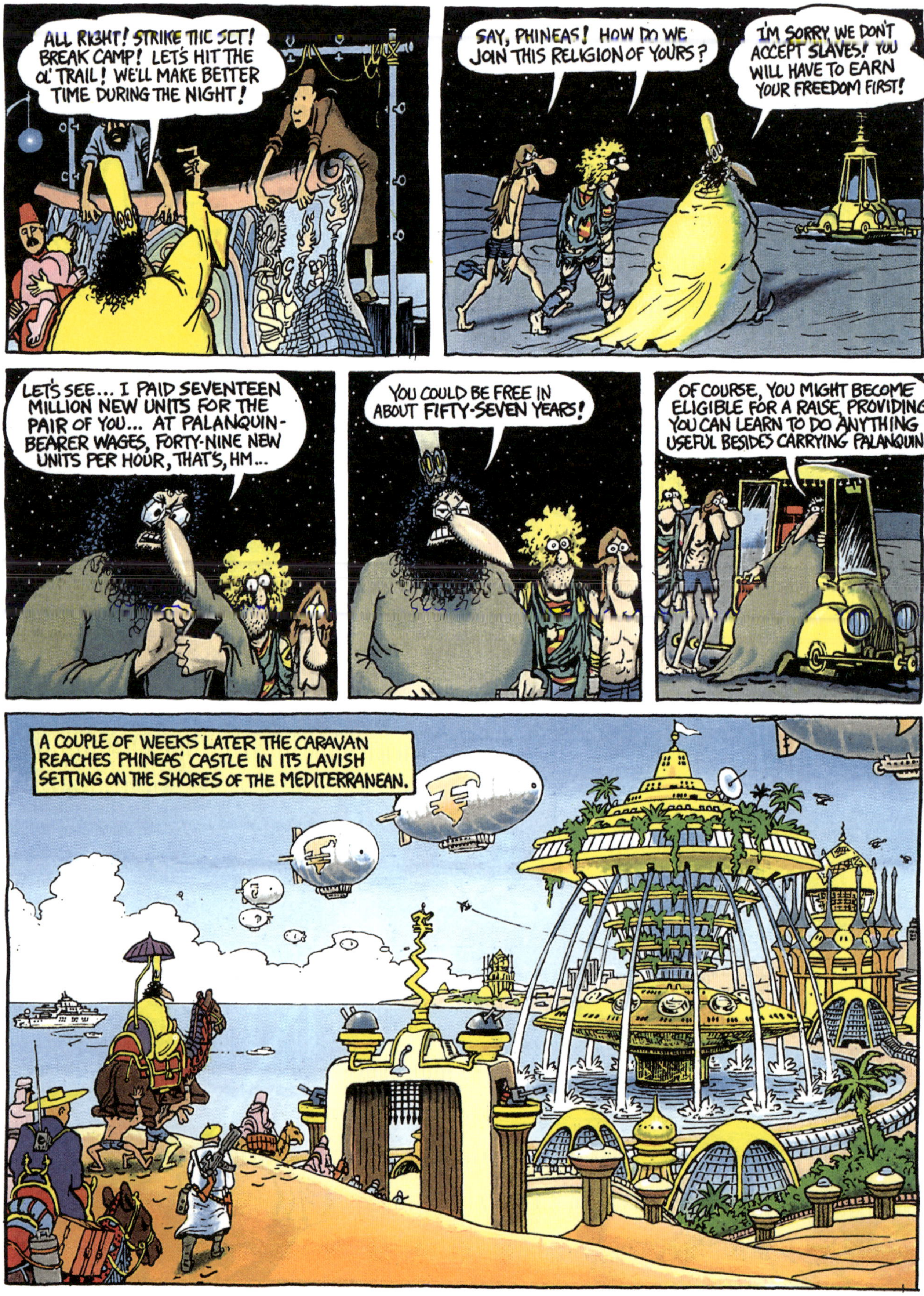
ALL RIGHT! STRIKE THE SET! BREAK CAMP! LET'S HIT THE OL' TRAIL! WE'LL MAKE BETTER TIME DURING THE NIGHT!
SAY, PHINEAS! HOW DO WE JOIN THIS RELIGION OF YOURS?
I'M SORRY, WE DON'T ACCEPT SLAVES! YOU WILL HAVE TO EARN YOUR FREEDOM FIRST!
LET'S SEE... I PAID SEVENTEEN MILLION NEW UNITS FOR THE PAIR OF YOU... AT PALANQUIN-BEARER WAGES, FORTY-NINE NEW UNITS PER HOUR, THAT'S, HM...
YOU COULD BE FREE IN ABOUT FIFTY-SEVEN YEARS!
OF COURSE, YOU MIGHT BECOME ELIGIBLE FOR A RAISE, PROVIDING YOU CAN LEARN TO DO ANYTHING USEFUL BESIDES CARRYING PALANQUINS!
A COUPLE OF WEEKS LATER THE CARAVAN REACHES PHINEAS' CASTLE IN ITS LAVISH SETTING ON THE SHORES OF THE MEDITERRANEAN.

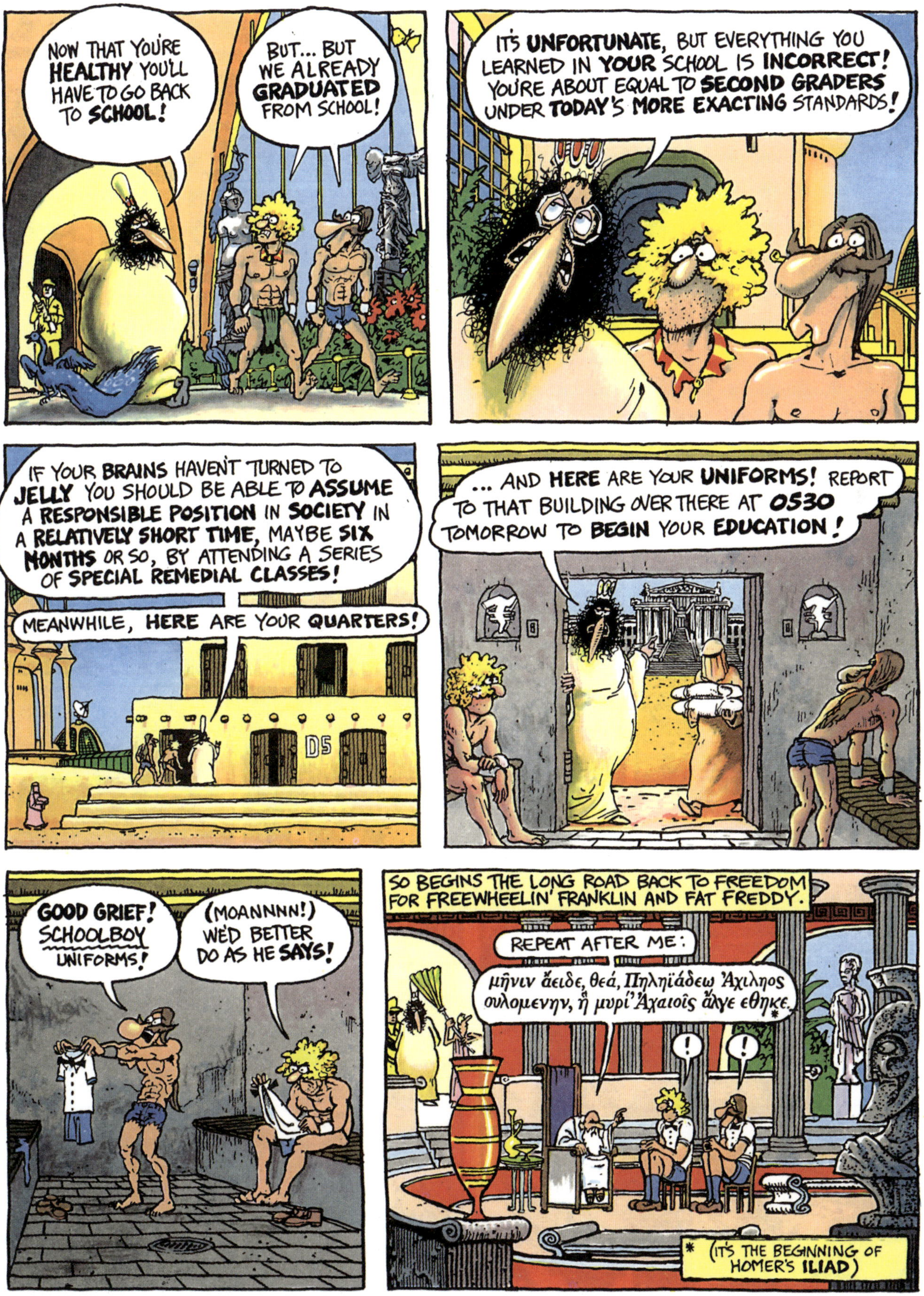
NOW THAT YOU'RE HEALTHY YOU'LL HAVE TO GO BACK TO SCHOOL!
BUT... BUT WE ALREADY GRADUATED FROM SCHOOL!
IT'S UNFORTUNATE, BUT EVERYTHING YOU LEARNED IN YOUR SCHOOL IS INCORRECT! YOU'RE ABOUT EQUAL TO SECOND GRADERS UNDER TODAY'S MORE EXACTING STANDARDS!
IF YOUR BRAINS HAVEN'T TURNED TO JELLY YOU SHOULD BE ABLE TO ASSUME A RESPONSIBLE POSITION IN SOCIETY IN A RELATIVELY SHORT TIME, MAYBE SIX MONTHS OR SO, BY ATTENDING A SERIES OF SPECIAL REMEDIAL CLASSES!
MEANWHILE, HERE ARE YOUR QUARTERS!
D5
... AND HERE ARE YOUR UNIFORMS! REPORT TO THAT BUILDING OVER THERE AT 0530 TOMORROW TO BEGIN YOUR EDUCATION!
GOOD GRIEF! SCHOOLBOY UNIFORMS!
(MOANNNN!) WE'D BETTER DO AS HE SAYS!
SO BEGINS THE LONG ROAD BACK TO FREEDOM FOR FREEWHEELIN' FRANKLIN AND FAT FREDDY.
REPEAT AFTER ME:
μῆνιν ἄειδε, θεά, Πηληϊάδεω Ἀχιληος ουλομενην, ἣ μυρί' Ἀχαιοῖς ἄλγε εθηκε.*
!
!
* (IT'S THE BEGINNING OF HOMER'S ILIAD)

RELENTLESSLY THEY ARE FORCE-TAUGHT A CURRICULUM OF PHILOSOPHY, POETRY, RELIGIONS, HISTORY, LITERATURE, GEOLOGY, BIOLOGY, CHEMISTRY, PHYSICS, ASTRONOMY, AGRICULTURE AND MEDICINE.

THEIR BRAINS ARE FED WITH THE WORDS AND THOUGHTS OF CONFUCIUS AND MOHAMMED, PLATO AND ARISTOTLE, VIRGIL AND DANTE, NEWTON AND DESCARTES, CHAUCER, SHAKESPEARE, SWIFT, NIETZCHE, MARX, EINSTEIN AND SARTRE.

ALSO:

 SENECA
 MACHIAVELLI
 THE BUDDHA
 BACON
 SPINOZA

 SCHOPENHAUER
 VOLTAIRE
 JEFFERSON
 LEIBNIZ
 WM. JAMES

NOT TO MENTION:

 PYTHAGORAS
 ERASMUS
 ROUSSEAU
 GANDHI

AND, OF COURSE...
 PHINEAS

THEY ARE TAUGHT ALL THE IMPORTANT LANGUAGES OF THE WORLD, INCLUDING (BESIDES ENGLISH) CHINESE, HEBREW, GREEK, LATIN, FRENCH, GERMAN, SPANISH, PORTUGUESE, JAPANESE, RUSSIAN, ITALIAN, DUTCH, DANISH, HINDI & ARABIC.

YOU MUST ALSO BE FAMILIAR WITH THE ANCIENT LANGUAGES, SANSKRIT AND EGYPTIAN, AS SOURCES OF OUR OWN CULTURE! AND LANGUE D'OC AND GAELIC TO GUIDE US THROUGH THE MIDDLE AGES!

IT IS ALSO NECESSARY TO LEARN THE REST OF THE SCANDANAVIAN LANGUAGES, SWEDISH, NORWEGIAN, AND ICELANDIC, AS WELL AS THE FINNISH TONGUE AND ITS ONLY EUROPEAN RELATIVE, HUNGARIAN!

OTHER CRUCIAL LANGUAGES INCLUDE URDU, SINDHI, PUNJABI, BENGALI, PUSHTU, FARSI, VIETNAMESE, RUMANIAN, POLISH, THAI, SLOVENIAN, TURKISH, CATALAN, CZECH, CAMBODIAN, BULGARIAN, BURMESE AND POLYNESIAN!

AND THERE'S NO IGNORING TAGALOG, SERBO-CROATIAN, ARMENIAN, ALBANIAN, KOREAN, MALAY, LAOTIAN, BASQUE, WELSH, KURDISH, NEPALESE, MALTESE, LAPP, MONGOLIAN, INUIT, TIBETAN, NAVAJO, RUMANSCH, LATVIAN, BRETON, LITHUANIAN & FRISIAN!

YOU WILL NEED TO KNOW SWAHILI AND THE AFRICAN LANGUAGES MINA, MASSA, AMHARIC, SETSWANA, SOMALI, SANGO, SONGHAI, MALAGASY, IBO, BANTU, LINGALA AND DAGBANI, NOT TO MENTION AFRIKAANS, YIDDISH AND PIDGIN, PLUS THE UNIVERSAL ESPERANTO!

THEN THERE'S DZONG-KHA AND KIKUYU AND YAQUI AND CHICHEWA AND FANTI AND EWE AND CHIPPEWA AND FANG AND BUBI AND TWI AND GA AND BALUCHI AND MAYAN AND BASSA AND EWONDO AND BARASA AND SINDEBELE AND OUDDAI AND KABYE AND GORANE AND ORIYA AND ISHILUBA AND COTOCOLI AND...

THEY LEARN MATHEMATICS AND CALCULUS, ENGINEERING AND DESIGN, COMPUTER SKILLS, LOGIC, RHETORIC, GRAMMAR AND LINGUISTICS, CIPHERING, CRYPTOLOGY AND PUBLIC RELATIONS.

SPORTS ARE NOT NEGLECTED: INCLUDED IN THE ACADEMIC SCHEDULE ARE EQUESTRIAN SKILLS, SAILING, SCUBADIVING, MOUNTAIN CLIMBING, FLYING, MOTORCYCLE ICE-RACING, AND MARTIAL ARTS.

EQUESTRIAN? IT MEANS "ON HORSEBACK"!
OHH!

...AND MORE MARTIAL ARTS.

TO INSURE THAT THEIR CHARACTERS WILL BE WELL-ROUNDED THEY ALSO TAKE LESSONS IN MUSIC, ART, DANCE, AND DRAMA, AS WELL AS COOKING CLASSES, FOLLOWED BY COURSES IN WINE APPRECIATION AND ORCHID GROWING.

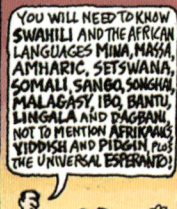

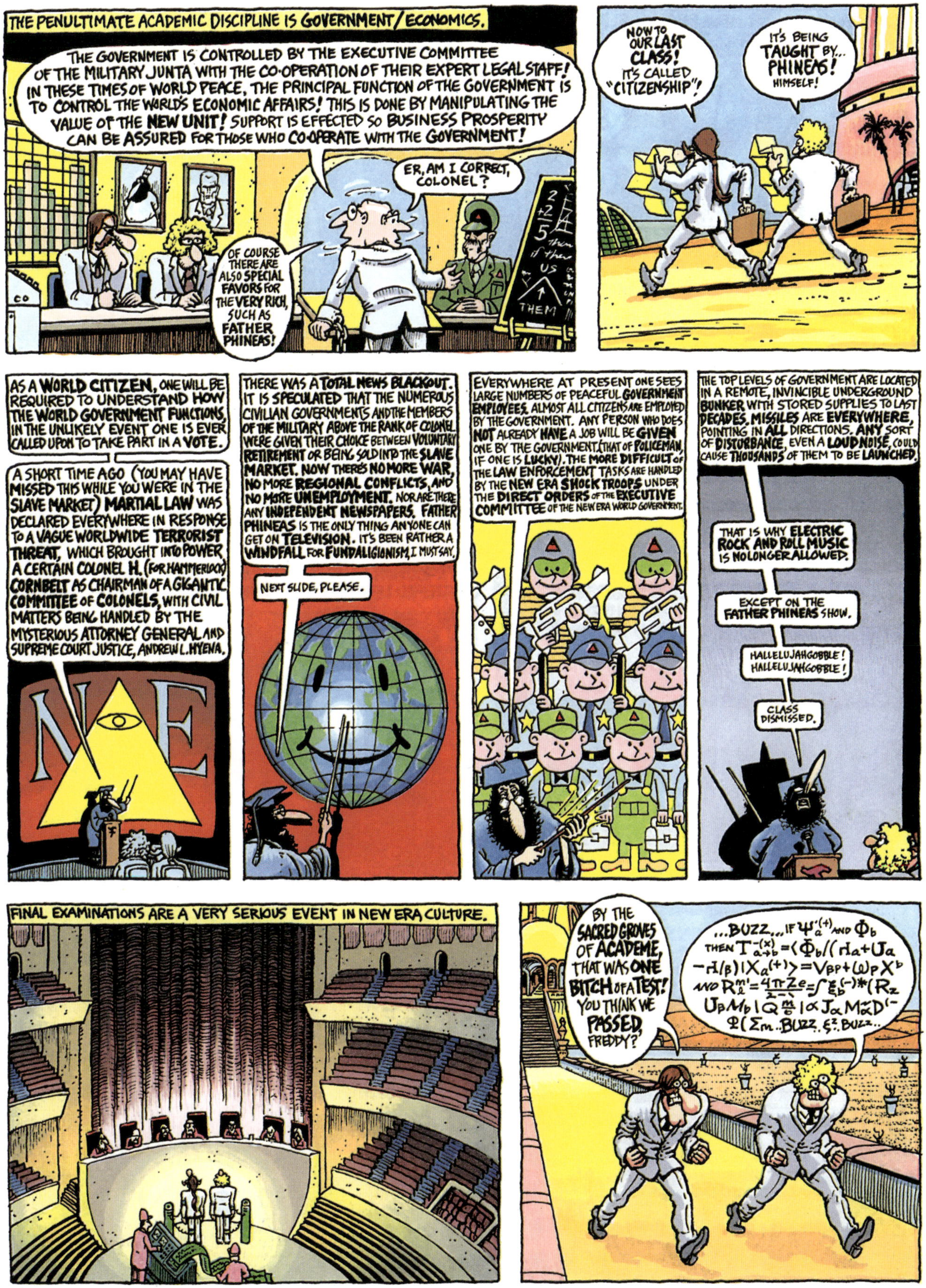
THE PENULTIMATE ACADEMIC DISCIPLINE IS GOVERNMENT/ECONOMICS.
THE GOVERNMENT IS CONTROLLED BY THE EXECUTIVE COMMITTEE OF THE MILITARY JUNTA WITH THE CO-OPERATION OF THEIR EXPERT LEGAL STAFF! IN THESE TIMES OF WORLD PEACE, THE PRINCIPAL FUNCTION OF THE GOVERNMENT IS TO CONTROL THE WORLD'S ECONOMIC AFFAIRS! THIS IS DONE BY MANIPULATING THE VALUE OF THE NEW UNIT! SUPPORT IS EFFECTED SO BUSINESS PROSPERITY CAN BE ASSURED FOR THOSE WHO CO-OPERATE WITH THE GOVERNMENT!
ER, AM I CORRECT, COLONEL?
OF COURSE THERE ARE ALSO SPECIAL FAVORS FOR THE VERY RICH, SUCH AS FATHER PHINEAS!
NOW TO OUR LAST CLASS! IT'S CALLED "CITIZENSHIP"!
IT'S BEING TAUGHT BY... PHINEAS! HIMSELF!
AS A WORLD CITIZEN, ONE WILL BE REQUIRED TO UNDERSTAND HOW THE WORLD GOVERNMENT FUNCTIONS, IN THE UNLIKELY EVENT ONE IS EVER CALLED UPON TO TAKE PART IN A VOTE.
A SHORT TIME AGO (YOU MAY HAVE MISSED THIS WHILE YOU WERE IN THE SLAVE MARKET) MARTIAL LAW WAS DECLARED EVERYWHERE IN RESPONSE TO A VAGUE WORLDWIDE TERRORIST THREAT, WHICH BROUGHT INTO POWER A CERTAIN COLONEL H. (FOR HAMMERLOCK) CORNBELT AS CHAIRMAN OF A GIGANTIC COMMITTEE OF COLONELS, WITH CIVIL MATTERS BEING HANDLED BY THE MYSTERIOUS ATTORNEY GENERAL AND SUPREME COURT JUSTICE, ANDREW L. HYENA.
NAE
THERE WAS A TOTAL NEWS BLACKOUT. IT IS SPECULATED THAT THE NUMEROUS CIVILIAN GOVERNMENTS AND THE MEMBERS OF THE MILITARY ABOVE THE RANK OF COLONEL WERE GIVEN THEIR CHOICE BETWEEN VOLUNTARY RETIREMENT OR BEING SOLD INTO THE SLAVE MARKET. NOW THERE'S NO MORE WAR, NO MORE REGIONAL CONFLICTS, AND NO MORE UNEMPLOYMENT. NOR ARE THERE ANY INDEPENDENT NEWSPAPERS. FATHER PHINEAS IS THE ONLY THING ANYONE CAN GET ON TELEVISION. IT'S BEEN RATHER A WINDFALL FOR FUNDALIGIONISM, I MUST SAY.
NEXT SLIDE, PLEASE.
EVERYWHERE AT PRESENT ONE SEES LARGE NUMBERS OF PEACEFUL GOVERNMENT EMPLOYEES. ALMOST ALL CITIZENS ARE EMPLOYED BY THE GOVERNMENT. ANY PERSON WHO DOES NOT ALREADY HAVE A JOB WILL BE GIVEN ONE BY THE GOVERNMENT (THAT OF POLICEMAN, IF ONE IS LUCKY). THE MORE DIFFICULT OF THE LAW ENFORCEMENT TASKS ARE HANDLED BY THE NEW ERA SHOCK TROOPS UNDER THE DIRECT ORDERS OF THE EXECUTIVE COMMITTEE OF THE NEW ERA WORLD GOVERNMENT.
THE TOP LEVELS OF GOVERNMENT ARE LOCATED IN A REMOTE, INVINCIBLE UNDERGROUND BUNKER WITH STORED SUPPLIES TO LAST DECADES. MISSILES ARE EVERYWHERE, POINTING IN ALL DIRECTIONS. ANY SORT OF DISTURBANCE, EVEN A LOUD NOISE, COULD CAUSE THOUSANDS OF THEM TO BE LAUNCHED.
THAT IS WHY ELECTRIC ROCK AND ROLL MUSIC IS NO LONGER ALLOWED.
EXCEPT ON THE FATHER PHINEAS SHOW.
HALLELUJAHGOBBLE! HALLELUJAHGOBBLE!
CLASS DISMISSED.
FINAL EXAMINATIONS ARE A VERY SERIOUS EVENT IN NEW ERA CULTURE.
BY THE SACRED GROVES OF ACADEME, THAT WAS ONE BITCH OF A TEST! YOU THINK WE PASSED, FREDDY?
...BUZZ... IF
BUZZ.. BUZZ..

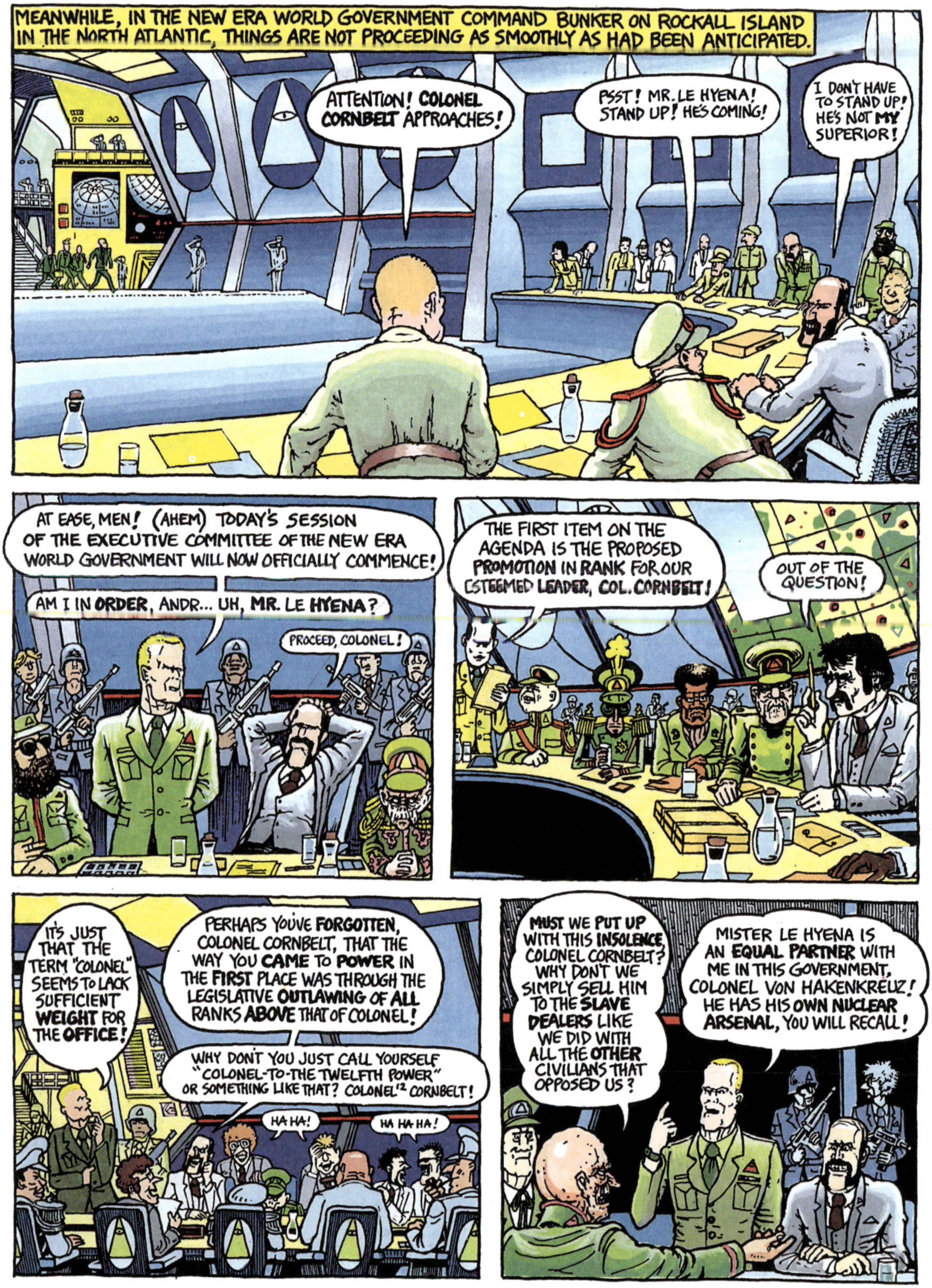

MEANWHILE, IN THE NEW ERA WORLD GOVERNMENT COMMAND BUNKER ON ROCKALL ISLAND IN THE NORTH ATLANTIC, THINGS ARE NOT PROCEEDING AS SMOOTHLY AS HAD BEEN ANTICIPATED.
ATTENTION! COLONEL CORNBELT APPROACHES!
PSST! MR. LE HYENA! STAND UP! HE'S COMING!
I DON'T HAVE TO STAND UP! HE'S NOT MY SUPERIOR!
AT EASE, MEN! (AHEM) TODAY'S SESSION OF THE EXECUTIVE COMMITTEE OF THE NEW ERA WORLD GOVERNMENT WILL NOW OFFICIALLY COMMENCE!
AM I IN ORDER, ANDR... UH, MR. LE HYENA?
PROCEED, COLONEL!
THE FIRST ITEM ON THE AGENDA IS THE PROPOSED PROMOTION IN RANK FOR OUR ESTEEMED LEADER, COL. CORNBELT!
OUT OF THE QUESTION!
IT'S JUST THAT THE TERM "COLONEL" SEEMS TO LACK SUFFICIENT WEIGHT FOR THE OFFICE!
PERHAPS YOU'VE FORGOTTEN, COLONEL CORNBELT, THAT THE WAY YOU CAME TO POWER IN THE FIRST PLACE WAS THROUGH THE LEGISLATIVE OUTLAWING OF ALL RANKS ABOVE THAT OF COLONEL!
WHY DON'T YOU JUST CALL YOURSELF "COLONEL-TO-THE TWELFTH POWER" OR SOMETHING LIKE THAT? COLONEL¹² CORNBELT!
HA HA!
HA HA HA!
MUST WE PUT UP WITH THIS INSOLENCE, COLONEL CORNBELT? WHY DON'T WE SIMPLY SELL HIM TO THE SLAVE DEALERS LIKE WE DID WITH ALL THE OTHER CIVILIANS THAT OPPOSED US?
MISTER LE HYENA IS AN EQUAL PARTNER WITH ME IN THIS GOVERNMENT, COLONEL VON HAKENKREUZ! HE HAS HIS OWN NUCLEAR ARSENAL, YOU WILL RECALL!

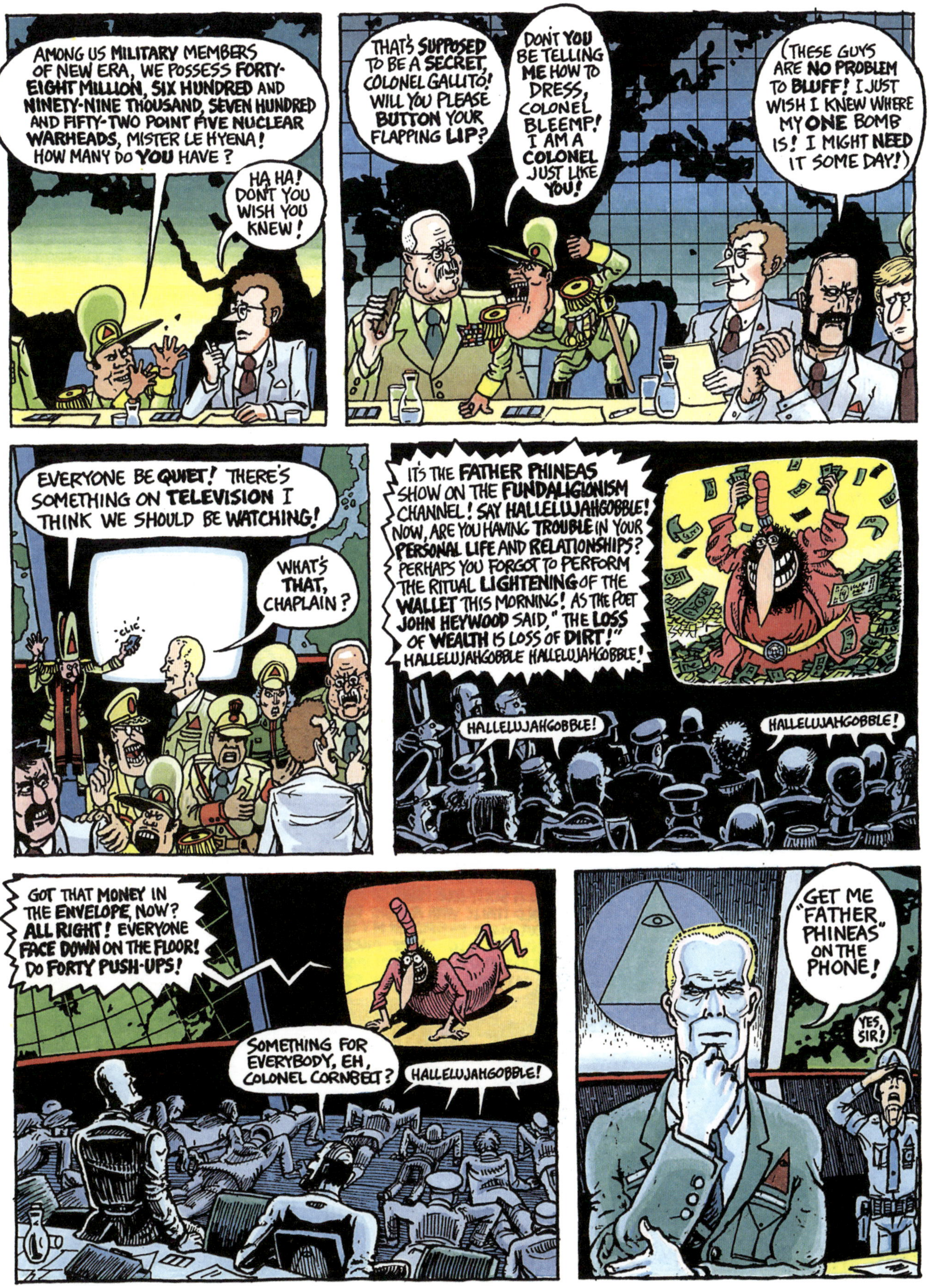
AMONG US MILITARY MEMBERS OF NEW ERA, WE POSSESS FORTY-EIGHT MILLION, SIX HUNDRED AND NINETY-NINE THOUSAND, SEVEN HUNDRED AND FIFTY-TWO POINT FIVE NUCLEAR WARHEADS, MISTER LE HYENA! HOW MANY DO YOU HAVE?
HA HA! DON'T YOU WISH YOU KNEW!
THAT'S SUPPOSED TO BE A SECRET, COLONEL GALLITO! WILL YOU PLEASE BUTTON YOUR FLAPPING LIP?
DON'T YOU BE TELLING ME HOW TO DRESS, COLONEL BLEEMP! I AM A COLONEL JUST LIKE YOU!
(THESE GUYS ARE NO PROBLEM TO BLUFF! I JUST WISH I KNEW WHERE MY ONE BOMB IS! I MIGHT NEED IT SOME DAY!)
EVERYONE BE QUIET! THERE'S SOMETHING ON TELEVISION I THINK WE SHOULD BE WATCHING!
CLIC
WHAT'S THAT, CHAPLAIN?
IT'S THE FATHER PHINEAS SHOW ON THE FUNDALIGIONISM CHANNEL! SAY HALLELUJAHGOBBLE! NOW, ARE YOU HAVING TROUBLE IN YOUR PERSONAL LIFE AND RELATIONSHIPS? PERHAPS YOU FORGOT TO PERFORM THE RITUAL LIGHTENING OF THE WALLET THIS MORNING! AS THE POET JOHN HEYWOOD SAID, "THE LOSS OF WEALTH IS LOSS OF DIRT!" HALLELUJAHGOBBLE HALLELUJAHGOBBLE!
HALLELUJAHGOBBLE!
HALLELUJAHGOBBLE!
GOT THAT MONEY IN THE ENVELOPE, NOW? ALL RIGHT! EVERYONE FACE DOWN ON THE FLOOR! DO FORTY PUSH-UPS!
SOMETHING FOR EVERYBODY, EH, COLONEL CORNBELT?
HALLELUJAHGOBBLE!
GET ME "FATHER PHINEAS" ON THE PHONE!
YES, SIR!

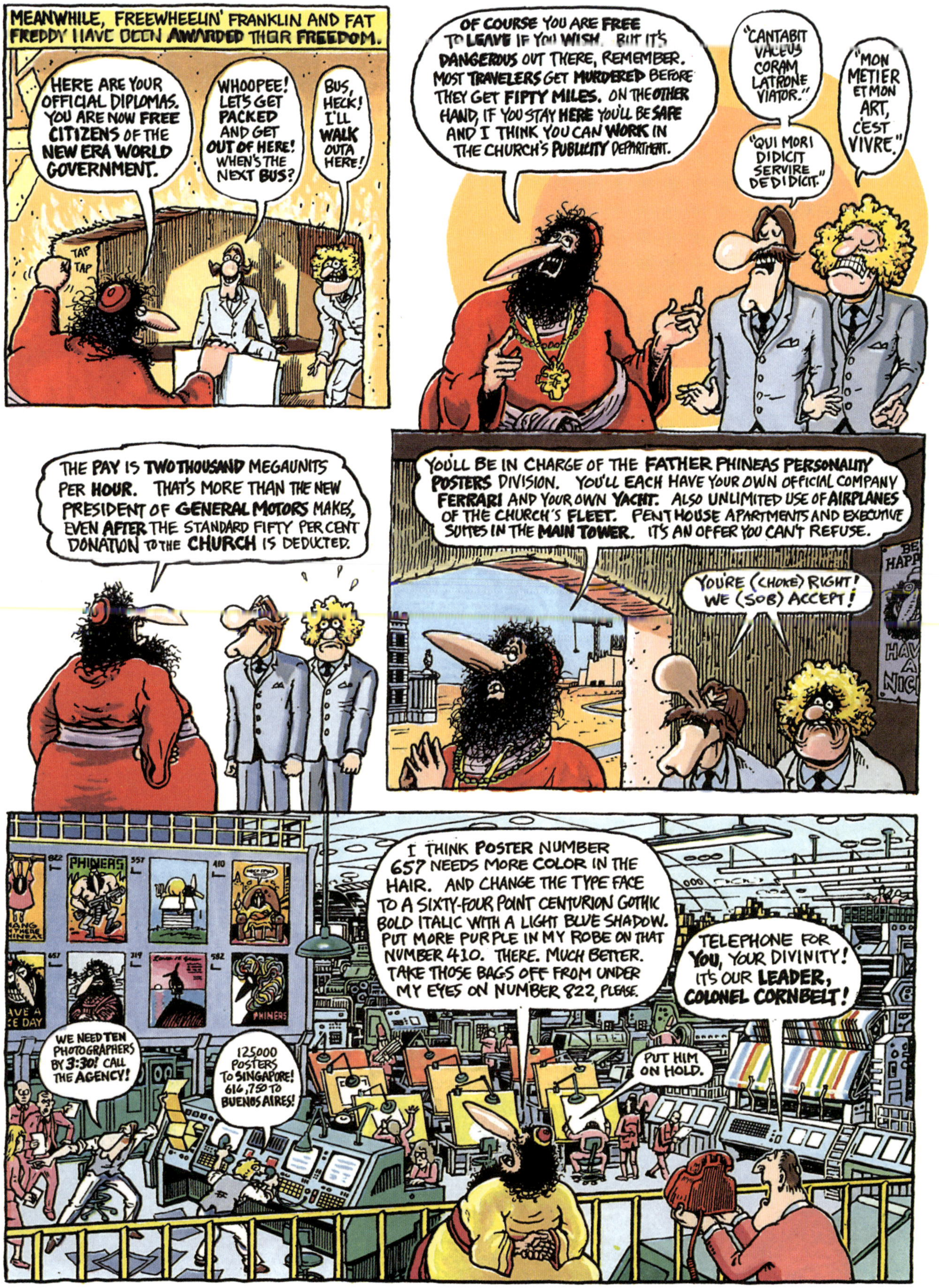
MEANWHILE, FREEWHEELIN' FRANKLIN AND FAT FREDDY HAVE BEEN AWARDED THEIR FREEDOM.
TAP TAP
HERE ARE YOUR OFFICIAL DIPLOMAS. YOU ARE NOW FREE CITIZENS OF THE NEW ERA WORLD GOVERNMENT.
WHOOPEE! LET'S GET PACKED AND GET OUT OF HERE! WHEN'S THE NEXT BUS?
BUS, HECK! I'LL WALK OUTA HERE!
OF COURSE YOU ARE FREE TO LEAVE IF YOU WISH. BUT IT'S DANGEROUS OUT THERE, REMEMBER. MOST TRAVELERS GET MURDERED BEFORE THEY GET FIFTY MILES. ON THE OTHER HAND, IF YOU STAY HERE YOU'LL BE SAFE AND I THINK YOU CAN WORK IN THE CHURCH'S PUBLICITY DEPARTMENT.
"CANTABIT VACUUS CORAM LATRONE VIATOR."
"QUI MORI DIDICIT SERVIRE DEDIDICIT."
"MON METIER ET MON ART, C'EST VIVRE."
THE PAY IS TWO THOUSAND MEGAUNITS PER HOUR. THAT'S MORE THAN THE NEW PRESIDENT OF GENERAL MOTORS MAKES, EVEN AFTER THE STANDARD FIFTY PER CENT DONATION TO THE CHURCH IS DEDUCTED.
YOU'LL BE IN CHARGE OF THE FATHER PHINEAS PERSONALITY POSTERS DIVISION. YOU'LL EACH HAVE YOUR OWN OFFICIAL COMPANY FERRARI AND YOUR OWN YACHT. ALSO UNLIMITED USE OF AIRPLANES OF THE CHURCH'S FLEET. PENTHOUSE APARTMENTS AND EXECUTIVE SUITES IN THE MAIN TOWER. IT'S AN OFFER YOU CAN'T REFUSE.
YOU'RE (CHOKE) RIGHT! WE (SOB) ACCEPT!
I THINK POSTER NUMBER 657 NEEDS MORE COLOR IN THE HAIR. AND CHANGE THE TYPE FACE TO A SIXTY-FOUR POINT CENTURION GOTHIC BOLD ITALIC WITH A LIGHT BLUE SHADOW. PUT MORE PURPLE IN MY ROBE ON THAT NUMBER 410. THERE. MUCH BETTER. TAKE THOSE BAGS OFF FROM UNDER MY EYES ON NUMBER 822, PLEASE.
TELEPHONE FOR YOU, YOUR DIVINITY! IT'S OUR LEADER, COLONEL CORNBELT!
WE NEED TEN PHOTOGRAPHERS BY 3:30! CALL THE AGENCY!
125,000 POSTERS TO SINGAPORE! 616,750 TO BUENOS AIRES!
PUT HIM ON HOLD.

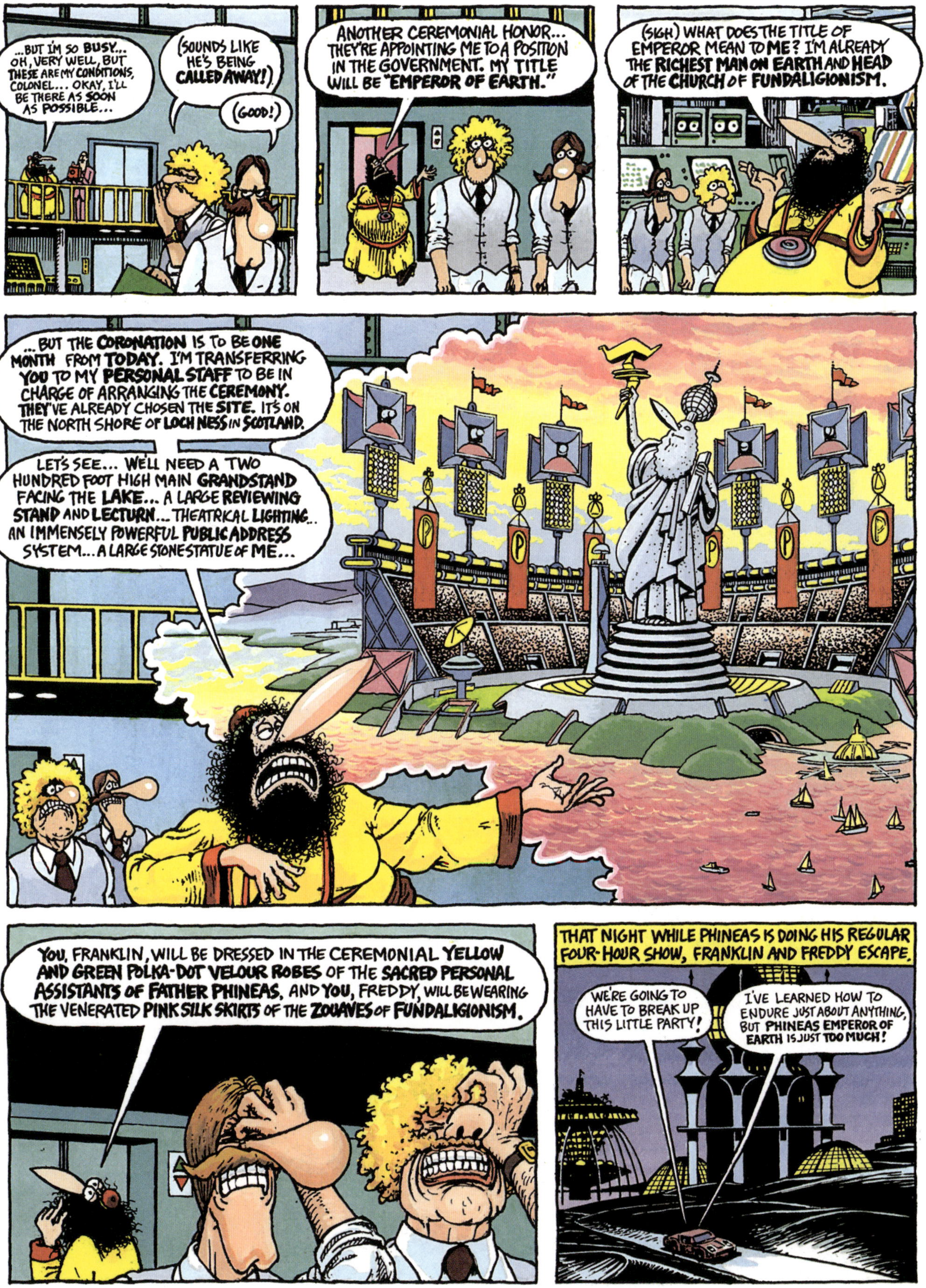
...BUT I'M SO BUSY... OH, VERY WELL, BUT THESE ARE MY CONDITIONS, COLONEL... OKAY, I'LL BE THERE AS SOON AS POSSIBLE...
(SOUNDS LIKE HE'S BEING CALLED AWAY!)
(GOOD!)
ANOTHER CEREMONIAL HONOR... THEY'RE APPOINTING ME TO A POSITION IN THE GOVERNMENT. MY TITLE WILL BE "EMPEROR OF EARTH."
(SIGH) WHAT DOES THE TITLE OF EMPEROR MEAN TO ME? I'M ALREADY THE RICHEST MAN ON EARTH AND HEAD OF THE CHURCH OF FUNDALIGIONISM.
...BUT THE CORONATION IS TO BE ONE MONTH FROM TODAY. I'M TRANSFERRING YOU TO MY PERSONAL STAFF TO BE IN CHARGE OF ARRANGING THE CEREMONY. THEY'VE ALREADY CHOSEN THE SITE. IT'S ON THE NORTH SHORE OF LOCH NESS IN SCOTLAND.
LET'S SEE... WE'LL NEED A TWO HUNDRED FOOT HIGH MAIN GRANDSTAND FACING THE LAKE... A LARGE REVIEWING STAND AND LECTURN... THEATRICAL LIGHTING.. AN IMMENSELY POWERFUL PUBLIC ADDRESS SYSTEM... A LARGE STONE STATUE OF ME...
YOU, FRANKLIN, WILL BE DRESSED IN THE CEREMONIAL YELLOW AND GREEN POLKA-DOT VELOUR ROBES OF THE SACRED PERSONAL ASSISTANTS OF FATHER PHINEAS, AND YOU, FREDDY, WILL BE WEARING THE VENERATED PINK SILK SKIRTS OF THE ZOUAVES OF FUNDALIGIONISM.
THAT NIGHT WHILE PHINEAS IS DOING HIS REGULAR FOUR-HOUR SHOW, FRANKLIN AND FREDDY ESCAPE.
WE'RE GOING TO HAVE TO BREAK UP THIS LITTLE PARTY!
I'VE LEARNED HOW TO ENDURE JUST ABOUT ANYTHING, BUT PHINEAS EMPEROR OF EARTH IS JUST TOO MUCH!

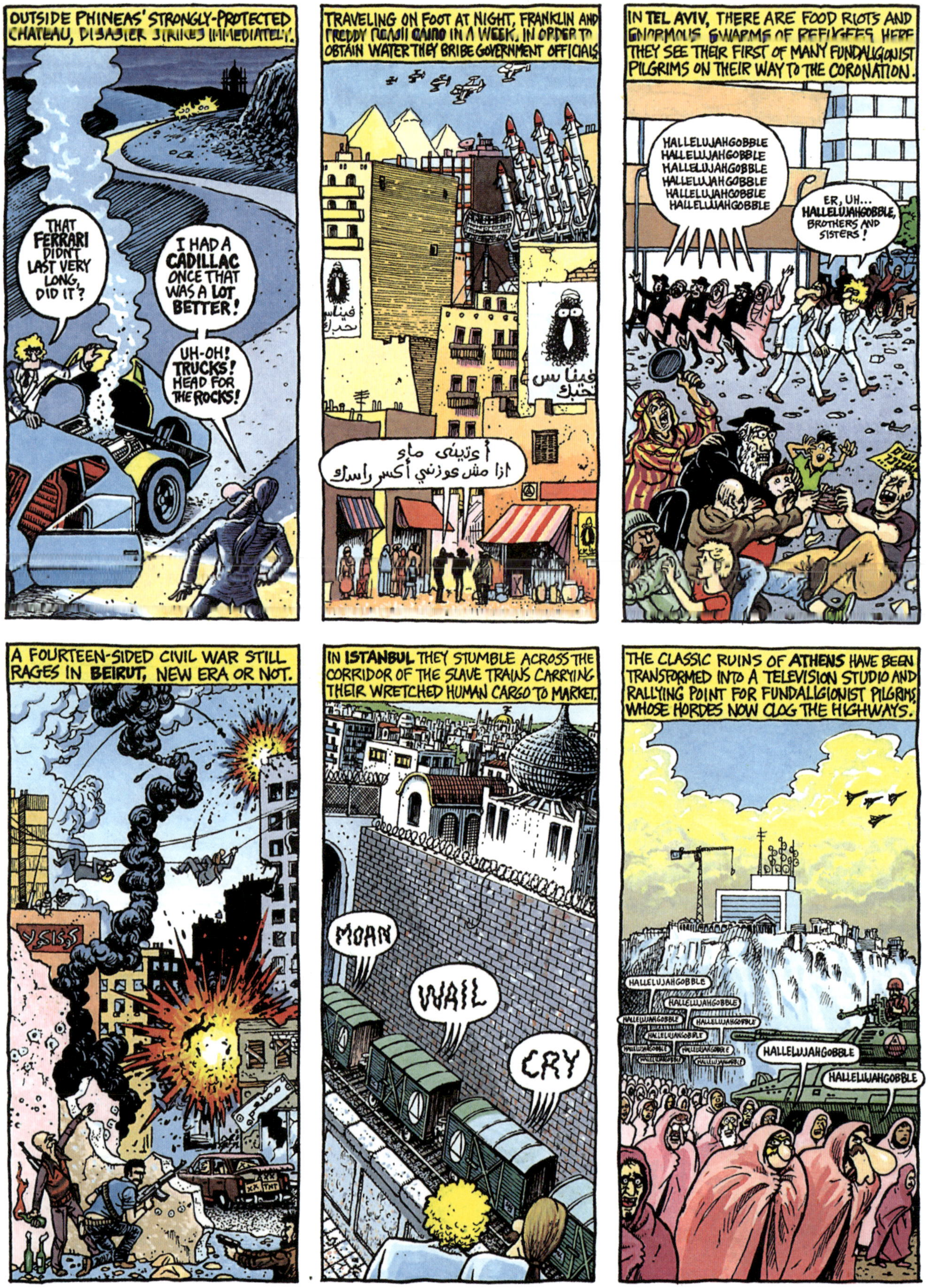
OUTSIDE PHINEAS' STRONGLY-PROTECTED CHATEAU, DISASTER STRIKES IMMEDIATELY.
THAT FERRARI DIDN'T LAST VERY LONG, DID IT?
I HAD A CADILLAC ONCE THAT WAS A LOT BETTER!
UH-OH! TRUCKS! HEAD FOR THE ROCKS!
TRAVELING ON FOOT AT NIGHT, FRANKLIN AND FREDDY REACH CAIRO IN A WEEK. IN ORDER TO OBTAIN WATER THEY BRIBE GOVERNMENT OFFICIALS
أوتيني ماء
ازا مش عوزني أكسر راسك
IN TEL AVIV, THERE ARE FOOD RIOTS AND ENORMOUS SWARMS OF REFUGEES. HERE THEY SEE THEIR FIRST OF MANY FUNDALIGONIST PILGRIMS ON THEIR WAY TO THE CORONATION.
HALLELUJAHGOBBLE HALLELUJAHGOBBLE HALLELUJAHGOBBLE HALLELUJAHGOBBLE HALLELUJAHGOBBLE HALLELUJAHGOBBLE
ER, UH... HALLELUJAHGOBBLE, BROTHERS AND SISTERS!
A FOURTEEN-SIDED CIVIL WAR STILL RAGES IN BEIRUT, NEW ERA OR NOT.
IN ISTANBUL THEY STUMBLE ACROSS THE CORRIDOR OF THE SLAVE TRAINS CARRYING THEIR WRETCHED HUMAN CARGO TO MARKET.
MOAN
WAIL
CRY
THE CLASSIC RUINS OF ATHENS HAVE BEEN TRANSFORMED INTO A TELEVISION STUDIO AND RALLYING POINT FOR FUNDALIGONIST PILGRIMS WHOSE HORDES NOW CLOG THE HIGHWAYS.
HALLELUJAHGOBBLE
HALLELUJAHGOBBLE
HALLELUJAHGOBBLE
HALLELUJAHGOBBLE

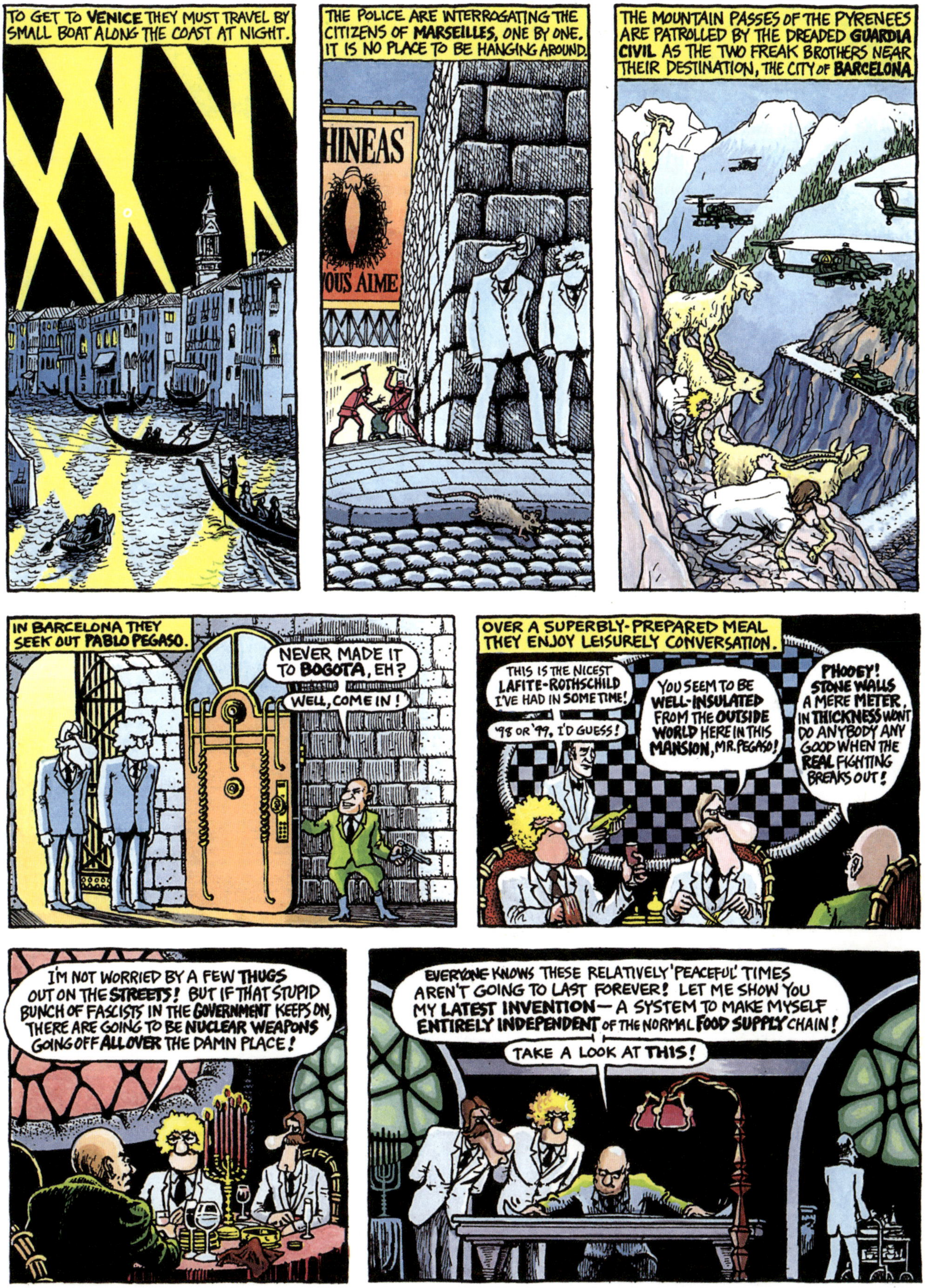
TO GET TO VENICE THEY MUST TRAVEL BY SMALL BOAT ALONG THE COAST AT NIGHT.
THE POLICE ARE INTERROGATING THE CITIZENS OF MARSEILLES, ONE BY ONE. IT IS NO PLACE TO BE HANGING AROUND.
THE MOUNTAIN PASSES OF THE PYRENEES ARE PATROLLED BY THE DREADED GUARDIA CIVIL AS THE TWO FREAK BROTHERS NEAR THEIR DESTINATION, THE CITY OF BARCELONA.
IN BARCELONA THEY SEEK OUT PABLO PEGASO.
NEVER MADE IT TO BOGOTA, EH?
WELL, COME IN!
OVER A SUPERBLY-PREPARED MEAL THEY ENJOY LEISURELY CONVERSATION.
THIS IS THE NICEST LAFITE-ROTHSCHILD I'VE HAD IN SOME TIME!
'98 OR '99, I'D GUESS!
YOU SEEM TO BE WELL-INSULATED FROM THE OUTSIDE WORLD HERE IN THIS MANSION, MR. PEGASO!
PHOOEY! STONE WALLS A MERE METER IN THICKNESS WON'T DO ANYBODY ANY GOOD WHEN THE REAL FIGHTING BREAKS OUT!
I'M NOT WORRIED BY A FEW THUGS OUT ON THE STREETS! BUT IF THAT STUPID BUNCH OF FASCISTS IN THE GOVERNMENT KEEPS ON, THERE ARE GOING TO BE NUCLEAR WEAPONS GOING OFF ALL OVER THE DAMN PLACE!
EVERYONE KNOWS THESE RELATIVELY 'PEACEFUL' TIMES AREN'T GOING TO LAST FOREVER! LET ME SHOW YOU MY LATEST INVENTION — A SYSTEM TO MAKE MYSELF ENTIRELY INDEPENDENT OF THE NORMAL FOOD SUPPLY CHAIN!
TAKE A LOOK AT THIS!

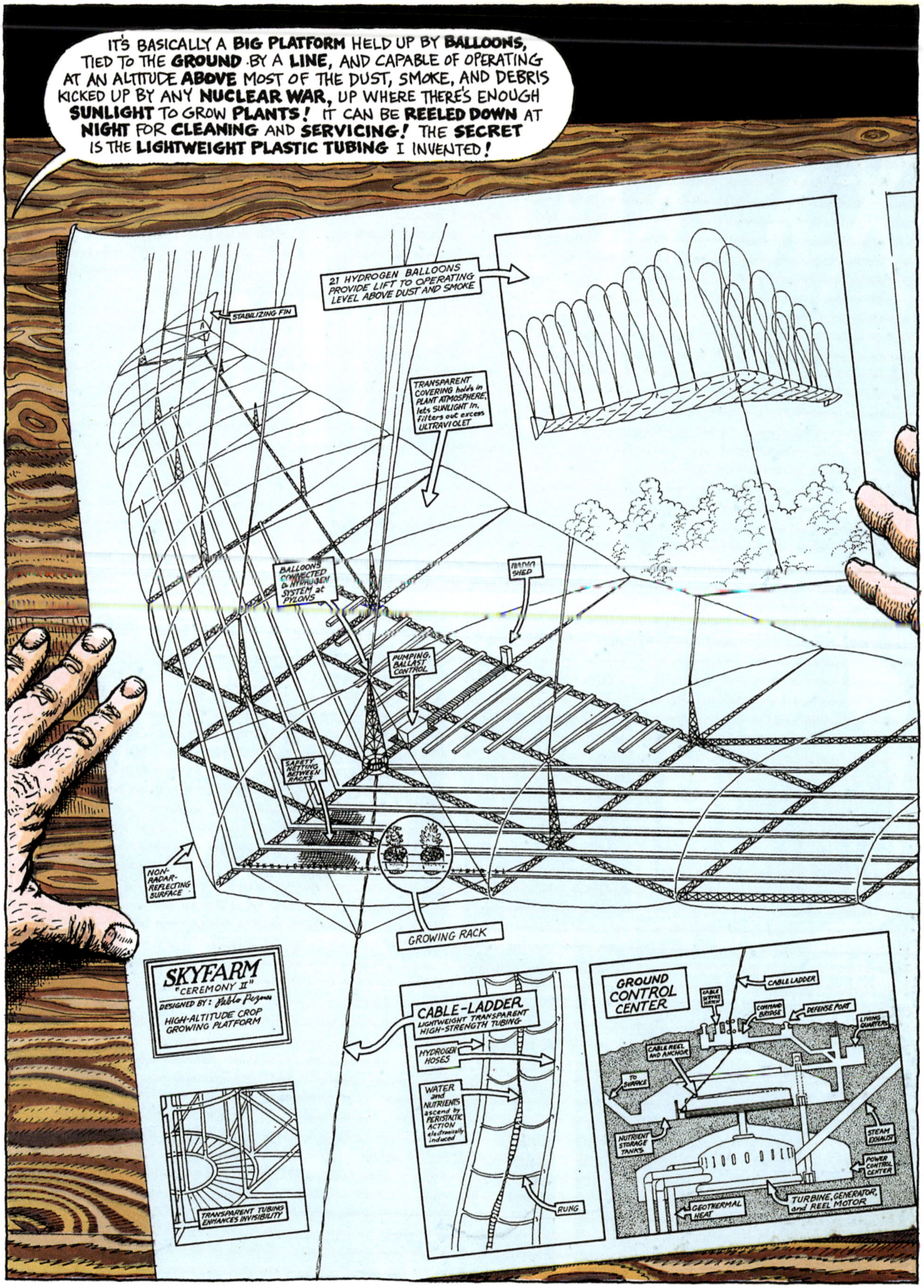
IT'S BASICALLY A BIG PLATFORM HELD UP BY BALLOONS, TIED TO THE GROUND BY A LINE, AND CAPABLE OF OPERATING AT AN ALTITUDE ABOVE MOST OF THE DUST, SMOKE, AND DEBRIS KICKED UP BY ANY NUCLEAR WAR, UP WHERE THERE'S ENOUGH SUNLIGHT TO GROW PLANTS! IT CAN BE REELED DOWN AT NIGHT FOR CLEANING AND SERVICING! THE SECRET IS THE LIGHTWEIGHT PLASTIC TUBING I INVENTED!
21 HYDROGEN BALLOONS PROVIDE LIFT TO OPERATING LEVEL ABOVE DUST AND SMOKE
STABILIZING FIN
TRANSPARENT COVERING holds in PLANT ATMOSPHERE, lets SUNLIGHT in, filters out excess ULTRAVIOLET
BALLOONS CONNECTED & HYDROGEN SYSTEM at PYLONS
RADIO SHED
PUMPING, BALLAST CONTROL
SAFETY NETTING BETWEEN RACKS
NON-RADAR-REFLECTING SURFACE
GROWING RACK
SKYFARM "CEREMONY II" DESIGNED BY: Pablo Pezones HIGH-ALTITUDE CROP GROWING PLATFORM
TRANSPARENT TUBING ENHANCES INVISIBILITY
CABLE-LADDER LIGHTWEIGHT TRANSPARENT HIGH-STRENGTH TUBING
HYDROGEN HOSES
WATER and NUTRIENTS ascend by PERISTALTIC ACTION electronically induced
RUNG
GROUND CONTROL CENTER
CABLE LADDER
COMMAND BRIDGE
DEFENSE PORT
LIVING QUARTERS
CABLE REEL AND ANCHOR
TO SURFACE
NUTRIENT STORAGE TANKS
STEAM EXHAUST
POWER CONTROL CENTER
TURBINE, GENERATOR, and REEL MOTOR
GEOTHERMAL HEAT

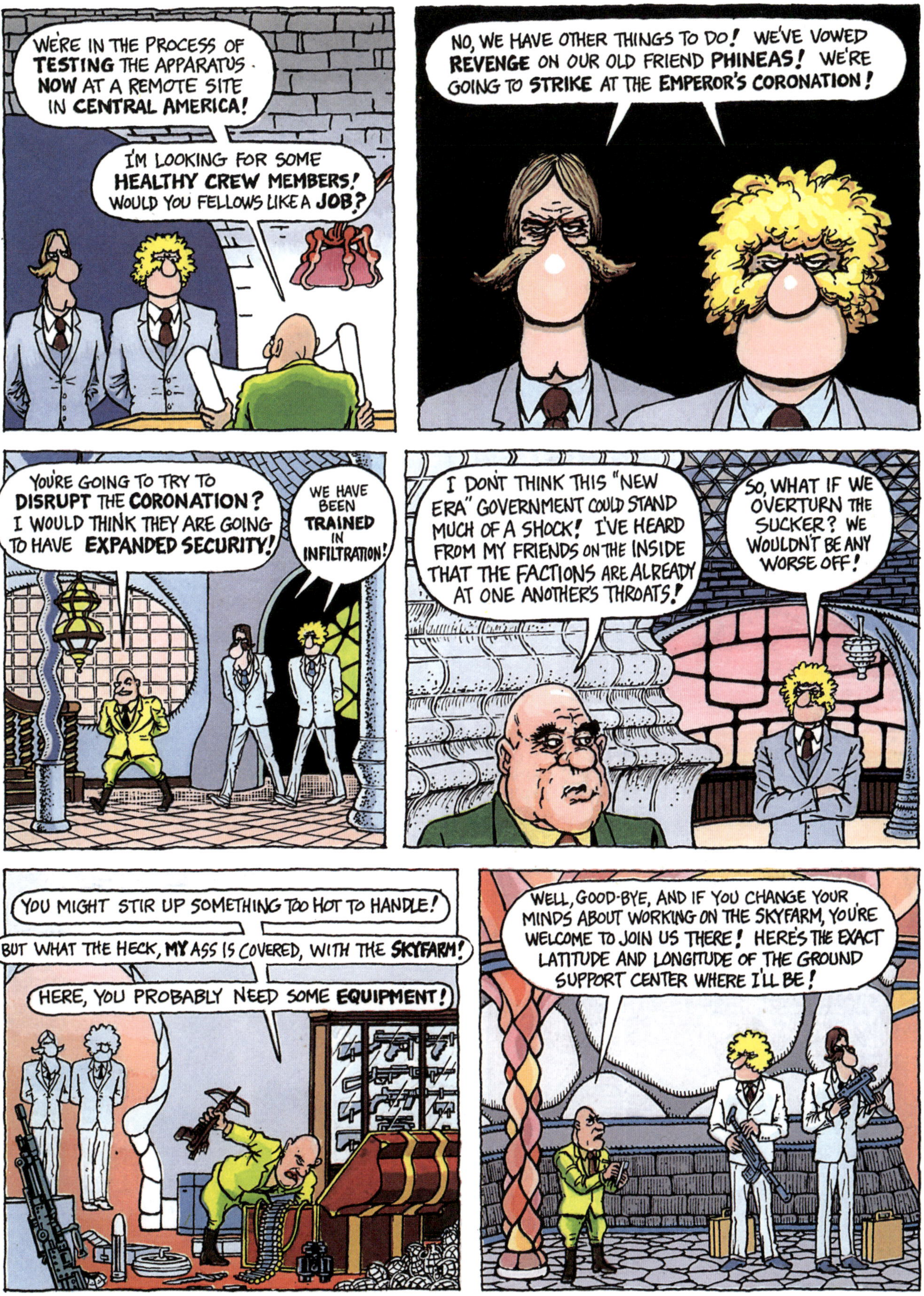
WE'RE IN THE PROCESS OF TESTING THE APPARATUS NOW AT A REMOTE SITE IN CENTRAL AMERICA!
I'M LOOKING FOR SOME HEALTHY CREW MEMBERS! WOULD YOU FELLOWS LIKE A JOB?
NO, WE HAVE OTHER THINGS TO DO! WE'VE VOWED REVENGE ON OUR OLD FRIEND PHINEAS! WE'RE GOING TO STRIKE AT THE EMPEROR'S CORONATION!
YOU'RE GOING TO TRY TO DISRUPT THE CORONATION? I WOULD THINK THEY ARE GOING TO HAVE EXPANDED SECURITY!
WE HAVE BEEN TRAINED IN INFILTRATION!
I DON'T THINK THIS "NEW ERA" GOVERNMENT COULD STAND MUCH OF A SHOCK! I'VE HEARD FROM MY FRIENDS ON THE INSIDE THAT THE FACTIONS ARE ALREADY AT ONE ANOTHER'S THROATS!
SO, WHAT IF WE OVERTURN THE SUCKER? WE WOULDN'T BE ANY WORSE OFF!
YOU MIGHT STIR UP SOMETHING TOO HOT TO HANDLE!
BUT WHAT THE HECK, MY ASS IS COVERED, WITH THE SKYFARM!
HERE, YOU PROBABLY NEED SOME EQUIPMENT!
WELL, GOOD-BYE, AND IF YOU CHANGE YOUR MINDS ABOUT WORKING ON THE SKYFARM, YOU'RE WELCOME TO JOIN US THERE! HERE'S THE EXACT LATITUDE AND LONGITUDE OF THE GROUND SUPPORT CENTER WHERE I'LL BE!

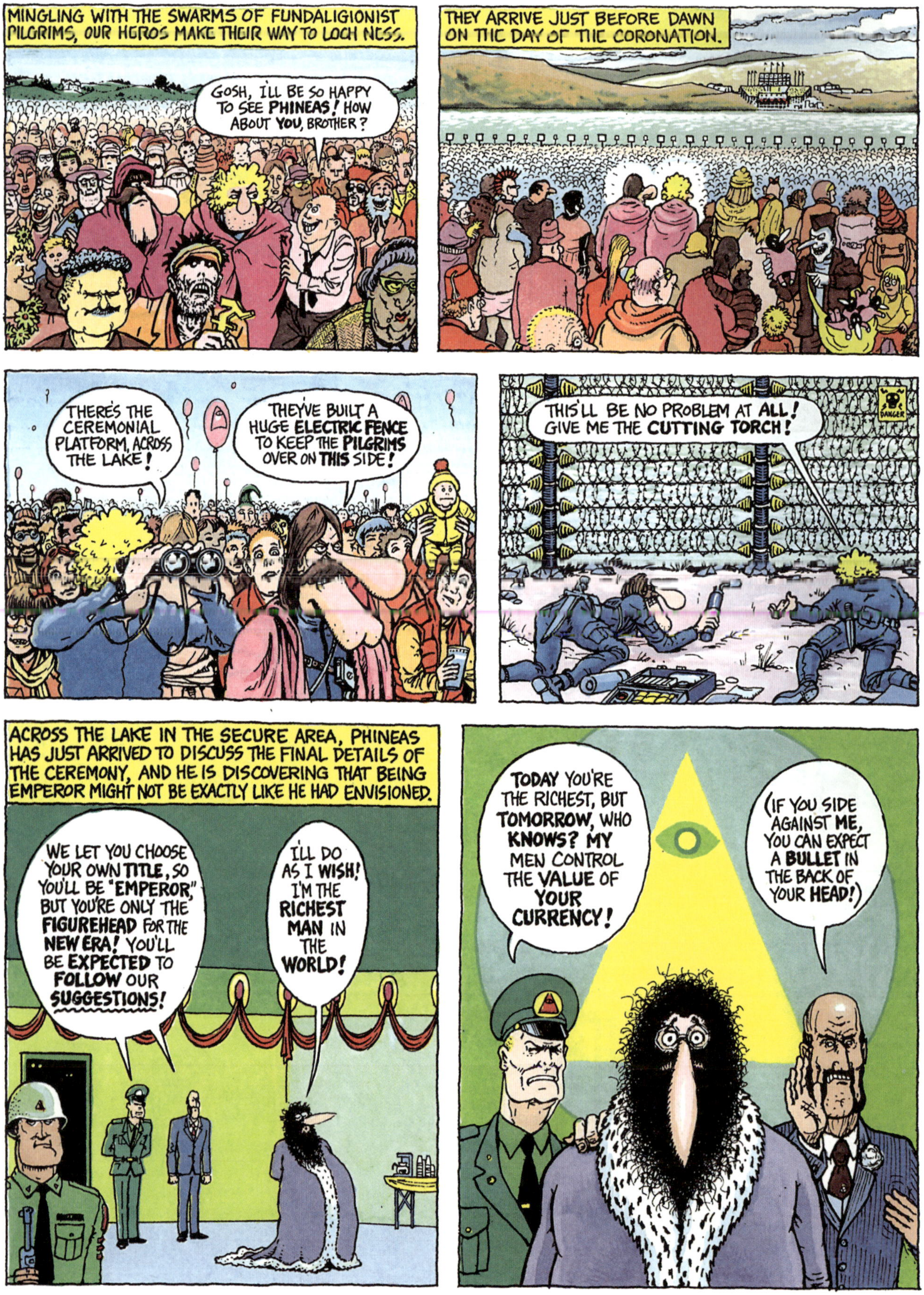
MINGLING WITH THE SWARMS OF FUNDALIGIONIST PILGRIMS, OUR HEROS MAKE THEIR WAY TO LOCH NESS.
GOSH, I'LL BE SO HAPPY TO SEE PHINEAS! HOW ABOUT YOU, BROTHER?
THEY ARRIVE JUST BEFORE DAWN ON THE DAY OF THE CORONATION.
THERE'S THE CEREMONIAL PLATFORM, ACROSS THE LAKE!
THEY'VE BUILT A HUGE ELECTRIC FENCE TO KEEP THE PILGRIMS OVER ON THIS SIDE!
THIS'LL BE NO PROBLEM AT ALL! GIVE ME THE CUTTING TORCH!
DANGER
ACROSS THE LAKE IN THE SECURE AREA, PHINEAS HAS JUST ARRIVED TO DISCUSS THE FINAL DETAILS OF THE CEREMONY, AND HE IS DISCOVERING THAT BEING EMPEROR MIGHT NOT BE EXACTLY LIKE HE HAD ENVISIONED.
WE LET YOU CHOOSE YOUR OWN TITLE, SO YOU'LL BE "EMPEROR," BUT YOU'RE ONLY THE FIGUREHEAD FOR THE NEW ERA! YOU'LL BE EXPECTED TO FOLLOW OUR SUGGESTIONS!
I'LL DO AS I WISH! I'M THE RICHEST MAN IN THE WORLD!
TODAY YOU'RE THE RICHEST, BUT TOMORROW, WHO KNOWS? MY MEN CONTROL THE VALUE OF YOUR CURRENCY!
(IF YOU SIDE AGAINST ME, YOU CAN EXPECT A BULLET IN THE BACK OF YOUR HEAD!)

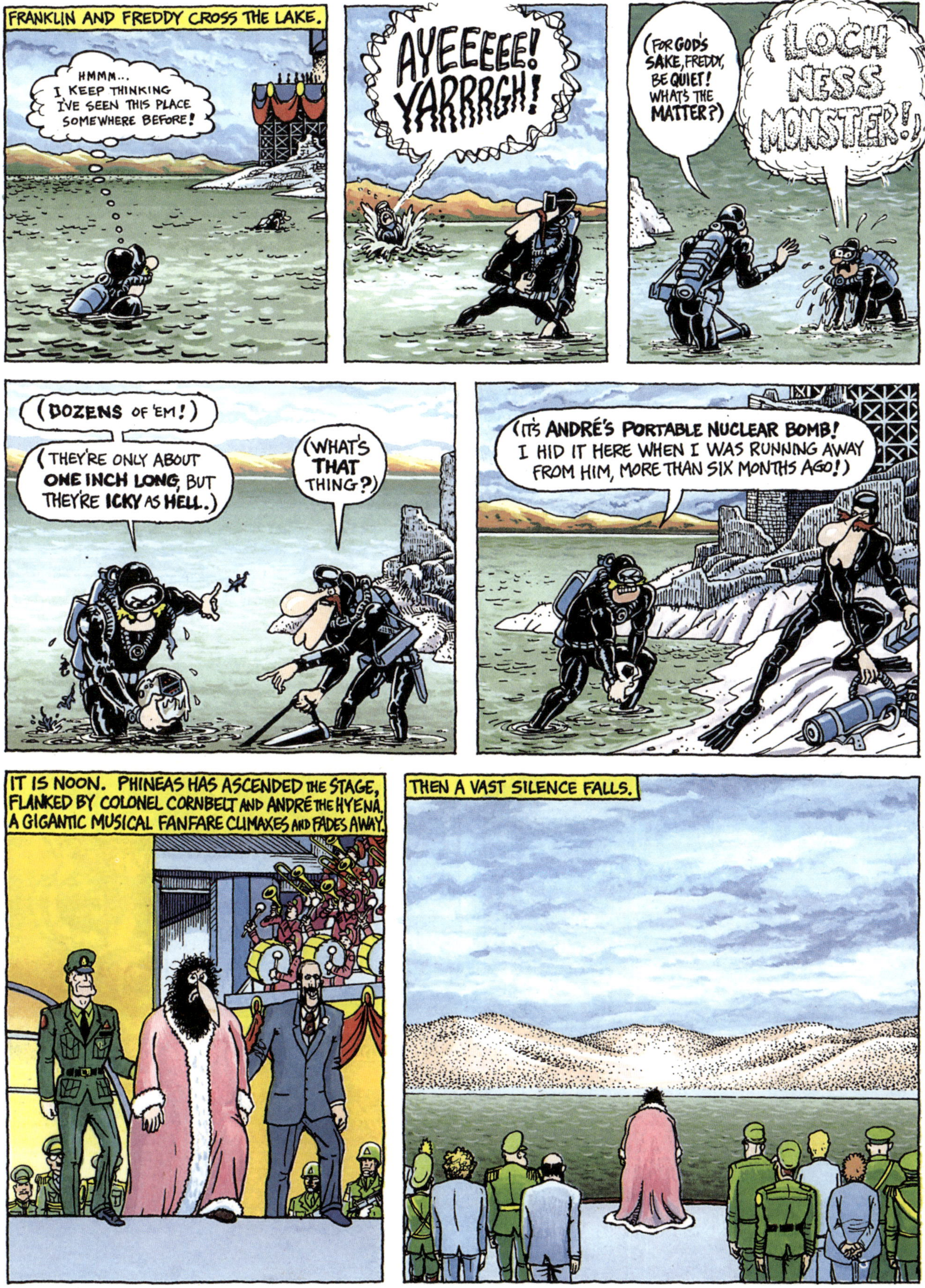
FRANKLIN AND FREDDY CROSS THE LAKE.
HMMM... I KEEP THINKING I'VE SEEN THIS PLACE SOMEWHERE BEFORE!
AYEEEEE! YARRRGH!
(FOR GOD'S SAKE, FREDDY, BE QUIET! WHAT'S THE MATTER?)
(LOCH NESS MONSTER!)
(DOZENS OF 'EM!)
(THEY'RE ONLY ABOUT ONE INCH LONG, BUT THEY'RE ICKY AS HELL.)
(WHAT'S THAT THING?)
(IT'S ANDRÉ'S PORTABLE NUCLEAR BOMB! I HID IT HERE WHEN I WAS RUNNING AWAY FROM HIM, MORE THAN SIX MONTHS AGO!)
IT IS NOON. PHINEAS HAS ASCENDED THE STAGE, FLANKED BY COLONEL CORNBELT AND ANDRÉ THE HYENA. A GIGANTIC MUSICAL FANFARE CLIMAXES AND FADES AWAY.
THEN A VAST SILENCE FALLS.

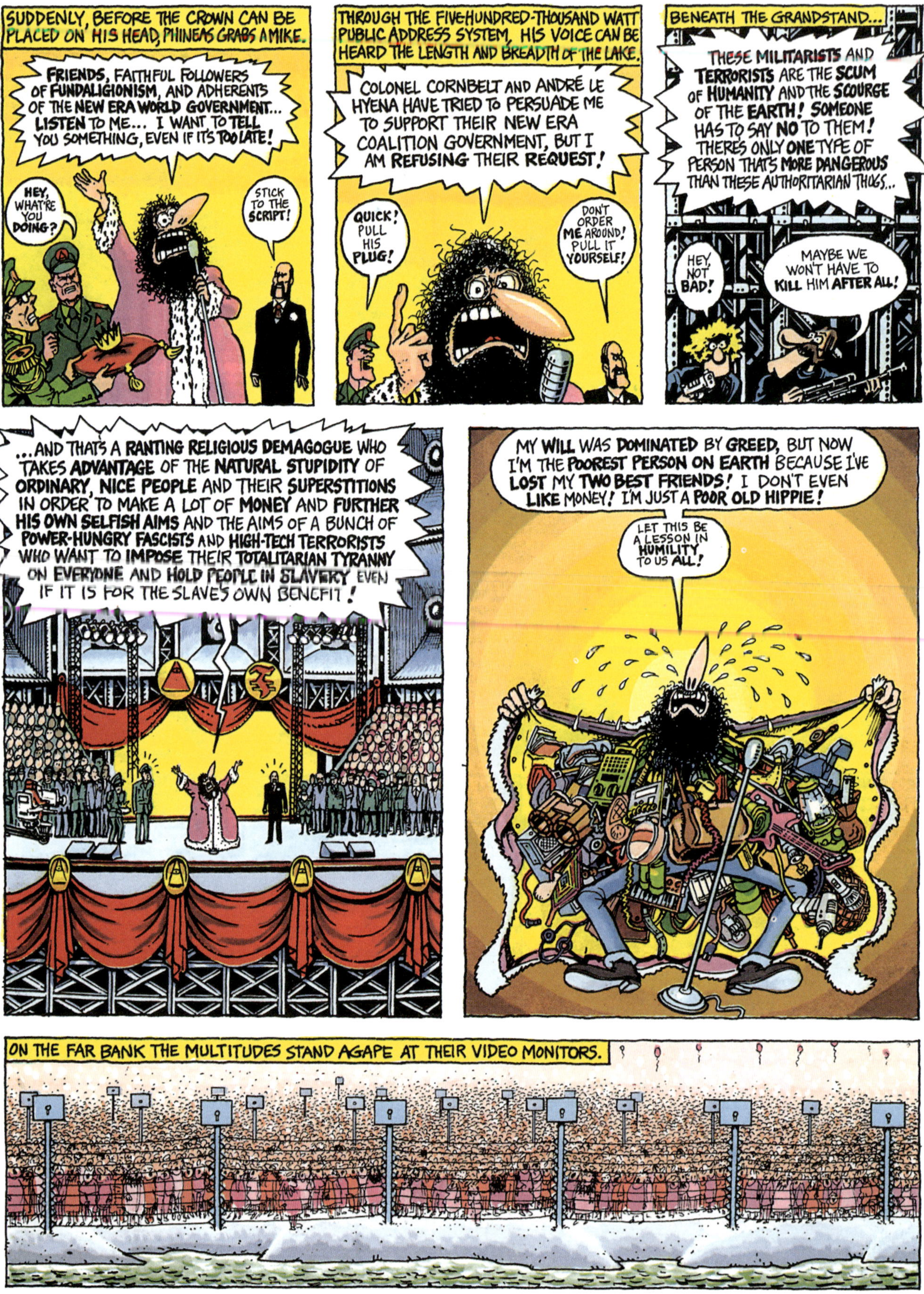
SUDDENLY, BEFORE THE CROWN CAN BE PLACED ON HIS HEAD, PHINEAS GRABS A MIKE.
FRIENDS, FAITHFUL FOLLOWERS OF FUNDALIGIONISM, AND ADHERENTS OF THE NEW ERA WORLD GOVERNMENT... LISTEN TO ME... I WANT TO TELL YOU SOMETHING, EVEN IF IT'S TOO LATE!
HEY, WHAT'RE YOU DOING?
STICK TO THE SCRIPT!
THROUGH THE FIVE-HUNDRED-THOUSAND WATT PUBLIC ADDRESS SYSTEM, HIS VOICE CAN BE HEARD THE LENGTH AND BREADTH OF THE LAKE.
COLONEL CORNBELT AND ANDRÉ LE HYENA HAVE TRIED TO PERSUADE ME TO SUPPORT THEIR NEW ERA COALITION GOVERNMENT, BUT I AM REFUSING THEIR REQUEST!
QUICK! PULL HIS PLUG!
DON'T ORDER ME AROUND! PULL IT YOURSELF!
BENEATH THE GRANDSTAND...
THESE MILITARISTS AND TERRORISTS ARE THE SCUM OF HUMANITY AND THE SCOURGE OF THE EARTH! SOMEONE HAS TO SAY NO TO THEM! THERE'S ONLY ONE TYPE OF PERSON THAT'S MORE DANGEROUS THAN THESE AUTHORITARIAN THUGS...
HEY, NOT BAD!
MAYBE WE WON'T HAVE TO KILL HIM AFTER ALL!
...AND THAT'S A RANTING RELIGIOUS DEMAGOGUE WHO TAKES ADVANTAGE OF THE NATURAL STUPIDITY OF ORDINARY, NICE PEOPLE AND THEIR SUPERSTITIONS IN ORDER TO MAKE A LOT OF MONEY AND FURTHER HIS OWN SELFISH AIMS AND THE AIMS OF A BUNCH OF POWER-HUNGRY FASCISTS AND HIGH-TECH TERRORISTS WHO WANT TO IMPOSE THEIR TOTALITARIAN TYRANNY ON EVERYONE AND HOLD PEOPLE IN SLAVERY EVEN IF IT IS FOR THE SLAVE'S OWN BENEFIT!
MY WILL WAS DOMINATED BY GREED, BUT NOW I'M THE POOREST PERSON ON EARTH BECAUSE I'VE LOST MY TWO BEST FRIENDS! I DON'T EVEN LIKE MONEY! I'M JUST A POOR OLD HIPPIE!
LET THIS BE A LESSON IN HUMILITY TO US ALL!
ON THE FAR BANK THE MULTITUDES STAND AGAPE AT THEIR VIDEO MONITORS.

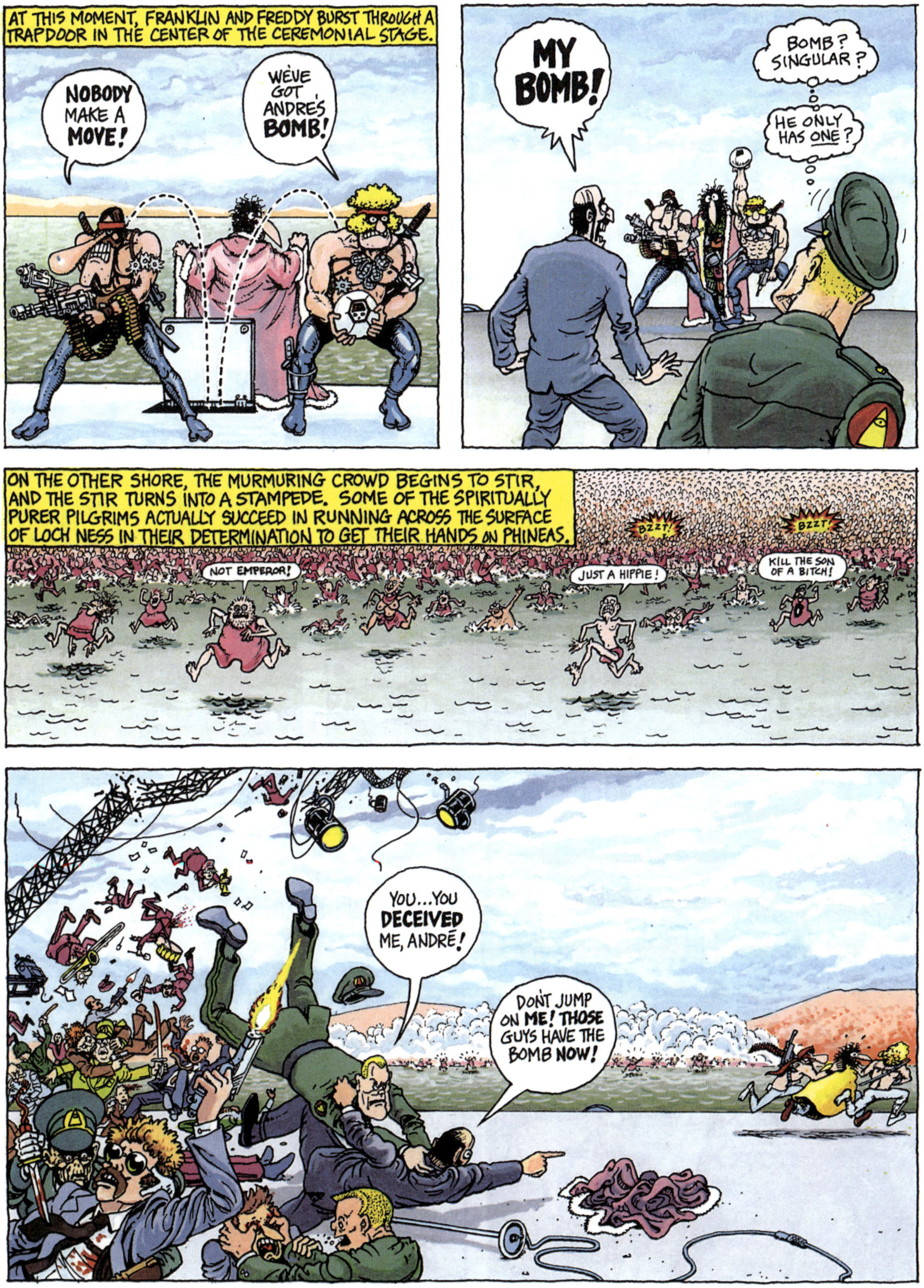
AT THIS MOMENT, FRANKLIN AND FREDDY BURST THROUGH A TRAPDOOR IN THE CENTER OF THE CEREMONIAL STAGE.
NOBODY MAKE A MOVE!
WE'VE GOT ANDRÉ'S BOMB!
MY BOMB!
BOMB? SINGULAR?
HE ONLY HAS ONE?
ON THE OTHER SHORE, THE MURMURING CROWD BEGINS TO STIR, AND THE STIR TURNS INTO A STAMPEDE. SOME OF THE SPIRITUALLY PURER PILGRIMS ACTUALLY SUCCEED IN RUNNING ACROSS THE SURFACE OF LOCH NESS IN THEIR DETERMINATION TO GET THEIR HANDS ON PHINEAS.
BZZT!
BZZT!
NOT EMPEROR!
JUST A HIPPIE!
KILL THE SON OF A BITCH!
YOU... YOU DECEIVED ME, ANDRÉ!
DON'T JUMP ON ME! THOSE GUYS HAVE THE BOMB NOW!

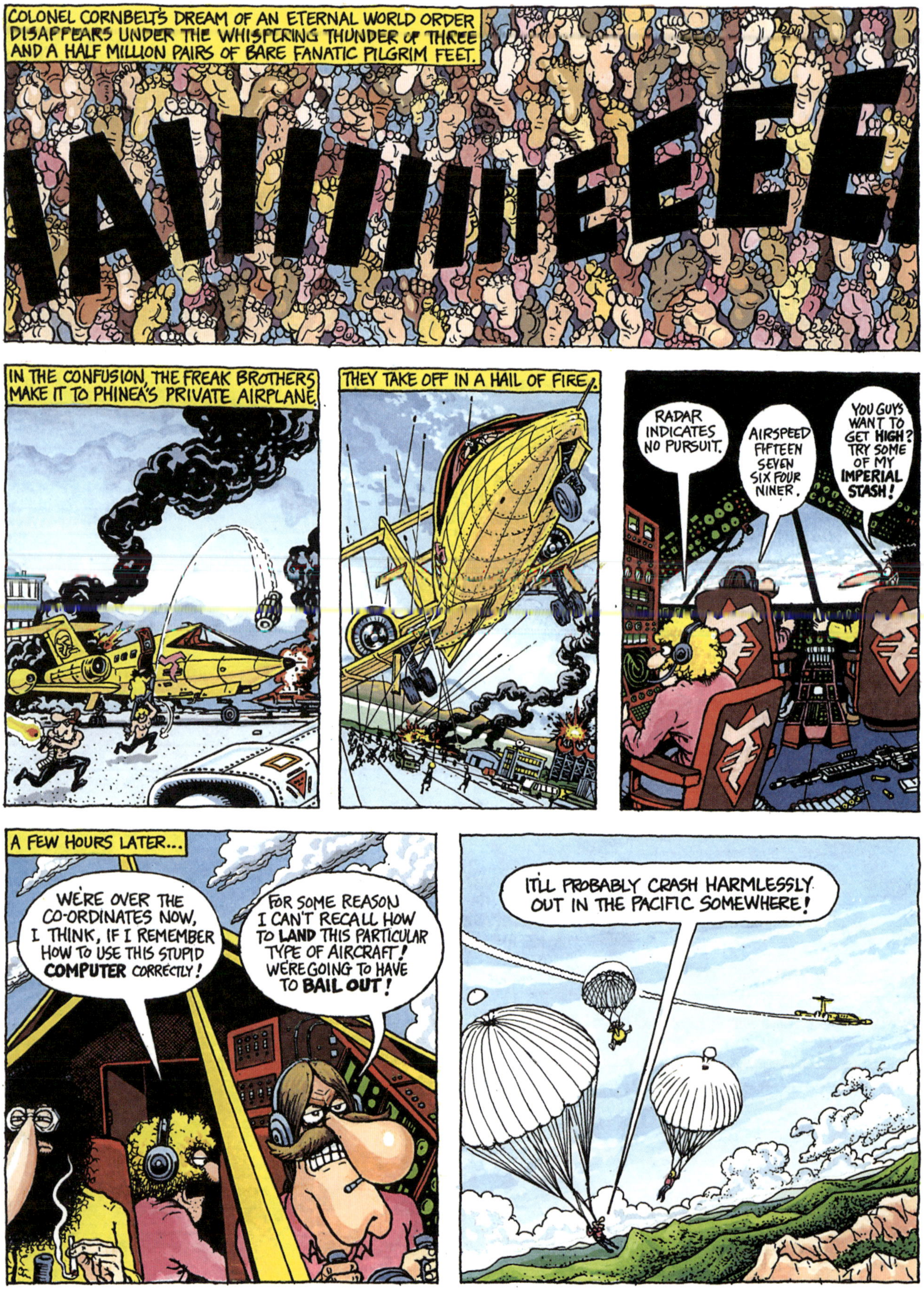
COLONEL CORNBELT'S DREAM OF AN ETERNAL WORLD ORDER DISAPPEARS UNDER THE WHISPERING THUNDER OF THREE AND A HALF MILLION PAIRS OF BARE FANATIC PILGRIM FEET.
AIIIIIIIEEEE
IN THE CONFUSION, THE FREAK BROTHERS MAKE IT TO PHINEA'S PRIVATE AIRPLANE.
THEY TAKE OFF IN A HAIL OF FIRE.
RADAR INDICATES NO PURSUIT.
AIRSPEED FIFTEEN SEVEN SIX FOUR NINER.
YOU GUYS WANT TO GET HIGH? TRY SOME OF MY IMPERIAL STASH!
A FEW HOURS LATER...
WE'RE OVER THE CO-ORDINATES NOW, I THINK, IF I REMEMBER HOW TO USE THIS STUPID COMPUTER CORRECTLY!
FOR SOME REASON I CAN'T RECALL HOW TO LAND THIS PARTICULAR TYPE OF AIRCRAFT! WE'RE GOING TO HAVE TO BAIL OUT!
IT'LL PROBABLY CRASH HARMLESSLY OUT IN THE PACIFIC SOMEWHERE!

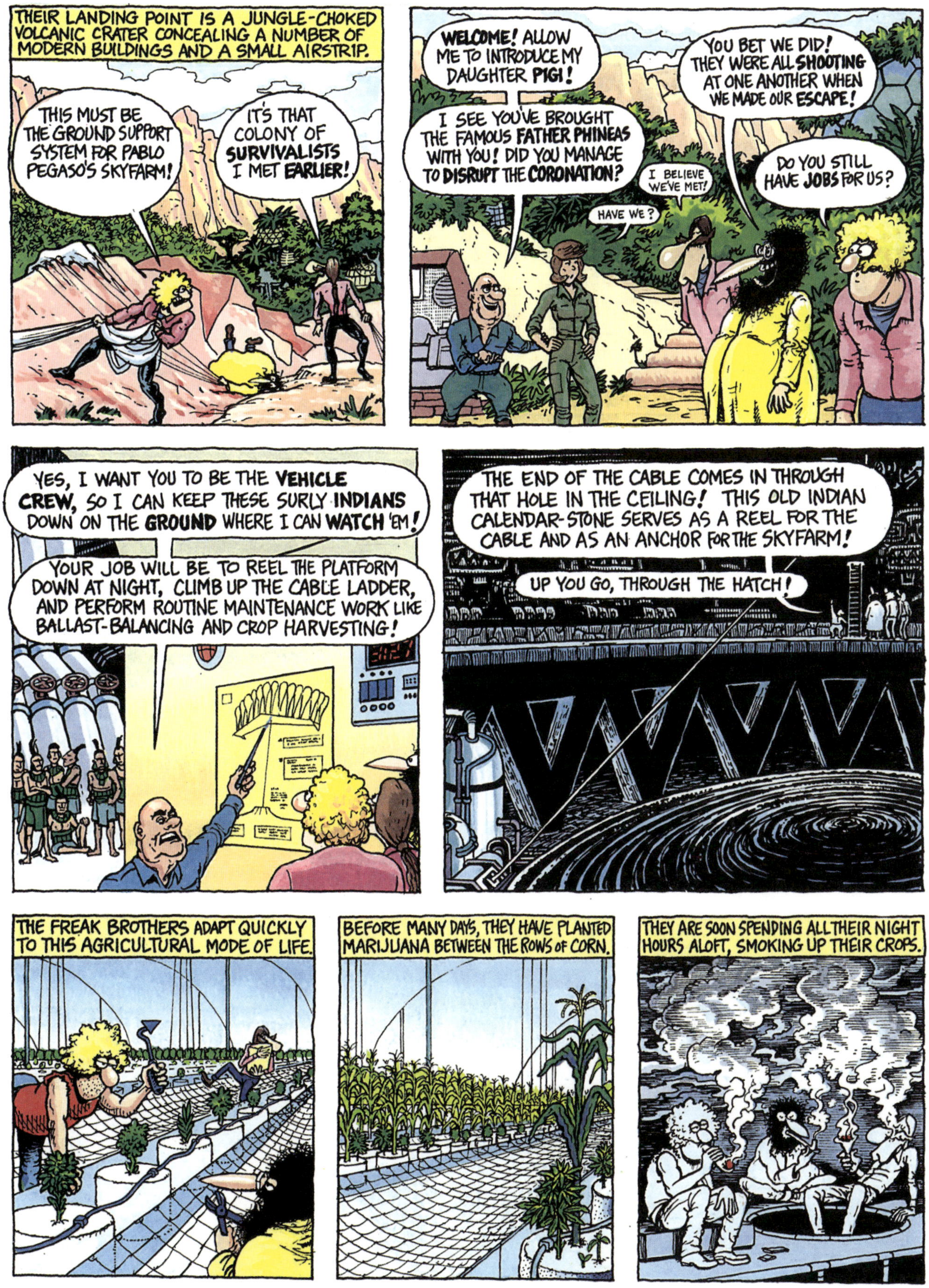
THEIR LANDING POINT IS A JUNGLE-CHOKED VOLCANIC CRATER CONCEALING A NUMBER OF MODERN BUILDINGS AND A SMALL AIRSTRIP.
THIS MUST BE THE GROUND SUPPORT SYSTEM FOR PABLO PEGASO'S SKYFARM!
IT'S THAT COLONY OF SURVIVALISTS I MET EARLIER!
WELCOME! ALLOW ME TO INTRODUCE MY DAUGHTER PIGI!
I SEE YOU'VE BROUGHT THE FAMOUS FATHER PHINEAS WITH YOU! DID YOU MANAGE TO DISRUPT THE CORONATION?
YOU BET WE DID! THEY WERE ALL SHOOTING AT ONE ANOTHER WHEN WE MADE OUR ESCAPE!
I BELIEVE WE'VE MET!
HAVE WE?
DO YOU STILL HAVE JOBS FOR US?
YES, I WANT YOU TO BE THE VEHICLE CREW, SO I CAN KEEP THESE SURLY INDIANS DOWN ON THE GROUND WHERE I CAN WATCH 'EM!
YOUR JOB WILL BE TO REEL THE PLATFORM DOWN AT NIGHT, CLIMB UP THE CABLE LADDER, AND PERFORM ROUTINE MAINTENANCE WORK LIKE BALLAST-BALANCING AND CROP HARVESTING!
THE END OF THE CABLE COMES IN THROUGH THAT HOLE IN THE CEILING! THIS OLD INDIAN CALENDAR-STONE SERVES AS A REEL FOR THE CABLE AND AS AN ANCHOR FOR THE SKYFARM!
UP YOU GO, THROUGH THE HATCH!
THE FREAK BROTHERS ADAPT QUICKLY TO THIS AGRICULTURAL MODE OF LIFE.
BEFORE MANY DAYS, THEY HAVE PLANTED MARIJUANA BETWEEN THE ROWS OF CORN.
THEY ARE SOON SPENDING ALL THEIR NIGHT HOURS ALOFT, SMOKING UP THEIR CROPS.

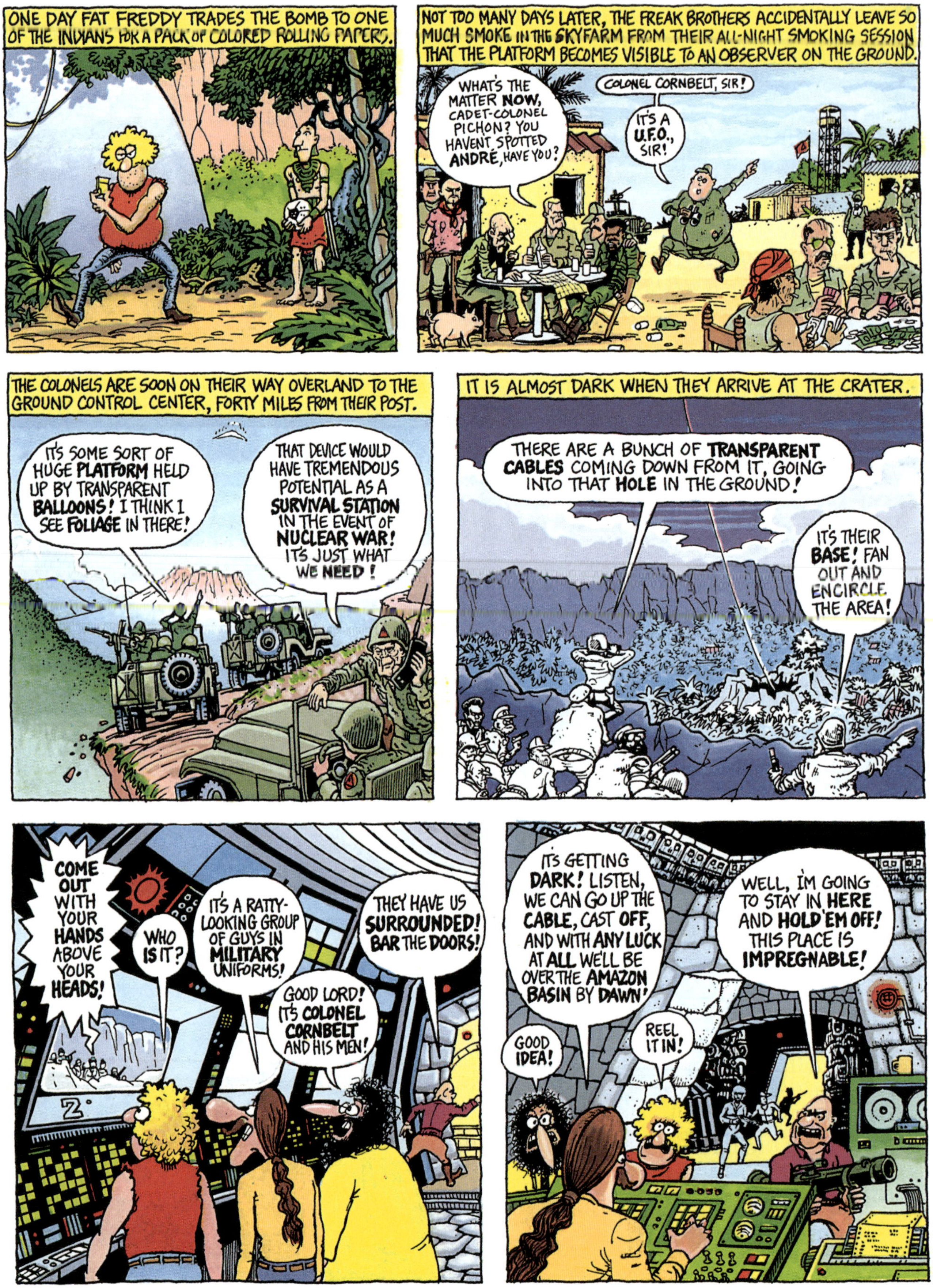
ONE DAY FAT FREDDY TRADES THE BOMB TO ONE OF THE INDIANS FOR A PACK OF COLORED ROLLING PAPERS.
NOT TOO MANY DAYS LATER, THE FREAK BROTHERS ACCIDENTALLY LEAVE SO MUCH SMOKE IN THE SKYFARM FROM THEIR ALL-NIGHT SMOKING SESSION THAT THE PLATFORM BECOMES VISIBLE TO AN OBSERVER ON THE GROUND.
COLONEL CORNBELT, SIR!
WHAT'S THE MATTER NOW, CADET-COLONEL PICHON? YOU HAVEN'T SPOTTED ANDRÉ, HAVE YOU?
IT'S A U.F.O., SIR!
THE COLONELS ARE SOON ON THEIR WAY OVERLAND TO THE GROUND CONTROL CENTER, FORTY MILES FROM THEIR POST.
IT'S SOME SORT OF HUGE PLATFORM HELD UP BY TRANSPARENT BALLOONS! I THINK I SEE FOLIAGE IN THERE!
THAT DEVICE WOULD HAVE TREMENDOUS POTENTIAL AS A SURVIVAL STATION IN THE EVENT OF NUCLEAR WAR! IT'S JUST WHAT WE NEED!
IT IS ALMOST DARK WHEN THEY ARRIVE AT THE CRATER.
THERE ARE A BUNCH OF TRANSPARENT CABLES COMING DOWN FROM IT, GOING INTO THAT HOLE IN THE GROUND!
IT'S THEIR BASE! FAN OUT AND ENCIRCLE THE AREA!
COME OUT WITH YOUR HANDS ABOVE YOUR HEADS!
WHO IS IT?
IT'S A RATTY-LOOKING GROUP OF GUYS IN MILITARY UNIFORMS!
GOOD LORD! IT'S COLONEL CORNBELT AND HIS MEN!
THEY HAVE US SURROUNDED! BAR THE DOORS!
IT'S GETTING DARK! LISTEN, WE CAN GO UP THE CABLE, CAST OFF, AND WITH ANY LUCK AT ALL WE'LL BE OVER THE AMAZON BASIN BY DAWN!
GOOD IDEA!
REEL IT IN!
WELL, I'M GOING TO STAY IN HERE AND HOLD 'EM OFF! THIS PLACE IS IMPREGNABLE!

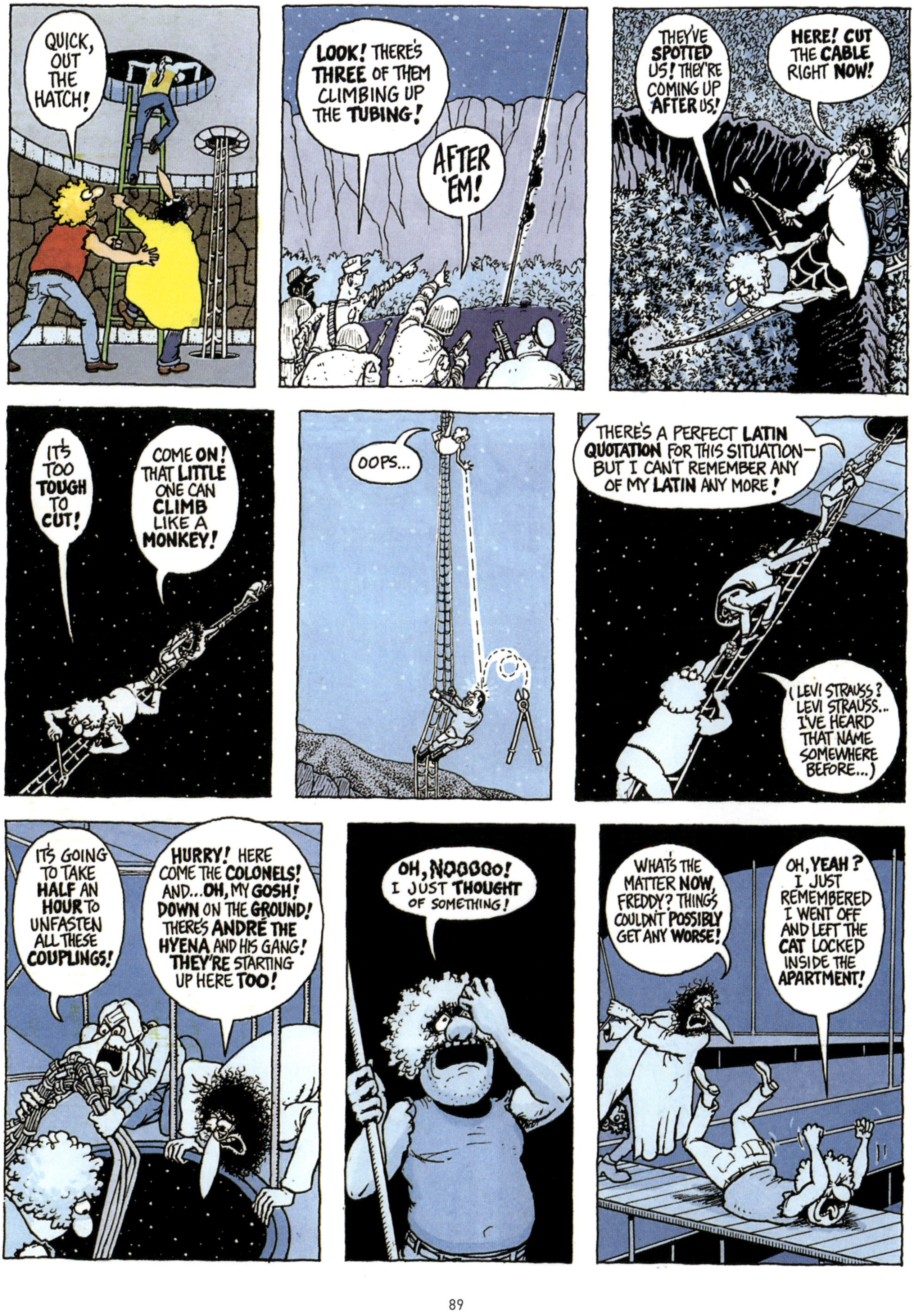
QUICK, OUT THE HATCH!
LOOK! THERE'S THREE OF THEM CLIMBING UP THE TUBING!
AFTER 'EM!
THEY'VE SPOTTED US! THEY'RE COMING UP AFTER US!
HERE! CUT THE CABLE RIGHT NOW!
IT'S TOO TOUGH TO CUT!
COME ON! THAT LITTLE ONE CAN CLIMB LIKE A MONKEY!
OOPS...
THERE'S A PERFECT LATIN QUOTATION FOR THIS SITUATION— BUT I CAN'T REMEMBER ANY OF MY LATIN ANY MORE!
(LEVI STRAUSS? LEVI STRAUSS... I'VE HEARD THAT NAME SOMEWHERE BEFORE...)
IT'S GOING TO TAKE HALF AN HOUR TO UNFASTEN ALL THESE COUPLINGS!
HURRY! HERE COME THE COLONELS! AND...OH, MY GOSH! DOWN ON THE GROUND! THERE'S ANDRÉ THE HYENA AND HIS GANG! THEY'RE STARTING UP HERE TOO!
OH, NOOOOO! I JUST THOUGHT OF SOMETHING!
WHAT'S THE MATTER NOW, FREDDY? THINGS COULDN'T POSSIBLY GET ANY WORSE!
OH, YEAH? I JUST REMEMBERED I WENT OFF AND LEFT THE CAT LOCKED INSIDE THE APARTMENT!

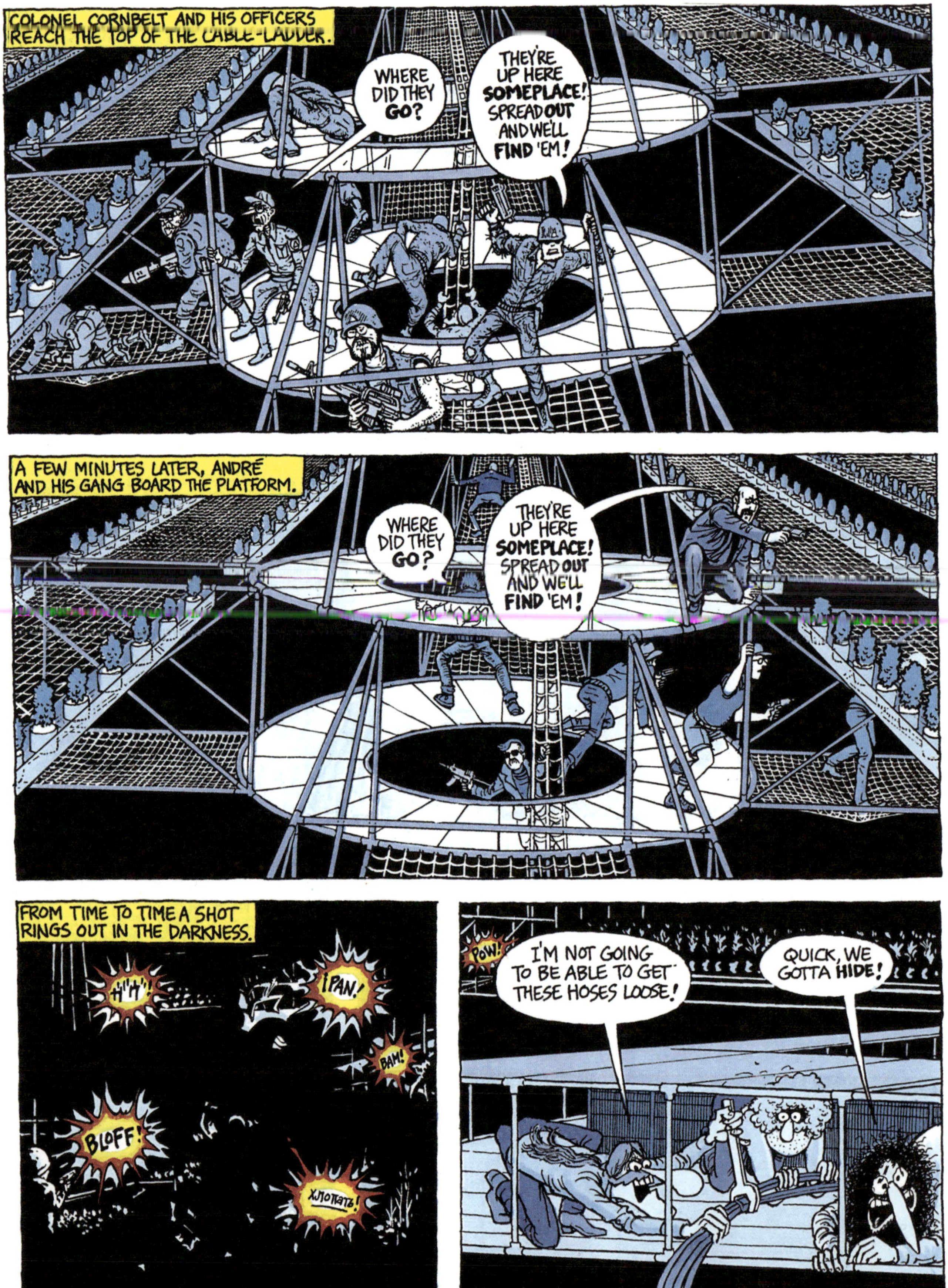
COLONEL CORNBELT AND HIS OFFICERS REACH THE TOP OF THE CABLE-LADDER.
WHERE DID THEY GO?
THEY'RE UP HERE SOMEPLACE! SPREAD OUT AND WE'LL FIND 'EM!
A FEW MINUTES LATER, ANDRÉ AND HIS GANG BOARD THE PLATFORM.
WHERE DID THEY GO?
THEY'RE UP HERE SOMEPLACE! SPREAD OUT AND WE'LL FIND 'EM!
FROM TIME TO TIME A SHOT RINGS OUT IN THE DARKNESS.
¡PAN!
BAM!
BLOFF!
ХЛОПАТЬ!
POW!
I'M NOT GOING TO BE ABLE TO GET THESE HOSES LOOSE!
QUICK, WE GOTTA HIDE!

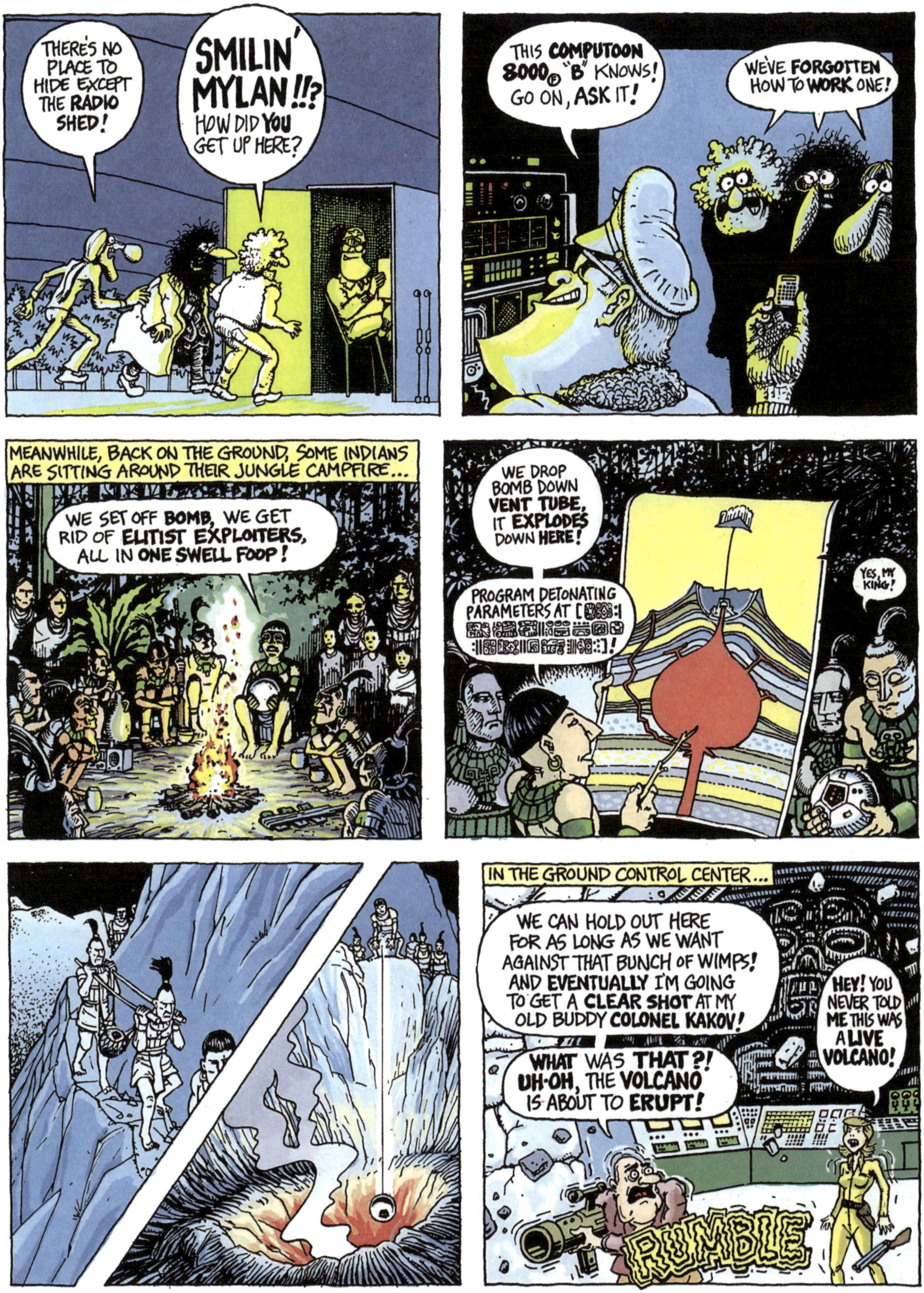
THERE'S NO PLACE TO HIDE EXCEPT THE RADIO SHED!
SMILIN' MYLAN!!? HOW DID YOU GET UP HERE?
THIS COMPUTOON 8000® "B" KNOWS! GO ON, ASK IT!
WE'VE FORGOTTEN HOW TO WORK ONE!
MEANWHILE, BACK ON THE GROUND, SOME INDIANS ARE SITTING AROUND THEIR JUNGLE CAMPFIRE...
WE SET OFF BOMB, WE GET RID OF ELITIST EXPLOITERS, ALL IN ONE SWELL FOOP!
WE DROP BOMB DOWN VENT TUBE, IT EXPLODES DOWN HERE!
PROGRAM DETONATING PARAMETERS AT
YES, MY KING!
IN THE GROUND CONTROL CENTER...
WE CAN HOLD OUT HERE FOR AS LONG AS WE WANT AGAINST THAT BUNCH OF WIMPS! AND EVENTUALLY I'M GOING TO GET A CLEAR SHOT AT MY OLD BUDDY COLONEL KAKOV!
HEY! YOU NEVER TOLD ME THIS WAS A LIVE VOLCANO!
WHAT WAS THAT?! UH-OH, THE VOLCANO IS ABOUT TO ERUPT!
RUMBLE

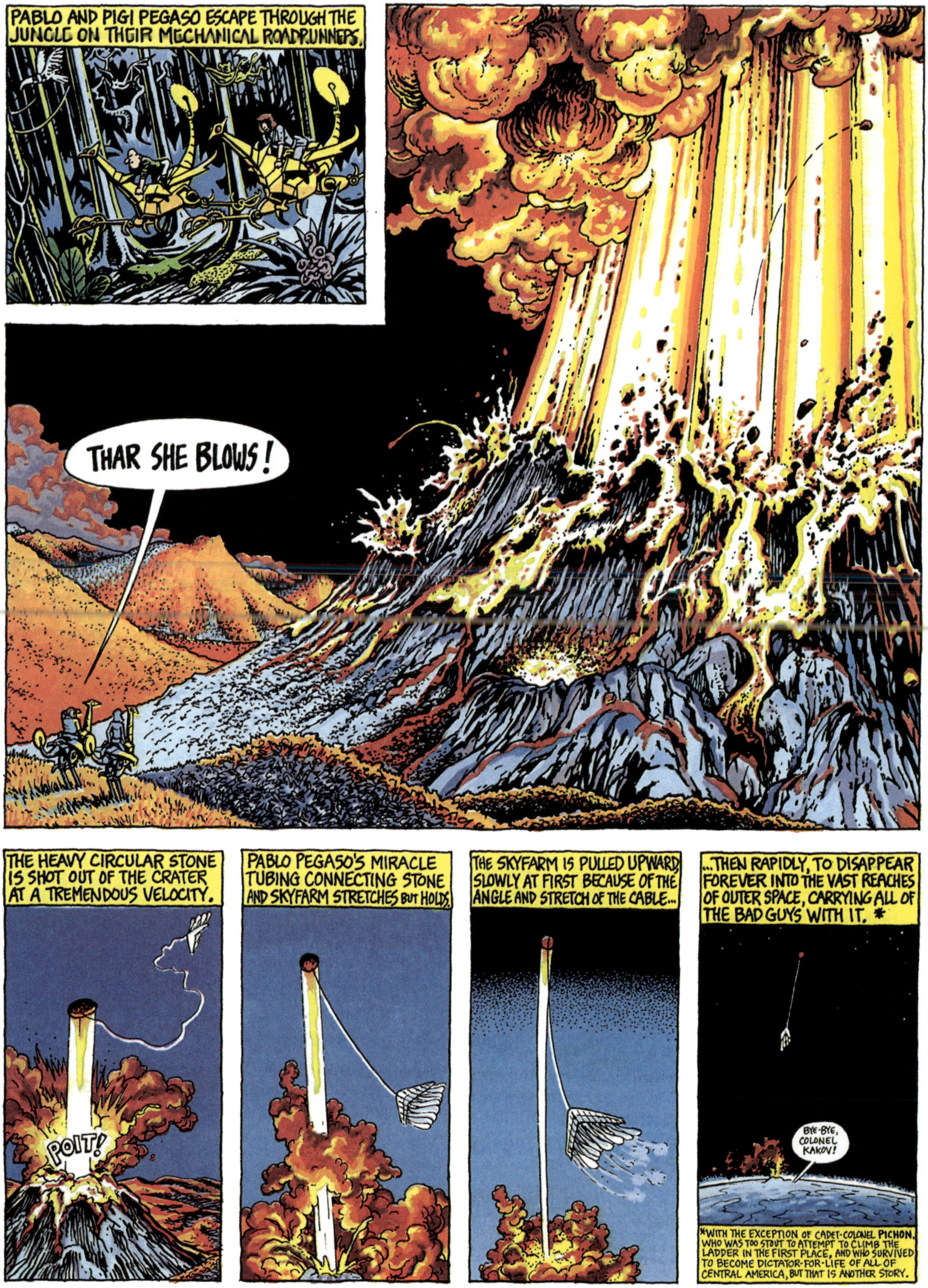
PABLO AND PIGI PEGASO ESCAPE THROUGH THE JUNGLE ON THEIR MECHANICAL ROADRUNNERS.
THAR SHE BLOWS!
THE HEAVY CIRCULAR STONE IS SHOT OUT OF THE CRATER AT A TREMENDOUS VELOCITY.
POIT!
PABLO PEGASO'S MIRACLE TUBING CONNECTING STONE AND SKYFARM STRETCHES BUT HOLDS.
THE SKYFARM IS PULLED UPWARD, SLOWLY AT FIRST BECAUSE OF THE ANGLE AND STRETCH OF THE CABLE...
...THEN RAPIDLY, TO DISAPPEAR FOREVER INTO THE VAST REACHES OF OUTER SPACE, CARRYING ALL OF THE BAD GUYS WITH IT. *
BYE-BYE, COLONEL KAKOV!
* WITH THE EXCEPTION OF CADET-COLONEL PICHON, WHO WAS TOO STOUT TO ATTEMPT TO CLIMB THE LADDER IN THE FIRST PLACE, AND WHO SURVIVED TO BECOME DICTATOR-FOR-LIFE OF ALL OF CENTRAL AMERICA, BUT THAT IS ANOTHER STORY.

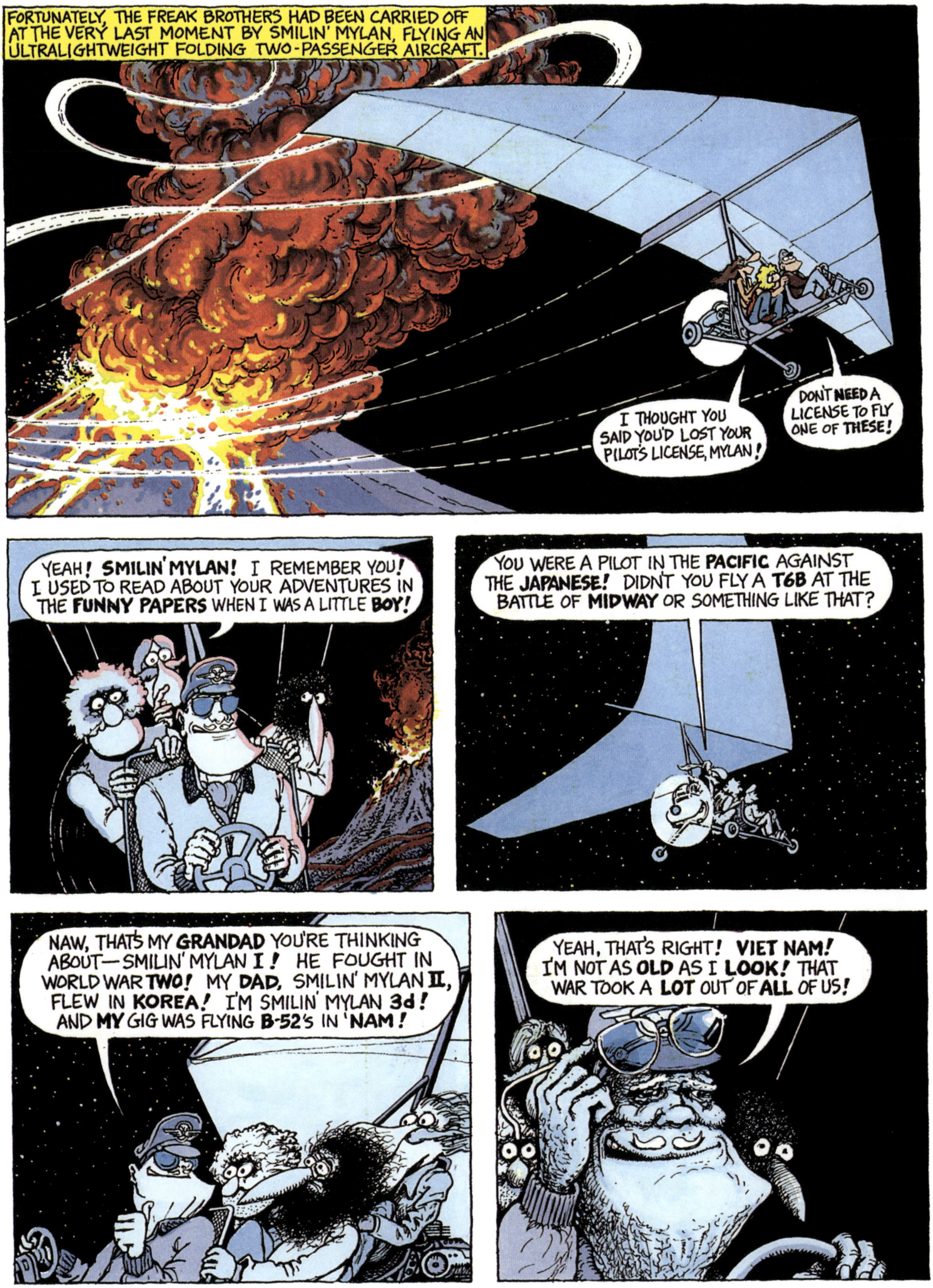

FORTUNATELY, THE FREAK BROTHERS HAD BEEN CARRIED OFF AT THE VERY LAST MOMENT BY SMILIN' MYLAN, FLYING AN ULTRALIGHTWEIGHT FOLDING TWO-PASSENGER AIRCRAFT.
I THOUGHT YOU SAID YOU'D LOST YOUR PILOT'S LICENSE, MYLAN!
DON'T NEED A LICENSE TO FLY ONE OF THESE!
YEAH! SMILIN' MYLAN! I REMEMBER YOU! I USED TO READ ABOUT YOUR ADVENTURES IN THE FUNNY PAPERS WHEN I WAS A LITTLE BOY!
YOU WERE A PILOT IN THE PACIFIC AGAINST THE JAPANESE! DIDN'T YOU FLY A T6B AT THE BATTLE OF MIDWAY OR SOMETHING LIKE THAT?
NAW, THAT'S MY GRANDAD YOU'RE THINKING ABOUT—SMILIN' MYLAN I! HE FOUGHT IN WORLD WAR TWO! MY DAD, SMILIN' MYLAN II, FLEW IN KOREA! I'M SMILIN' MYLAN 3d! AND MY GIG WAS FLYING B-52's IN 'NAM!
YEAH, THAT'S RIGHT! VIET NAM! I'M NOT AS OLD AS I LOOK! THAT WAR TOOK A LOT OUT OF ALL OF US!

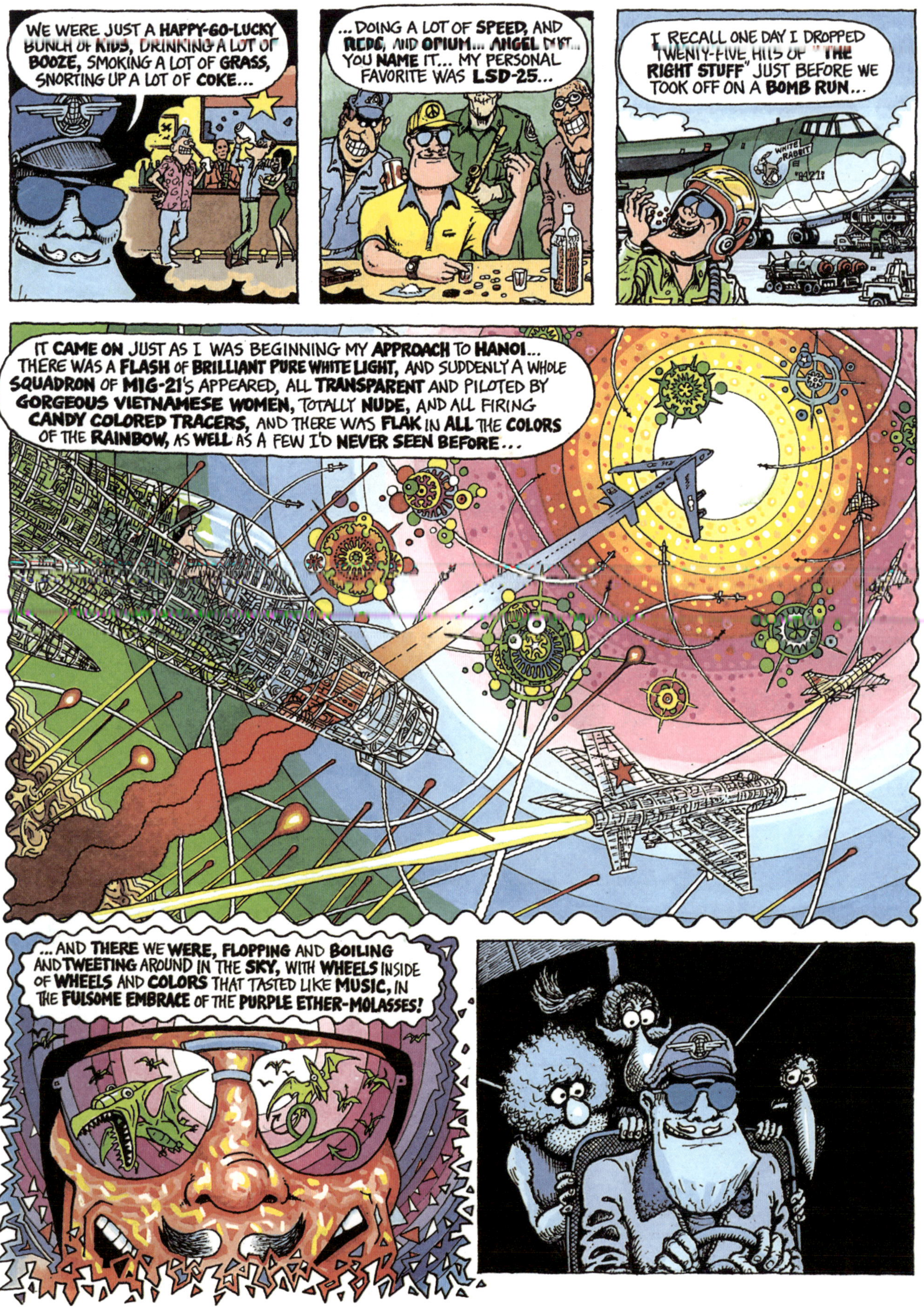
WE WERE JUST A HAPPY-GO-LUCKY BUNCH OF KIDS, DRINKING A LOT OF BOOZE, SMOKING A LOT OF GRASS, SNORTING UP A LOT OF COKE...
...DOING A LOT OF SPEED, AND REDS, AND OPIUM... ANGEL DUST... YOU NAME IT... MY PERSONAL FAVORITE WAS LSD-25...
I RECALL ONE DAY I DROPPED TWENTY-FIVE HITS OF "THE RIGHT STUFF" JUST BEFORE WE TOOK OFF ON A BOMB RUN...
WHITE RABBIT
IT CAME ON JUST AS I WAS BEGINNING MY APPROACH TO HANOI... THERE WAS A FLASH OF BRILLIANT PURE WHITE LIGHT, AND SUDDENLY A WHOLE SQUADRON OF MIG-21'S APPEARED, ALL TRANSPARENT AND PILOTED BY GORGEOUS VIETNAMESE WOMEN, TOTALLY NUDE, AND ALL FIRING CANDY COLORED TRACERS, AND THERE WAS FLAK IN ALL THE COLORS OF THE RAINBOW, AS WELL AS A FEW I'D NEVER SEEN BEFORE...
...AND THERE WE WERE, FLOPPING AND BOILING AND TWEETING AROUND IN THE SKY, WITH WHEELS INSIDE OF WHEELS AND COLORS THAT TASTED LIKE MUSIC, IN THE FULSOME EMBRACE OF THE PURPLE ETHER-MOLASSES!

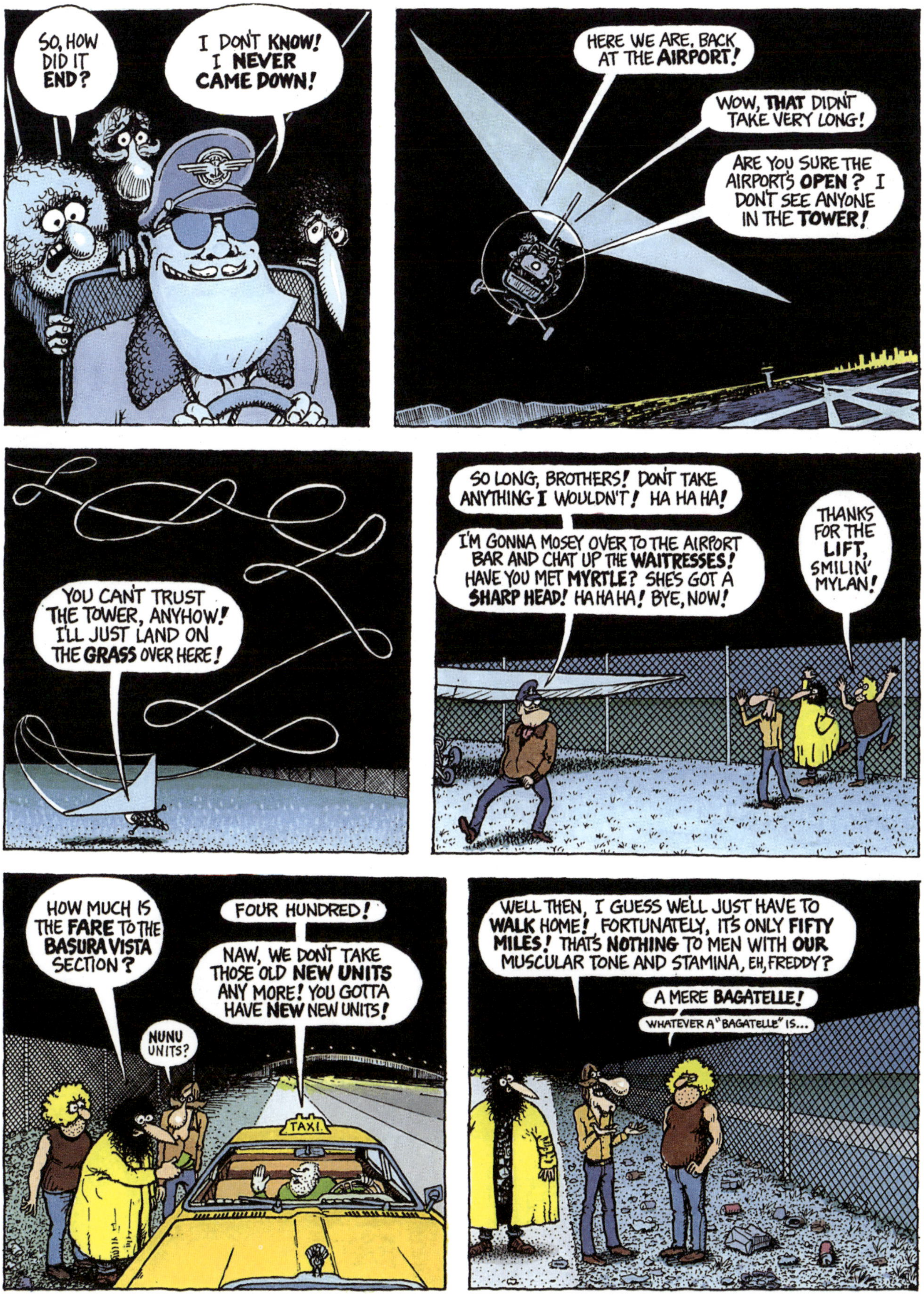
SO, HOW DID IT END?
I DON'T KNOW! I NEVER CAME DOWN!
HERE WE ARE, BACK AT THE AIRPORT!
WOW, THAT DIDN'T TAKE VERY LONG!
ARE YOU SURE THE AIRPORT'S OPEN? I DON'T SEE ANYONE IN THE TOWER!
YOU CAN'T TRUST THE TOWER, ANYHOW! I'LL JUST LAND ON THE GRASS OVER HERE!
SO LONG, BROTHERS! DON'T TAKE ANYTHING I WOULDN'T! HA HA HA!
I'M GONNA MOSEY OVER TO THE AIRPORT BAR AND CHAT UP THE WAITRESSES! HAVE YOU MET MYRTLE? SHE'S GOT A SHARP HEAD! HA HA HA! BYE, NOW!
THANKS FOR THE LIFT, SMILIN' MYLAN!
HOW MUCH IS THE FARE TO THE BASURA VISTA SECTION?
FOUR HUNDRED!
NAW, WE DON'T TAKE THOSE OLD NEW UNITS ANY MORE! YOU GOTTA HAVE NEW NEW UNITS!
NUNU UNITS?
TAXI
WELL THEN, I GUESS WE'LL JUST HAVE TO WALK HOME! FORTUNATELY, IT'S ONLY FIFTY MILES! THAT'S NOTHING TO MEN WITH OUR MUSCULAR TONE AND STAMINA, EH, FREDDY?
A MERE BAGATELLE!
WHATEVER A "BAGATELLE" IS...

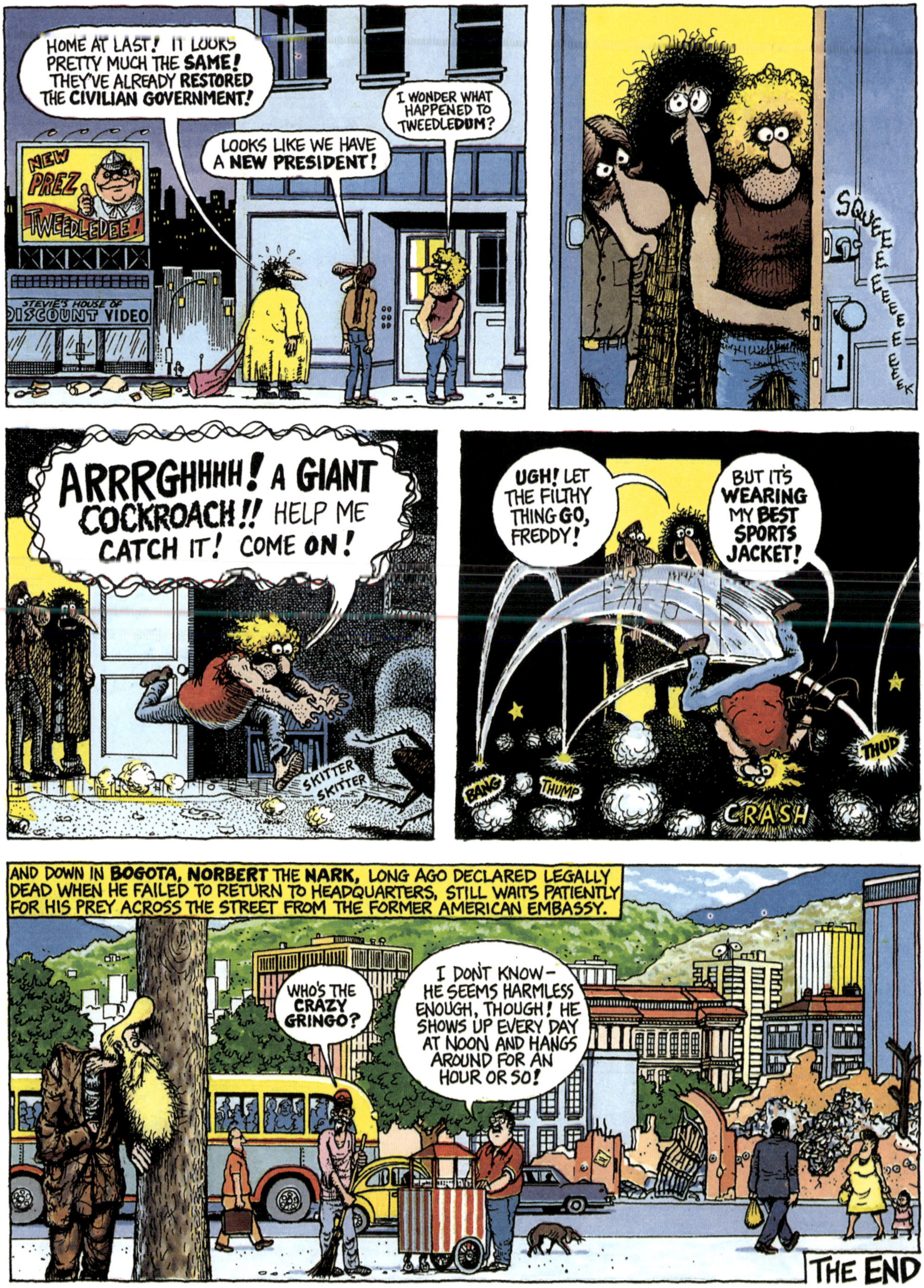

HOME AT LAST! IT LOOKS PRETTY MUCH THE SAME! THEY'VE ALREADY RESTORED THE CIVILIAN GOVERNMENT!
LOOKS LIKE WE HAVE A NEW PRESIDENT!
I WONDER WHAT HAPPENED TO TWEEDLEDUM?
NEW PREZ TWEEDLEDEE!
STEVIE'S HOUSE OF DISCOUNT VIDEO
SQUEEEEEEEEEEEEK
ARRRGHHHH! A GIANT COCKROACH!! HELP ME CATCH IT! COME ON!
SKITTER SKITTER
UGH! LET THE FILTHY THING GO, FREDDY!
BUT IT'S WEARING MY BEST SPORTS JACKET!
BANG
THUMP
CRASH
THUD
AND DOWN IN BOGOTA, NORBERT THE NARK, LONG AGO DECLARED LEGALLY DEAD WHEN HE FAILED TO RETURN TO HEADQUARTERS, STILL WAITS PATIENTLY FOR HIS PREY ACROSS THE STREET FROM THE FORMER AMERICAN EMBASSY.
WHO'S THE CRAZY GRINGO?
I DON'T KNOW— HE SEEMS HARMLESS ENOUGH, THOUGH! HE SHOWS UP EVERY DAY AT NOON AND HANGS AROUND FOR AN HOUR OR SO!
THE END

by way of explanation...

...continued from inside front cover

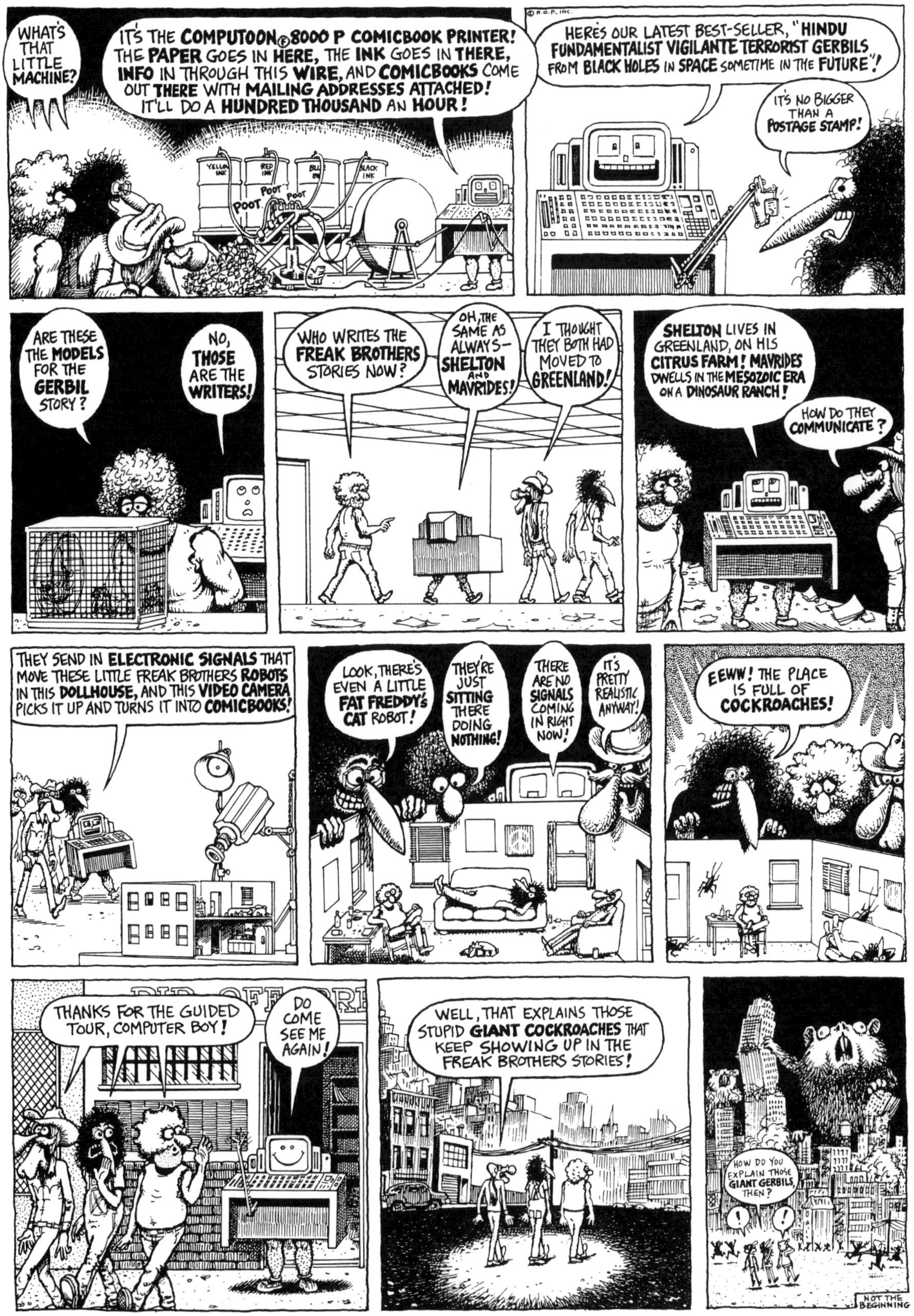
© R.O.P., INC.
WHAT'S THAT LITTLE MACHINE?
IT'S THE COMPUTOON® 8000 P COMICBOOK PRINTER! THE PAPER GOES IN HERE, THE INK GOES IN THERE, INFO IN THROUGH THIS WIRE, AND COMICBOOKS COME OUT THERE WITH MAILING ADDRESSES ATTACHED! IT'LL DO A HUNDRED THOUSAND AN HOUR!
YELLOW INK
RED INK
BLUE INK
BLACK INK
POOT POOT POOT
HERE'S OUR LATEST BEST-SELLER, "HINDU FUNDAMENTALIST VIGILANTE TERRORIST GERBILS FROM BLACK HOLES IN SPACE SOMETIME IN THE FUTURE"!
IT'S NO BIGGER THAN A POSTAGE STAMP!
ARE THESE THE MODELS FOR THE GERBIL STORY?
NO, THOSE ARE THE WRITERS!
WHO WRITES THE FREAK BROTHERS STORIES NOW?
OH, THE SAME AS ALWAYS— SHELTON AND MAVRIDES!
I THOUGHT THEY BOTH HAD MOVED TO GREENLAND!
SHELTON LIVES IN GREENLAND, ON HIS CITRUS FARM! MAVRIDES DWELLS IN THE MESOZOIC ERA ON A DINOSAUR RANCH!
HOW DO THEY COMMUNICATE?
THEY SEND IN ELECTRONIC SIGNALS THAT MOVE THESE LITTLE FREAK BROTHERS ROBOTS IN THIS DOLLHOUSE, AND THIS VIDEO CAMERA PICKS IT UP AND TURNS IT INTO COMICBOOKS!
LOOK, THERE'S EVEN A LITTLE FAT FREDDY'S CAT ROBOT!
THEY'RE JUST SITTING THERE DOING NOTHING!
THERE ARE NO SIGNALS COMING IN RIGHT NOW!
IT'S PRETTY REALISTIC ANYWAY!
EEWW! THE PLACE IS FULL OF COCKROACHES!
THANKS FOR THE GUIDED TOUR, COMPUTER BOY!
DO COME SEE ME AGAIN!
WELL, THAT EXPLAINS THOSE STUPID GIANT COCKROACHES THAT KEEP SHOWING UP IN THE FREAK BROTHERS STORIES!
HOW DO YOU EXPLAIN THOSE GIANT GERBILS, THEN?
!
!
NOT THE BEGINNING

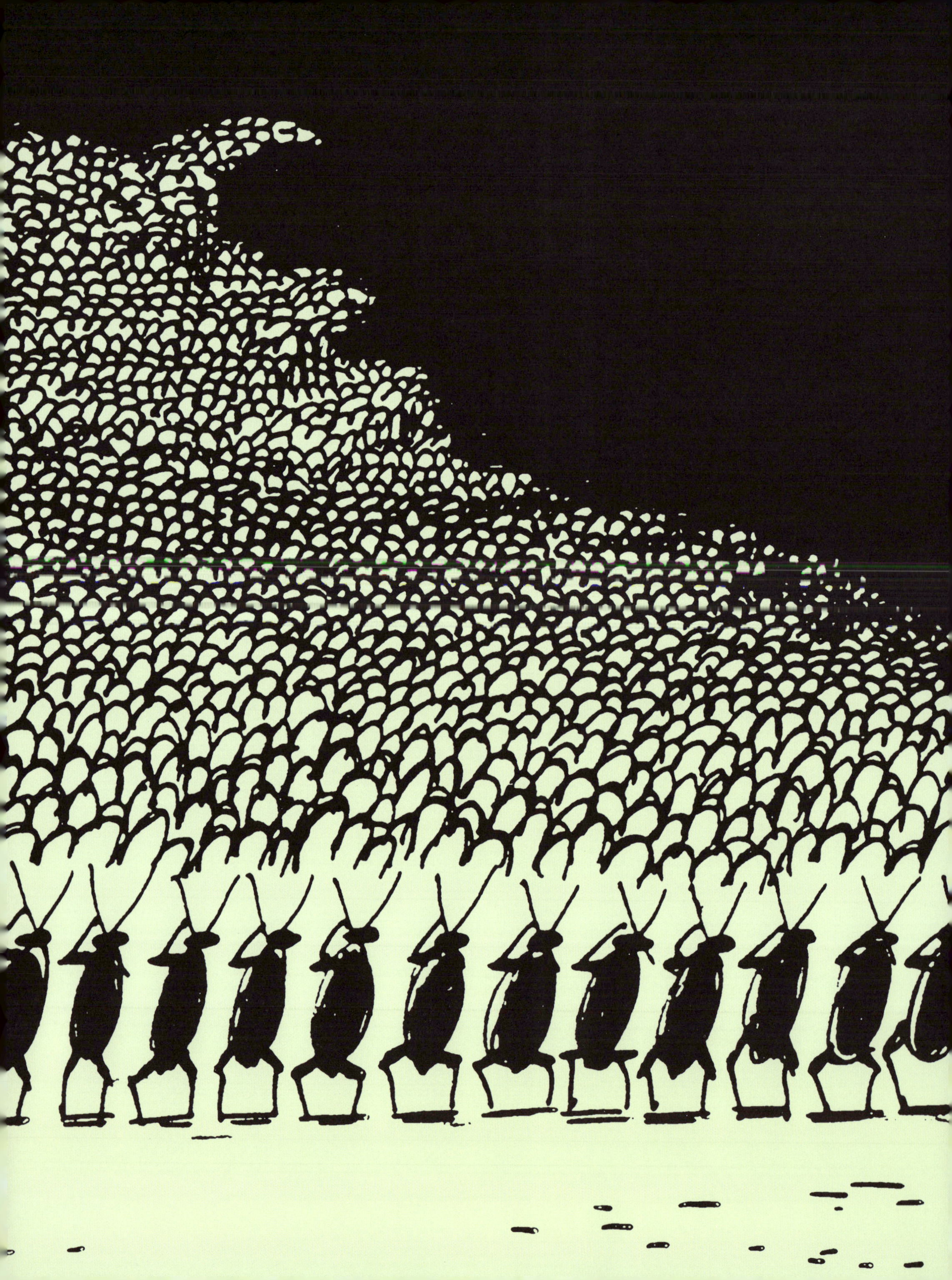

FAT FREDDY'S CAT

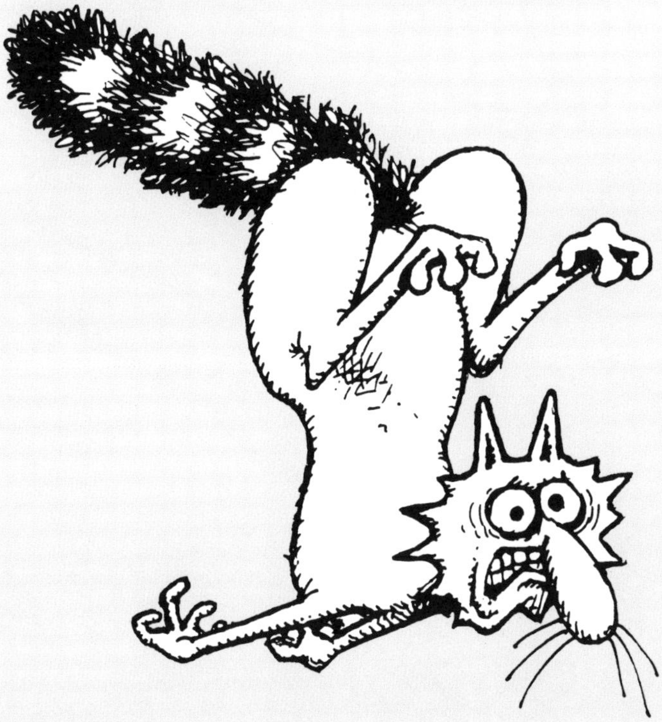

COCKROACH *FACTS*

by GILBERT SHELTON

There are thousands of species of cockroaches, including tropical forest & semiaquatic varieties, woodborers, underground dwellers and species that are parasitic on other insects. Fortunately, only a few are house pests. The four types most commonly encountered are the **American Cockroach** (*Periplaneta americana*), the German Cockroach (*Blattella germanica*), the Oriental Cockroach (*Blatta orientalis*), and the Brown-Banded Cockroach (*Supella longipalpa*). Of these, the largest is the *Periplaneta americana*, a prime specimen of which can be up to two inches long. All of these species came originally from the old world, perhaps Africa. In the summer of 1979, over a million German cockroaches were found in a house in Schenectady, New York. Since then, this city has been known as the **Cockroach Capital of the World.**

Foreign words for cockroach:

German:	*Küchenschabe*
French:	*blatte* or *cafard*
Spanish:	*cucaracha*
Italian:	*blatta*
Russian:	*tarakán*
Dutch:	*kakkerlak*
Chinese:	*chang-liang*
Portuguese:	*bicho-de-conta*
Danish:	*kakerlak*
Norwegian:	*kakerlakk*
Swedish:	*mort*
Polish:	*karaluch*
Japanese:	*abula mushi*
Hebrew:	*juke*

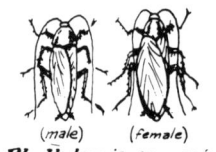

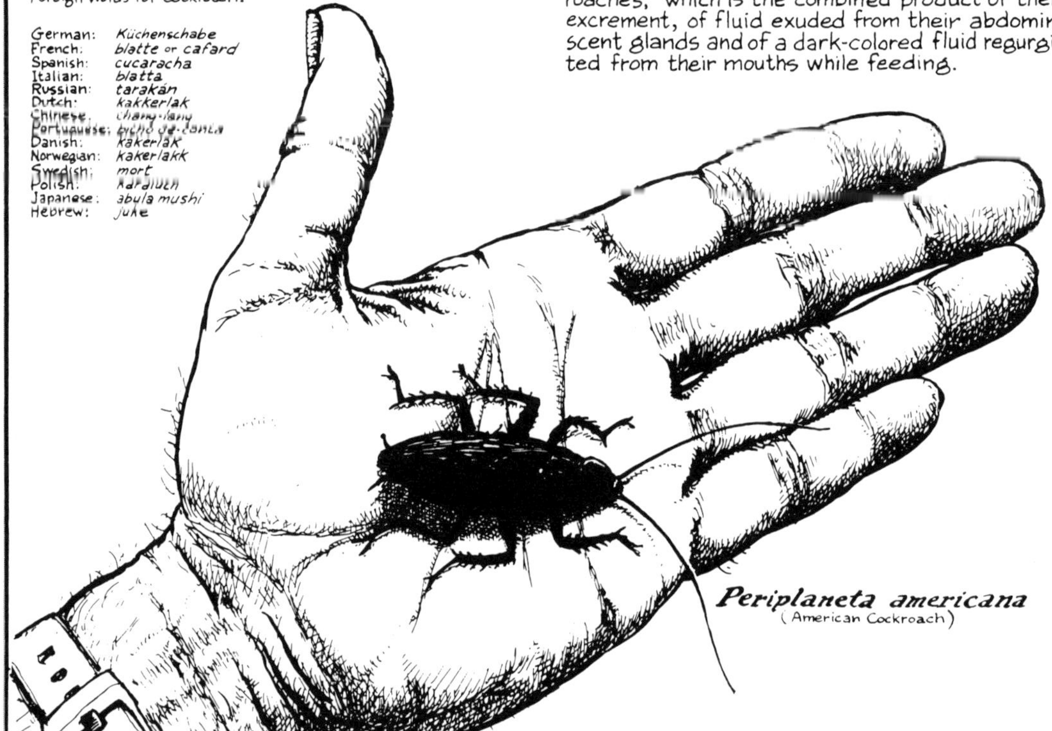

Phyllodromia germanica
(German Cockroach)
(male) (female)

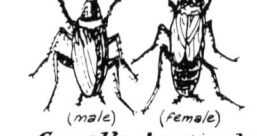

Supella longipalpa
(Brown-banded Cockroach)
(male) (female)

The cockroach picks up vibrations with its antennae in the front and the **cerci** in the rear, which are attached directly to its legs, avoiding the need for its sensations to be processed by the brain before the legs start in motion. Roaches eat almost anything, a thin layer of grease being enough to keep them happy. They will eat bread, fruit, crackers, grease, sweets, vegetables, pet food, garbage, beer, marijuana, tobacco, cereal, paper, soap, glue, fingernails, toenails, pus, urine, feces, and each other. They produce an unpleasant odor called "attar of roaches," which is the combined product of their excrement, of fluid exuded from their abdominal scent glands and of a dark-colored fluid regurgitated from their mouths while feeding.

Periplaneta americana
(American Cockroach)

Cockroaches have a life span of more than two years, and can go for over two weeks without food or water. They lay eggs in capsules containing up to forty-eight eggs which, depending on the species, may mature in as few as thirty-six days. One roach is therefore able to produce four hundred thousand descendants in one year. Cockroaches are able to withstand exposure to atomic radiation at levels far in excess of what humans can tolerate. It is said that the cockroach represents the culmination of psychic evolution toward pure instinct, as opposed to man, who represents the culmination of psychic evolution toward pure intellect. This is not necessarily true, however; there are numerous people, some at the highest levels of government, who seem less intelligent than roaches.

Blatta Orientalis
(Oriental Cockroach)
(Female) (male)

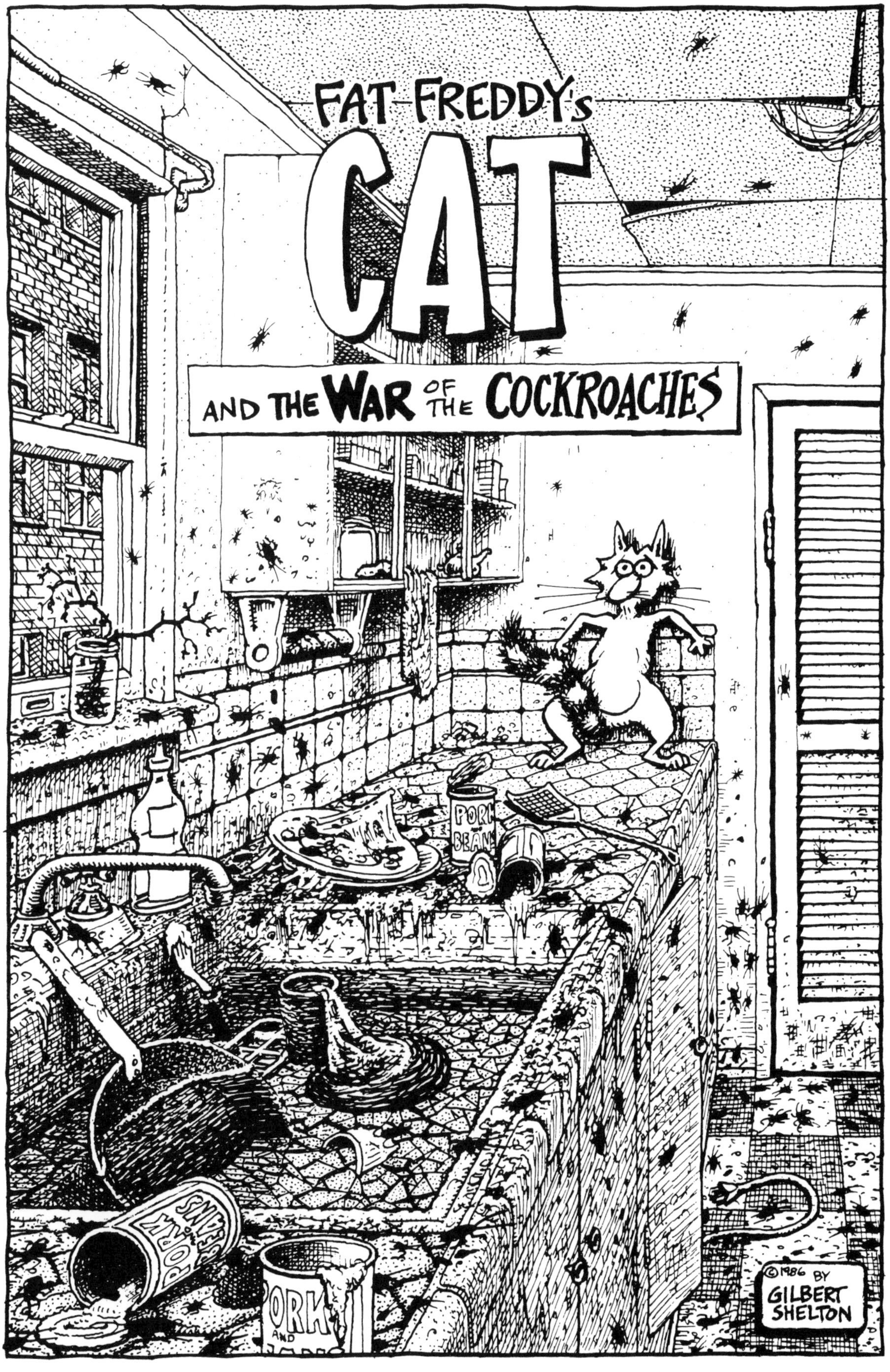
FAT FREDDY'S
CAT
AND THE WAR OF THE COCKROACHES
PORK BEANS
PORK AND BEANS
PORK
©1986 BY GILBERT SHELTON

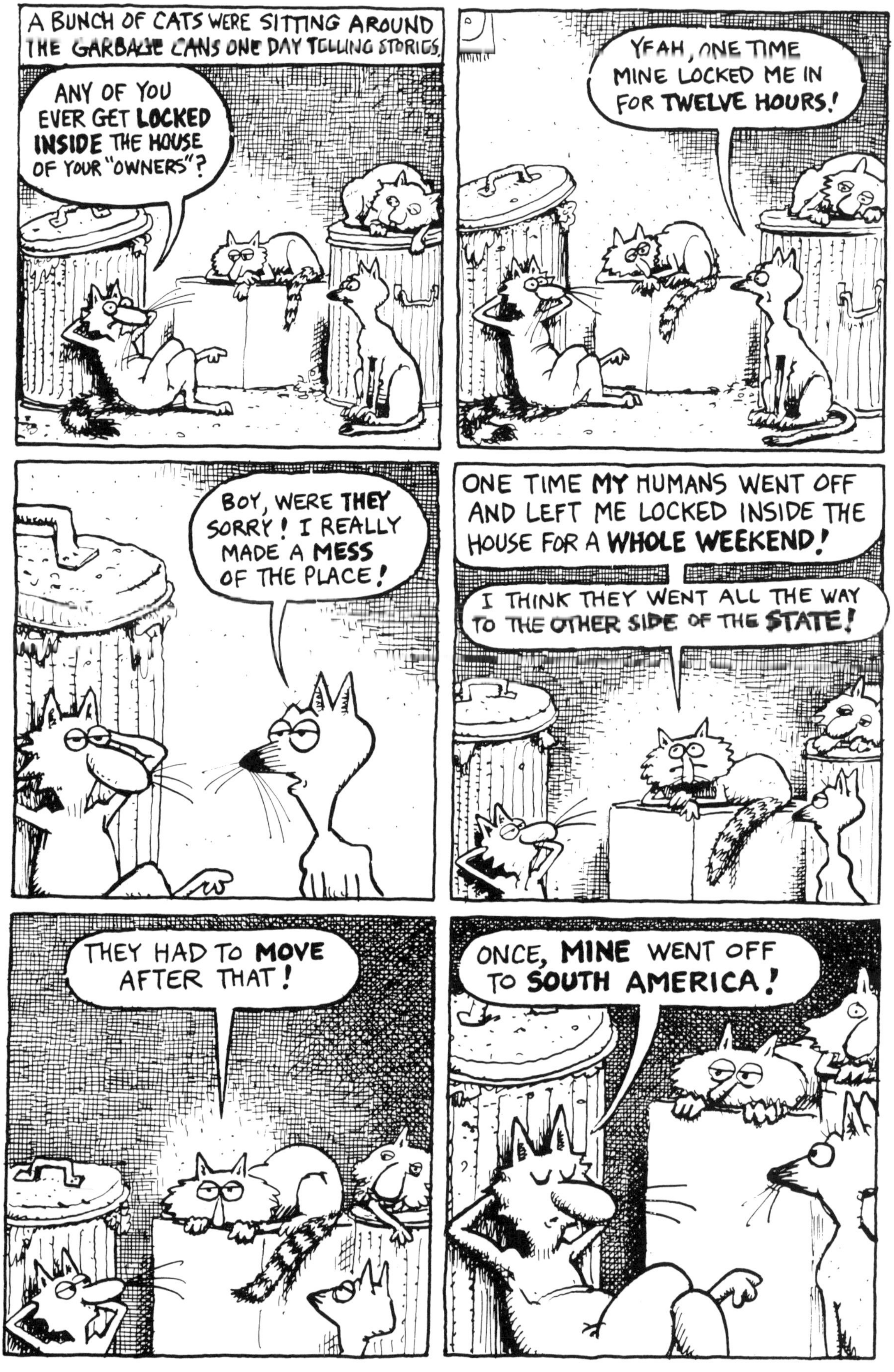
A BUNCH OF CATS WERE SITTING AROUND THE GARBAGE CANS ONE DAY TELLING STORIES.
ANY OF YOU EVER GET LOCKED INSIDE THE HOUSE OF YOUR "OWNERS"?
YEAH, ONE TIME MINE LOCKED ME IN FOR TWELVE HOURS!
BOY, WERE THEY SORRY! I REALLY MADE A MESS OF THE PLACE!
ONE TIME MY HUMANS WENT OFF AND LEFT ME LOCKED INSIDE THE HOUSE FOR A WHOLE WEEKEND!
I THINK THEY WENT ALL THE WAY TO THE OTHER SIDE OF THE STATE!
THEY HAD TO MOVE AFTER THAT!
ONCE, MINE WENT OFF TO SOUTH AMERICA!

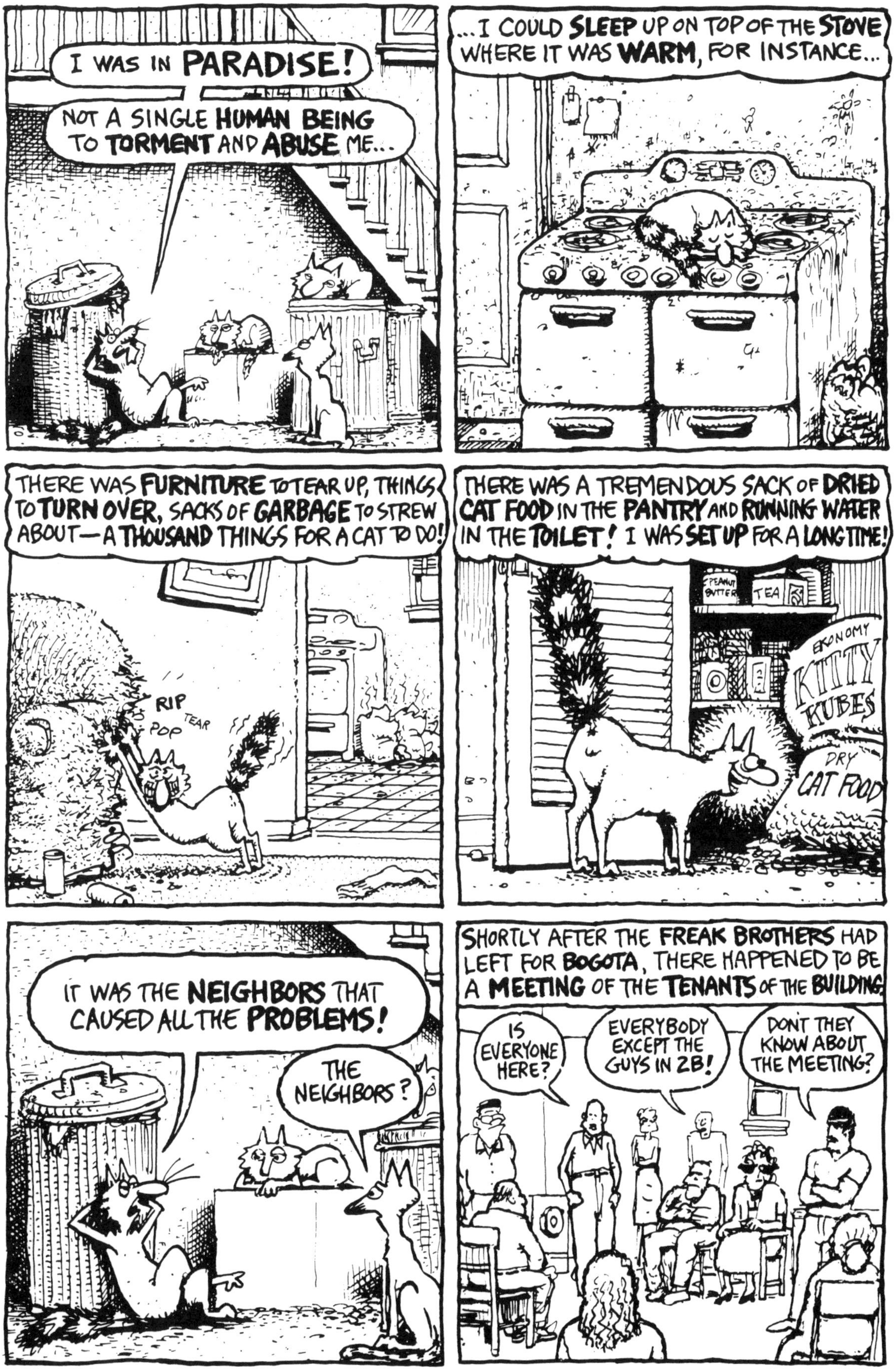
I WAS IN PARADISE!
NOT A SINGLE HUMAN BEING TO TORMENT AND ABUSE ME...
...I COULD SLEEP UP ON TOP OF THE STOVE WHERE IT WAS WARM, FOR INSTANCE...
THERE WAS FURNITURE TO TEAR UP, THINGS TO TURN OVER, SACKS OF GARBAGE TO STREW ABOUT—A THOUSAND THINGS FOR A CAT TO DO!
RIP
TEAR
POP
THERE WAS A TREMENDOUS SACK OF DRIED CAT FOOD IN THE PANTRY AND RUNNING WATER IN THE TOILET! I WAS SET UP FOR A LONG TIME!
PEANUT BUTTER
TEA
EKONOMY KITTY KUBES DRY CAT FOOD
IT WAS THE NEIGHBORS THAT CAUSED ALL THE PROBLEMS!
THE NEIGHBORS?
SHORTLY AFTER THE FREAK BROTHERS HAD LEFT FOR BOGOTA, THERE HAPPENED TO BE A MEETING OF THE TENANTS OF THE BUILDING.
IS EVERYONE HERE?
EVERYBODY EXCEPT THE GUYS IN 2B!
DON'T THEY KNOW ABOUT THE MEETING?

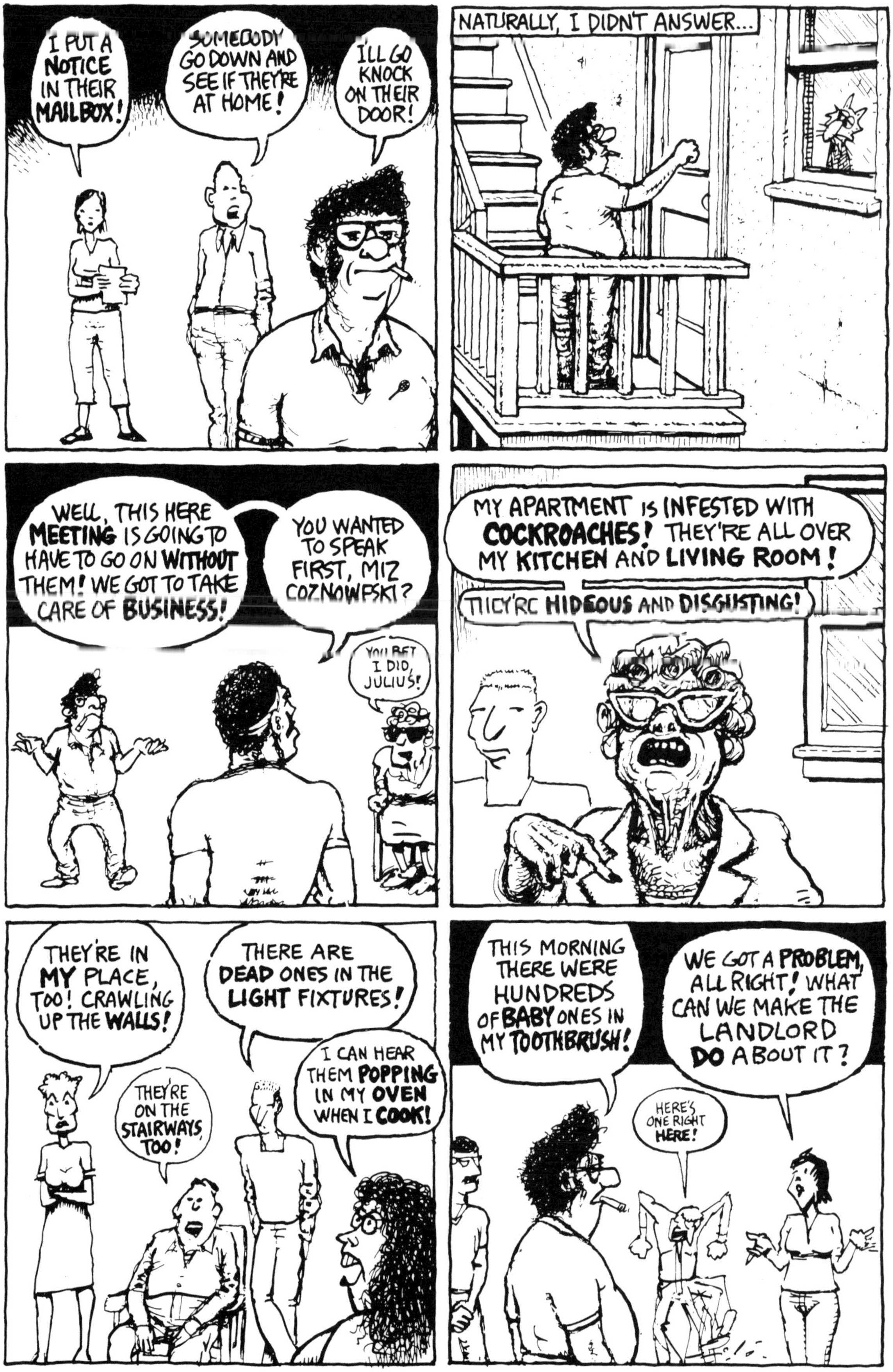
I PUT A NOTICE IN THEIR MAILBOX!
SOMEBODY GO DOWN AND SEE IF THEY'RE AT HOME!
I'LL GO KNOCK ON THEIR DOOR!
NATURALLY, I DIDN'T ANSWER...
WELL, THIS HERE MEETING IS GOING TO HAVE TO GO ON WITHOUT THEM! WE GOT TO TAKE CARE OF BUSINESS!
YOU WANTED TO SPEAK FIRST, MIZ COZNOWFSKI?
YOU BET I DID, JULIUS!
MY APARTMENT IS INFESTED WITH COCKROACHES! THEY'RE ALL OVER MY KITCHEN AND LIVING ROOM!
THEY'RE HIDEOUS AND DISGUSTING!
THEY'RE IN MY PLACE, TOO! CRAWLING UP THE WALLS!
THEY'RE ON THE STAIRWAYS TOO!
THERE ARE DEAD ONES IN THE LIGHT FIXTURES!
I CAN HEAR THEM POPPING IN MY OVEN WHEN I COOK!
THIS MORNING THERE WERE HUNDREDS OF BABY ONES IN MY TOOTHBRUSH!
HERE'S ONE RIGHT HERE!
WE GOT A PROBLEM, ALL RIGHT! WHAT CAN WE MAKE THE LANDLORD DO ABOUT IT?

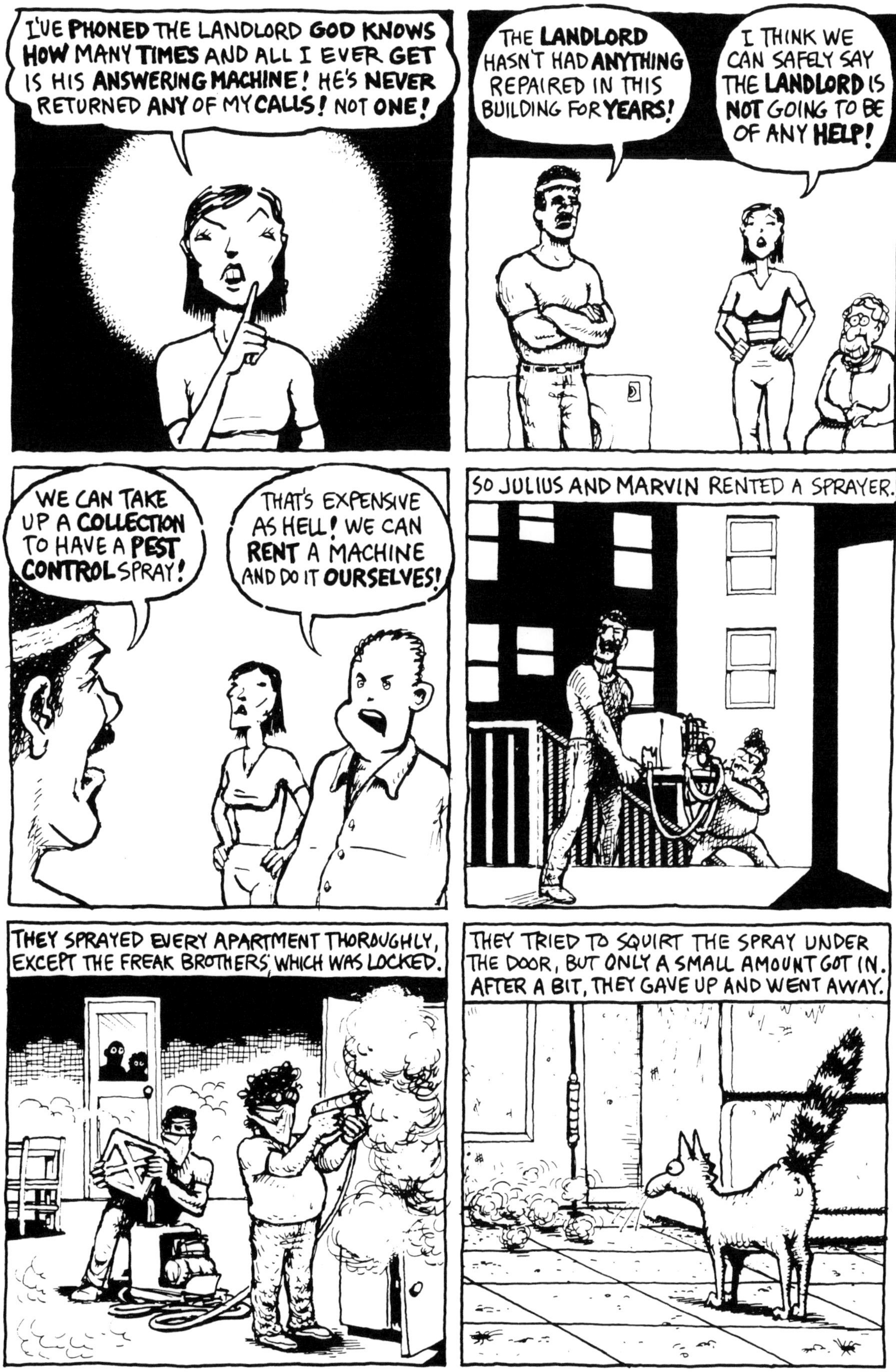
I'VE PHONED THE LANDLORD GOD KNOWS HOW MANY TIMES AND ALL I EVER GET IS HIS ANSWERING MACHINE! HE'S NEVER RETURNED ANY OF MY CALLS! NOT ONE!
THE LANDLORD HASN'T HAD ANYTHING REPAIRED IN THIS BUILDING FOR YEARS!
I THINK WE CAN SAFELY SAY THE LANDLORD IS NOT GOING TO BE OF ANY HELP!
WE CAN TAKE UP A COLLECTION TO HAVE A PEST CONTROL SPRAY!
THAT'S EXPENSIVE AS HELL! WE CAN RENT A MACHINE AND DO IT OURSELVES!
SO JULIUS AND MARVIN RENTED A SPRAYER.
THEY SPRAYED EVERY APARTMENT THOROUGHLY, EXCEPT THE FREAK BROTHERS' WHICH WAS LOCKED.
THEY TRIED TO SQUIRT THE SPRAY UNDER THE DOOR, BUT ONLY A SMALL AMOUNT GOT IN. AFTER A BIT, THEY GAVE UP AND WENT AWAY.

WHEN THE NEIGHBORS WERE ABLE TO RE-ENTER THEIR APARTMENTS, THEY WERE PLEASANTLY SHOCKED.

THE **COCKROACHES** ARE **ALL GONE!**

I DON'T EVEN SEE ANY **DEAD** ONES!

THEY HAD ALL COME INTO **OUR** APARTMENT.

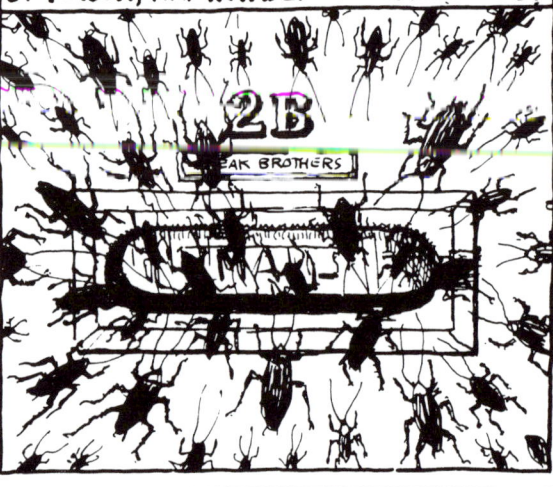

APARTMENT **2B**, BEING IN THE **CENTER** OF THE BUILDING AND THE ONLY PLACE **FREE** OF **POISON**, WAS **INVADED** FROM **ALL SIDES**.

2B
EAK BROTHERS

NOW, SINCE 2B WAS THE **DIRTIEST** APARTMENT OF **ALL**, IT NATURALLY HAD AN **INDIGENOUS** COCKROACH POPULATION ALREADY...

THERE WERE, IN FACT, TWO LARGE CULTURES: THE **CAPITALIST** COCKROACHES, WHICH LIVED IN THE FECUND AND RESOURCE-RICH **KITCHEN**...

...AND THE **COMMUNIST** COCKROACHES, WHICH INHABITED THE VAST BUT RELATIVELY BARREN REGIONS OF THE **LIVING ROOM** AND **BATHROOM**.

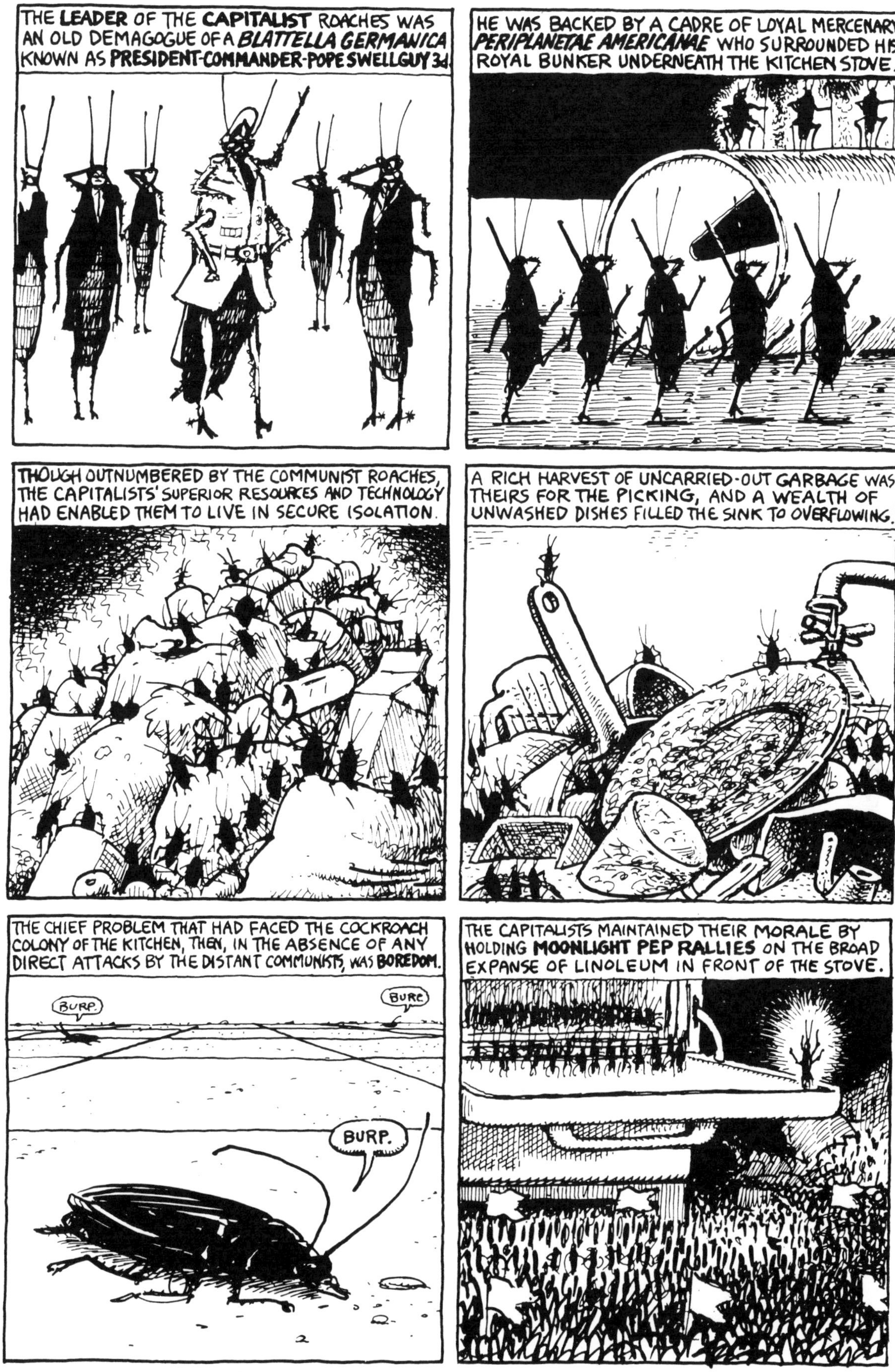
THE LEADER OF THE CAPITALIST ROACHES WAS AN OLD DEMAGOGUE OF A BLATTELLA GERMANICA KNOWN AS PRESIDENT-COMMANDER-POPE SWELLGUY 3d.
HE WAS BACKED BY A CADRE OF LOYAL MERCENARY PERIPLANETAE AMERICANAE WHO SURROUNDED HIS ROYAL BUNKER UNDERNEATH THE KITCHEN STOVE.
THOUGH OUTNUMBERED BY THE COMMUNIST ROACHES, THE CAPITALISTS' SUPERIOR RESOURCES AND TECHNOLOGY HAD ENABLED THEM TO LIVE IN SECURE ISOLATION.
A RICH HARVEST OF UNCARRIED-OUT GARBAGE WAS THEIRS FOR THE PICKING, AND A WEALTH OF UNWASHED DISHES FILLED THE SINK TO OVERFLOWING.
THE CHIEF PROBLEM THAT HAD FACED THE COCKROACH COLONY OF THE KITCHEN, THEN, IN THE ABSENCE OF ANY DIRECT ATTACKS BY THE DISTANT COMMUNISTS, WAS BOREDOM.
BURP.
BURP.
BURP.
THE CAPITALISTS MAINTAINED THEIR MORALE BY HOLDING MOONLIGHT PEP RALLIES ON THE BROAD EXPANSE OF LINOLEUM IN FRONT OF THE STOVE.

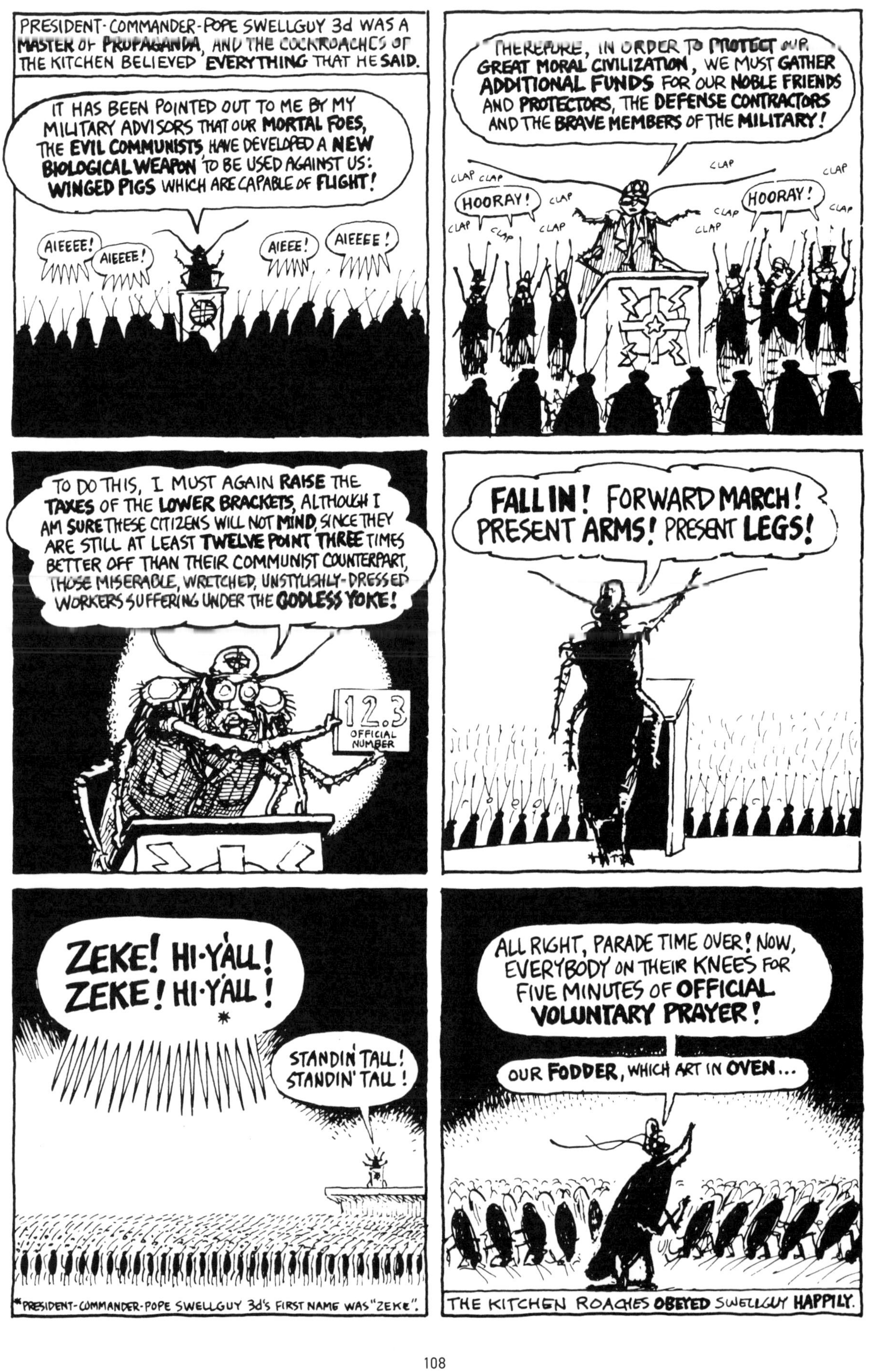
PRESIDENT-COMMANDER-POPE SWELLGUY 3d WAS A MASTER OF PROPAGANDA, AND THE COCKROACHES OF THE KITCHEN BELIEVED EVERYTHING THAT HE SAID.
IT HAS BEEN POINTED OUT TO ME BY MY MILITARY ADVISORS THAT OUR MORTAL FOES, THE EVIL COMMUNISTS, HAVE DEVELOPED A NEW BIOLOGICAL WEAPON TO BE USED AGAINST US: WINGED PIGS WHICH ARE CAPABLE OF FLIGHT!
AIEEEE!
AIEEEE!
AIEEE!
AIEEEE!
THEREFORE, IN ORDER TO PROTECT OUR GREAT MORAL CIVILIZATION, WE MUST GATHER ADDITIONAL FUNDS FOR OUR NOBLE FRIENDS AND PROTECTORS, THE DEFENSE CONTRACTORS AND THE BRAVE MEMBERS OF THE MILITARY!
CLAP CLAP
HOORAY!
CLAP
CLAP
CLAP
CLAP
CLAP
CLAP
HOORAY!
CLAP
CLAP
CLAP
TO DO THIS, I MUST AGAIN RAISE THE TAXES OF THE LOWER BRACKETS, ALTHOUGH I AM SURE THESE CITIZENS WILL NOT MIND, SINCE THEY ARE STILL AT LEAST TWELVE POINT THREE TIMES BETTER OFF THAN THEIR COMMUNIST COUNTERPART, THOSE MISERABLE, WRETCHED, UNSTYLISHLY-DRESSED WORKERS SUFFERING UNDER THE GODLESS YOKE!
12.3 OFFICIAL NUMBER
FALL IN! FORWARD MARCH! PRESENT ARMS! PRESENT LEGS!
ZEKE! HI-Y'ALL! ZEKE! HI-Y'ALL! *
STANDIN' TALL! STANDIN' TALL!
*PRESIDENT-COMMANDER-POPE SWELLGUY 3d's FIRST NAME WAS "ZEKE".
ALL RIGHT, PARADE TIME OVER! NOW, EVERYBODY ON THEIR KNEES FOR FIVE MINUTES OF OFFICIAL VOLUNTARY PRAYER!
OUR FODDER, WHICH ART IN OVEN...
THE KITCHEN ROACHES OBEYED SWELLGUY HAPPILY.

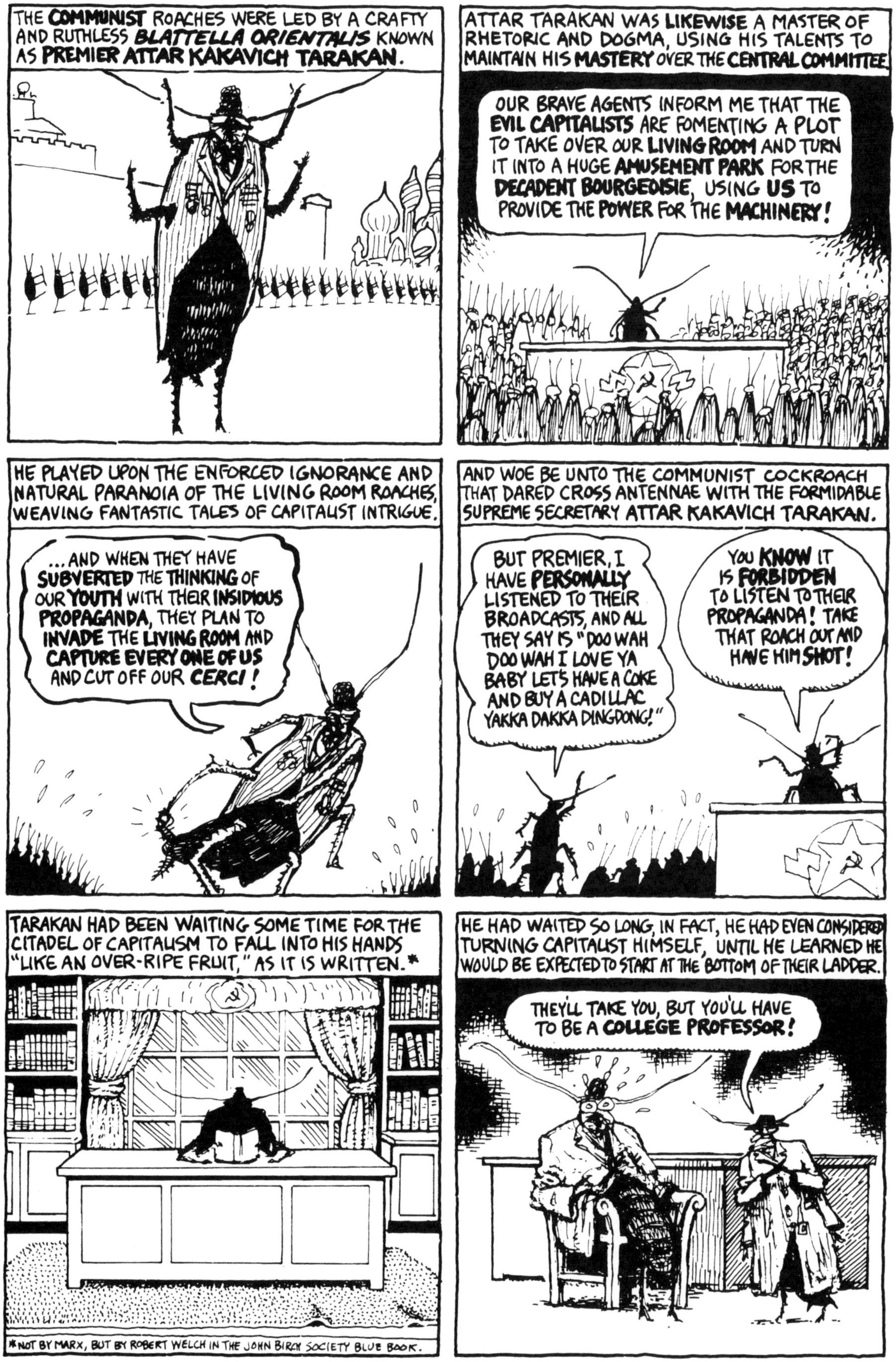

THE COMMUNIST ROACHES WERE LED BY A CRAFTY AND RUTHLESS BLATTELLA ORIENTALIS KNOWN AS PREMIER ATTAR KAKAVICH TARAKAN.
ATTAR TARAKAN WAS LIKEWISE A MASTER OF RHETORIC AND DOGMA, USING HIS TALENTS TO MAINTAIN HIS MASTERY OVER THE CENTRAL COMMITTEE.
OUR BRAVE AGENTS INFORM ME THAT THE EVIL CAPITALISTS ARE FOMENTING A PLOT TO TAKE OVER OUR LIVING ROOM AND TURN IT INTO A HUGE AMUSEMENT PARK FOR THE DECADENT BOURGEOISIE, USING US TO PROVIDE THE POWER FOR THE MACHINERY!
HE PLAYED UPON THE ENFORCED IGNORANCE AND NATURAL PARANOIA OF THE LIVING ROOM ROACHES, WEAVING FANTASTIC TALES OF CAPITALIST INTRIGUE.
...AND WHEN THEY HAVE SUBVERTED THE THINKING OF OUR YOUTH WITH THEIR INSIDIOUS PROPAGANDA, THEY PLAN TO INVADE THE LIVING ROOM AND CAPTURE EVERY ONE OF US AND CUT OFF OUR CERCI!
AND WOE BE UNTO THE COMMUNIST COCKROACH THAT DARED CROSS ANTENNAE WITH THE FORMIDABLE SUPREME SECRETARY ATTAR KAKAVICH TARAKAN.
BUT PREMIER, I HAVE PERSONALLY LISTENED TO THEIR BROADCASTS, AND ALL THEY SAY IS "DOO WAH DOO WAH I LOVE YA BABY LET'S HAVE A COKE AND BUY A CADILLAC YAKKA DAKKA DINGDONG!"
YOU KNOW IT IS FORBIDDEN TO LISTEN TO THEIR PROPAGANDA! TAKE THAT ROACH OUT AND HAVE HIM SHOT!
TARAKAN HAD BEEN WAITING SOME TIME FOR THE CITADEL OF CAPITALISM TO FALL INTO HIS HANDS "LIKE AN OVER-RIPE FRUIT," AS IT IS WRITTEN.*
*NOT BY MARX, BUT BY ROBERT WELCH IN THE JOHN BIRCH SOCIETY BLUE BOOK.
HE HAD WAITED SO LONG, IN FACT, HE HAD EVEN CONSIDERED TURNING CAPITALIST HIMSELF, UNTIL HE LEARNED HE WOULD BE EXPECTED TO START AT THE BOTTOM OF THEIR LADDER.
THEY'LL TAKE YOU, BUT YOU'LL HAVE TO BE A COLLEGE PROFESSOR!

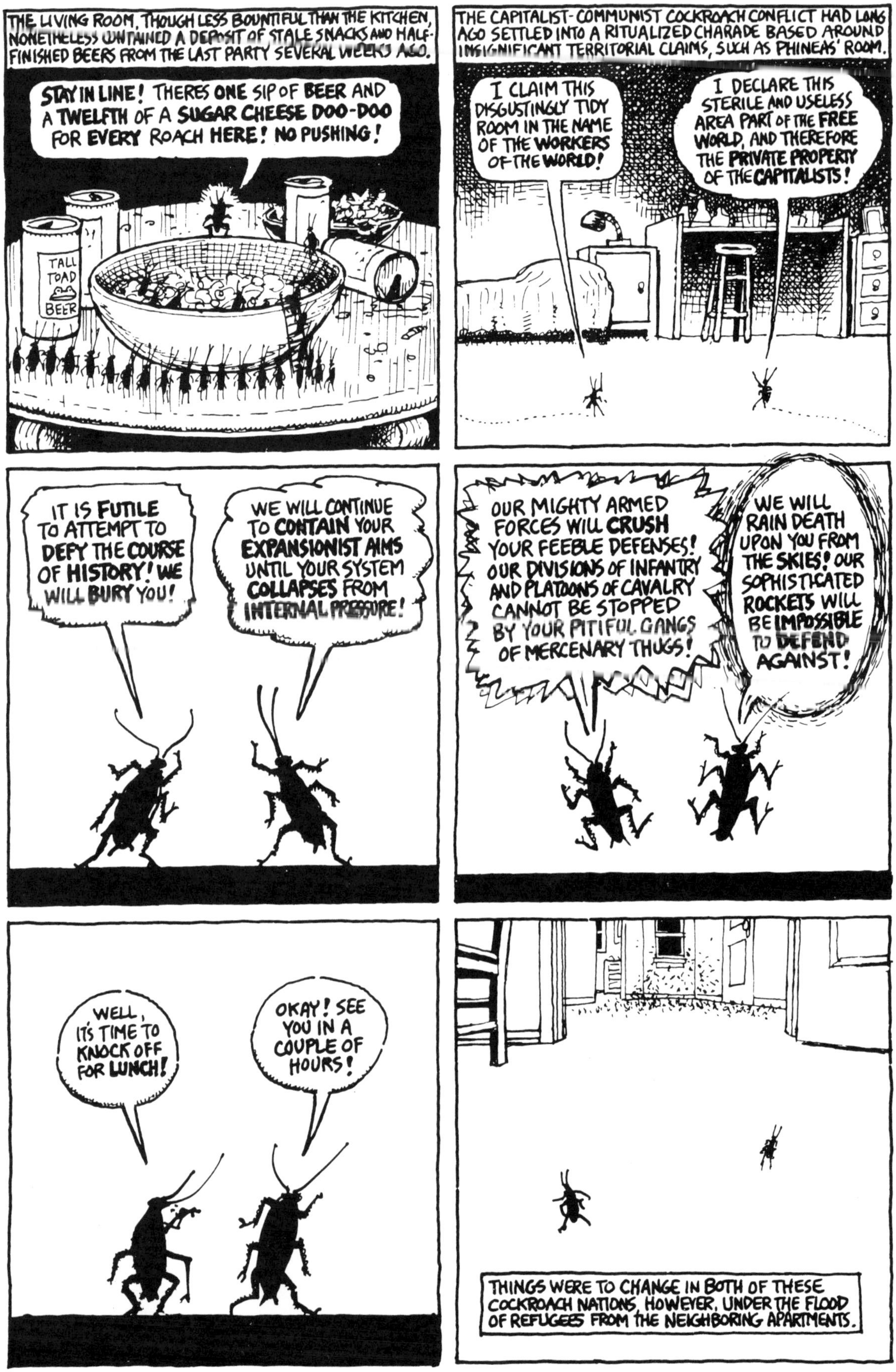

THE LIVING ROOM, THOUGH LESS BOUNTIFUL THAN THE KITCHEN, NONETHELESS CONTAINED A DEPOSIT OF STALE SNACKS AND HALF-FINISHED BEERS FROM THE LAST PARTY SEVERAL WEEKS AGO.
STAY IN LINE! THERES ONE SIP OF BEER AND A TWELFTH OF A SUGAR CHEESE DOO-DOO FOR EVERY ROACH HERE! NO PUSHING!
TALL TOAD BEER
THE CAPITALIST-COMMUNIST COCKROACH CONFLICT HAD LONG AGO SETTLED INTO A RITUALIZED CHARADE BASED AROUND INSIGNIFICANT TERRITORIAL CLAIMS, SUCH AS PHINEAS' ROOM.
I CLAIM THIS DISGUSTINGLY TIDY ROOM IN THE NAME OF THE WORKERS OF THE WORLD!
I DECLARE THIS STERILE AND USELESS AREA PART OF THE FREE WORLD, AND THEREFORE THE PRIVATE PROPERTY OF THE CAPITALISTS!
IT IS FUTILE TO ATTEMPT TO DEFY THE COURSE OF HISTORY! WE WILL BURY YOU!
WE WILL CONTINUE TO CONTAIN YOUR EXPANSIONIST AIMS UNTIL YOUR SYSTEM COLLAPSES FROM INTERNAL PRESSURE!
OUR MIGHTY ARMED FORCES WILL CRUSH YOUR FEEBLE DEFENSES! OUR DIVISIONS OF INFANTRY AND PLATOONS OF CAVALRY CANNOT BE STOPPED BY YOUR PITIFUL GANGS OF MERCENARY THUGS!
WE WILL RAIN DEATH UPON YOU FROM THE SKIES! OUR SOPHISTICATED ROCKETS WILL BE IMPOSSIBLE TO DEFEND AGAINST!
WELL, IT'S TIME TO KNOCK OFF FOR LUNCH!
OKAY! SEE YOU IN A COUPLE OF HOURS!
THINGS WERE TO CHANGE IN BOTH OF THESE COCKROACH NATIONS, HOWEVER, UNDER THE FLOOD OF REFUGEES FROM THE NEIGHBORING APARTMENTS.

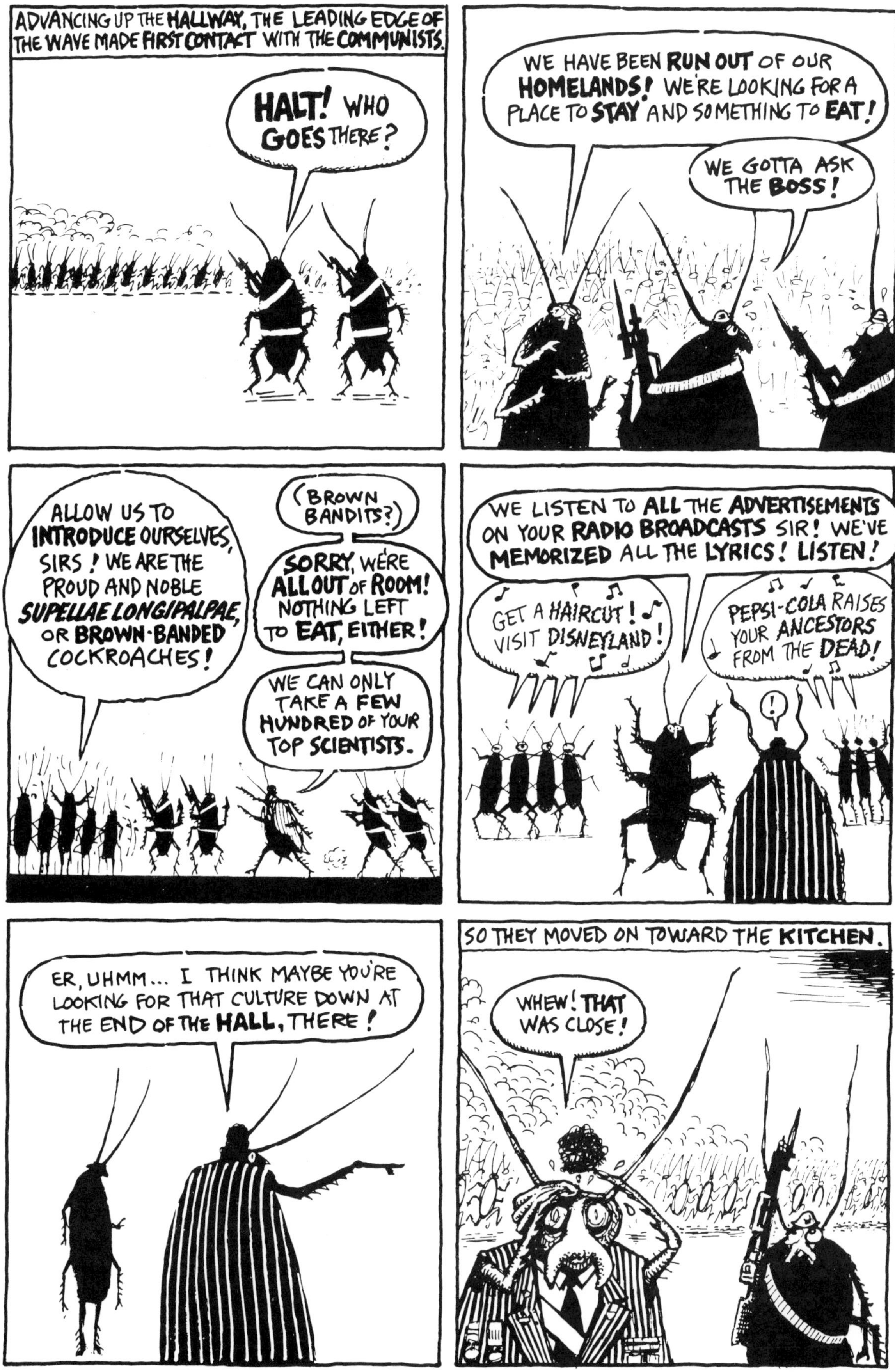

ADVANCING UP THE HALLWAY, THE LEADING EDGE OF THE WAVE MADE FIRST CONTACT WITH THE COMMUNISTS.
HALT! WHO GOES THERE?
WE HAVE BEEN RUN OUT OF OUR HOMELANDS! WE'RE LOOKING FOR A PLACE TO STAY AND SOMETHING TO EAT!
WE GOTTA ASK THE BOSS!
ALLOW US TO INTRODUCE OURSELVES, SIRS! WE ARE THE PROUD AND NOBLE SUPELLAE LONGIPALPAE, OR BROWN-BANDED COCKROACHES!
(BROWN BANDITS?)
SORRY, WE'RE ALL OUT OF ROOM! NOTHING LEFT TO EAT, EITHER!
WE CAN ONLY TAKE A FEW HUNDRED OF YOUR TOP SCIENTISTS.
WE LISTEN TO ALL THE ADVERTISEMENTS ON YOUR RADIO BROADCASTS SIR! WE'VE MEMORIZED ALL THE LYRICS! LISTEN!
GET A HAIRCUT! VISIT DISNEYLAND!
PEPSI-COLA RAISES YOUR ANCESTORS FROM THE DEAD!
!
ER, UHMM... I THINK MAYBE YOU'RE LOOKING FOR THAT CULTURE DOWN AT THE END OF THE HALL, THERE!
SO THEY MOVED ON TOWARD THE KITCHEN.
WHEW! THAT WAS CLOSE!

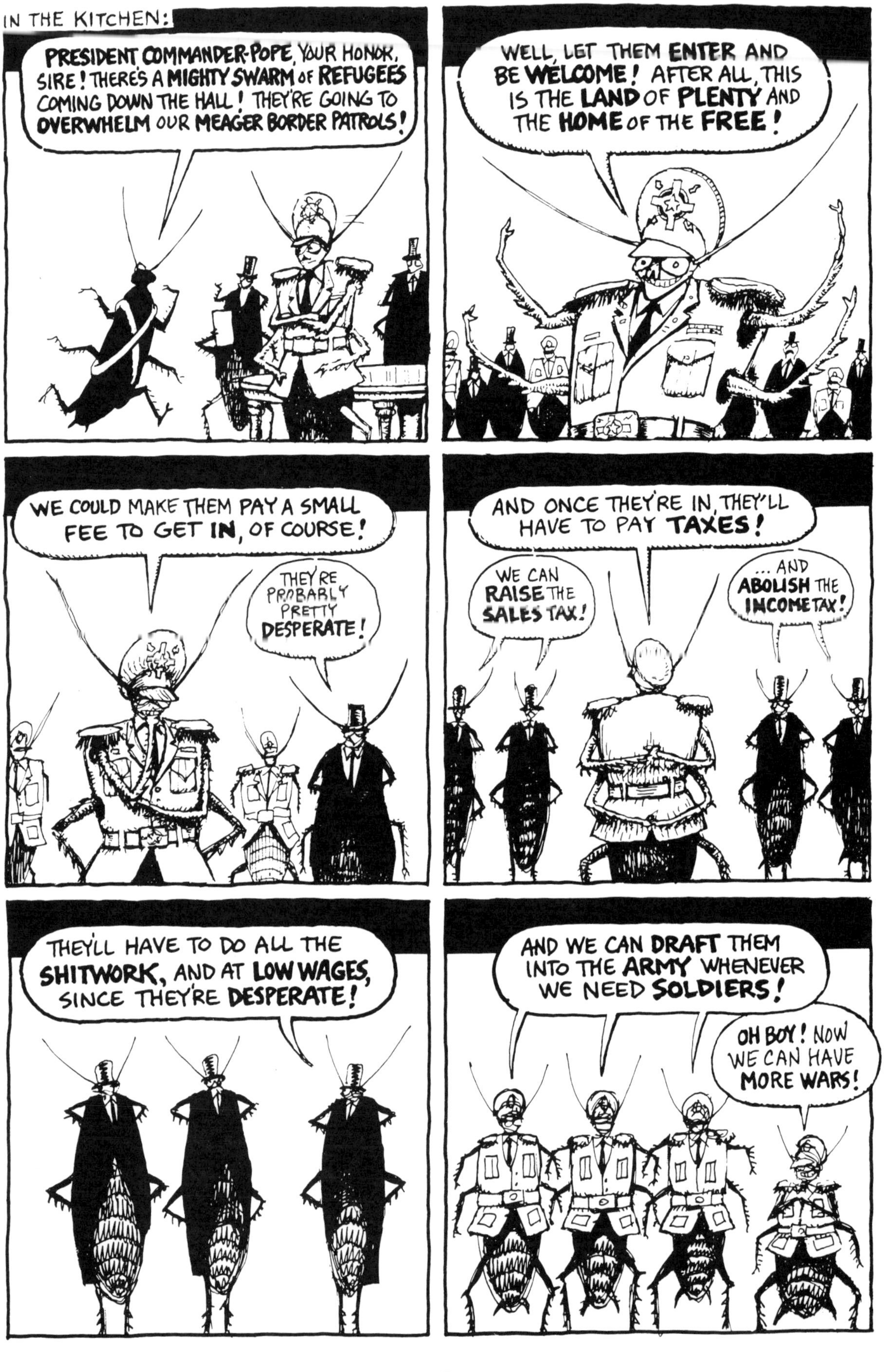
IN THE KITCHEN:
PRESIDENT COMMANDER-POPE, YOUR HONOR, SIRE! THERE'S A MIGHTY SWARM OF REFUGEES COMING DOWN THE HALL! THEY'RE GOING TO OVERWHELM OUR MEAGER BORDER PATROLS!
WELL, LET THEM ENTER AND BE WELCOME! AFTER ALL, THIS IS THE LAND OF PLENTY AND THE HOME OF THE FREE!
WE COULD MAKE THEM PAY A SMALL FEE TO GET IN, OF COURSE!
THEY'RE PROBABLY PRETTY DESPERATE!
AND ONCE THEY'RE IN, THEY'LL HAVE TO PAY TAXES!
WE CAN RAISE THE SALES TAX!
... AND ABOLISH THE INCOME TAX!
THEY'LL HAVE TO DO ALL THE SHITWORK, AND AT LOW WAGES, SINCE THEY'RE DESPERATE!
AND WE CAN DRAFT THEM INTO THE ARMY WHENEVER WE NEED SOLDIERS!
OH BOY! NOW WE CAN HAVE MORE WARS!

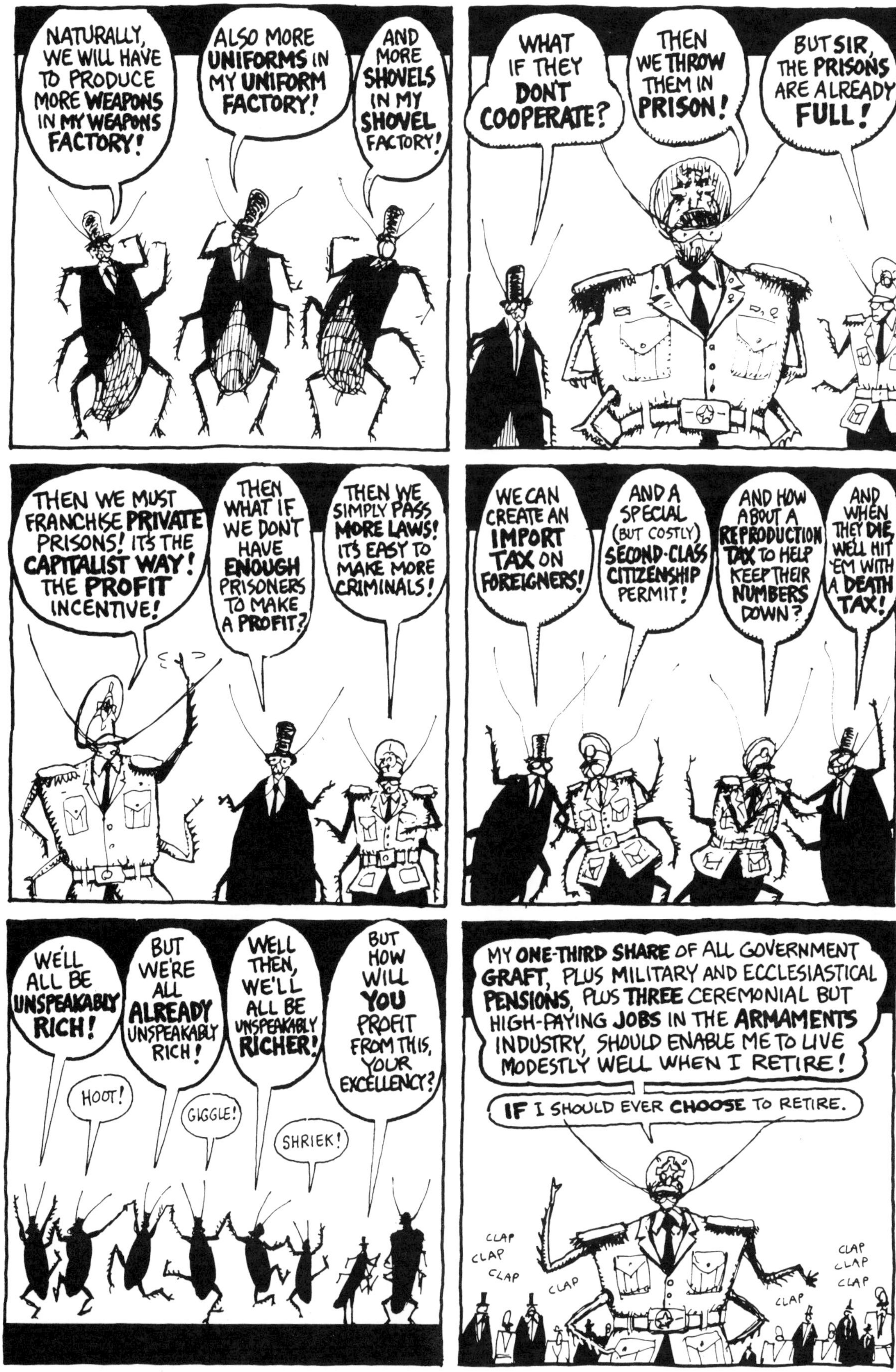
NATURALLY, WE WILL HAVE TO PRODUCE MORE WEAPONS IN MY WEAPONS FACTORY!
ALSO MORE UNIFORMS IN MY UNIFORM FACTORY!
AND MORE SHOVELS IN MY SHOVEL FACTORY!
WHAT IF THEY DON'T COOPERATE?
THEN WE THROW THEM IN PRISON!
BUT SIR, THE PRISONS ARE ALREADY FULL!
THEN WE MUST FRANCHISE PRIVATE PRISONS! IT'S THE CAPITALIST WAY! THE PROFIT INCENTIVE!
THEN WHAT IF WE DON'T HAVE ENOUGH PRISONERS TO MAKE A PROFIT?
THEN WE SIMPLY PASS MORE LAWS! IT'S EASY TO MAKE MORE CRIMINALS!
WE CAN CREATE AN IMPORT TAX ON FOREIGNERS!
AND A SPECIAL (BUT COSTLY) SECOND-CLASS CITIZENSHIP PERMIT!
AND HOW ABOUT A REPRODUCTION TAX TO HELP KEEP THEIR NUMBERS DOWN?
AND WHEN THEY DIE, WE'LL HIT 'EM WITH A DEATH TAX!
WE'LL ALL BE UNSPEAKABLY RICH!
BUT WE'RE ALL ALREADY UNSPEAKABLY RICH!
WELL THEN, WE'LL ALL BE UNSPEAKABLY RICHER!
BUT HOW WILL YOU PROFIT FROM THIS, YOUR EXCELLENCY?
HOOT!
GIGGLE!
SHRIEK!
MY ONE-THIRD SHARE OF ALL GOVERNMENT GRAFT, PLUS MILITARY AND ECCLESIASTICAL PENSIONS, PLUS THREE CEREMONIAL BUT HIGH-PAYING JOBS IN THE ARMAMENTS INDUSTRY, SHOULD ENABLE ME TO LIVE MODESTLY WELL WHEN I RETIRE!
IF I SHOULD EVER CHOOSE TO RETIRE.
CLAP CLAP CLAP
CLAP
CLAP
CLAP CLAP CLAP

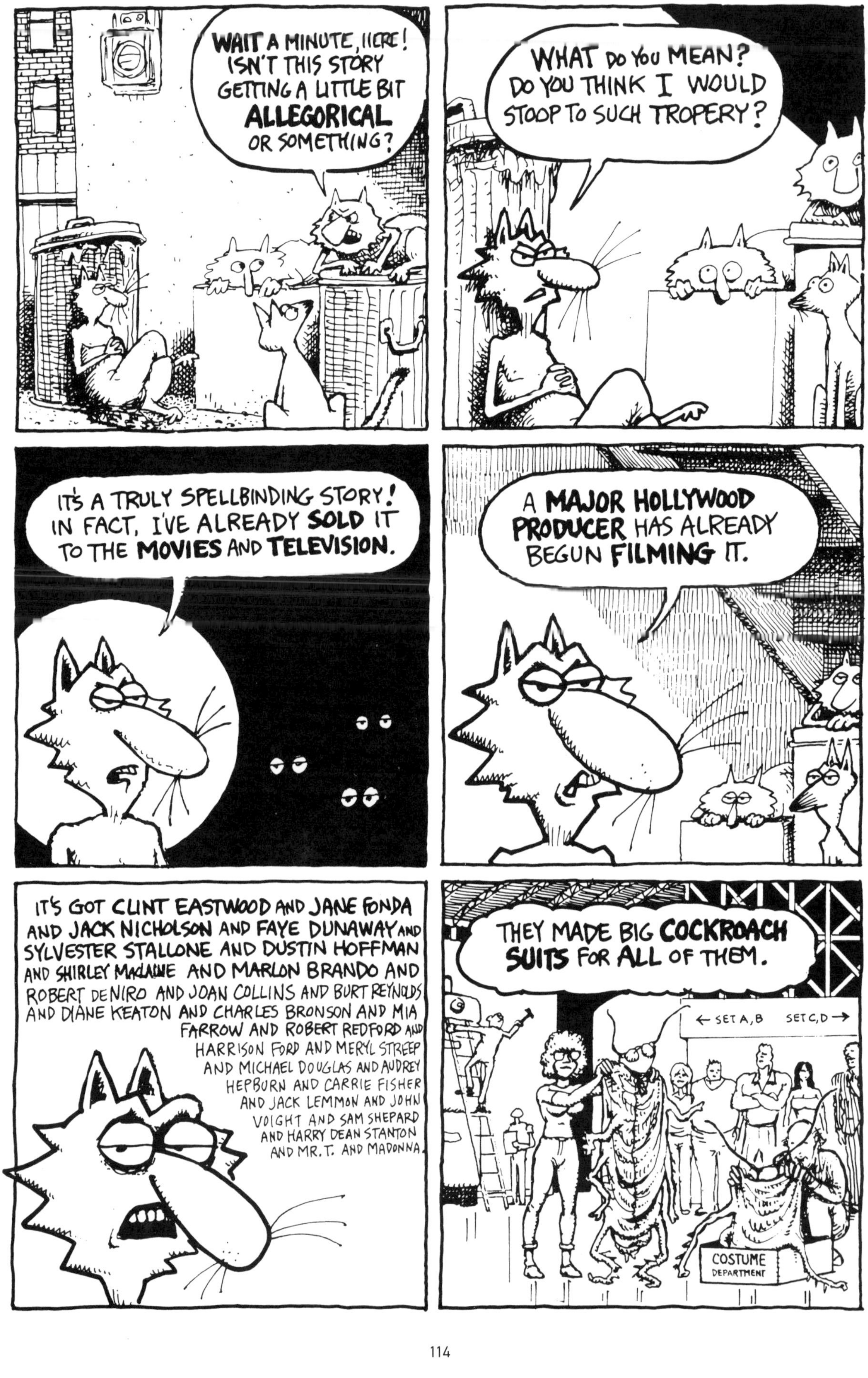
WAIT A MINUTE, HERE! ISN'T THIS STORY GETTING A LITTLE BIT ALLEGORICAL OR SOMETHING?
WHAT DO YOU MEAN? DO YOU THINK I WOULD STOOP TO SUCH TROPERY?
IT'S A TRULY SPELLBINDING STORY! IN FACT, I'VE ALREADY SOLD IT TO THE MOVIES AND TELEVISION.
A MAJOR HOLLYWOOD PRODUCER HAS ALREADY BEGUN FILMING IT.
IT'S GOT CLINT EASTWOOD AND JANE FONDA AND JACK NICHOLSON AND FAYE DUNAWAY AND SYLVESTER STALLONE AND DUSTIN HOFFMAN AND SHIRLEY MACLAINE AND MARLON BRANDO AND ROBERT DENIRO AND JOAN COLLINS AND BURT REYNOLDS AND DIANE KEATON AND CHARLES BRONSON AND MIA FARROW AND ROBERT REDFORD AND HARRISON FORD AND MERYL STREEP AND MICHAEL DOUGLAS AND AUDREY HEPBURN AND CARRIE FISHER AND JACK LEMMON AND JOHN VOIGHT AND SAM SHEPARD AND HARRY DEAN STANTON AND MR. T. AND MADONNA.
THEY MADE BIG COCKROACH SUITS FOR ALL OF THEM.
← SET A, B
SET C, D →
COSTUME DEPARTMENT

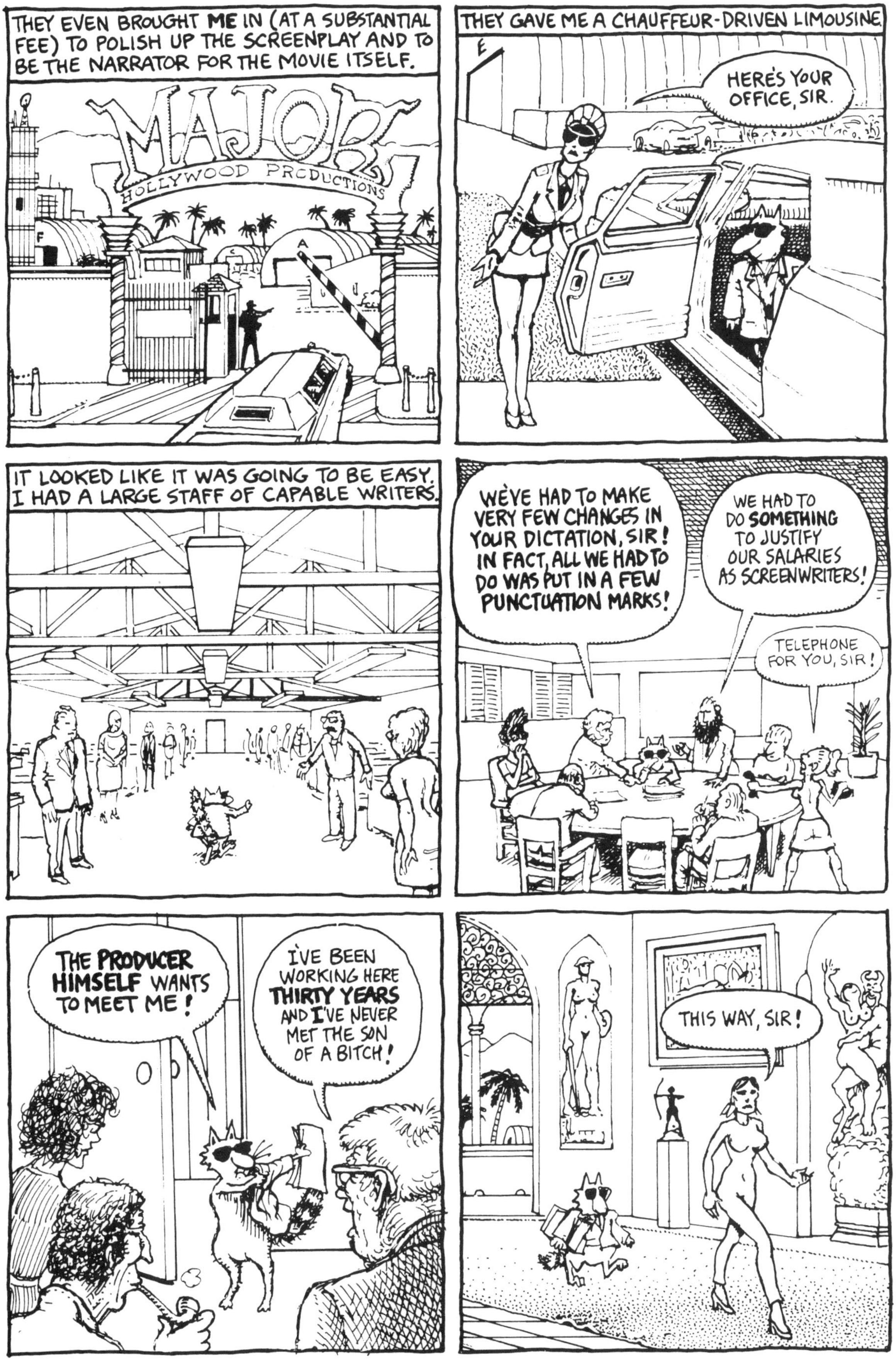
THEY EVEN BROUGHT **ME** IN (AT A SUBSTANTIAL FEE) TO POLISH UP THE SCREENPLAY AND TO BE THE NARRATOR FOR THE MOVIE ITSELF.
MAJOR
HOLLYWOOD PRODUCTIONS
THEY GAVE ME A CHAUFFEUR-DRIVEN LIMOUSINE.
HERE'S YOUR OFFICE, SIR.
IT LOOKED LIKE IT WAS GOING TO BE EASY. I HAD A LARGE STAFF OF CAPABLE WRITERS.
WE'VE HAD TO MAKE VERY FEW CHANGES IN YOUR DICTATION, SIR! IN FACT, ALL WE HAD TO DO WAS PUT IN A FEW PUNCTUATION MARKS!
WE HAD TO DO **SOMETHING** TO JUSTIFY OUR SALARIES AS SCREENWRITERS!
TELEPHONE FOR YOU, SIR!
THE **PRODUCER HIMSELF** WANTS TO MEET ME!
I'VE BEEN WORKING HERE **THIRTY YEARS** AND **I'VE** NEVER MET THE SON OF A BITCH!
THIS WAY, SIR!

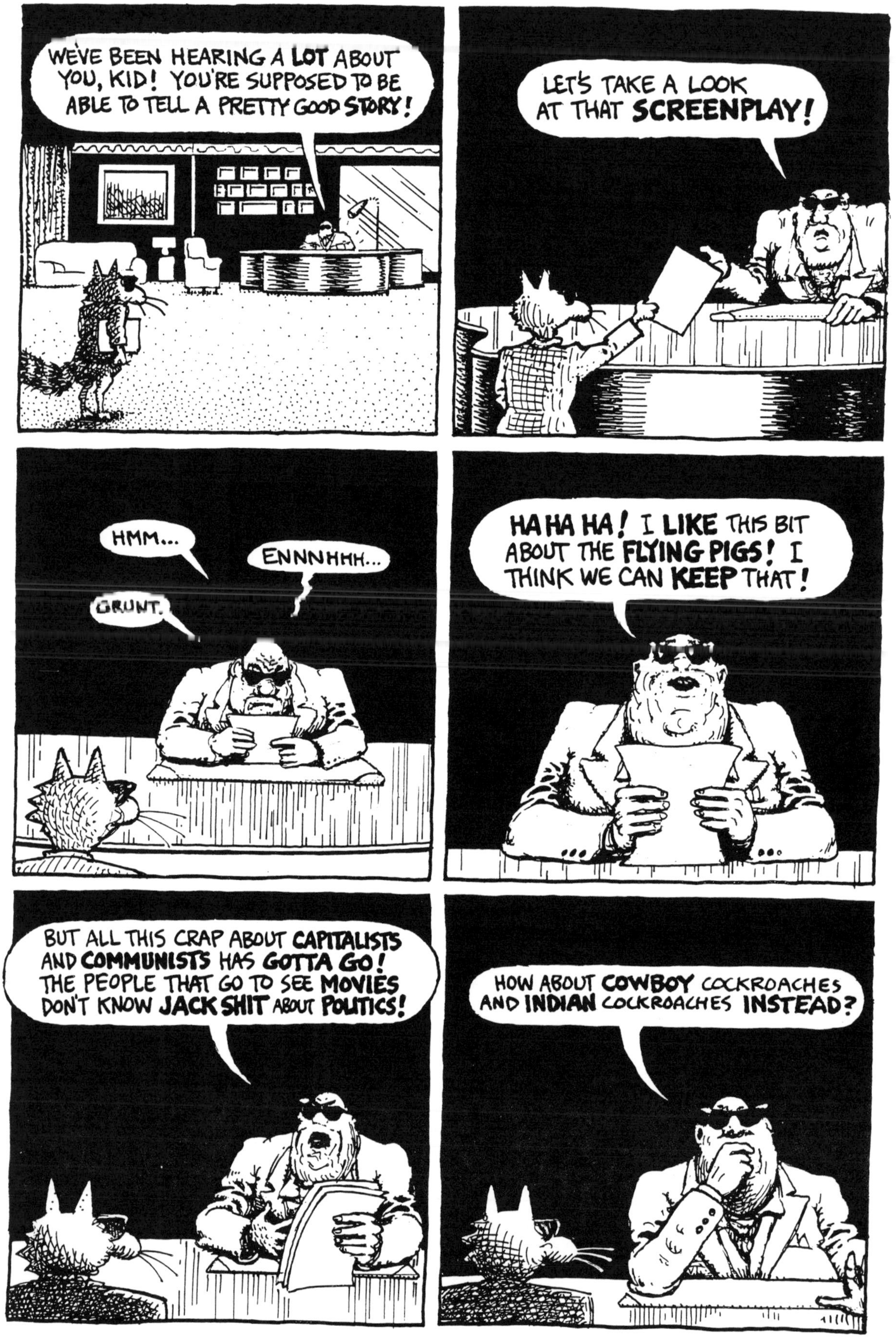
WE'VE BEEN HEARING A LOT ABOUT YOU, KID! YOU'RE SUPPOSED TO BE ABLE TO TELL A PRETTY GOOD STORY!
LET'S TAKE A LOOK AT THAT SCREENPLAY!
HMM...
ENNNHHH...
GRUNT.
HA HA HA! I LIKE THIS BIT ABOUT THE FLYING PIGS! I THINK WE CAN KEEP THAT!
BUT ALL THIS CRAP ABOUT CAPITALISTS AND COMMUNISTS HAS GOTTA GO! THE PEOPLE THAT GO TO SEE MOVIES DON'T KNOW JACK SHIT ABOUT POLITICS!
HOW ABOUT COWBOY COCKROACHES AND INDIAN COCKROACHES INSTEAD?

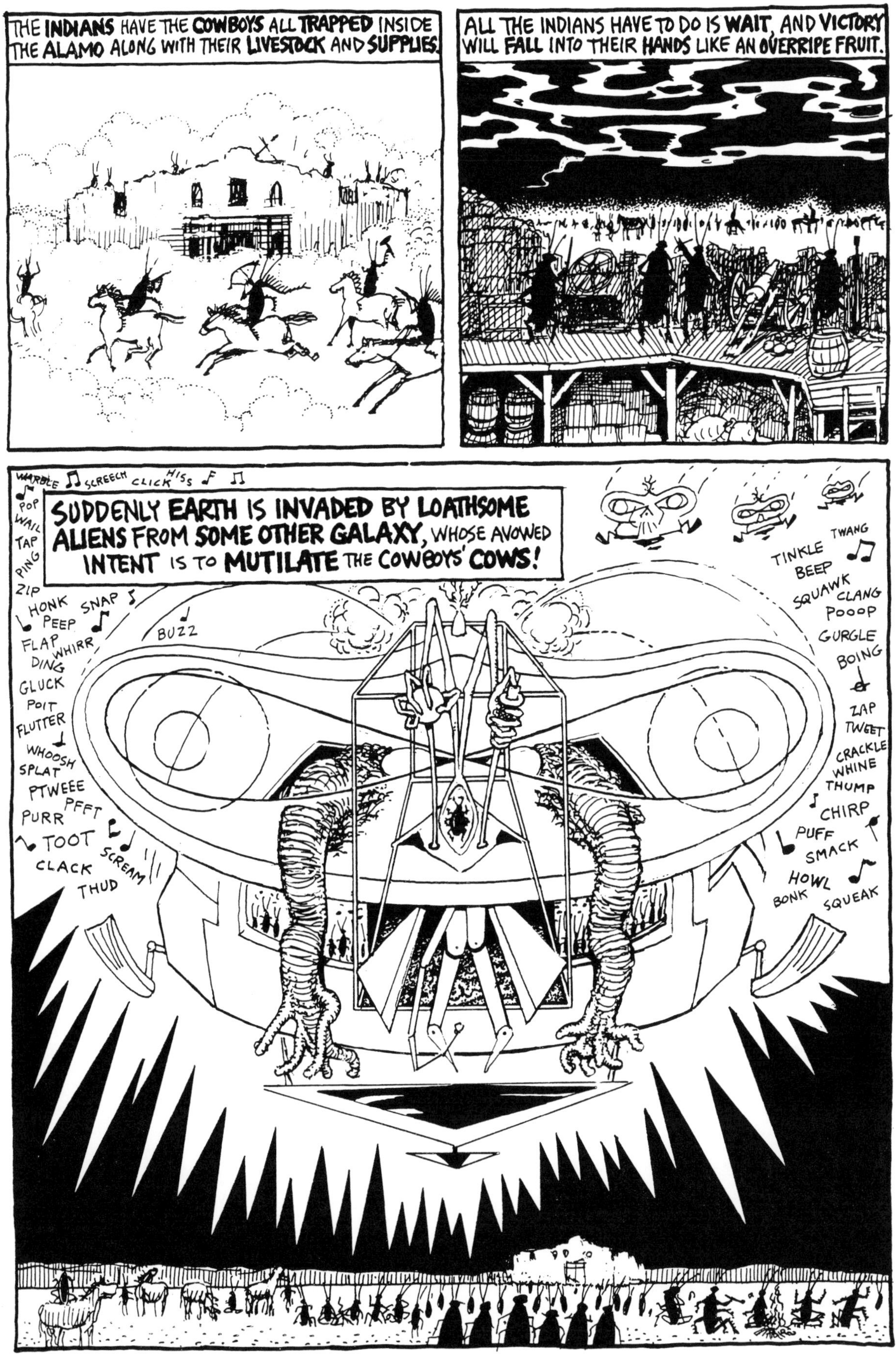
THE INDIANS HAVE THE COWBOYS ALL TRAPPED INSIDE THE ALAMO ALONG WITH THEIR LIVESTOCK AND SUPPLIES.
ALL THE INDIANS HAVE TO DO IS WAIT, AND VICTORY WILL FALL INTO THEIR HANDS LIKE AN OVERRIPE FRUIT.
WARBLE SCREECH CLICK HISS
POP WAIL TAP PING
SUDDENLY EARTH IS INVADED BY LOATHSOME ALIENS FROM SOME OTHER GALAXY, WHOSE AVOWED INTENT IS TO MUTILATE THE COWBOYS' COWS!
TWANG TINKLE BEEP SQUAWK CLANG POOOP GURGLE BOING ZAP TWEET CRACKLE WHINE THUMP CHIRP PUFF SMACK HOWL BONK SQUEAK
ZIP HONK PEEP SNAP FLAP WHIRR BUZZ DING GLUCK POIT FLUTTER WHOOSH SPLAT PTWEEE PFFT PURR TOOT SCREAM CLACK THUD

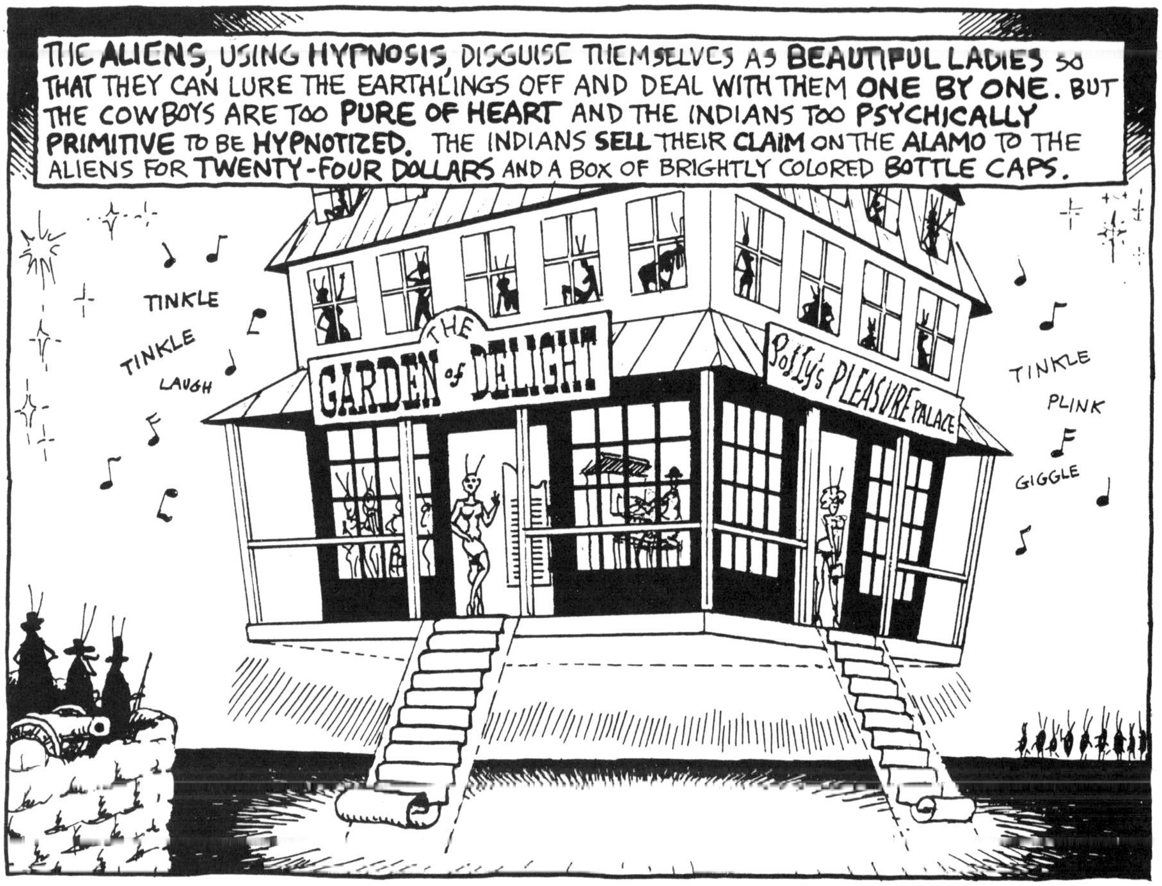
THE ALIENS, USING HYPNOSIS, DISGUISE THEMSELVES AS BEAUTIFUL LADIES SO THAT THEY CAN LURE THE EARTHLINGS OFF AND DEAL WITH THEM ONE BY ONE. BUT THE COWBOYS ARE TOO PURE OF HEART AND THE INDIANS TOO PSYCHICALLY PRIMITIVE TO BE HYPNOTIZED. THE INDIANS SELL THEIR CLAIM ON THE ALAMO TO THE ALIENS FOR TWENTY-FOUR DOLLARS AND A BOX OF BRIGHTLY COLORED BOTTLE CAPS.
TINKLE
TINKLE
LAUGH
THE GARDEN of DELIGHT
Polly's PLEASURE PALACE
TINKLE
PLINK
GIGGLE

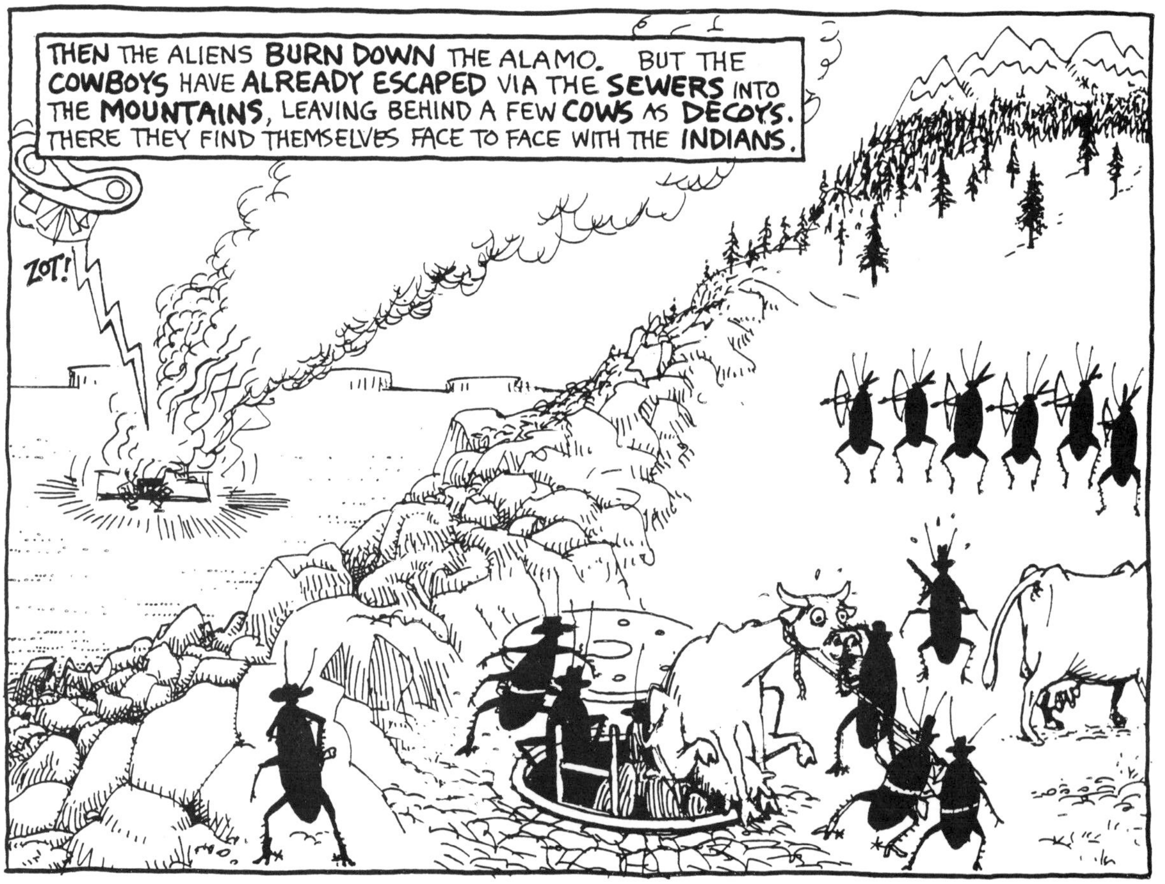
THEN THE ALIENS BURN DOWN THE ALAMO. BUT THE COWBOYS HAVE ALREADY ESCAPED VIA THE SEWERS INTO THE MOUNTAINS, LEAVING BEHIND A FEW COWS AS DECOYS. THERE THEY FIND THEMSELVES FACE TO FACE WITH THE INDIANS.
ZOT!

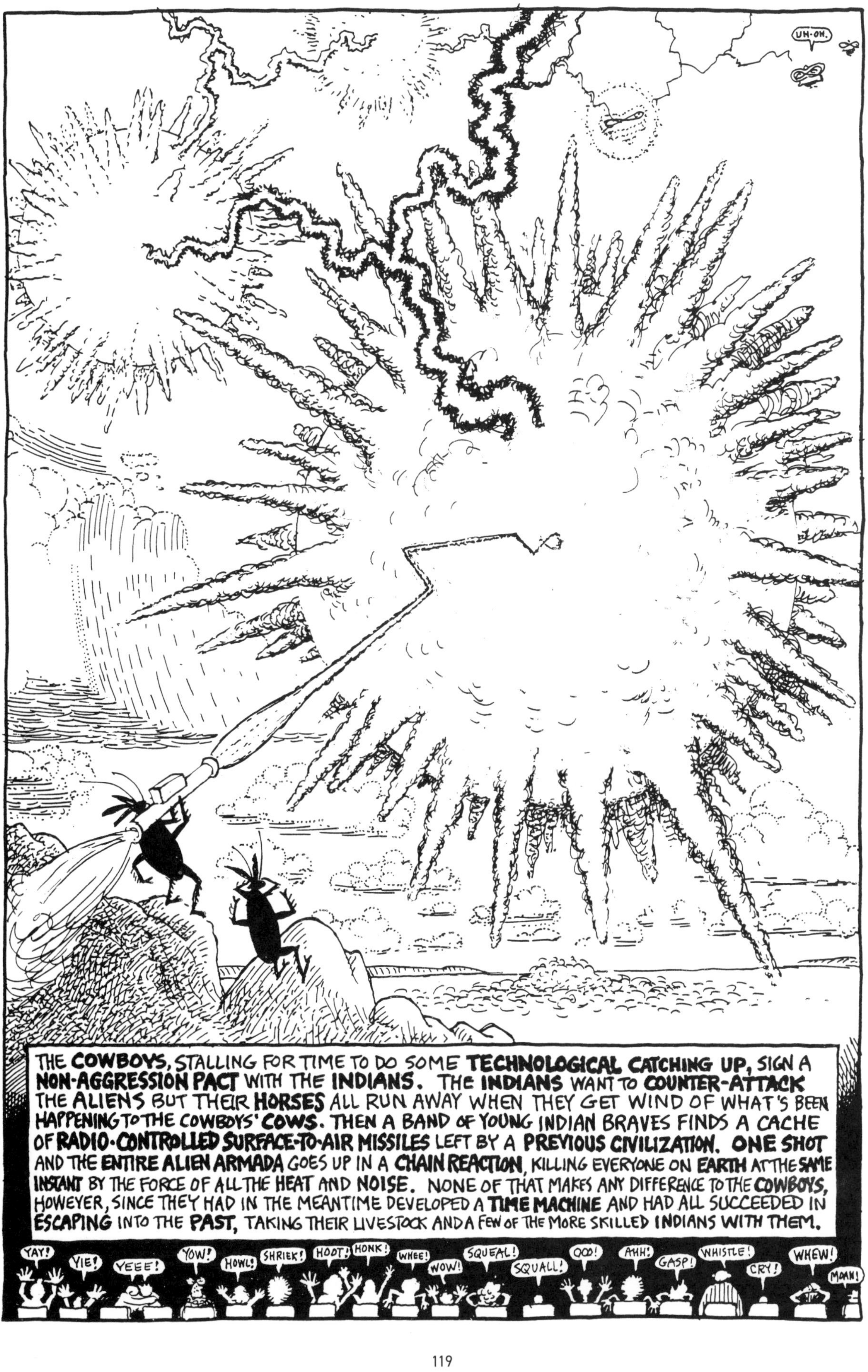
UH-OH.
THE COWBOYS, STALLING FOR TIME TO DO SOME TECHNOLOGICAL CATCHING UP, SIGN A NON-AGGRESSION PACT WITH THE INDIANS. THE INDIANS WANT TO COUNTER-ATTACK THE ALIENS BUT THEIR HORSES ALL RUN AWAY WHEN THEY GET WIND OF WHAT'S BEEN HAPPENING TO THE COWBOYS' COWS. THEN A BAND OF YOUNG INDIAN BRAVES FINDS A CACHE OF RADIO-CONTROLLED SURFACE-TO-AIR MISSILES LEFT BY A PREVIOUS CIVILIZATION. ONE SHOT AND THE ENTIRE ALIEN ARMADA GOES UP IN A CHAIN REACTION, KILLING EVERYONE ON EARTH AT THE SAME INSTANT BY THE FORCE OF ALL THE HEAT AND NOISE. NONE OF THAT MAKES ANY DIFFERENCE TO THE COWBOYS, HOWEVER, SINCE THEY HAD IN THE MEANTIME DEVELOPED A TIME MACHINE AND HAD ALL SUCCEEDED IN ESCAPING INTO THE PAST, TAKING THEIR LIVESTOCK AND A FEW OF THE MORE SKILLED INDIANS WITH THEM.
YAY!
YIE!
YEEE!
YOW!
HOWL!
SHRIEK!
HOOT!
HONK!
WHEE!
WOW!
SQUEAL!
SQUALL!
OOO!
AHH!
GASP!
WHISTLE!
CRY!
WHEW!
MOAN!

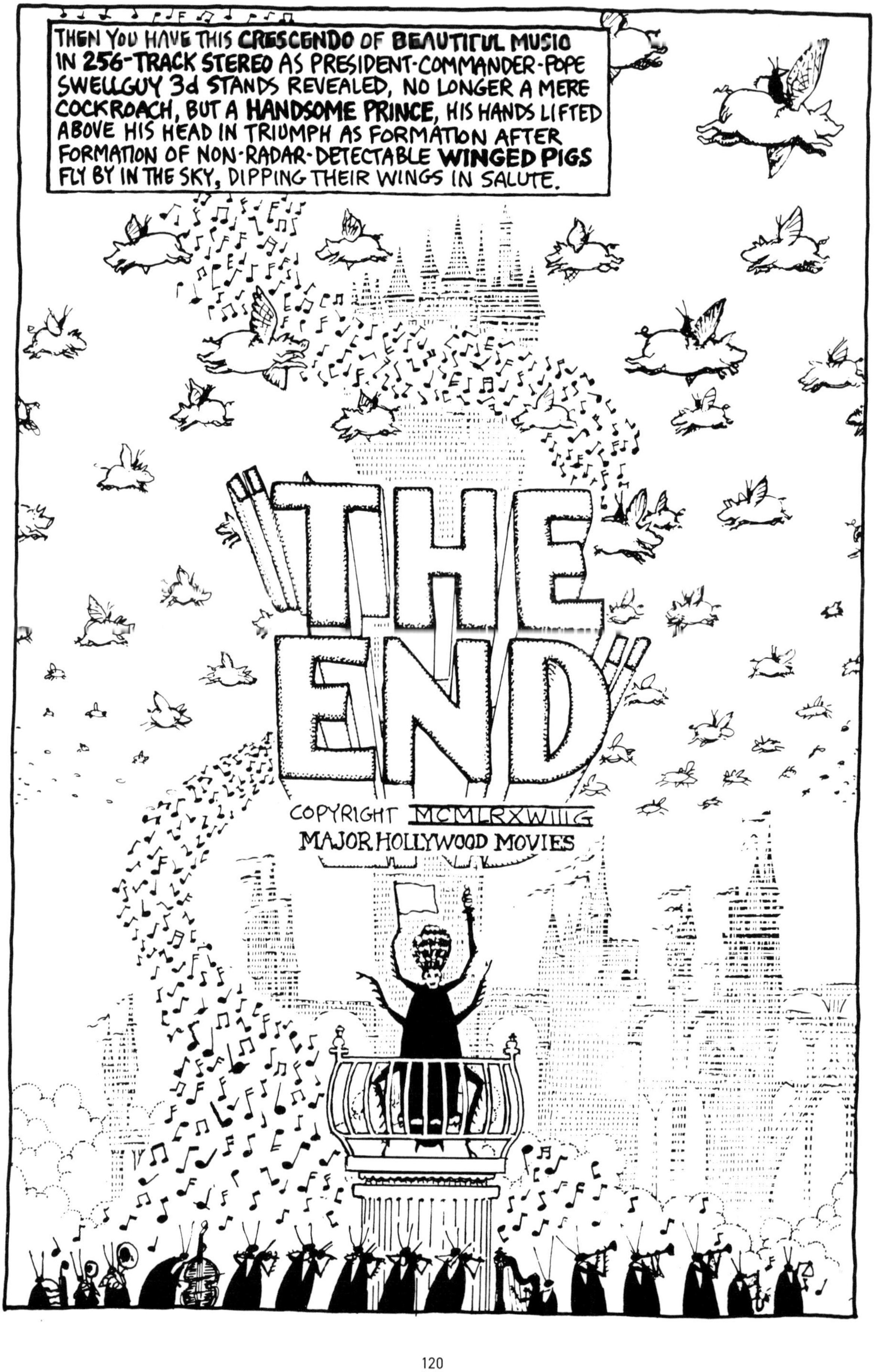
THEN YOU HAVE THIS CRESCENDO OF BEAUTIFUL MUSIC IN 256-TRACK STEREO AS PRESIDENT-COMMANDER-POPE SWELLGUY 3d STANDS REVEALED, NO LONGER A MERE COCKROACH, BUT A HANDSOME PRINCE, HIS HANDS LIFTED ABOVE HIS HEAD IN TRIUMPH AS FORMATION AFTER FORMATION OF NON-RADAR-DETECTABLE WINGED PIGS FLY BY IN THE SKY, DIPPING THEIR WINGS IN SALUTE.
"THE END"
COPYRIGHT MCMLRXWIIIG
MAJOR HOLLYWOOD MOVIES

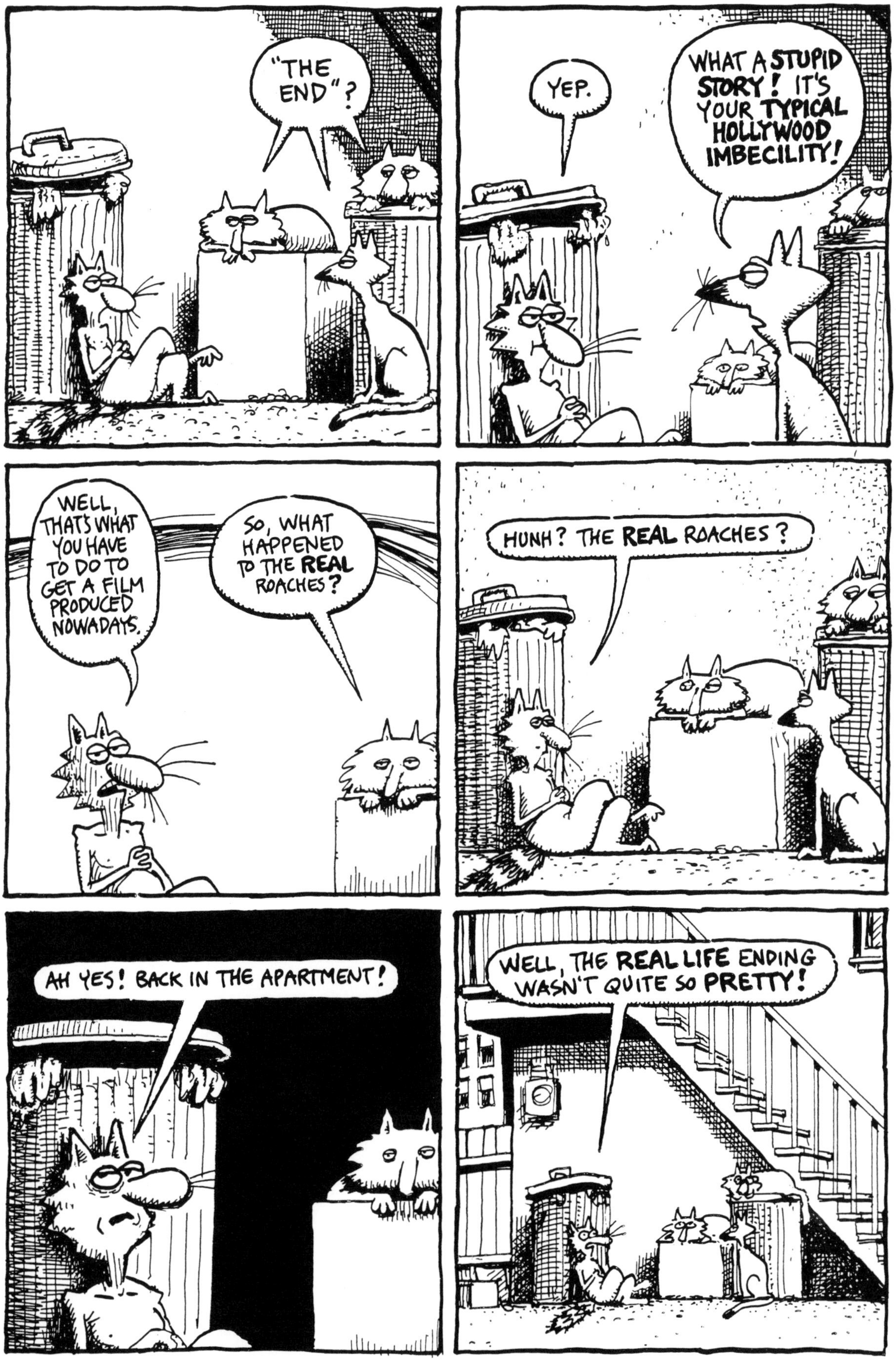
"THE END"?
YEP.
WHAT A STUPID STORY! IT'S YOUR TYPICAL HOLLYWOOD IMBECILITY!
WELL, THAT'S WHAT YOU HAVE TO DO TO GET A FILM PRODUCED NOWADAYS.
SO, WHAT HAPPENED TO THE REAL ROACHES?
HUNH? THE REAL ROACHES?
AH YES! BACK IN THE APARTMENT!
WELL, THE REAL LIFE ENDING WASN'T QUITE SO PRETTY!

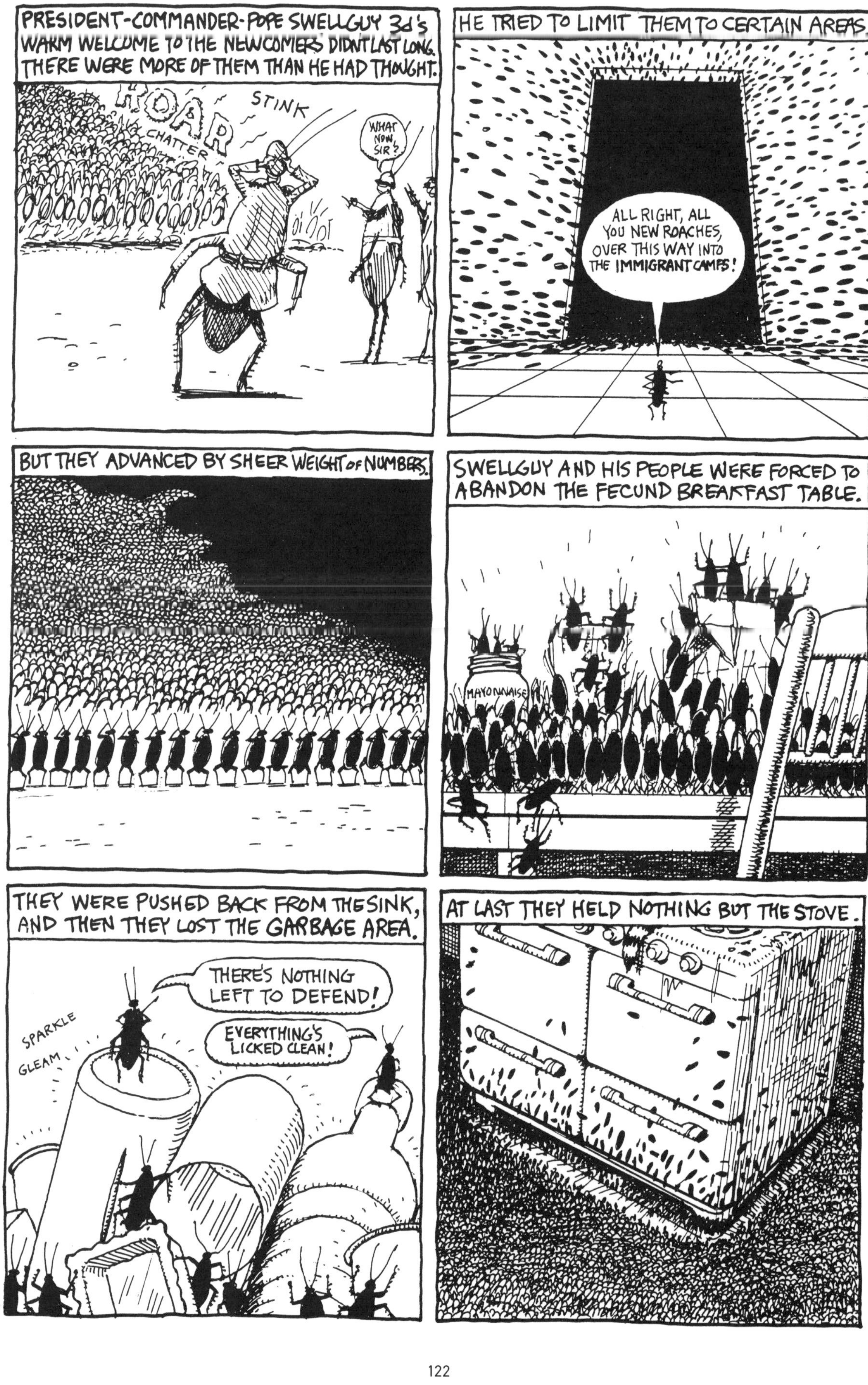
PRESIDENT-COMMANDER-POPE SWELLGUY 3d's WARM WELCOME TO THE NEWCOMERS DIDN'T LAST LONG. THERE WERE MORE OF THEM THAN HE HAD THOUGHT.
ROAR
CHATTER
STINK
WHAT NOW, SIR?
HE TRIED TO LIMIT THEM TO CERTAIN AREAS.
ALL RIGHT, ALL YOU NEW ROACHES, OVER THIS WAY INTO THE IMMIGRANT CAMPS!
BUT THEY ADVANCED BY SHEER WEIGHT OF NUMBERS.
SWELLGUY AND HIS PEOPLE WERE FORCED TO ABANDON THE FECUND BREAKFAST TABLE.
MAYONNAISE
THEY WERE PUSHED BACK FROM THE SINK, AND THEN THEY LOST THE GARBAGE AREA.
SPARKLE
GLEAM
THERE'S NOTHING LEFT TO DEFEND!
EVERYTHING'S LICKED CLEAN!
AT LAST THEY HELD NOTHING BUT THE STOVE.

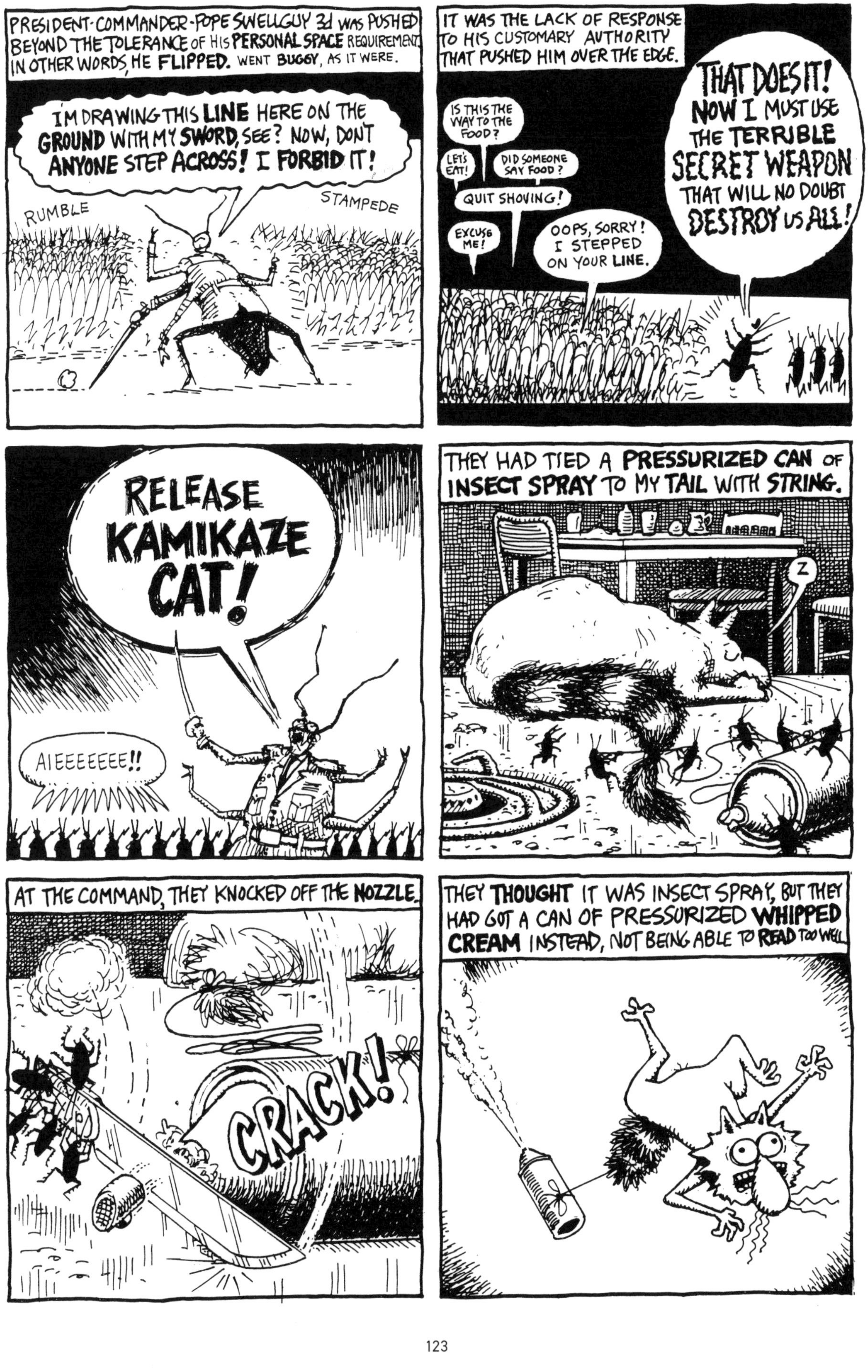

PRESIDENT-COMMANDER-POPE SWELLGUY 3d WAS PUSHED BEYOND THE TOLERANCE OF HIS PERSONAL SPACE REQUIREMENT. IN OTHER WORDS, HE FLIPPED. WENT BUGGY, AS IT WERE.
I'M DRAWING THIS LINE HERE ON THE GROUND WITH MY SWORD, SEE? NOW, DON'T ANYONE STEP ACROSS! I FORBID IT!
RUMBLE
STAMPEDE
IT WAS THE LACK OF RESPONSE TO HIS CUSTOMARY AUTHORITY THAT PUSHED HIM OVER THE EDGE.
IS THIS THE WAY TO THE FOOD?
LET'S EAT!
DID SOMEONE SAY FOOD?
QUIT SHOVING!
EXCUSE ME!
OOPS, SORRY! I STEPPED ON YOUR LINE.
THAT DOES IT! NOW I MUST USE THE TERRIBLE SECRET WEAPON THAT WILL NO DOUBT DESTROY US ALL!
RELEASE KAMIKAZE CAT!
AIEEEEEEE!!
THEY HAD TIED A PRESSURIZED CAN OF INSECT SPRAY TO MY TAIL WITH STRING.
Z
AT THE COMMAND, THEY KNOCKED OFF THE NOZZLE.
CRACK!
THEY THOUGHT IT WAS INSECT SPRAY, BUT THEY HAD GOT A CAN OF PRESSURIZED WHIPPED CREAM INSTEAD, NOT BEING ABLE TO READ TOO WELL

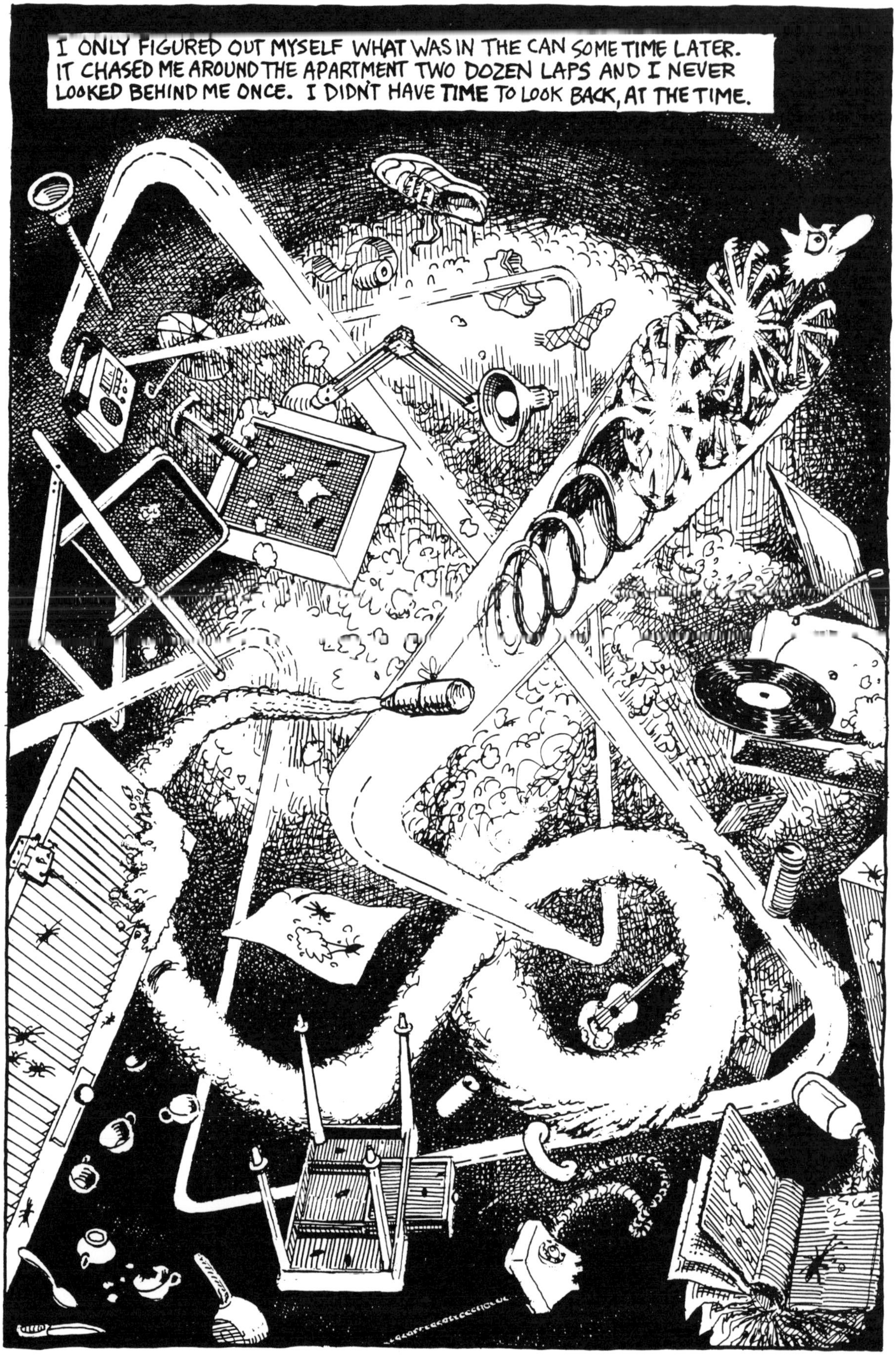
I ONLY FIGURED OUT MYSELF WHAT WAS IN THE CAN SOME TIME LATER. IT CHASED ME AROUND THE APARTMENT TWO DOZEN LAPS AND I NEVER LOOKED BEHIND ME ONCE. I DIDN'T HAVE TIME TO LOOK BACK, AT THE TIME.

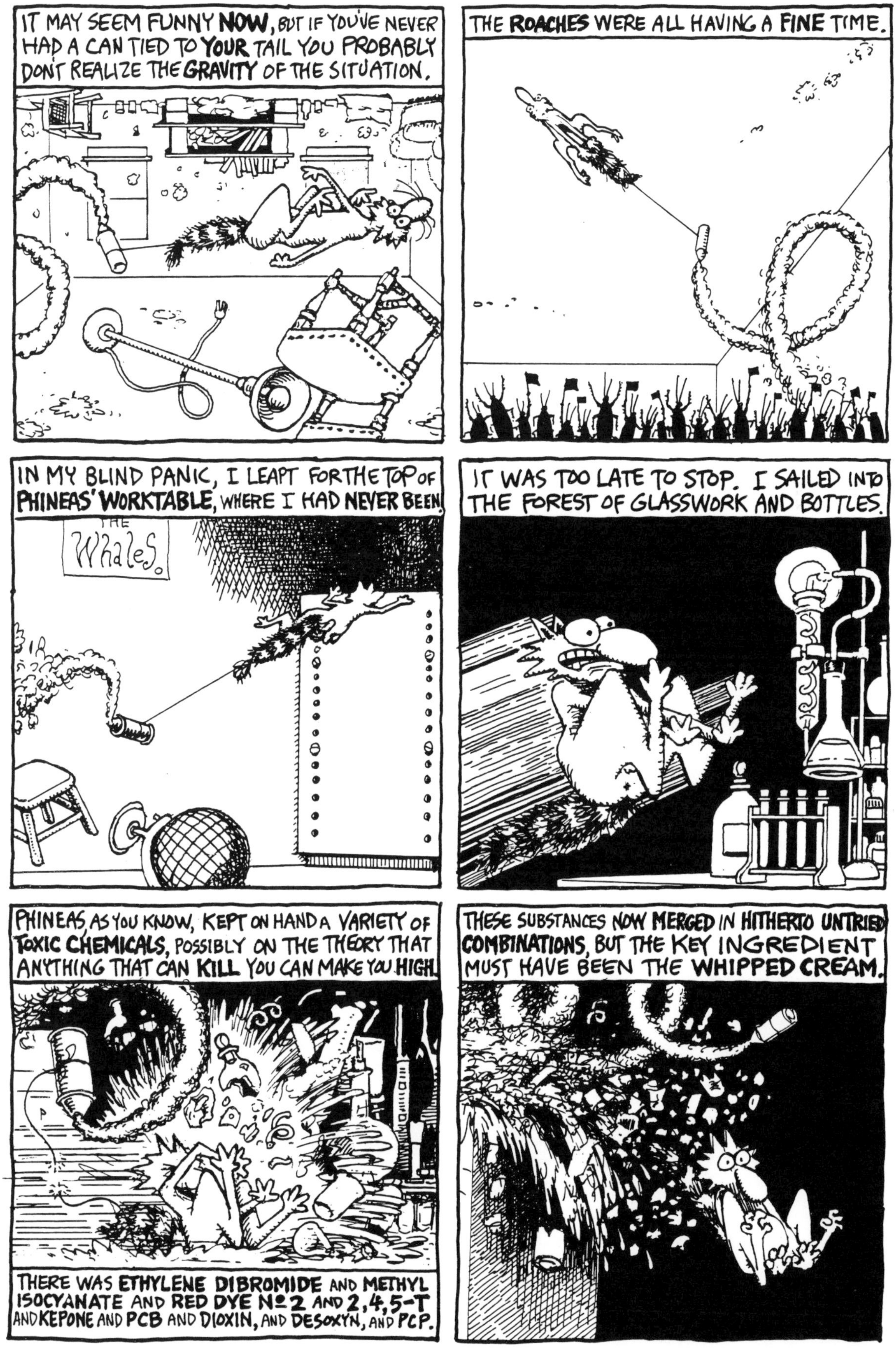
IT MAY SEEM FUNNY NOW, BUT IF YOU'VE NEVER HAD A CAN TIED TO YOUR TAIL YOU PROBABLY DON'T REALIZE THE GRAVITY OF THE SITUATION.
THE ROACHES WERE ALL HAVING A FINE TIME.
IN MY BLIND PANIC, I LEAPT FOR THE TOP OF PHINEAS' WORKTABLE, WHERE I HAD NEVER BEEN!
THE Whales.
IT WAS TOO LATE TO STOP. I SAILED INTO THE FOREST OF GLASSWORK AND BOTTLES.
PHINEAS, AS YOU KNOW, KEPT ON HAND A VARIETY OF TOXIC CHEMICALS, POSSIBLY ON THE THEORY THAT ANYTHING THAT CAN KILL YOU CAN MAKE YOU HIGH.
THERE WAS ETHYLENE DIBROMIDE AND METHYL ISOCYANATE AND RED DYE № 2 AND 2,4,5-T AND KEPONE AND PCB AND DIOXIN, AND DESOXYN, AND PCP.
THESE SUBSTANCES NOW MERGED IN HITHERTO UNTRIED COMBINATIONS, BUT THE KEY INGREDIENT MUST HAVE BEEN THE WHIPPED CREAM.

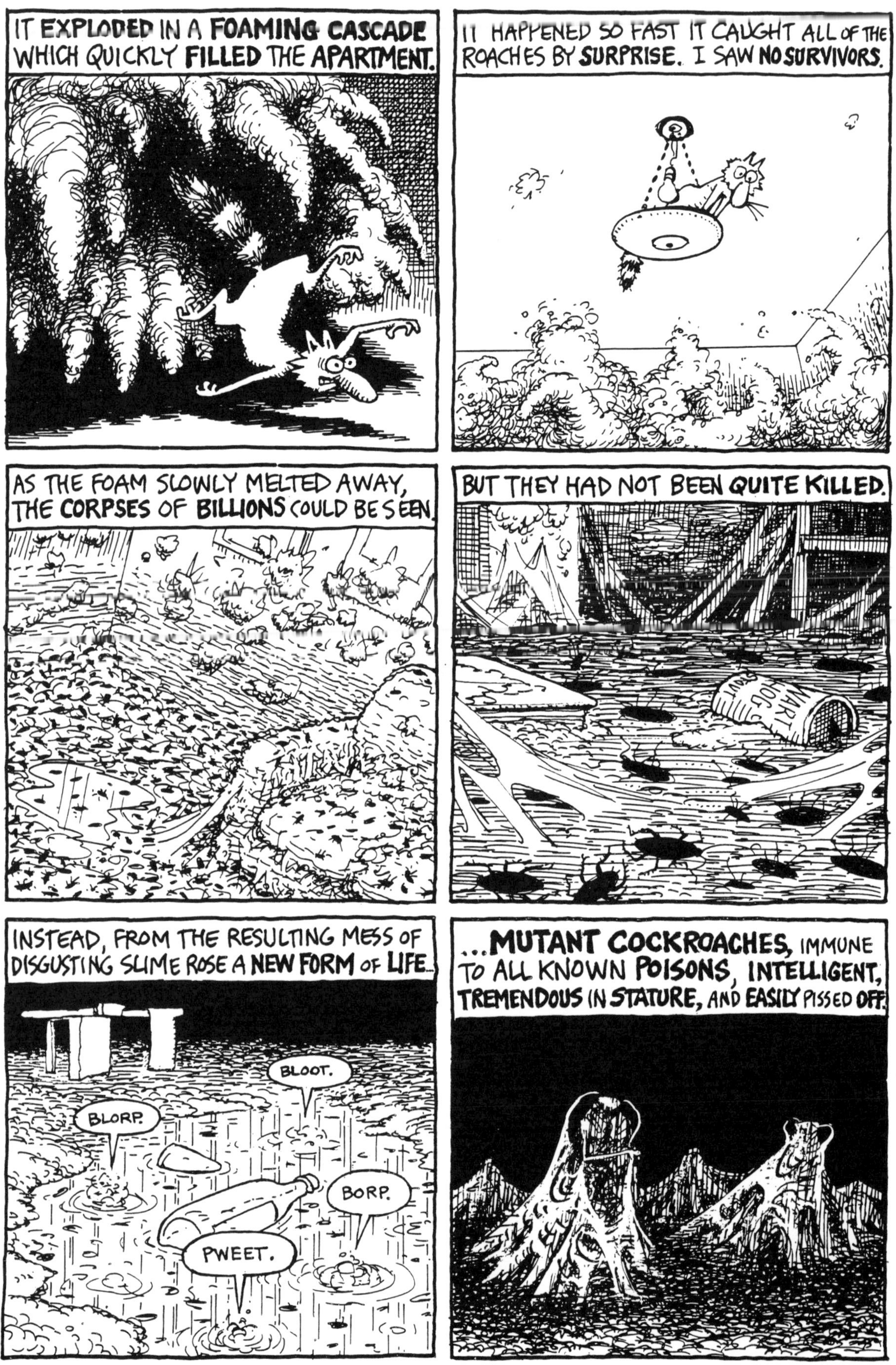
IT EXPLODED IN A FOAMING CASCADE WHICH QUICKLY FILLED THE APARTMENT.
IT HAPPENED SO FAST IT CAUGHT ALL OF THE ROACHES BY SURPRISE. I SAW NO SURVIVORS.
AS THE FOAM SLOWLY MELTED AWAY, THE CORPSES OF BILLIONS COULD BE SEEN.
BUT THEY HAD NOT BEEN QUITE KILLED.
INSTEAD, FROM THE RESULTING MESS OF DISGUSTING SLIME ROSE A NEW FORM OF LIFE...
BLOOT.
BLORP.
BORP.
PWEET.
...MUTANT COCKROACHES, IMMUNE TO ALL KNOWN POISONS, INTELLIGENT, TREMENDOUS IN STATURE, AND EASILY PISSED OFF.

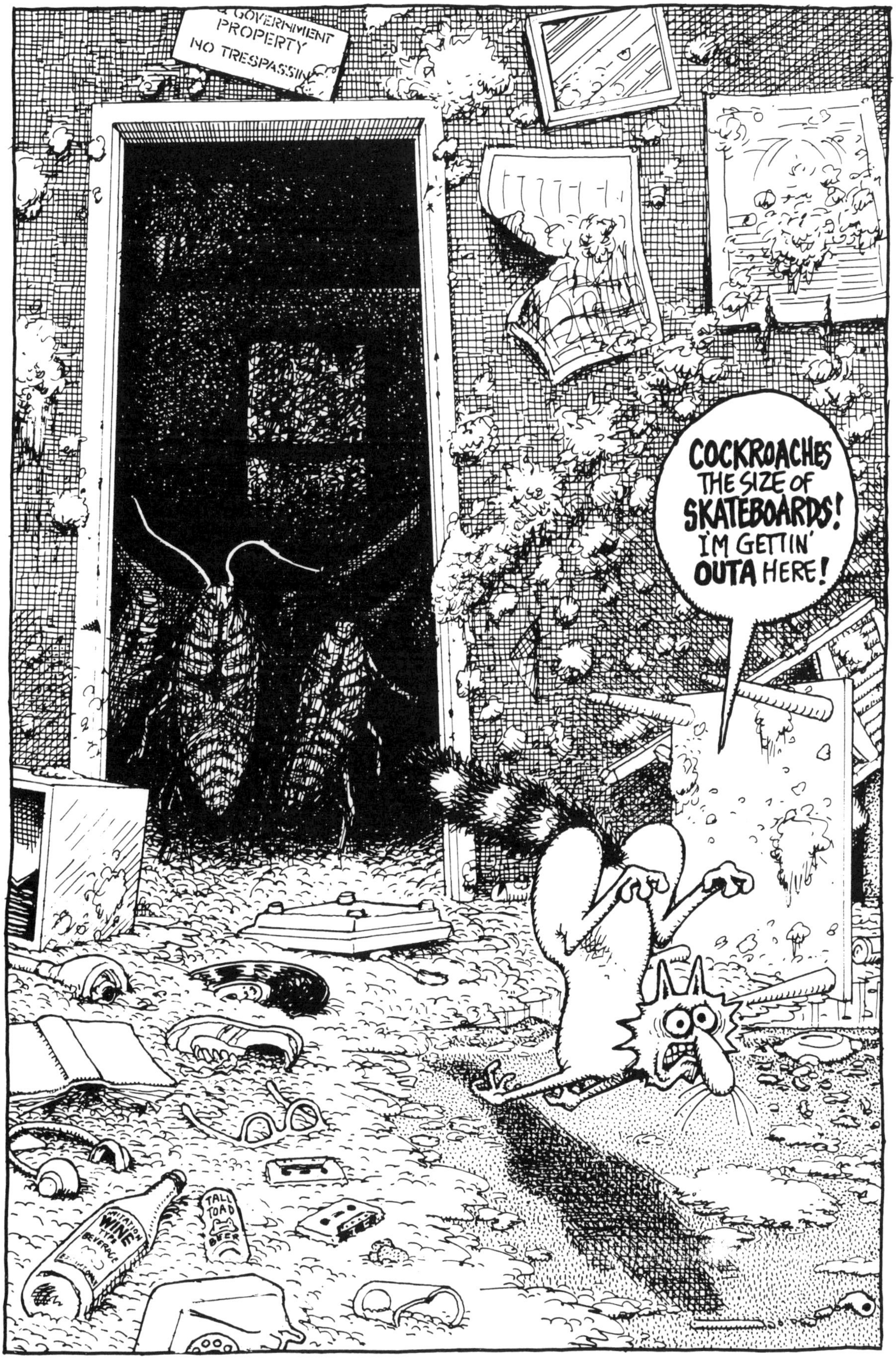
GOVERNMENT PROPERTY NO TRESPASSIN
COCKROACHES THE SIZE OF SKATEBOARDS! I'M GETTIN' OUTA HERE!
IMITATION WINE TYPE BEVERAGE
TALL TOAD BEER

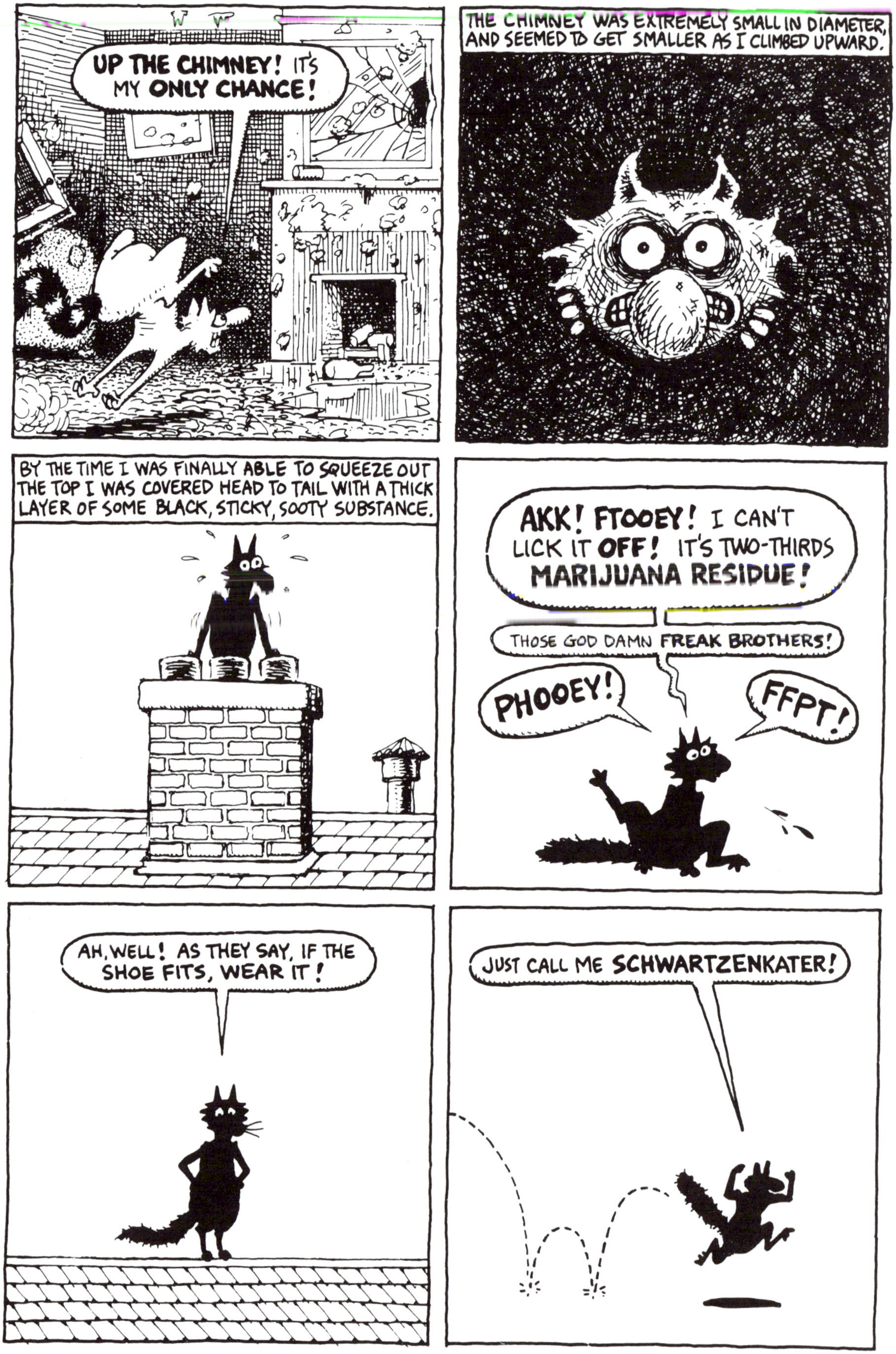
UP THE CHIMNEY! IT'S MY ONLY CHANCE!
THE CHIMNEY WAS EXTREMELY SMALL IN DIAMETER, AND SEEMED TO GET SMALLER AS I CLIMBED UPWARD.
BY THE TIME I WAS FINALLY ABLE TO SQUEEZE OUT THE TOP I WAS COVERED HEAD TO TAIL WITH A THICK LAYER OF SOME BLACK, STICKY, SOOTY SUBSTANCE.
AKK! FTOOEY! I CAN'T LICK IT OFF! IT'S TWO-THIRDS MARIJUANA RESIDUE!
THOSE GOD DAMN FREAK BROTHERS!
PHOOEY!
FFPT!
AH, WELL! AS THEY SAY, IF THE SHOE FITS, WEAR IT!
JUST CALL ME SCHWARTZENKATER!

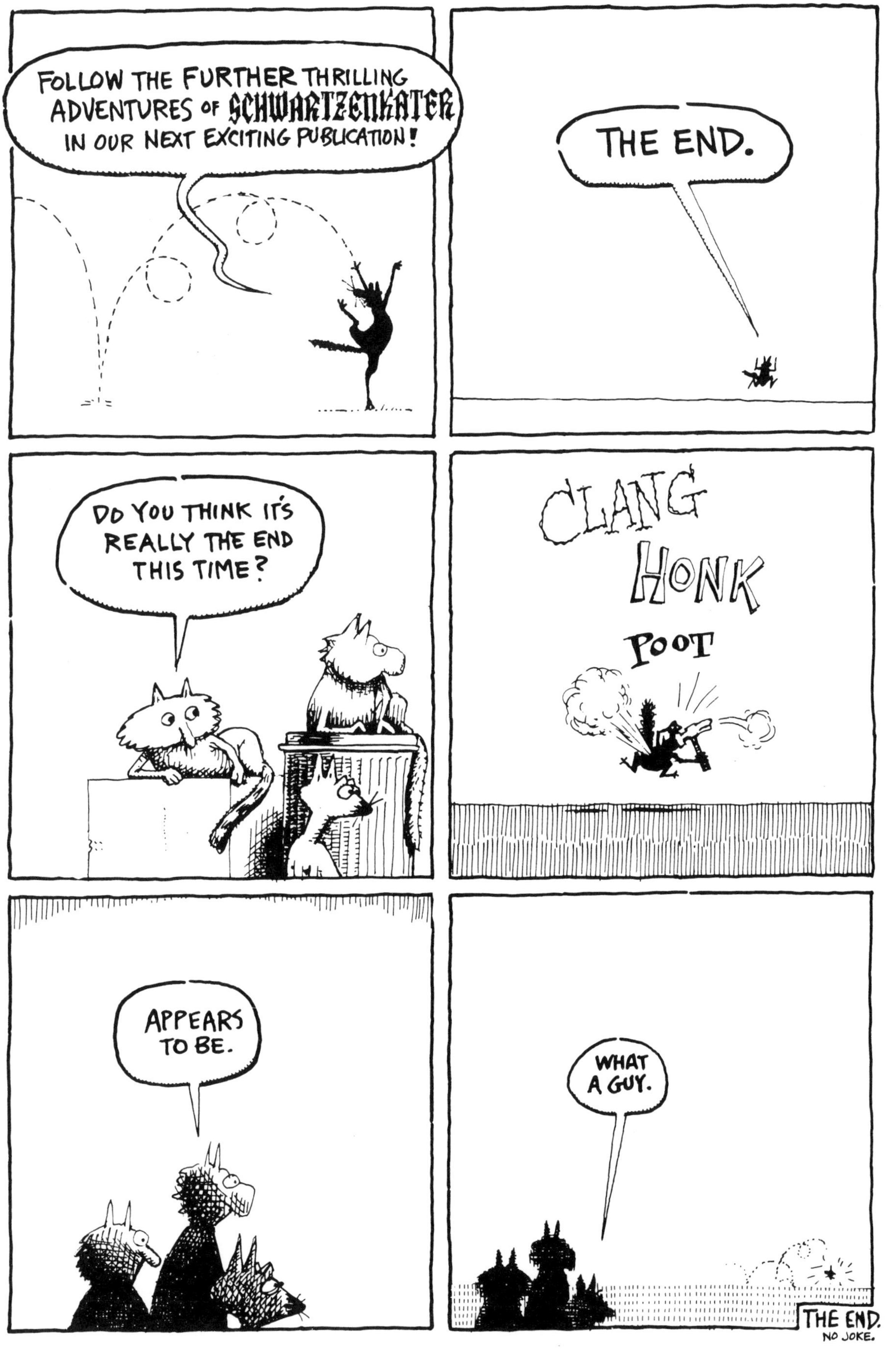
FOLLOW THE FURTHER THRILLING ADVENTURES OF SCHWARTZENKATER IN OUR NEXT EXCITING PUBLICATION!
THE END.
DO YOU THINK IT'S REALLY THE END THIS TIME?
CLANG
HONK
POOT
APPEARS TO BE.
WHAT A GUY.
THE END.
NO JOKE.

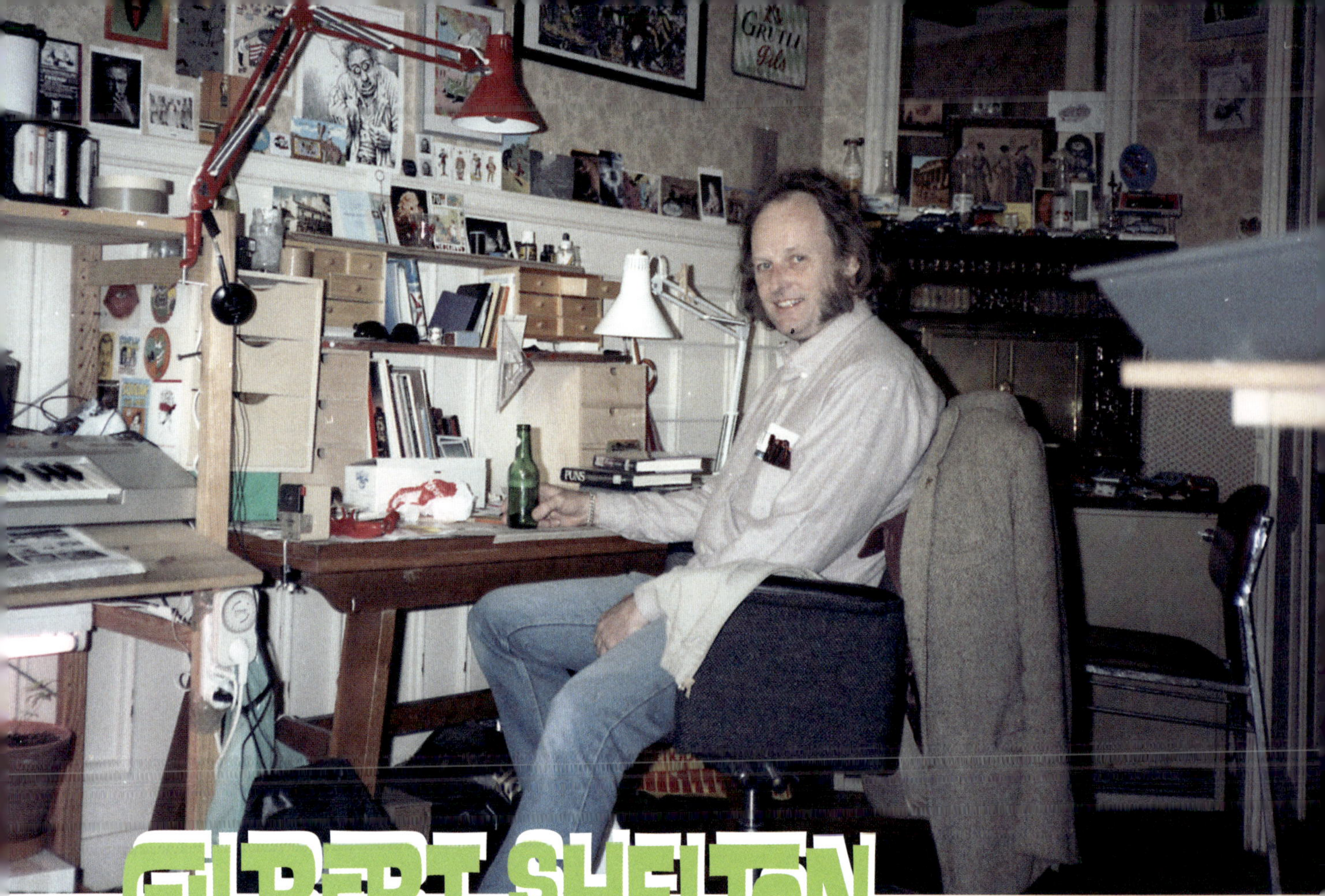

GILBERT SHELTON

by Patrick Rosenkranz

Gilbert Shelton (b. May 31, 1940, Dallas, Texas) enjoyed drawing funny pictures from an early age. He signed up to be a member of the Lamar High School cartoon club in Houston, but he lost his amateur status when he enrolled at the University of Texas in Austin. To his great surprise and delight, the *Texas Ranger* at UT actually paid people to draw cartoons. When editor Frank Stack hired him to work on the college humor magazine during his sophomore year, he discovered his true path in life. He determined to never again have a regular job, but instead to apply his talents to humor publications.

Drawing was hard and tedious work and used up a lot of what could be beer-drinking time, so he also tried his hand at better-paying, more glamorous jobs. He drove Formula 8 stock cars for a while. He even made music, going so far as to form the Gilbert Shelton Ensemble in 1966 and to release a 45-rpm record on ESP Records ("If I Was a Hell's Angel" backed with "Southern Stock Car Man"). He always returned to comics.

Shelton earned his bachelor's degree in history in 1961 and moved to New York City, where he found employment as an editorial assistant for two hot-rod magazines, *Custom Rodder* and *Speed and Custom*. The Berlin Wall crisis caused a lot of people to get drafted during that time, he said, and created job openings just when he needed one. He also introduced himself to Harvey Kurtzman and Terry Gilliam at *Help!* magazine, which published some Wonder Wart-Hog strips a few years later.

The inspirations for the Hog of Steel came to him while walking along the Avenue of the Americas that fall. He drew some sketches of his porcine superhero and filed them away. The

ABOVE: Shelton in his Paris studio, 1986, during the time he was working on "The Idiots Abroad." Photo by Glenn Bray.

next spring, he returned to UT to reactivate his student draft deferment by starting a new bachelor's degree, this time in art. He drew his first Wonder Wart-Hog story that summer for *Bacchanal*, an off-campus humor magazine. Further adventures of the well-intentioned — but easily angered — mutant antihero later appeared in the *Ranger* as well as in *Charlatan*, a Florida college humor magazine without the burden of a college affiliation or administration censors.

Shelton became the editor of the *Ranger* during the 1962–1963 school year, operating out of an office in the journalism department building. Tony Bell, Jack Jackson (a.k.a. Jaxon), and other writers and cartoonists on staff would continue to work with Shelton throughout his life. The *Ranger* reached a peak circulation of about 12,000 just before his tenure, and the staff always held a big party with their share of the proceeds from the monthly sales. Beer and liquor were the drugs of choice in those days, although a little weed and peyote were known to make a surreptitious appearance. *The Ranger* created a social scene so big and obnoxious that law enforcement and university officials launched several investigations into their activities, he said.

After leaving college and convincing his draft board he was not suitable military material, he spent time in Cleveland, Ohio, with his girlfriend, Pat Brown. Shelton applied for a job at American Greetings, where Robert Crumb was working, but he was not hired. He spent time with the Cleveland Gooses, a bohemian motorcycle and drinking club, and organized a road trip to California with them via Austin and points west. Shelton settled into Venice and reconnected with Tony Bell.

The Hog of Steel found a new home at *Drag Cartoons*, which published monthly Wonder Wart-Hog comics from March 1966 through April 1968. Shelton and Bell collaborated on writing and drawing the strips, which now took on hot rod themes, and, with the addition of Joe Brown, continued producing them after moving back to Austin.

The publisher, Pete Millar, decided to gamble on two mass-circulation, 64-page *Wonder Wart-Hog Quarterly* magazines, but appallingly bad sales drove him out of business.

The counterculture was making slow inroads into urban Texas when Shelton and friends opened the first head shop, Underground City Hall, at 1606 Lavaca Street in Austin, not far from the state capitol building.

Houston White launched a dance and concert hall on Congress Avenue — the Vulcan Gas Company, which was Austin's version of the Fillmore and Avalon Ballrooms in San Francisco. White hired Shelton as art director and charged him with producing psychedelic dance posters in the style of Wes Wilson and the other West Coast poster artists. This was Texas, though, so their posters were larger, said Shelton.

He also drew comic strips for the underground newspaper *Austin Rag*, which included the earliest appearance of the gleesome threesome that would make him famous, the Fabulous Furry Freak Brothers, whose comics stories have been among the most informative and honest looks at the drug culture ever to see print. Their first adventure was actually done as an ad for a movie made by Shelton and Renée Tooley. But the comic strip was better.

Sophisticated political satire was often blended with slapstick humor in Shelton's comic strips and reflected his interest in the radical politics of the emerging counterculture, which attracted a hip young adult audience who appreciated where he was coming from.

After seeing copies of *R. Crumb's Head Comix* and *Zap #1* in 1968, Shelton drew and self-published a twenty-four-page comic book, *Feds 'N' Heads*, on a Multilith press in Terry Raines's garage in Austin. He hand-collated, folded, and stapled several thousand copies.

He sold some around town and then put the rest in his trunk and drove to San Francisco, where Gary Arlington at the San Francisco Comic Book Company gladly took them all in exchange for a used car. Print Mint soon reprinted them, and these few new underground comix began to spread everywhere that backpackers and jet-setters went.

Shelton joined the *Zap* artists' group in *Zap #3* with the nine-page story "Wonder Wart-Hog Blows an Easy One." Finally freed from censors and advertisers, the Hog of Steel runs around bare-assed with a toilet stuck on his head.

Shelton and three of his friends from Texas—Fred Todd, Jack Jackson, and David Moriarty—decided to try their own hand at printing and publishing, so they all chipped in to put a down payment on a used press from Printer's Exchange. They set up shop on the third floor of Mowry's Opera House alongside Don Donahue's Apex Novelties. They called themselves Rip Off Press.

They learned the printing process the hard way, starting with posters for Soundproof Productions and working their way up to comic books. They spent several months reprinting Jaxon's *God Nose Comics* and then *R. Crumb's Comics and Stories*. More titles followed, including Crumb's *Motor City Comics* and *Big Ass Comics*. These early struggles were later memorialized in Jaxon's comic story, "Rip Off Press: The Golden Years" in *Rip Off Comix #21* in 1998.

Suspicious fires broke out all over the Fillmore neighborhood that summer, forcing out many local tenants and making urban improvement projects easier for the city's redevelopment commission. A fire next door to Mowry's Opera House leaped across to its roof and burned out the top floor, where Rip Off had its offices. After the firemen left, the transplanted Texans rescued what they could of their equipment—the presses themselves were still usable—and moved into the empty former Family Dog headquarters nearby.

When the city discovered them there a few months later, they were relocated to another site at the corner of Golden Gate and Franklin Streets. The building, a four-story hotel, was empty and slated for destruction, but they bored through the shop walls into the rest of the space and filled it with friends and squatters. It wasn't luxurious, but you couldn't beat the rent. By then, they had become reasonably competent commercial printers, with comic books, posters, T-shirts, and other jobs under their belts. When they weren't printing, they were partying.

At their next location, in a modern production plant—on 17th Street, near Potrero Hill—they added to their "museum grade" printing equipment and even bought a large web press, enjoying a successful business during the peak years of the comix boom. They had fifteen employees at one point, and new customers ordered everything in their catalog.

The publication of a new book was all the excuse necessary for another rip-snorting Rip Off Press party, with kegs and live bands and hundreds of people. Just when it seemed to be too good to last, boom turned to bust. Sales slipped. Interest waned. Retailers sent back returns. Sometime during the winter of 1973, when orders had dwindled to a trickle, the sheriff came by to repossess their web press.

One day that same winter, Shelton showed up at the office and began to draw what would become *A Year Passes Like Nothing With the Fabulous Furry Freak Brothers*, (a.k.a. *The Fabulous Furry Freak Brothers #3*), the third issue in the top-selling series. The regular appearance of new issues of the fabulously popular Freak Brothers comic books kept Rip Off Press solvent for many years. Dave Sheridan and Paul Mavrides collaborated with Shelton to meet the public's demand for more misadventures and drug-addled hilarity with Phineas, Fat Freddy, and Freewheelin' Franklin as they confronted irate landladies, rabid federal agents, bullshit artists, and changing sexual politics, each time narrowly avoiding disaster thanks to savvy survival instincts.

"People always enjoy laughing at stupid hippies," said Shelton.

Many of the one-page adventures in this series originally appeared in college newspapers and alternative weeklies, distributed by the Rip Off Syndicate. Our hairy heroes were also translated and published in Finland, France, and Italy in 1975. Remnants of the Underground Press Syndicate continued to reprint unauthorized editions all over the globe. Despite the decline of the underground press, Shelton's comics continued to find new readers.

Over the years, there have been several attempts to bring the Freak Brothers to life on the screen, but only one has come to fruition. *The Freak Brothers* — an animated series produced by WTG Enterprises and executive-produced by Courtney Solomon, Mark Canton, Alan Cohen, and Alan Freedland — began streaming in late 2021 on Tubi. The series stars Woody Harrelson, John Goodman, Pete Davidson, and Tiffany Haddish (www.thefreakbrothers.com).

Shelton and his wife, Lora Fountain, moved to Europe in the 1980s, living in Barcelona and London before settling in Paris, all the while issuing comics albums through European publishers. Shelton also introduced many European cartoonists to American audiences through reprints translated to English in *Rip Off Comix*. He also began a new comic series starring a dysfunctional rock band, called *Not Quite Dead*, in collaboration with French artist Pic.

European editions of Shelton's work were published simultaneously in several languages, and nearly every comic he ever drew is still in print in English, Danish, French, German, Spanish, and Portuguese, "though not in Icelandic, Catalan, Frisian, Gaelic, Romansh, Basque, or any of the minor dialects," Shelton said with a sigh, dreaming of worlds yet unconquered.

Gilbert Shelton was honored with a Will Eisner Lifetime Achievement Award at Comic-Con International: San Diego in 2012.

Now, at long last, Phineas, Fat Freddy, and Freewheelin' Franklin have returned to the U.S. with this new series of Freak Brothers books from Fantagraphics.

BELOW:Gilbert Shelton by Gilbert Shelton, 1974

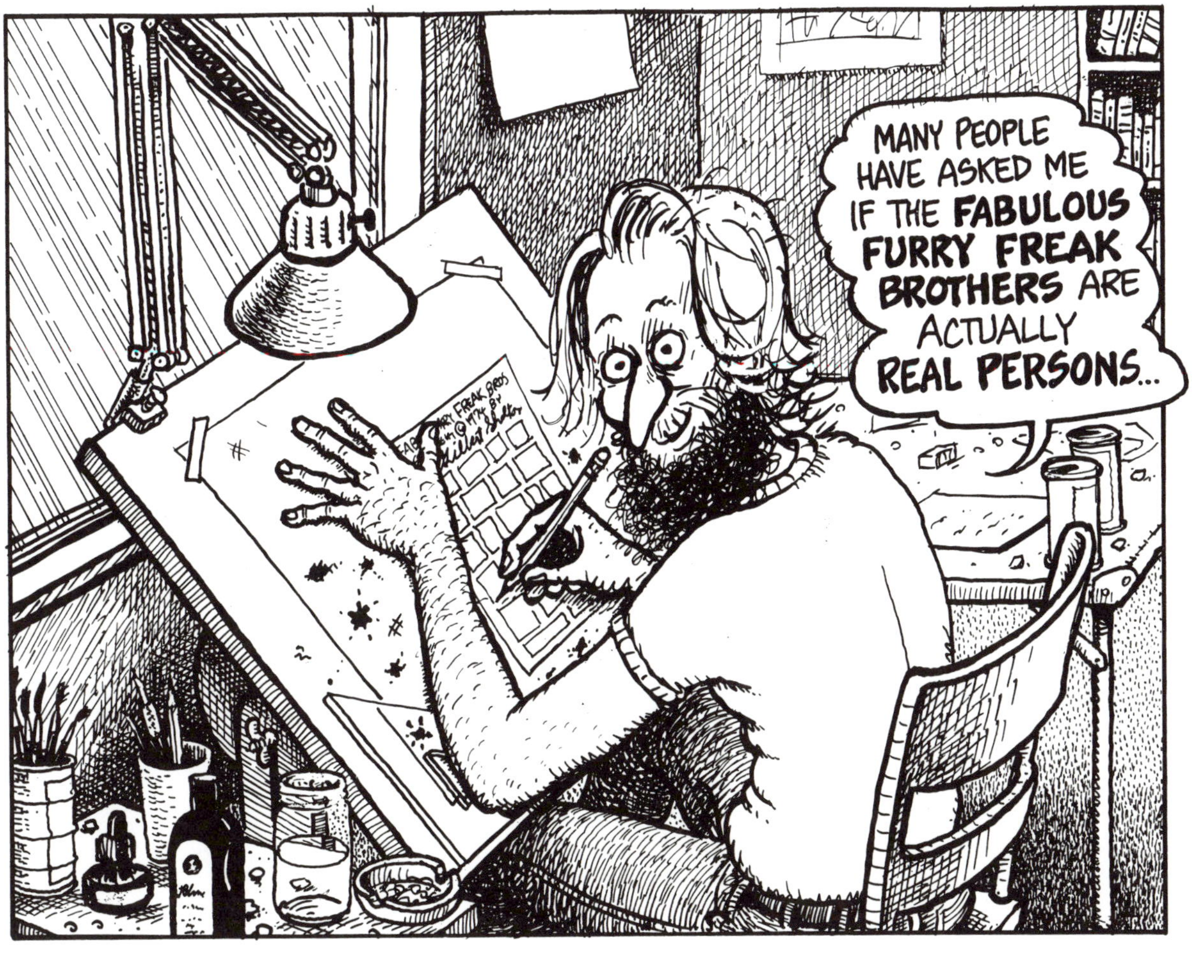
MANY PEOPLE HAVE ASKED ME IF THE FABULOUS FURRY FREAK BROTHERS ARE ACTUALLY REAL PERSONS...

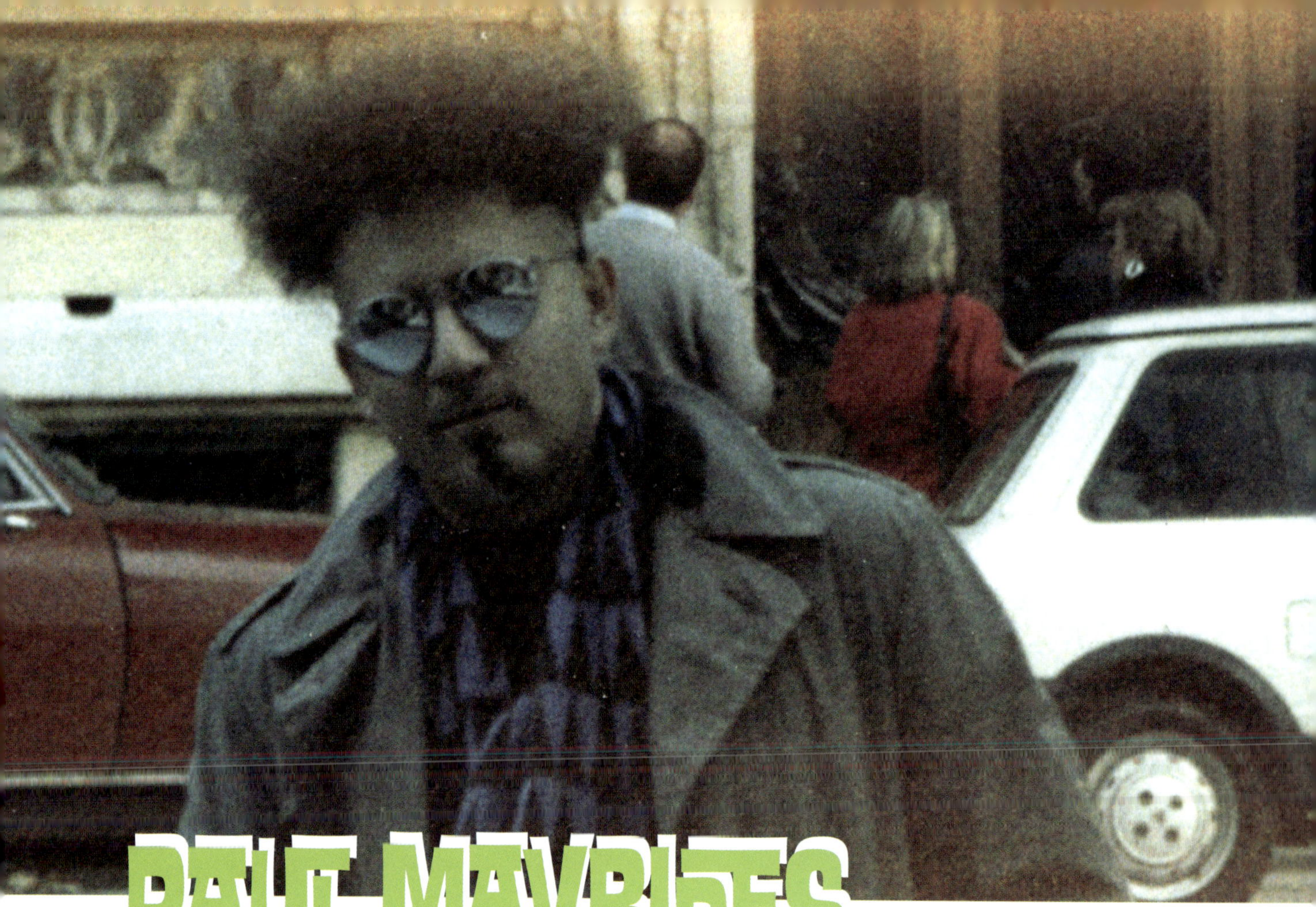

PAUL MAVRIDES

by Patrick Rosenkranz

Paul Mavrides (b. 1952, Duckburg, Calisota), discovered, at two years of age, that the contents of his diaper were a suitable medium for the creation of a large-scale mural across his grandmother's hallway. His father spent several hours deconstructing this seminal work, and — none too happy about this unwelcome curatorial task — strongly encouraged his son to switch to more traditional painting media.

Personal details about Mavrides's life are often hard to come by, since he takes great pains to spread as much disinformation about himself as possible: claiming multiple birthdates (that sometimes turn out to be off by as much as twenty years in either direction) or simply lying about his profession, gender, religion(s), and birthplace.

The mysterious Mavrides is today an enigmatic figure in underground art and antiart circles, an artist whose fingers and toes are often dipped in more esoteric and populist genres than sequential art.

Still smarting to this day from having his childhood collection of EC and *Mad* comics burned by his well-meaning parents, Mavrides vividly remembers his first encounter with *Zap Comix* as an Ohio teenager in 1968, when the UPS man delivered a shipment to a friend who ran the only head shop in Akron. Together, they unpacked several cartons of underground comic books from San Francisco that included copies of *Zap*, Gilbert Shelton's *Feds 'N' Heads*, and *Yellow Dog* — the initial lineup of brand new, subversive, hippie funny books. Reading them all in one intensive sitting, he said, he found his brain had dissolved from the concentrated perceptual assault.

Mavrides is an example of how blunt force trauma applied to sensitive adolescent psyches

ABOVE: Paul Mavrides, Avenue Rapp, Paris, c. 1986, during the time he was working on "The Idiots Abroad." Photo by Gilbert Shelton.

made at just the right moment (through exposure to insidious visions and seditious insights, such as those delivered via the seemingly innocent comic book) can lead either directly to a life squandered in the gutter, or, even more improbably, to a long and distinguished art career—or both. If he'd known then that he'd one day be working on the *Fabulous Furry Freak Brothers* and *Zap* comix, he might have saved himself time and trouble by heading straight to San Francisco. Instead, the encounter inspired him to learn all his could about these comix and their creators, and eventually he did meet them all—as a member of the tribe.

His first job in the underground press was during the tail end of the '60s era, on the *New Times* (*NT*), an alternative weekly newspaper in Tucson, Arizona. It wasn't really "underground," he said, but the *NT* was the only media waterhole in that hyperconservative desert state that would run in-depth investigative reporting alongside countercultural news.

Mavrides moved to the San Francisco Bay Area in 1975, where a mutual acquaintance, David Ossman of the Firesign Theater, introduced him to Jay Kinney. Within a few months, Kinney and Mavrides created the first four *Cover Up Lowdown* cartoons for the *Berkeley Barb*. It was an unusual approach to comics, combining fact and fiction to examine ecological dangers, political scandals, and conspiracy theories in a serious yet humorous way. They successfully pitched an expansion of the single-panel series to the Rip Off Press Syndicate, and several dozen cartoons followed, finding a wide readership in the national alternative press. Rip Off Press eventually collected and published the series as a comic book with the same title.

That led Mavrides and Kinney to create *Anarchy Comics #1*, which Last Gasp published in 1978. Three more issues followed over the next ten years, featuring the work of a radical and eclectic group of cartoonists from across America and Europe, including a translation of "Liberty Through the Ages" by French artists Epistolier and Volny. The comic book's

marriage of historical anarchist traditions with post-hippie punk sensibilities and abhorrence of capitalism, consumerism, and pop culture, along with stripped-down graphic stylings, made it one of the more insightful political publications to document the greed and elitism of the 1980s.

Following the creation of his first velvet painting in 1979, *'63 Election* (a depiction of Zapruder Film Frame #374), Mavrides offered up a portrait called *The Chairman*—black velvet in the "big eyes" style of Margaret Keane—for the back cover of *Anarchy #2*. Several gallery shows featuring black-velvet paintings of consumer products and iconographic political events followed, including Mavrides's looks at the Jack Ruby assassination, the HIV virus, the Challenger explosion, microwave ovens, crack pipes, Operation Desert Storm, and the Jonestown massacre.

It was mildew that really brought Mavrides to the attention of Gilbert Shelton. After an extensive rainy period in the Bay Area, Mavrides discovered that, thanks to his porous Berkeley apartment, many of his drawings were in danger of suffering mold damage. He received permission from Rip Off Press to spread the musty paper all over their warehouse to dry it out under the skylights—which provided Shelton an ample opportunity to look over the art. He decided to try out Mavrides as an art assistant—which quickly led to a full partnership—and they cocreated the further adventures of the immensely popular Fabulous Furry Freak Brothers.

After they produced *Six Snappy Sockeroos From the Archives of the Fabulous Furry Freak Brothers* (*Freak Brothers #6*) in 1979, Dave Sheridan briefly reunited with the team, and the trio produced *Several Short Stories From the Fabulous Furry Freak Brothers* (*Freak Brothers #7*) in 1980. After Sheridan's untimely death in 1982, Mavrides and Shelton continued, publishing *The Idiots Abroad* saga and many other Freak Brothers projects over the next two decades. They shared writing, penciling, and inking responsibilities, and Mavrides would regularly commute to Europe, working side by side with Shelton at his Paris studio.

Mavrides's critique-laden comics, cartoons, paintings, graphics, performances, and writings encompass a disturbing yet humorous catalog of the social ills and shortcomings of human civilization. His projects expose, explore, and exploit the edge between truth and propaganda. Mavrides is known for his bludgeon-like proselytizing on behalf of J.R. "Bob" Dobbs's SubGenius Foundation, a do-it-yourself, antipsychotronic religious cult, for which he still serves as official apostate. He is one of the multiheaded coauthors and main designer of *Revelation X: The "Bob" Apocryphon: Hidden Teachings and Deuterocanonical Texts of J.R. "Bob" Dobbs*.

One of the least-visible, yet fastest-growing religions of the 21st century, the Church of the SubGenius resembles a brain tumor — one that tears down the philosophical scrim of "well being" that the average human personality depends on for stability and replaces it with cellular replicas of itself stamped with the meme "think for yourself."

Mavrides designed the opening title sequence for filmmaker Ron Mann's 1988 comic book documentary feature, *Comic Book Confidential*. He was art director, head artist, CG animator, and uncredited codirector on Mann's 2000 theatrical documentary *Grass*, a history of marijuana prohibition in America.

In 1991, Mavrides led a well-publicized and hard-fought six-year battle against the California State Board of Equalization (the state's sales tax board) over the legal definition of cartoonists as authors. With assistance from the Comic Book Legal Defense Fund and the American Civil Liberties Union, he argued that original comic strip pages constitute a work of authorship — a manuscript that should be regarded as identical in legal status to those of prose authors.

The ramifications of allowing the tax board's radical reinterpretation of the regulatory sales tax law to stand unopposed could have meant a loss of legal literary status for comics, mandatory licensing of cartoonists, and a downgrade of the fundamental free speech rights of comics creators — a chain of legal disasters that, in the end, would have created a drastic constriction of experimental work in the field.

Mavrides vehemently disagreed with the Board's opinion that original comics pages were "merely templates for printing manufacturing," rather than an author's original manuscript. In early 1997, at the final hearing, the California State Board of Equalization handed down a regulatory ruling in Mavrides's favor, which also benefited his cartoonist peers; magazine, comics, and newspaper publishers; and newspaper comic strip syndicates. Over the following two years, the Graphic Artists Guild and The American Federation of Labor and Congress of Industrial Organizations (AFL-CIO) used this case ruling to successfully lobby the California state legislature to change the direct wording of the tax laws to reflect the Board's decision.

Mavrides's time-consuming and expensive sacrifice for the greater good was to be acknowledged by the Zap Collective.

The only way to leave *Zap Comix* was to die, according to S. Clay Wilson (1941–2021). When Rick Griffin was killed in a traffic accident in 1991, it created an opening to be filled, and the surviving band of brothers met to discuss a new recruit. They chose to promote someone from within the ranks of underground comix and invited Mavrides to join them. He became the first new member of the Zap Collective in nearly three decades with his two-page story "My Big Break" in *Zap #14* in 1998. He was also shown the secret handshake and given a key to the art supply cabinet.

Paul Mavrides is a kinesthetic artist whose life comprises his art. The territories of his earliest underground comix were autonomy, liberation, and enlightened self-expression — themes that still resonate through his work, no matter the subject or medium. 🍁

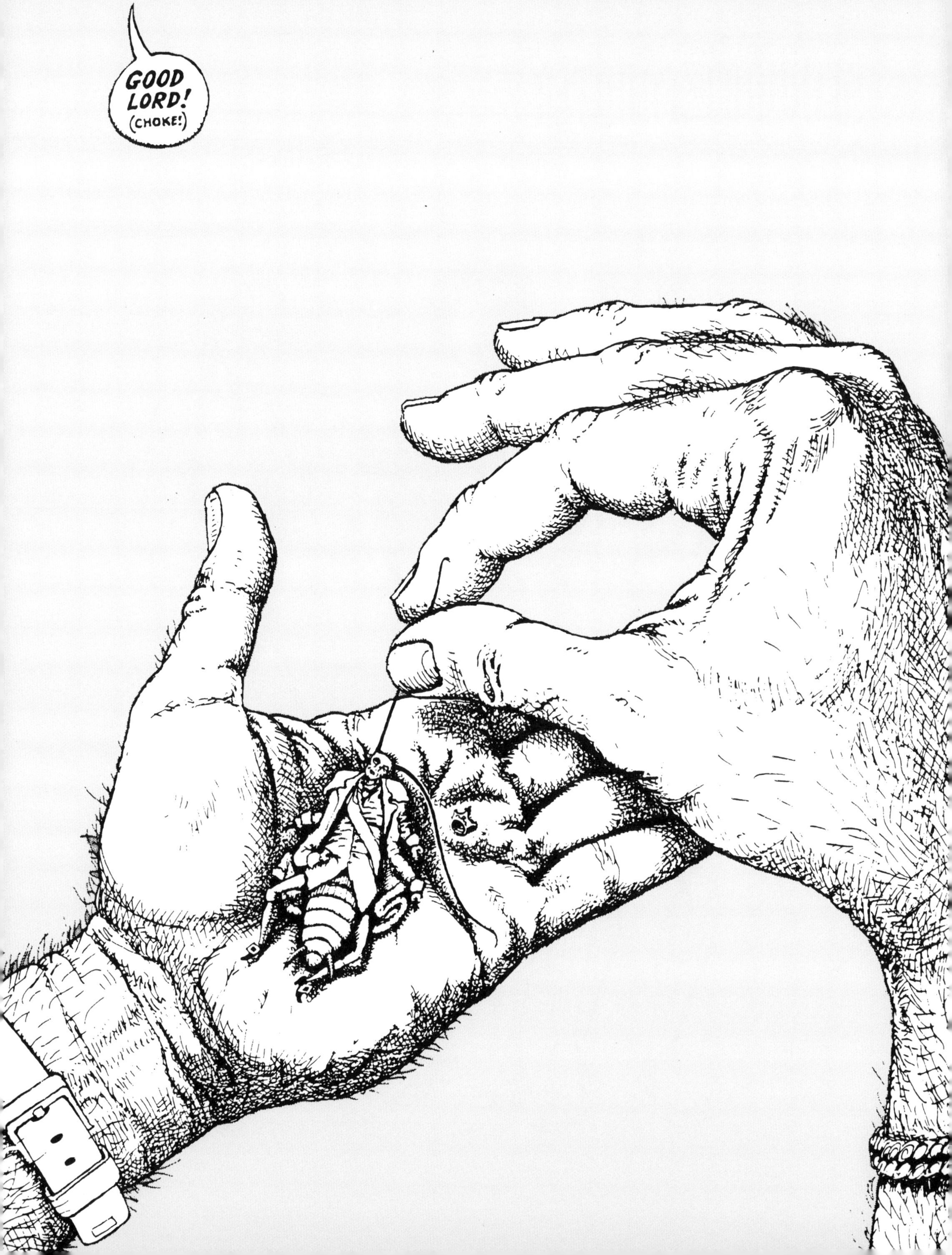
GOOD LORD! (CHOKE!)

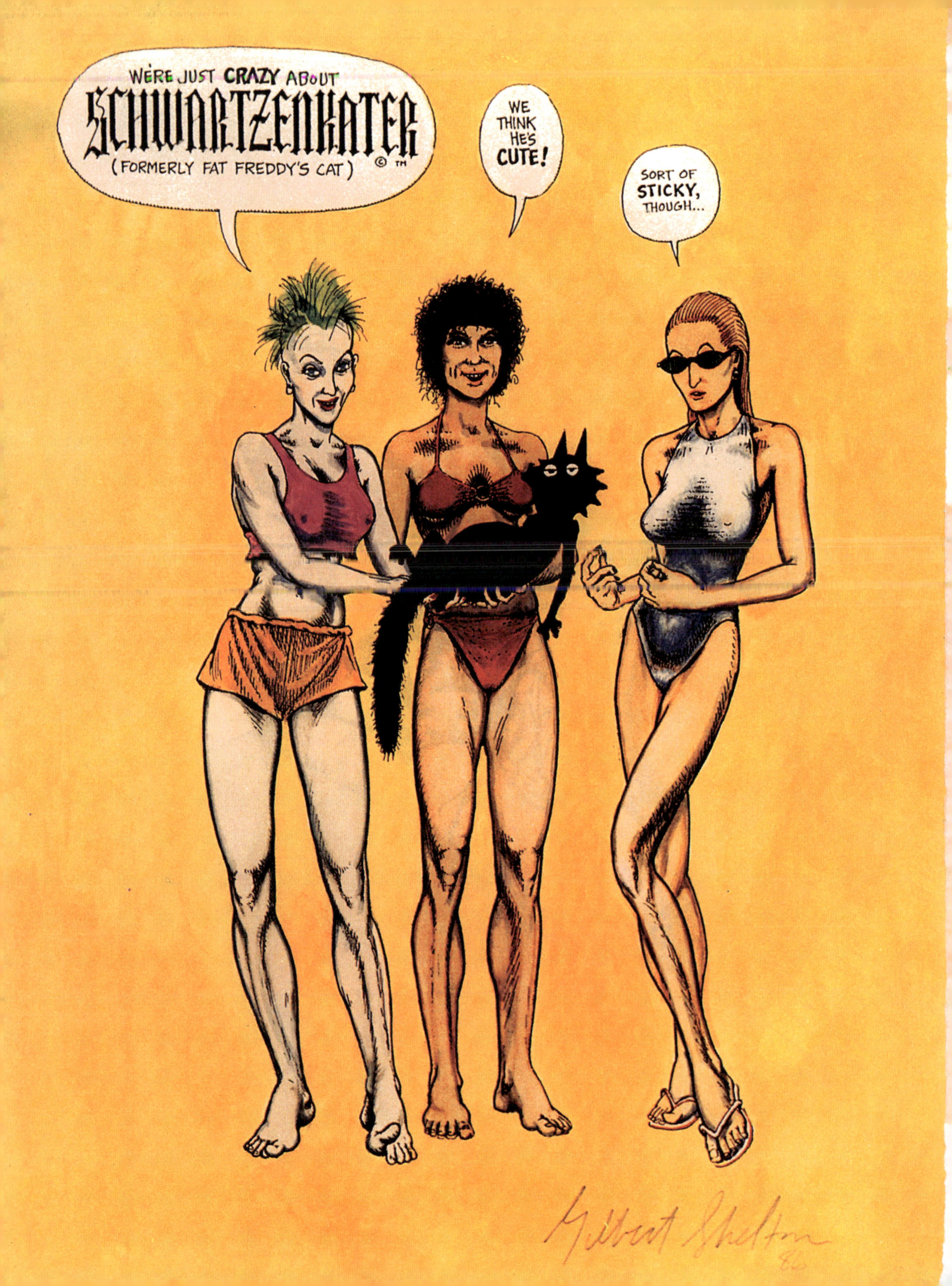
WE'RE JUST CRAZY ABOUT SCHWARTZENKATER (FORMERLY FAT FREDDY'S CAT) © TM
WE THINK HE'S CUTE!
SORT OF STICKY, THOUGH...

FREEWHEELIN'
FRANKLIN
&
FREDDY
PRINCES
& FAT FREDDY'S CAT

The

FABULOU

FREAK B

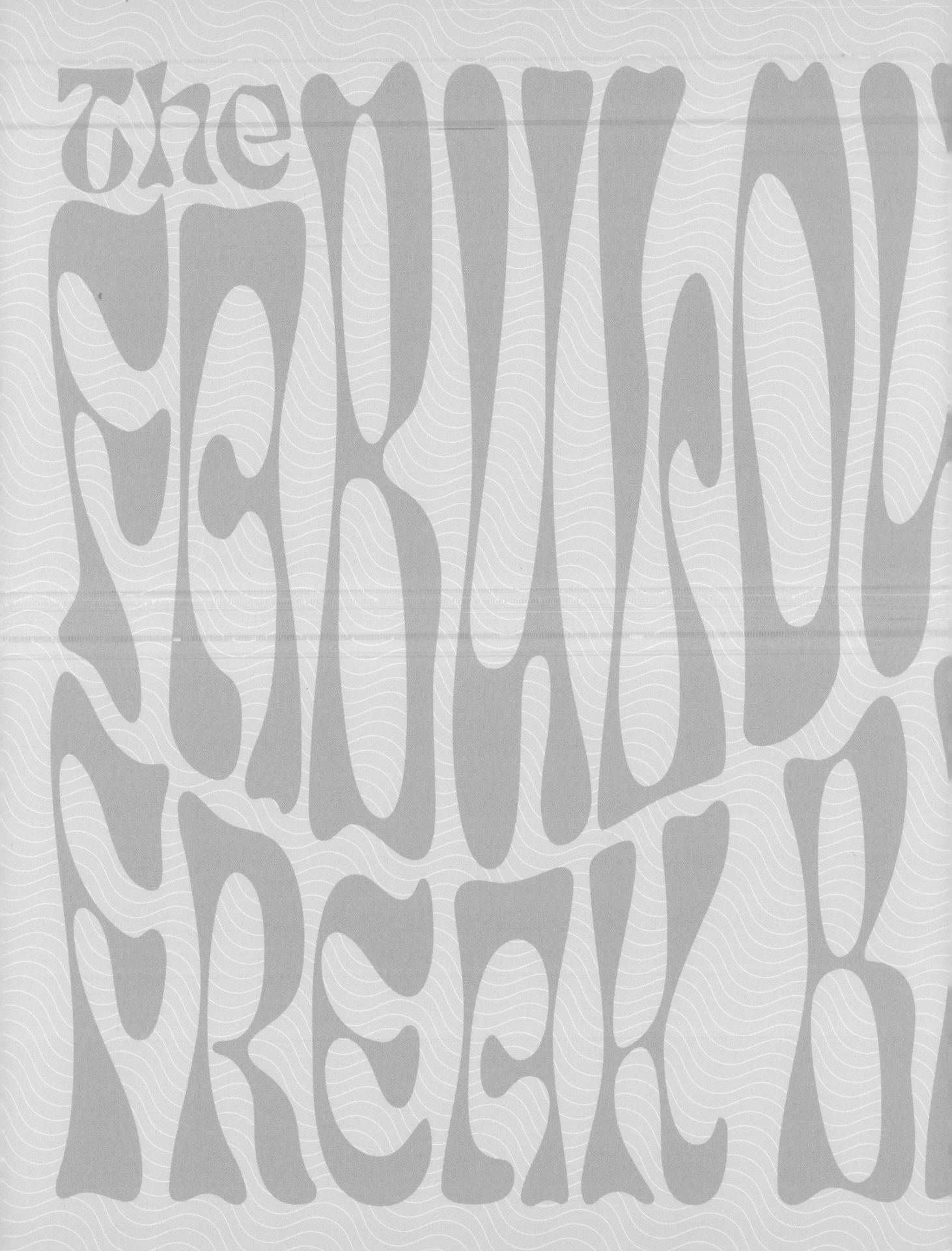